Lake Classical Series

ELEMENTARY LATIN

AN INTRODUCTORY COURSE

BY

HARRY FLETCHER SCOTT, A. M.

OHIO UNIVERSITY,
ATHENS, OHIO

SCOTT, FORESMAN AND COMPANY

CHICAGO   ATLANTA   NEW YORK

PREFACE

In the preparation of these lessons, the author has kept in view the necessity for simplicity of statement and for the avoidance of unnecessary details. The purpose has been to furnish drill on the forms and constructions of most frequent occurrence, leaving the more difficult syntactical relations and the forms less frequently employed for a later point in the course. A few topics included in the lessons near the end of the book have been given place in order to meet the needs of teachers who prefer a more complete presentation of Latin grammar in the first year. These topics may, however, be omitted and the work of the lessons made to consist of the translation exercises and drill on the essential constructions and forms previously given.

Instead of the usual arrangement of lessons which must be divided into two or three assignments, the plan has been adopted of providing short lessons which can usually be covered in single recitations. Naturally, no such plan can be made to correspond absolutely to the needs of every class, and occasionally a teacher may find it necessary to omit or to leave for later review, part of the exercises of a lesson. But the presentation of forms and syntax in small units will, it is hoped, tend to prevent confusion in the mind of the pupil and to aid the teacher in planning the work of the class.

The number of new words in each lesson has been kept as nearly uniform as possible and review lessons have been provided for special drill on vocabulary. These review lessons, however, with the exception of the first and second, are not an essential part of the plan of the book and may be omitted by teachers who prefer to arrange reviews in a different way. In connection with these lessons, lists of English derivatives have been given which may serve to relate the work in Latin more closely to the pupil's study of English, and to make clear the great importance of the Latin element in the English language. The vocabulary is for the greater part based on Caesar.

The reading lessons are planned to make the translation of Caesar easier, by giving in simple Latin the story of the first two books of the Gallic war, and by the frequent use of phrases and constructions from Caesar. The pupil who studies Latin but one year will at least have the opportunity to learn something of Caesar's narrative which may contribute to his interest in ancient history.

The selections from Eutropius are based on the text of Ruehl, with some changes and omissions. Since to many the tales of early Rome are unfamiliar, a good introduction to Roman history is furnished by this material.

The recommendations of the Joint Committee on Grammatical Nomenclature have been followed, with a few exceptions. The tense name "imperfect" has been retained in the indicative and subjunctive, and a different term from that suggested by the Committee has been employed to designate conditional sentences with the present and past tenses of the indicative.

Acknowledgment is made of the many helpful suggestions which were received from Professor Frederick W. Sanford of the University of Nebraska, Professor Charles Knapp of Barnard College, Miss Mildred Dean of the Central High School of Washington, D. C., Professor Arthur Tappan Walker of the University of Kansas, and Professor Rollin H. Tanner of Illinois College, who read the manuscript. Professor Edward Capps of Princeton University, editor of the Lake Classical Series, has also given the book the benefit of his scholarly judgment on many points. Some features which have been most heartily commended by those to whom the manuscript has been submitted are due to the suggestions of the late Professor H. W. Johnston of the University of Indiana, to whom the plan of the lessons was submitted shortly before his death.

Chicago, Illinois, May, 1915.

                                        HARRY FLETCHER SCOTT.

CONTENTS

ILLUSTRATIONS AND MAPS

THE VALUE OF LATIN

A very large proportion of the words of the English language is derived from Latin. In some instances words have been taken directly, without change of form. For example, *terminus, stimulus, veto,* and *affidavit,* are Latin words in the form in which they were used by the Romans. Other words first became a part of the French language and after being modified by the pronunciation of that language were taken into English in this changed form. Such are *humble, count, blame,* and *sure.* The numerous English adjectives ending in *-ent* and *-ant,* such as *patient, intelligent, independent,* and *defiant,* are derived from Latin participles either directly or through the French. As an illustration of how large this element is in English, nearly three-fourths of the words in the Preamble to the Constitution of the United States (with the exception of prepositions and articles) are of Latin origin.

The study of Latin is, therefore, to a large extent, the study of the history of our own language. But it is more than merely a study of its history. One who has become familiar with the derivation of the words which he uses is likely to speak and write with greater clearness and accuracy. For this reason the best schools which afford training for those who wish to become newspaper writers advise or require the study of Latin as a preparation. For the same reason, law schools require that a student shall have some knowledge of Latin, and prominent lawyers have said that no other training can give the command of language which is necessary for the largest success in the legal profession. Schools of engineering advise or require Latin because the Latin student usually has the ability to state a plan of work or describe what is to be done with greater clearness than one who has not had the training afforded by Latin.

For business life the study of Latin is valuable in that it gives one a larger English vocabulary and through the experience of translation affords training in the careful choice of words. Even a brief course, of two or three years will give much help in these respects. One who has learned to look carefully at words is more likely to avoid errors in spelling and in the structure of sentences. Inaccuracy in the use of language may be the cause of failure in many situations in the business world. In proportion as one gains positions of greater importance, the ability to speak and write clearly and correctly becomes more valuable. The opportunities for success for one who lacks this ability are rapidly becoming less.

Another reason why the study of Latin is of importance to the English-speaking person is that his own literature is made clearer thereby. The greatest works of English literature have been written by men who knew Latin, and they contain innumerable passages which cannot be understood without a knowledge of Latin. This does not mean simply Latin quotations, but references and forms of expression in English. And this is true not merely of the writers of an early period, but of some of the most modern. Many English poems have as their titles famous Latin phrases which one must understand in order to appreciate the poems themselves.

The modern languages which have been developed from Latin are very important and widely spoken. Those of Italy, France, Spain, Portugal, and Roumania are modern forms of Latin. And since the languages spoken in the greater part of South America, and Mexico, and in parts of the southwestern states of our own country and of Canada belong to this group, they are of very direct concern to us. Further, one who wishes to become familiar with the great literatures of the world or to be able to read important scientific books must

**MAP SHOWING THE INFLUENCE OF LATIN ON THE LANGUAGES OF
MODERN EUROPE**

Heavy shading indicates languages directly derived from Latin
Light shading indicates languages largely influenced by Latin

know at least one of these languages. If he knows Latin he has the foundation of all of them and can learn any one of them with much less effort because of that knowledge.

In the Latin language there is also a great literature which one will appreciate better if he reads it in the original form. The works of the Roman poets and historians have had a powerful influence on the literature of modern nations. They are often quoted today, and parts of them have been imitated many times. In reading them one finds the source of a great number of the mythological stories which have been retold in so many forms in later literature. These stories become more vivid and real as they are read in the language in which they were originally written.

In these ways and in others, the study of Latin is closely connected with the life of the modern world, and it cannot well be disregarded by any one who wishes to become in the best sense efficient and intelligent.

INTRODUCTORY LESSON

1. The Latin alphabet is the same as the English, except that the Latin has no **j** or **w**.

VOWELS AND CONSONANTS

2. The vowels, as in English, are **a, e, i, o, u,** and **y.** The other letters are consonants. The letter **i** is usually a consonant when it stands at the beginning of a word and is followed by a vowel, or when it stands between vowels within a word.

SOUNDS OF THE LETTERS

3. The vowels in Latin are either long or short. In this book long vowels are indicated by a mark placed above them. A vowel which is unmarked is short. The vowel sounds are indicated in the following table:

ā = *a* in "father"	a = *a* in "comma"[1]
ē = *a* in "fade"	e = *e* in "net"
ī = *i* in "machine"	i = *i* in "this"
ō = *o* in "holy"	o = *o* in "domain"
ū = *u* in "rude"	u = *u* in "full"

y is seldom used. Its sound is the same as that of *u* in the French language or *ü* in German.

---

[1] Like ā, but pronounced more quickly.

1

4. The consonants have in general the same sounds as in English. The following exceptions are to be noted:

c and **ch** have the sound of *k*.

g has only one sound, that heard in *go*.

i as a consonant is equivalent to *y* in *yes*.

s has only the sound heard in *say*.

t always has the sound heard in *top*. It does not combine with *i* to give the sound of *sh* as in *nation*.

v has the sound of *w*.

x has only the sound of *ks*, as in *exercise*.

bs and **bt** are equivalent to *ps* and *pt*.

ph and **th** are nearly equivalent to *p* and *t*.

DIPHTHONGS

5. A diphthong is a combination of two vowels in one syllable. The diphthongs are **ae, au, ei, eu, oe,** and **ui.** Their sounds are as follows:

ae = *ai* in "aisle"	**eu** = *eu* in "feud"
au = *ou* in "out"	**oe** = *oi* in "boil"
ei = *ei* in "vein"	**ui** = almost[1] *ui* in "ruin"

SYLLABLES

6. (1) A syllable must contain a vowel or a diphthong, and may contain also one or more consonants.

(2) A consonant between two vowels is taken with the vowel which follows it: **pō-nō, ha-be-ō.**

(3) Two consonants between two vowels are divided, one going with the vowel which precedes and one with the vowel which follows. But if the second of two consonants is **l** or **r,** and if the combination can be pronounced at the beginning of a word, as **bl, br,** etc., the two are taken with the vowel which follows, like a single consonant:[2] **man-dā-re, car-dō;** but **fe-bris, ā-cris.**

---

[1] The **u** is shorter than in the English word, and the vowels are more closely blended.

[2] In the division of a compound verb into syllables in writing or printing, the prepositional element is separated from the simple verb.

LENGTH OF SYLLABLES

7. (1) A syllable is long if it contains a long vowel or a diphthong: **dō-num, cau-tus.**

(2) A syllable is long if its vowel is followed by two consonants, except when the first of these consonants is a mute, and the second is **l** or **r.** The mutes are **b, p, c, k, q, g, d, t,** and the combinations **ph, th,** and **ch: con-dō, mit-tō.**

(3) All other syllables are short: **me-mor, a-grī.**

　　a. **x** and **z** have the value of two consonants because they represent a combination of sounds. A syllable is long if its vowel is followed by either of these double consonants.

ACCENT

8. (1) In a word of two syllables the accent falls on the first syllable.

(2) In a word of more than two syllables the accent falls on the syllable before the last, if it is long, otherwise on the second syllable from the last: **lū′men, au-dī′re, con-ten′tus, me′mi-nī.**

(3) The syllable before the last is called the *penult*, the second from the last is called the *antepenult.*

LESSON I

NOUN INFLECTION: THE ARTICLE: POSITION OF VERB

THE USE OF CASE FORMS IN ENGLISH

9. In English, one form of the pronoun is used as the subject of the sentence, a different form as the object of a verb or of a preposition, and a third form to express possession.

> *He* walks (subject).
> We see *him* (object).
> *His* book is new (possessive).

CASE FORMS OF LATIN NOUNS

10. In Latin, nouns as well as pronouns have different forms to show how they are used in sentences.

> **Puella** (subject) **ambulat,** *the girl walks.*
> **Puellam** (object) **vidēmus,** *we see the girl.*
> **Liber puellae** (possessive), *the girl's book.*

NAMES OF CASES

11. The subject case is called the Nominative, the object case is called the Accusative, and the case of the possessor is called the Genitive.

> Nom. **puella** (subject).
> Gen. **puellae** (possessive).
> Acc. **puellam** (object).

TRANSLATION OF THE GENITIVE

12. The genitive is sometimes translated by the English possessive, as in the example above, and sometimes by *of* and the noun. **Puellae** may be translated *the girl's* or *of the girl.*

THE ARTICLE

13. The Latin has no article. With the English translation of a Latin noun, *a, an,* or *the* is generally supplied as the sense requires. **Puella** means *the girl* or *a girl* according to the meaning of the sentence in which it stands.

POSITION OF THE VERB

14. The verb of a Latin sentence, unless it is especially emphasized, usually stands at the end of the sentence.[1]

15. ### VOCABULARY

fēmina, woman   amat, loves
fīlia, daughter   dat, gives
puella, girl   laudat, praises
rosa, rose   vocat, calls

EXERCISES

16.
1. Fēmina puellam vocat.
2. Puella fēminam vocat.
3. Fīlia rosam dat.
4. Fēmina rosam puellae laudat.
5. Puella fīliam fēminae amat.
6. Fīlia fēminae rosam laudat.

17.
1. The woman loves the girl.
2. The girl loves the woman.
3. The woman praises the girl.
4. The woman's daughter gives a rose.
5. The girl praises the woman's rose.

SUGGESTED DRILL

(1) Divide the words of the vocabulary into syllables and indicate the accent of each word. (2) Give the genitive and the accusative of each noun in the vocabulary. (3) In the following sentences point out the subjects: (a) The boy has a gun. (b) We missed the first train. (c) You did not see us yesterday. (d) The engine of the aeroplane is small. (e) The boy's gun is not loaded. (f) The friends of this girl sent presents. (4) In the sentences of (3) point out the objects, and also the words or phrases which express possession. (5) Name the case in which each noun or pronoun in these sentences would stand if translated into Latin.

---

[1] The forms of the verb meaning *to be,* when equivalent to the English *there is,* or *there are,* usually stand first in the clause.

LESSON II

ADJECTIVES: PREDICATE ADJECTIVES AND NOUNS

CASE FORMS OF ADJECTIVES

18. Adjectives as well as nouns have different case forms in Latin. An adjective agrees in case with the noun to which it belongs.

NOM. **puella bona,** *a good girl.*
GEN. **puellae bonae,** *of a good girl.*
ACC. **puellam bonam,** *a good girl.*

POSITION OF ADJECTIVES

19. An adjective which tells some quality of a noun is placed after the noun to which it belongs, unless especially emphasized: **Fēmina benigna,** *the kind woman.*

PREDICATE ADJECTIVES

20. An adjective which is connected with a noun or pronoun by some form of the verb meaning *to be* is called a Predicate Adjective.

The girl is *good.*

A predicate adjective agrees with the subject of its clause.

Fēmina benigna est, *the woman is kind.*

PREDICATE NOUNS

21. A noun which is connected with the subject by some form of the verb meaning *to be* is called a Predicate Noun. A predicate noun stands in the same case as the subject.

Puella fīlia fēminae est, *the girl is the woman's daughter.*

22. VOCABULARY

benigna, kind
bona, good
magna, large
pulchra, beautiful

īnsula, island
statua, statue
est, is
et, and

EXERCISES

23. 1. Puella benigna est.
2. Statua pulchra est.
3. Insula magna et pulchra est.
4. Fīlia fēminae benignae bona est.
5. Fīlia fēminae bonae benigna est.
6. Fēmina statuam pulchram laudat.
7. Puella fēminam benignam amat.

24. 1. The woman is kind.
2. The rose is beautiful.
3. The woman's daughter is a good girl.
4. The girl gives a beautiful rose.
5. The woman praises the large statue.

SUGGESTED DRILL

(1) Name the case of each noun in the sentences of **23** and tell why each noun stands in the case in which it appears. (2) Point out the predicate adjectives in the sentences of **23** and **24**. (3) Point out the predicate nouns and the objects in the following sentences and state what the case of each would be in Latin: (a) The man was a stranger. (b) I have had no dinner. (c) You have been the leader. (d) This boy will never be a good player. (e) We saw your friend yesterday.

ROMAN CHILDREN AT PLAY

LESSON III

INDIRECT OBJECT: DATIVE WITH ADJECTIVES: POSITION OF GENITIVE AND DATIVE

THE INDIRECT OBJECT

25. The word denoting the person to whom something is given or said or shown is called the Indirect Object.

> He told the *boy* an interesting story.
> The girl gave her *sister* a picture.

THE DATIVE AS INDIRECT OBJECT

26. In Latin, the case of the indirect object is called the Dative. Nouns which end in -a in the nominative have the same form for the dative as for the genitive in the singular.

Fēmina puellae rosam dat, *the woman gives the girl a rose.*

a. In English the indirect object is often expressed by "to" and the noun.

> The woman gives a rose *to the girl.*

In Latin the phrase *to the girl* is expressed by the one word, **puellae.**

THE DATIVE WITH ADJECTIVES

27. In English, many adjectives, such as those meaning *kind, friendly, pleasing, useful, near,* are modified by a phrase consisting of the preposition *to* and a noun or pronoun.

> Every one is kind *to me.*

In Latin, such adjectives are modified by the dative.
Puellae benigna, *kind to the girl.*

POSITION OF THE GENITIVE AND THE DATIVE

28. (1) A noun in the genitive case, when not emphasized, commonly stands after the word to which it belongs.

(2) A noun in the dative case, when not emphasized, commonly stands before the word to which it belongs.

VERB ENDINGS OF THE THIRD PERSON

29. Verbs ending in -t are in the third person, singular number. The third person plural ends in **-nt**.

> Sing. **laudat,** *praises.*
> Plu. **laudant,** *praise.*

30. ## VOCABULARY

agricola, farmer   **grāta,** pleasing
amīcitia, friendship   **tua,** your, yours
aqua, water   **tibi,** to you (*dative*)
nauta, sailor   **portat,** carries

EXERCISES

31.
1. Puella aquam portat.
2. Amīcitia tibi grāta est.
3. Nauta et fēmina puellam laudant.
4. Amīcitia tua nautae est grāta.
5. Puella fēminae (*dative*) benigna est.
6. Agricola puellae rosam dat.
7. Puella fīliam agricolae amat.

32.
1. The good daughter gives a rose to the woman.
2. The girl and the woman call the sailor.
3. The large rose is pleasing to you.
4. Your friendship is pleasing to the good girl.
5. The farmer and the sailor praise the statue.

SUGGESTED DRILL

(1) Give the dative and the accusative forms of the nouns in the vocabulary above. (2) Give the third person plural of the verbs in the vocabulary of Lesson I. (3) Name the case which may be used after adjectives meaning *friendly, unfriendly, pleasing, opposed, injurious.* (4) Point out the indirect objects and also the direct objects in the following sentences: (a) They told us the reason for this. (b) No one gave the tramp money. (c) Who gave your brother this knife? (d) He said this to his father.

LESSON IV

THE ABLATIVE: THE VOCATIVE: THE FIRST DECLENSION

THE ABLATIVE CASE

33. The case used in Latin to express relations which are indicated in English by the prepositions *from, in,* and *with* is called the Ablative. There are additional uses of this case which have been developed from these. Latin prepositions are sometimes used with the ablative.

> **ex silvā,** *from the forest.*
> **in silvā,** *in the forest.*
> **cum nautā,** *with the sailor.*

a. The form of the ablative singular is to be distinguished from that of the nominative singular by the final long **a** in such nouns as those given above.

> Nom. **silva.**
> Abl. **silvā.**

THE VOCATIVE CASE

34. The case used in Latin to name the person directly addressed is called the Vocative. In most nouns the vocative singular is identical in form with the nominative singular. The vocative plural is always identical with the nominative plural.

Fīlia tua, Cornēlia, pulchra est, *Cornelia, your daughter is beautiful.*

POSITION OF THE VOCATIVE

35. In Latin, the vocative regularly stands after one or more words in the sentence, as in the example above. Its English equivalent usually stands either at the beginning or at the end of the sentence.

THE FIRST DECLENSION

36. The nouns which have been given thus far belong to what is called the First Declension. They are declined in full through the singular and plural according to the following model:[1]

rosa, *rose*

SINGULAR			TERMINATIONS
NOM.	rosa,	*a rose* (subject or predicate)	**-a**
GEN.	rosae,	*of a rose*	**-ae**
DAT.	rosae,	*to* or *for a rose*	**-ae**
ACC.	rosam,	*a rose* (object)	**-am**
ABL.	rosā,	*from, in, with a rose*	**-ā**
	PLURAL		
NOM.	rosae,	*roses* (subject or predicate)	**-ae**
GEN.	rosārum,	*of roses*	**-ārum**
DAT.	rosīs,	*to* or *for roses*	**-īs**
ACC.	rosās,	*roses* (object)	**-ās**
ABL.	rosīs,	*from, in, with roses*	**-īs**

a. The genitive singular ending, -ae, printed after a word in the vocabulary shows that the word belongs to the first declension.

IDENTICAL FORMS

37. The form **rosae** may be a genitive singular, a dative singular, a nominative plural, or a vocative plural. The meaning of the rest of the sentence will usually make it possible to determine what is the case of a doubtful form.

THE BASE

38. The part of a noun to which the terminations are added and which is not changed in declension, is called the Base. The base of **rosa** is **ros-**. The base of a noun is found by dropping the ending of the genitive singular.

---

[1] The noun **filia** has the irregular form **filiābus** in the dative and ablative plural.

39.   **VOCABULARY**

Cornēlia, Cornelia (*a woman's name*)

silva, -ae, forest

ambulat, walks

habitat, lives, dwells

cum, *prep. with abl.,* with

properat, hastens

ē, ex,[1] *prep. with abl.,* from, out of

in, *prep. with abl., in, on*

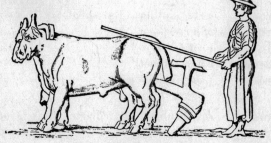

ROMAN FARMER WITH PLOW

EXERCISES

40. 1. Silva magna tibi est grāta. 2. Agricola in silvā magnā est. 3. Fēmina cum fīliā in īnsulā habitat. 4. Cornēlia ex silvā properat. 5. Fīliae agricolae rosam magnam laudant. 6. Puellae, Cornēlia, in silvā ambulant. 7. Amīcitia fēminārum tibi grāta est. 8. Fēmina puellīs rosās dat.

41. 1. The sailors live on the large island. 2. The woman walks with the girls. 3. The rose is pleasing to the girls. 4. The farmer hastens from the forest. 5. The woman praises the farmer's daughters.

SUGGESTED DRILL

(1) Give the case terminations of the first declension in the singular and plural. (2) Decline the nouns in the vocabularies of this lesson and of the preceding lesson. (3) Name the case of each noun in 40. (4) Point out the subjects of the sentences in 41. (5) Point out a direct object in 41.

---

[1] Before vowels and *h*, **ex** is used, before most consonants, **ē.**

LESSON V

PRESENT INDICATIVE: AGREEMENT OF VERB: THE INFINITIVE: FIRST CONJUGATION

THE THREE FORMS OF THE ENGLISH VERB

42. The English verb has three forms for the present tense; *walks, does walk,* and *is walking* are all present. In Latin, there is only one form for this tense. The form **ambulat** is translated *walks,* or *is walking,* or *does walk,* as the sense requires. **Nōn ambulat** is translated *does not walk,* or *is not walking.* **Ubi puella habitat** is translated *Where does the girl live?* or *Where is the girl living?*

PERSONAL ENDINGS OF THE VERB

43. The form **portō** is translated *I carry (am carrying, do carry).* The subject *I* is indicated by the ending **-ō,** and a pronoun is not expressed unless the subject is emphasized, or contrasted with another word.

In the form **portat,** the ending **-t** shows that the verb is third person, singular number. If no subject is expressed in the Latin, a pronoun of the third person, *he, she,* or *it,* is regularly to be supplied in translation. Thus **est** may be translated *he·is,* or *she is,* or *it is.*

The other personal pronouns when not emphatic are likewise indicated as subjects by verb endings.

AGREEMENT OF THE VERB

44. The verb agrees with its subject in person and number.

THE INFINITIVE

45. The present active infinitive of **portō** is **portāre,** *to carry.* All verbs given thus far, except the verb meaning *to be,* form the present active infinitive with the termination **-āre: laudāre,** *to praise;* **amāre,** *to love.*

    a. The infinitive **dare,** *to give,* is slightly irregular. in that the **a** is short.

THE FIRST CONJUGATION

46. Verbs which have the infinitive termination **-āre** form what is called the First Conjugation.

The forms of the first conjugation in the present tense, indicative mood, active voice, are as follows:

	SINGULAR		PERSONAL ENDINGS
1. portō,	*I carry, (am carrying, do carry)*	**-ō** (*I*)
2. portās,	*you* (singular) *carry,* etc.	**-s** (*you*)[1]
3. portat,	*he, she, it carries,* etc.	**-t** (*he, she, it*)

	PLURAL		
1. portāmus,	*we carry,* etc.	**-mus** (*we*)
2. portātis,	*you* (plural) *carry,* etc.	**-tis** (*you*)
3. portant,	*they carry,* etc.	**-nt** (*they*)

    a. In the vocabulary, either the infinitive or its termination is printed after the first form given, to indicate the conjugation.

    b. The main body of the verb, ending in the characteristic vowel, is called the Present Stem. The present stem of **portāre** is **portā-**. The present tense of the indicative mood is formed by uniting personal endings to the present stem. In the first person singular of the first conjugation the characteristic **ā** disappears. Before the endings **-t** and **-nt** it becomes short **a**.

47.   **VOCABULARY**

Britannia, -ae, Great Britain   **mea,** my, mine
Hibernia, -ae, Ireland   **mihi,** to me (*dat.*)
patria, -ae, native country   **nōn,** *adv.,* not
via, -ae, road, street   **sunt,** are, they are

---

    [1] In English, *you carry* may be either singular or plural. In Latin, the distinction between the singular and the plural of the verb in the second person is always indicated.

FIRST REVIEW LESSON

50. (1) The subject of a finite[1] verb is in the nominative case.

(2) The predicate noun used with a finite form of the verb meaning *to be* is in the nominative case.

(3) The genitive case is used to name a person or thing referred to as possessing something.

(4) The indirect object is in the dative case.

(5) The dative is used in sentences or phrases containing adjectives of attitude or quality or relation to denote that toward which the attitude, quality, or relation is directed or in reference to which it is said to exist.

(6) The direct object of a verb is in the accusative case.

(7) The ablative case is used to express relations indicated in English by the prepositions *from, with,* or *in*.

(8) The vocative case is used to denote the person addressed.

TERMINATIONS (First Declension)

	SINGULAR	PLURAL
NOM.	-a	-ae
GEN.	-ae	-ārum
DAT.	-ae	-īs
ACC.	-am	-ās
ABL.	-ā	-īs

PERSONAL ENDINGS (Active Voice)

	SINGULAR	PLURAL
1.	-ō or -m[2] (*I*)	-mus (*we*)
2.	-s (*you*)	-tis (*you*)
3.	-t (*he, she, it*)	-nt (*they*)

51. Give Latin words with which the following English words are connected in derivation:

amble	habitation	patriotic
aquatic	Hibernian	portable
benign	insular	rose
Britain	laudable	statue
feminine	magnify	via (*in time-tables*)
gratify	nautical	vocation

---

[1] That is, any verb form except the infinitives and participles.
[2] The use of the personal ending -m will be shown later.

EXERCISES

48. 1. Nōn in Hiberniā habitō. 2. Britannia et Hibern
sunt īnsulae. 3. Britannia nōn patria mea est. 4. In v.
cum nautā ambulāmus. 5. In īnsulā habitō. 6. Puella mil
rosam dat. 7. Tibi rosās dō. 8. Statuam pulchram laudā
tis. 9. Patriam meam amō et laudō. 10. Fīlia agricola(
cum fēminā in viā ambulat.

49. 1. I praise the daughter of the farmer. 2. You (*sin-gular*) are calling (call) the girl. 3. We do not live on the
island. 4. My native country is beautiful. 5. You (*plural*)
love the forest. 6. You love and praise your native country.

SUGGESTED DRILL

(1) Give the personal endings of the verb, and the English pronoun
for which each stands. (2) Translate **laudō** in three different ways.
(3) Give the infinitives of the verbs in the vocabularies of Lessons
I, III, and IV, with the meaning of each. (4) Divide the words
Britannia and **Hibernia** into syllables and indicate the accent. (5)
Form two English sentences, each of which contains a direct and an
indirect object. (6) Tell what would be the case of these objects in
Latin. (7) Form two English sentences containing predicate nouns
and tell what would be the case of these nouns in Latin.

ROMAN WALL IN BRITAIN

LESSON VI

GENDER OF NOUNS: SECOND DECLENSION, -*UM* NOUNS: AGREEMENT OF ADJECTIVES

GENDER

52. In Latin, gender is only in part a distinction based on sex. Many nouns referring to objects without life are either masculine or feminine. For example, **silva** and **rosa** are feminine.

GENDER IN THE FIRST DECLENSION

53. Nouns of the first declension are feminine, with the exception of a few words which regularly denote men. **Agricola** and **nauta** belong to this class and are masculine.

THE SECOND DECLENSION. NEUTER NOUNS

54. Nouns ending in -**um** are of the Second Declension and are neuter in gender. They are declined as follows:

templum, N., *temple*
BASE, **templ-**

	SINGULAR		TERMINATIONS
NOM.	templum,	*a temple*	-um
GEN.	templī,	*of a temple*	-ī
DAT.	templō,	*to* or *for a temple*	-ō
ACC.	templum,	*a temple*	-um
ABL.	templō,	*from, in, with a temple*	-ō

	PLURAL		
NOM.	templa,	*temples*	-a
GEN.	templōrum,	*of temples*	-ōrum
DAT.	templīs,	*to* or *for temples*	-īs
ACC.	templa,	*temples*	-a
ABL.	templīs,	*from, in, with temples*	-īs

a. The genitive ending -**ī** placed after a word in the vocabulary indicates that it is of the second declension.

AGREEMENT OF ADJECTIVES

55. Adjectives agree with their nouns in gender and number, as well as in case.

> **templum magnum,** *a great temple.*
> **silva magna,** *a great forest.*

56.   **VOCABULARY**

dōnum, -ī, N., gift, present

oppidum, -ī, N., town

perīculum, -ī, N., danger

saxum, -ī, N., rock, stone

sed, *conj.,* but

stō, stāre, stand

templum, -ī, N., temple

vītō, -āre, avoid

EXERCISES

57. 1. Agricola saxum magnum portat. 2. Templum pulchrum in īnsulā laudō. 3. In oppidō magnō habitāmus. 4. Dōnum grātum tibi nōn dant. 5. In īnsulā habitō, sed īnsula nōn mihi grāta est. 6. Agricola et nauta perīculum nōn vītant. 7. Puellae in viā cum fēminā stant. 8. In viā oppidī cum fīliā tuā ambulō.

58. 1. In the forest are large stones. 2. We give presents to the girls. 3. We are standing in the forest with the farmer. 4. Cornelia loves the woman, but she does not love the woman's daughter. 5. The woman gives a present to the sailor's daughter. 6. The sailor praises the beautiful town.

SUGGESTED DRILL

(1) Decline the nouns **oppidum, saxum,** and **dōnum.** (2) Conjugate the verbs in the vocabulary of this lesson, in the present tense. (3) Decline together **saxum magnum.** (4) Decline together **silva magna.** (5) Point out the adjectives in **57** and give the reason for their forms. (6) Point out an indirect object in **58.** (7) Give the case terminations of **templum.**

FIRST SUPPLEMENTARY REVIEW

The following Supplementary Reviews, which contain additional material for word study, may be substituted by teachers who wish to do so in place of the reviews following lessons 10, 20, 30, etc.

VOCABULARY REVIEW

1. agricola, -ae, M.
2. amīcitia, -ae, F.
3. amō, -āre
4. cum, *prep. with abl.*
5. dīligentia, -ae, F.
6. dō, dare
7. ē, ex, *prep. with abl.*
8. et, *conj.*
9. exemplum, -ī, N.
10. fāma, -ae, F.
11. fīlia, -ae, F.
12. ignōrō, -āre
13. īnsula, -ae, F.
14. līberō, -āre
15. nōn, *adv.*
16. oppidum, -ī, N.
17. perīculum, -ī, N.
18. portō, -āre
19. properō, -are
20. puella, -ae, F
21. sed, *conj.*
22. silva, -ae, F.
23. temptō, -āre
24. via, -ae, F.
25. vīlla, -ae, F.
26. vocō, -āre

---

1. farmer
2. friendship
3. love
4. with
5. painstaking, care
6. give
7. out from
8. and, also, even
9. example, precedent
10. reputation, report
11. daughter
12. be ignorant of
13. island
14. set free
15. not
16. town
17. trial, danger
18. carry
19. hurry
20. girl
21. but
22. forest
23. test, try, attempt
24. highway, road
25. farmhouse
26. call

WORD STUDY

1. We have seen (p. xvii) that many English words, such as *terminus, stimulus, veto, censor, census,* were originally Latin words, and have been taken into English without change of spelling. Others, such as *humble, count, blame, sure,* are greatly changed from their original Latin form, because they have not come directly from Latin, but were developed in French from Latin, with changed pronunciation and spelling,

and were taken from French into English. Some times the meaning as well as the form of these words has changed, but usually we can recognize the original meaning.

2. We often find a group of Latin words which are related in derivation and meaning. Thus, **amō, amor, amīcus, amīcitia, amābilis, inimīcus, inimīcitia** have a common element. We shall see later something of how Latin words are formed. We sometimes say that an English word is related in derivation to a certain Latin word, although it does not come directly from that word, but from another word which is derived from the Latin word given. Thus, we say the word *amiable* is related in derivation to the Latin **amō**, although it comes more directly from **amābilis**, which in turn is from **amō**. Some of the Latin words from which our English words are directly derived were not often used by good Latin writers, and therefore the derivation of the English word is more easily explained by a related Latin word of common use.

3. There are certain changes of spelling which we find in the development of English words from Latin. Thus, Latin words ending in -**tia** often give English words in -*ce* (occasionally -*cy*). For example, *temperance* is from **temperantia**, and *patience* from **patientia**. Other changes will be explained later.

In the following list of English words which are related to Latin words found in the vocabulary on the preceding page, look up in a dictionary the meaning of those which are not familiar.

4.   RELATED ENGLISH WORDS [1]

amiable	export	peninsula	tempt
diligence	fame	peril	via (in time
example	ignorant	porter	tables)
exemplary	insular	silvan	villa

[1] This list and similar lists which follow are not meant to be exhaustive. They may be extended by teachers who wish to do so.

LESSON VII

SECOND DECLENSION, -*US* AND -*IR* NOUNS: VOCATIVE FORMS: APPOSITION: POSITION OF ADVERBS

NOUNS OF THE SECOND DECLENSION IN -*US* AND -*IR*

59. In addition to the neuter nouns ending in -um, the second declension has masculine nouns ending in -us, -er, and -ir. The declension of those which end in -us and -ir is as follows:

amīcus, M., *friend*   vir, M., *man*
BASE, amīc-   BASE, vir-

	SINGULAR	TERMINATIONS		SINGULAR	TERMINATIONS
Nom.	amīcus, *a friend*	-us	vir, *man*	—
Gen.	amīcī, *of a friend,* etc.	-ī	virī, *of a man*	-ī
Dat.	amīcō	-ō	virō	-ō
Acc.	amīcum	-um	virum	-um
Abl.	amīcō	-ō	virō	-ō
Voc.	amīce	-e		

	PLURAL	TERMINATIONS		PLURAL	TERMINATIONS
Nom.	amīcī	-ī	virī	-ī
Gen.	amīcōrum	-ōrum	virōrum	-ōrum
Dat.	amīcīs	-īs	virīs	-īs
Acc.	amīcōs	-ōs	virōs	-ōs
Abl.	amīcīs	-īs	virīs	-īs

FORMS OF THE VOCATIVE

60. The vocative singular of nouns of the second declension in -us ends in -e. In all other Latin nouns the vocative singular is the same form as the nominative singular. The vocative plural of all nouns is the same as the nominative plural.

APPOSITION

61. A noun which serves to explain another noun referring to the same person or thing is said to be in Apposition with that noun.

Jones, *the captain* of the team, was hurt.

In this sentence, *captain* is in apposition with *Jones*.

THE APPIAN WAY IN THE TIME OF AUGUSTUS

THE CASE OF NOUNS IN APPOSITION

62. A noun in apposition stands in the same case as the noun it explains.

Cornēlia, fīlia agricolae, benigna est, *Cornelia, the farmer's daughter, is kind.*

POSITION OF ADVERBS

63. An adverb usually stands before the word which it modifies.

64. VOCABULARY

amīcus, -ī, M., friend
cūr, adv., why
errō, -āre, wander
labōrō, -āre, work
numquam, adv., never

nunc, adv., now
servus, -ī, M., slave
Sextus, -ī, M., Sextus, *name of a man*
vir, virī, M., man

EXERCISES

65. 1. Cūr dōna nōn tibi grāta sunt? 2. Sextus, servus, cum agricolā labōrat. 3. Amīcus agricolae in silvā errat. 4. Cornēlia, fīlia nautae, nunc in oppidō est. 5. Amīcum Cornēliae numquam laudō. 6. Fīliam tuam, Sexte, laudō. 7. Servus in templō cum virō stat. 8. Virī mihi dōna dant. 9. Vir nauta est et in īnsulā habitat. 10. Agricola Sextum servum laudat.

66. 1. The slaves are wandering in the forest. 2. The man is standing in the street with the slave and the sailor. 3. Why is Sextus, the slave, working in the town? 4. Friend, you never praise your native country. 5. The man's native country is Ireland, but he lives in Great Britain.

SUGGESTED DRILL

(1) Form the vocative singular of **servus, Sextus, agricola,** and **fēmina.** (2) Divide into syllables the words **amīcōrum** and **agricolae** and indicate the accent of each. (3) Point out the words used in apposition in 65. (4) Name the cases which have the same forms in the plural of masculine nouns of the second declension. (5) Point out the appositives (nouns in apposition) and the predicate nouns in the following sentences, and name the case in which each would stand in Latin: (a) Maynard, the captain, was a hero. (b) We saw William, the boy who had been hurt. (c) I gave the papers to the lawyer, the man standing by the table. (d) This plan was the work of Franklin, the printer.

LESSON VIII

SECOND DECLENSION, *-ER* NOUNS: PRESENT INDICATIVE OF *SUM*: THE EXPLETIVE "THERE"

NOUNS OF THE SECOND DECLENSION IN *-ER*

67. Second declension nouns in **-er** are declined thus:

puer, M., *boy*   **ager**, M., *field*
BASE, **puer-**   BASE, **agr-**

	SINGULAR	PLURAL		SINGULAR	PLURAL
NOM.	puer	puerī	NOM.	ager	agrī
GEN.	puerī	puerōrum	GEN.	agrī	agrōrum
DAT.	puerō	puerīs	DAT.	agrō	agrīs
ACC.	puerum	puerōs	ACC.	agrum	agrōs
ABL.	puerō	puerīs	ABL.	agrō	agrīs

68. The case terminations of the second declension are:

	SINGULAR			PLURAL	
	Masc.	*Neut.*		*Masc.*	*Neut.*
NOM.	-us, -er, -ir	-um	NOM.	-ī	-a
GEN.	-ī	-ī	GEN.	-ōrum	-ōrum
DAT.	-ō	-ō	DAT.	-īs	-īs
ACC.	-um	-um	ACC.	-ōs	-a
ABL.	-ō	-ō	ABL.	-īs	-īs

(Vocative singular, -e in nouns ending in -us)

69. The genitive printed after a word in the vocabulary will show whether or not the **e** of the nominative appears in the other cases.

THE PRESENT INDICATIVE OF *SUM*

70. The irregular verb **sum** is conjugated as follows in the present indicative:

SINGULAR		PLURAL	
1. sum,	*I am*	1. sumus,	*we are*
2. es,	*you are*	2. estis,	*you are*
3. est,	*he, she, it is*	3. sunt,	*they are*

    a. The present infinitive is **esse,** *to be.*

THE EXPLETIVE "THERE"

71. The English word *there* is often used as an expletive; that is, it serves merely to introduce the sentence and has no adverbial force (no idea of place). In this use it has no equivalent in Latin, and is to be supplied in translation when the sense requires; **est perīculum** may be translated, *there is danger.*

72. **VOCABULARY**

accūsō, -āre, accuse, censure
ager, agrī, M., field
liber, librī, M., book
mūrus, -ī, M., wall

puer, puerī, M., boy
quod, *conj.,* because
tēlum, -ī, N., weapon
ubi, *adv.,* where, when

EXERCISES

73. 1. Puer in (*on*) mūrō ambulat. 2. Vir puerōs accūsat quod in agrō sunt. 3. Cūr puerī et puellae librōs portant? 4. Amīcus puerōrum et puellārum es. 5. Vir puellae bonae librum dat. 6. Perīculum virōrum et puerōrum est magnum. 7. In silvā cum puerīs sumus. 8. Ubi liber puerī est?

74. 1. The boys are walking on the island with the sailor. 2. There is danger in the forest. 3. The men are carrying weapons because there is danger. 4. The woman praises the roses and the books. 5. The boy is walking in the field and is carrying a stone. 6. Where does the sailor's friend live?

SUGGESTED DRILL

(1) Distinguish between the use of *there* as an expletive and as an adverb in the following sentences: (a) I lived there two years. (b) I did not stop, because there was no one at home. (c) There was thought to be no hope. (2) Form two English sentences containing appositives and explain the case use of the appositives. (3) Point out the case endings of the nouns in sentences 3, 4, 6, 7, **73.** (4) Give the accusative plural of **liber, puer,** and **tēlum.** (5) Give the vocative singular of **amīcus** and **puer.**

LESSON IX

FIRST AND SECOND DECLENSION ADJECTIVES: IRREGULAR GENITIVE AND VOCATIVE FORMS

ADJECTIVES OF THE FIRST AND SECOND DECLENSIONS

75. There are many adjectives which have their masculine and neuter forms in the second declension and their feminine forms in the first declension. Those having the masculine ending in **-us** are declined as follows:

bonus, -a, -um, *good*

SINGULAR

	Masc.	*Fem.*	*Neut.*
NOM.	bonus	bona	bonum
GEN.	bonī	bonae	bonī
DAT.	bonō	bonae	bonō
ACC.	bonum	bonam	bonum
ABL.	bonō	bonā	bonō
VOC.	bone	bona	bonum

PLURAL

NOM.	bonī	bonae	bona
GEN.	bonōrum	bonārum	bonōrum
DAT.	bonīs	bonīs	bonīs
ACC.	bonōs	bonās	bona
ABL.	bonīs	bonīs	bonīs

The adjectives **benignus, grātus,** and **magnus,** the feminine forms of which have been given, are declined like **bonus.**

IRREGULAR GENITIVES OF THE SECOND DECLENSION

76. Nouns ending in **-ium** or **-ius** regularly form the genitive singular by replacing **-ium** or **-ius** by **-ī: beneficium,** gen., **beneficī; fīlius,** gen., **fīlī.** These shortened genitive forms are accented on the syllable before the last: **benefi'cī.** Adjectives are not thus contracted.

IRREGULAR VOCATIVE FORMS

77. Proper nouns ending in -ius and also the common noun fīlius regularly form the vocative singular in the same manner as the genitive singular; hence fīlī may be either genitive singular or vocative singular.

78. VOCABULARY

beneficium, beneficī, N., kindness, favor

fīlius, fīlī, M., son

lātus, -a, -um, wide, broad

longus, -a, -um, long

multus, -a, -um, much; *in the plural,* many

oculus, -ī, M., eye

porta, -ae, F., gate

saepe, *adv.,* often

a. The forms of the adjective **multus** precede the noun: **Multī virī,** *many men.* This is true in general of words which express an idea of quantity.

EXERCISES

79. 1. Oculī puellae magnī sunt. 2. Portae oppidī sunt lātae. 3. Amīcus benignus saepe dōna dat. 4. Cūr nōn patriam tuam amās? 5. Agricola in agrō magnō labōrat. 6. Viae oppidī longae et lātae sunt. 7. Multī virī in Britanniā habitant. 8. Puerī bonī estis et labōrātis. 9. Beneficia amīcōrum sunt grāta.

80. 1. Why do you walk in the street? 2. The island is long but it is not wide. 3. The girl is carrying many roses. 4. The sons of the sailor live in Ireland. 5. The wall of the town is not long. 6. The farmer often praises the good slaves.

SUGGESTED DRILL

(1) Decline together **vir benignus.** (2) Decline together **ager lātus.** (3) Give the genitive singular and the accusative plural of the phrase **auxilium magnum.** (4) Decline together **fīlius bonus.** (5) Give the nominative plural of **longus** in the three genders. (6) Decline together the words meaning *many books.*

LESSON X

FIRST AND SECOND DECLENSION ADJECTIVES (Continued): POSSESSIVE ADJECTIVES

ADJECTIVES IN -ER OF THE FIRST AND SECOND DECLENSIONS

81. Some adjectives of the first and second declensions have the masculine singular nominative ending in **-er**. Of these, some are declined by adding the case endings to the nominative singular of the masculine. In others the **e** before **r** appears only in the nominative and vocative singular of the masculine.

miser, -a, -um, *unhappy*

SINGULAR

	Masc.	*Fem.*	*Neut.*
NOM.	miser	misera	miserum
GEN.	miserī	miserae	miserī
DAT.	miserō	miserae	miserō
ACC.	miserum	miseram	miserum
ABL.	miserō	miserā	miserō

PLURAL

	Masc.	*Fem.*	*Neut.*
NOM.	miserī	miserae	misera
GEN.	miserōrum	miserārum	miserōrum
DAT.	miserīs	miserīs	miserīs
ACC.	miserōs	miserās	misera
ABL.	miserīs	miserīs	miserīs

pulcher, -chra, -chrum, *beautiful*

SINGULAR

NOM.	pulcher	pulchra	pulchrum
GEN.	pulchrī	pulchrae	pulchrī
DAT.	pulchrō	pulchrae	pulchrō
ACC.	pulchrum	pulchram	pulchrum
ABL.	pulchrō	pulchrā	pulchrō

PLURAL

Nom.	pulchrī	pulchrae	pulchra
Gen.	pulchrōrum	pulchrārum	pulchrōrum
Dat.	pulchrīs	pulchrīs	pulchrīs
Acc.	pulchrōs	pulchrās	pulchra
Abl.	pulchrīs	pulchrīs	pulchrīs

82. The adjective does not always have the same ending as the noun with which it agrees.

The use of adjectives with masculine nouns of the first declension is as follows:

nauta bonus, *the good sailor.*

	SINGULAR	PLURAL
Nom.	nauta bonus	nautae bonī
Gen.	nautae bonī	nautārum bonōrum
Dat.	nautae bonō	nautīs bonīs
Acc.	nautam bonum	nautās bonōs
Abl.	nautā bonō	nautīs bonīs
Voc.	nauta bone	nautae bonī

POSSESSIVE ADJECTIVES

83. The possessive words **meus,** *my* or *mine,* **tuus,** *your* (referring to one person), **noster,** *our,* and **vester,** *your* (referring to more than one person) are adjectives, and are declined throughout. They take their gender, number, and case from the thing possessed and not from the persons to whom they refer as possessors.

> **liber meus,** *my book.*
> **rosa mea,** *my rose.*
> **dōnum meum,** *my gift.*

a. The vocative of **meus** in the masculine singular is **mī. Tuus** has no vocative.

84.   VOCABULARY

auxilium, auxilī, N., aid, help,
  assistance
equus, -ī, M., horse
impiger, impigra, impigrum,
  energetic, industrious
līber, lībera, līberum, free

miser, misera, miserum, unhappy, unfortunate
noster, nostra, nostrum, our,
  ours
piger, pigra, pigrum, lazy
postulō, -āre, demand

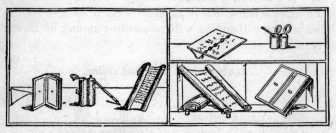

ROMAN WRITING MATERIALS

EXERCISES

85. 1. Virī auxilium nostrum postulant quod perīculum
magnum est. 2. Amīcus noster equum pulchrum tuum
laudat. 3. Fēmina misera est quod puerī pigrī sunt.
4. Agricola impiger cum servō labōrat. 5. Servus miser est
quod nōn līber est. 6. Puer bonus es et amīcōs tuōs amās.
7. Amīcī virōrum benignī sunt. 8. Aquam nōn portātis
quod pigrī estis.

86. 1. A good slave is not lazy. 2. Your daughter loves
beautiful horses. 3. The kind farmer praises the boy.
4. We often praise the good sailor. 5. We are unhappy
because our friends are in danger.

SUGGESTED DRILL

(1) Decline together **nauta miser**. (2) Give the genitive singular
and the vocative singular of the phrase meaning *my son*. (3) Decline together **servus piger**. (4) Decline **noster** in full. (5) Give all
the endings of the second declension in the nominative singular.

SECOND REVIEW LESSON

87.   VOCABULARY REVIEW

ager, agrī, M.   saxum, -ī, N.   dō, dare[1]
agricola, -ae, M.   servus, -ī, M.   errō, -āre
amīcitia, -ae, F.   silva, -ae, F.   habitō, -āre
amīcus, -ī, M.   tēlum, -ī. N.   labōrō, -āre
aqua, -ae, F.   templum, -ī, N.   portō, -āre
auxilium, -ī, N.   via, -ae, F. *road*   postulō, -āre
beneficium, -ī, N.   vir, virī, M.   stō, stāre
dōnum, -ī, N.   benignus, -a, -um   sum, esse
equus, -ī, M.   bonus, -a, -um   vītō, -āre
fēmina, -ae, F.   grātus, -a, -um   vocō, -āre
fīlia, -ae, F.   lātus, -a, -um *wide*   cūr
fīlius, -ī, M.   līber, lībera, līberum *free* nōn
liber, librī, M. *book*   magnus, -a, -um   numquam
mūrus, -ī, M. *wall*   meus, mea, meum   nunc
nauta, -ae, M.   miser, misera, miserum   saepe
oculus, -ī, M.   multus, -a, -um *many*   cum
oppidum, -ī, N. *town*   noster, nostra, nostrum   ē, ex
patria, -ae, F.   piger, pigra, pigrum   in
perīculum, -ī, N.   pulcher, -chra, -chrum   et
porta, -ae, F.   tuus, tua, tuum   quod
puella, -ae, F.   accūsō, -āre   sed
puer, puerī, M.   amō, -āre   ubi

88.   RELATED ENGLISH WORDS

accusation   error   mural
agriculture   filial   oculist
amicable   laborious   peril
auxiliary   liberty   puerile
beneficial   library   servant
donation   miserable   temple
equine   multiply   station

---

[1] The verb **dō** is irregular in that the **a** is short in the infinitive (45, *a*) and in almost all the other forms except the second person singular, **dās**.

ROMAN MATRONS OFFERING GIFTS

LESSON XI

DEMONSTRATIVES: DECLENSION OF *HIC:*   POSITION OF DEMONSTRATIVES

DEMONSTRATIVE ADJECTIVES AND PRONOUNS

89. The demonstratives in Latin, like their most general English equivalents, *this* and *that*, are used to point out objects without describing them.

DECLENSION OF *HIC*

90. The forms of the demonstrative **hic,** *this,* pointing out an object near at hand, are as follows:

	SINGULAR			PLURAL		
	Masc.	*Fem.*	*Neut.*	*Masc.*	*Fem.*	*Neut.*
NOM.	hic	haec	hoc	hī	hae	haec
GEN.	huius	huius	huius	hōrum	hārum	hōrum
DAT.	huie	huic	huic	hīs	hīs	hīs
ACC.	hunc	hanc	hoc	hōs	hās	haec
ABL.	hōc	hāc	hōc	hīs	hīs	hīs

91. The demonstratives may be used as adjectives or as pronouns. As adjectives they agree in gender, number, and case with the nouns to which they belong. As pronouns they agree in gender and number with the nouns to which they refer, but their case is determined by their use in the clauses in which they stand.

POSITION OF DEMONSTRATIVES

92. Demonstrative adjectives, like words which express quantity (**78,** *a*), unless especially emphasized, precede the nouns to which they belong: **hic vir,** *this man.* This is also true of words which denote number.

93.   VOCABULARY

bellum, -ī, N., war
dēmōnstrō, -āre, show, point
     out
hic, haec, hoc, this, *pl.* these
lēgātus, -ī, M., lieutenant,
     envoy

locus, -ī, M. (*usually neuter in*
     the plural), place
vester, -tra, -trum, your, *of*
     more than one
vulnerō, -āre, wound

EXERCISES

94. 1. Hī virī bonī bellum nōn laudant. 2. Lēgātus hoc perīculum vītat. 3. Hunc locum amō ubi amīcī vestrī habitant. 4. Hae puellae numquam magna dōna postulant. 5. Huic agricolae bellum nōn grātum est. 6. Cūr amīcum tuum vulnerās? 7. Fīlia huius virī impigrī nōn impigra est. 8. Hanc puellam laudāmus quod labōrat. 9. Amīcī huius fēminae ex hōc oppidō properant. 10. Hic nauta benignus perīculum dēmōnstrat.

95. 1. We are hastening from the forest with our friends. 2. This girl loves the farmer's daughter. 3. This gift is not pleasing to you. 4. The slave wounds the sailor. 5. There is a large forest on this island. 6. This man points out the forest. 7. Boys, your friends are in great danger.

SUGGESTED DRILL

(1) Decline together **hic ager.** (2) Decline together **haec silva.** (3) Decline together the words meaning *this sailor.* (4) In the following sentences state which occurrences of *your* will be translated by a form of **tuus,** and which by a form of **vester:** (a) Soldiers, your courage has saved us. (b) Mary, where are your books? (c) Your cap has fallen on the ground. (d) Gentlemen, we need your help. (e) Your hand is small.

LESSON XII

FIRST CONJUGATION, PRESENT INDICATIVE PASSIVE: ABLATIVE OF AGENT

THE PASSIVE VOICE

96. The passive voice represents the subject of the clause as acted upon.

Puer laudātur, *the boy is praised.*

97. The passive forms of **portō** in the present tense, indicative mood, are as follows:

SINGULAR

	TERMINATIONS
portor, *I am carried*	-r (-or)
portāris *or* portāre, *you are carried*	-ris (-re)
portātur, *he, she, it is carried*	-tur

PLURAL

portāmur, *we are carried*	-mur
portāminī, *you are carried*	-minī
portantur, *they are carried*	-ntur

a. The passive present forms may also be translated, *I am being carried, you are being carried,* etc.

THE ABLATIVE OF AGENT

98. With passive verbs, the noun or pronoun which indicates the person by whom the act is done is put in the ablative case, governed by the preposition **ā** or **ab.** This is called the Ablative of Agent.

Liber ā puerō portātur, *the book is carried by the boy*

a. There are three points to be noted with regard to the ablative of agent: (1) It always has a preposition. (2) It is used only with a passive verb. (3) It regularly denotes a *person.*

99. **VOCABULARY**

ā, ab,[1] *prep. with abl.*, from, by
carrus, -ī, M., cart
cōnsilium, -ī, N., plan, counsel, advice
exspectō, -āre, wait for, expect

impigrē, *adv.*, industriously, energetically
iuvō, -āre, help, assist
probō, -āre, approve, approve of

EXERCISES

100. 1. Bellum longum ab hīs virīs nōn exspectātur. 2. Hoc cōnsilium ā multīs puerīs probātur. 3. Laudāris quod impigrē labōrās. 4. Ab amīcīs tuīs iuvāmur et laudāmur. 5. Multa tēla ab hīs puerīs portantur. 6. Haec puella laudātur quod impigrē labōrat. 7. Perīculum ā lēgātō numquam vītātur. 8. Carrus agricolae in viā est. 9. Hic nauta auxilium postulat quod in perīculō est. 10. Saxa magna ab hōc agricolā portantur.

101. 1. The slave is helped by this kind man. 2. Gifts are expected by many boys. 3. This plan is praised because it is good. 4. The good farmer praises these horses. 5. This sailor now works energetically. 6. This boy's cart is not large. 7. We approve of your plan and we are your friends.

SUGGESTED DRILL

(1) Conjugate the verbs of the vocabulary in the present passive. (2) Point out the examples of the ablative of agent in the sentences of **100.** (3) Point out the personal endings of the verbs in **100.** (4) Decline together **hoc cōnsilium.** (5) Distinguish between the active and the passive voice in the following phrases: (a) He is praised, he is praising, he is being praised. (b) He is working, he approves, he is called.

---

[1] Before vowels or *h,* **ab** is used, before most consonants, **ā.**

LESSON XIII

ILLE AND *IPSE:* ABLATIVE OF ACCOMPANIMENT

DECLENSION OF *ILLE*

102. The demonstrative **ille,** *that,* is used to refer to an object which is somewhat remote from the speaker in time, place, or thought. It is declined as follows:

	SINGULAR			PLURAL		
	Masc.	*Fem.*	*Neut.*	*Masc.*	*Fem.*	*Neut.*
Nom.	ille	illa	illud	illī	illae	illa
Gen.	illīus	illīus	illīus	illōrum	illārum	illōrum
Dat.	illī	illī	illī	illīs	illīs	illīs
Acc.	illum	illam	illud	illōs	illās	illa
Abl.	illō	illā	illō	illīs	illīs	illīs

DECLENSION OF *IPSE*

103. The intensive pronoun **ipse, ipsa, ipsum,** *himself, herself, itself, myself, yourself,* is used to emphasize a noun or another pronoun, with which it agrees. It is declined as follows:

	SINGULAR			PLURAL		
	Masc.	*Fem.*	*Neut.*	*Masc.*	*Fem.*	*Neut.*
Nom.	ipse	ipsa	ipsum	ipsī	ipsae	ipsa
Gen.	ipsīus	ipsīus	ipsīus	ipsōrum	ipsārum	ipsōrum
Dat.	ipsī	ipsī	ipsī	ipsīs	ipsīs	ipsīs
Acc.	ipsum	ipsam	ipsum	ipsōs	ipsās	ipsa
Abl.	ipsō	ipsā	ipsō	ipsīs	ipsīs	ipsīs

THE ABLATIVE OF ACCOMPANIMENT

104. The use of the ablative with **cum** to name the person with whom one is associated in doing an act is called the Ablative of Accompaniment.

Cum amīcō ambulō, *I walk with a friend.*

105. VOCABULARY

convocō, -āre, call together
ille, illa, illud, that (*pl.* those);
  as pron., he, she, it (*pl.* they)
ipse, ipsa, ipsum, himself, herself, *etc.; pl.* themselves, *etc.*

numerus, -ī, M., number
parvus, -a, -um, small
semper, *adv.*, always
vix, *adv.*, scarcely, with difficulty

EXERCISES

106. 1. Ille puer piger est, hic vir impiger est. 2. Illud saxum ā virō ipsō vix portātur. 3. Servus ipse impigrē labōrat. 4. Perīculum illī virō semper grātum est. 5. Puer magnum numerum amīcōrum convocat. 6. Illa silva magna in īnsulā est. 7. In illō oppidō cum amīcīs habitāmus. 8. Oppidum ipsum nōn grātum est. 9. Illa puella parva librōs amat. 10. Fīlia illīus fēminae benigna est.

107. 1. The boy himself always works. 2. The small temple is praised by my friend. 3. Those girls are not always lazy. 4. We avoid the danger with difficulty. 5. The man himself calls together a large number of small boys. 6. The walls of those towns are large. 7. That farmer always loves good horses. 8. The small boy is helped by the energetic farmer.

SUGGESTED DRILL

(1) Write two Latin sentences containing ablatives of accompaniment, using the verbs **labōrō** and **stō**. (2) Point out an ablative of accompaniment and an ablative of agent in the sentences of **106**. (3) Decline together **illa statua**. (4) Decline together the words meaning *that farmer*. (5) Give the accusative singular and plural of **hic** in all genders.

SECOND SUPPLEMENTARY REVIEW

VOCABULARY REVIEW

1. ā, ab, *prep. with abl.*
2. aequus, -a, -um
3. ager, agrī, M.
4. amīcus, -a, -um (*as noun,* amīcus, -ī, M.)
5. auxilium, -ī, N.
6. barbarus, -a, -um
7. bellum, -ī, N.
8. beneficium, -ī, N.
9. bonus, -a, -um
10. cōnsilium, -ī, N.
11. convocō, -āre
12. cūr, *adv.*
13. dēmōnstrō, -āre
14. equus, -ī, M.
15. exspectō, -āre
16. hic, haec, hoc (*adv.* hīc)
17. fīlius, -ī, M.
18. ille, illa, illud
19. ipse, ipsa, ipsum
20. labōrō, -āre
21. liber, librī, M.
22. līber, lībera, līberum
23. locus, -ī, M. (*pl.* loca, -ōrum, N.)
24. longus, -a, -um
25. magnus, -a, -um
26. meus, -a, -um
27. multus, -a, -um
28. noster, -tra, -trum
29. numerus, -ī, M.
30. nunc, *adv.*
31. parvus, -a, -um
32. porta, -ae, F.
33. puer, puerī, M.
34. pulcher, -chra, -chrum
35. quod, *conj.*
36. sacer, -cra, -crum
37. servus, -ī, M.
38. sum, esse
39. tuus, -a, -um
40. ubi, *adv.*
41. vester, -tra, -trum
42. vir, virī, M.
43. vīvus, -a, -um
44. vulnerō, -āre

---

1. away from, by
2. level, even, just, fair
3. field
4. friendly (*as noun,* friend)
5. aid, help
6. foreign, barbarous
7. war
8. kindness
9. good.
10. advice, plan
11. call together, summon
12. why
13. point out, show
14. horse

15. expect, wait, await
16. this (*as adj.*); he (*as pron.*); (*adv.* here)
17. son
18. that, he
19. self, the very
20. labor, suffer
21. book
22. free
23. place
24. long
25. large
26. my, mine
27. much, many
28. our
29. number
30. now
31. small
32. gate
33. boy
34. beautiful
35. because
36. sacred
37. slave
38. be
39. your (*of one person*)
40. where, when
41. your (*of more than one person*)
42. man, hero
43. alive
44. wound

WORD STUDY

1. In the previous supplementary lesson we have seen certain changes in the spelling of some Latin words which have been brought into English. Another change is that from **ae** to *e* as seen in the derivation of *equal,* and other words from **aequus**. Also, there are certain Latin words beginning with **ex** followed by **s,** in which the related English word omits s. Thus, *exist* is from Latin **exsistō**. Sometimes, however, these Latin words are spelled without **s**.

2.

RELATED ENGLISH WORDS

agriculture	equestrian	magnify
amicable	expect	numeral
auxiliary	filial	puerile
belligerent	laborious	virile
counsel	liberty	vivacious
equalize	library	vulnerable

NOTE.—For form of note books to be used in word study, see page 314.

LESSON XIV

THE FOUR CONJUGATIONS: PRESENT INDICATIVE OF THE SECOND CONJUGATION: ABLATIVE OF PLACE

THE FOUR CONJUGATIONS

108. There are four conjugations of verbs in Latin. They are distinguished by the final vowel of the present stem. The termination of the present active infinitive shows to which conjugation a verb belongs.

	Infinitive	Termination	Characteristic Vowel
I.	portāre	-āre	ā
II.	monēre	-ēre	ē
III.	dūcere	-ere	e
IV.	audīre	-īre	ī

PRESENT INDICATIVE OF THE SECOND CONJUGATION

109. The characteristic vowel of the second conjugation, ē, appears in all the forms of the present tense. It becomes short before another vowel and before the personal endings -t, -nt, and -ntur. (The same change of quantity takes place in the other conjugations when a long vowel is followed by another vowel or by the endings given above.)

ACTIVE	PASSIVE
SINGULAR	SINGULAR
moneō, *I warn, am warning,* etc.	moneor, *I am warned*
monēs, *you warn,* etc.	monēris, -re, *you are warned*
monet, *he, she, it warns,* etc.	monētur, *he, she, it is warned*
PLURAL	PLURAL
monēmus, *we warn*	monēmur, *we are warned*
monētis, *you warn*	monēminī, *you are warned*
monent, *they warn*	monentur, *they are warned*

　　a. The personal endings are the same as in the first conjugation.

THE ABLATIVE OF PLACE

110. The use of the ablative with **in** to refer to the place where something is or is done is called the Ablative of Place or the Locative Ablative.

111.   VOCABULARY

domicilium, -ī, N., home, dwelling place, residence

habeō, -ēre, have

iniūria, -ae, F., injury

Ītalia, -ae, F., Italy

moneō, -ēre, warn, advise, remind

proelium, -ī, N., battle

timeō, -ēre, fear

videō, -ēre, see

EXERCISES

112. 1. Hunc puerum pigrum monēmus. 2. Illum puerum impigrum semper laudāmus. 3. Iniūriae tuae multae sunt. 4. Ille puer parvus equum magnum timet. 5. Perīculum ab illō virō nōn timētur. 6. Puella saepe in silvā ambulat et ab agricolā vidētur. 7. Hic vir in proeliō nōn timet. 8. Cūr hoc perīculum magnum nōn vidēs? 9. Ītalia ā multīs amātur et laudātur. 10. Agricola bonus semper equōs bonōs habet. 11. Domicilium meum in illā īnsulā est.

113. 1. We do not live in Italy. 2. The sailors see the small island. 3. The boys are walking with the sailor and do not fear danger. 4. The man is feared because he has a weapon. 5. We are in danger and we are warned by our friends. 6. They see the town where you live. 7. My friend has a residence in this town.

———

SUGGESTED DRILL

(1) Explain the reason for the case of each noun in sentences 5, 6, and 7, of **113**. (2) Indicate the personal endings of the verbs in sentences 8, 9, and 10, **112**. (3) Conjugate **timeō** and **videō** in the present indicative, active and passive. (4) Give the genitive plural and the accusative plural of **iniūria** and **proelium**. (5) Give the genitive singular of the words meaning *this kindness*.

ROMAN FESTIVAL PROCESSION

LESSON XV

IMPERFECT, INDICATIVE ACTIVE, FIRST AND SECOND CONJUGATIONS: *HIC* AND *ILLE* AS CORRELATIVES

THE IMPERFECT[1] INDICATIVE ACTIVE

114. The imperfect tense of the indicative mood represents an act as going on or a situation as existing at a past time.

Vocābam, *I was calling.*

It is sometimes translated by the simple form of the past tense, *I called.*

ENTRANCE TO A ROMAN FORTIFIED CAMP

---

[1] This tense is sometimes called the "past" or (in the indicative mood) the "past descriptive." Teachers who prefer to employ either of these names instead of "imperfect" for this tense in connection with the paradigms and exercises which are given in this book may easily indicate the change which is desired by a general direction to the pupils.

115. The imperfect tense is formed on the present stem. It has the tense sign **bā** connecting the stem and the personal endings. In the active the vowel **ā** becomes short before the endings -m, -t, and -nt.

The endings are the same as in the present tense, except that the first person singular ends in -m. **Portō** and **moneō** are conjugated in the imperfect indicative active as follows:

SINGULAR

portābam, *I was carrying* or *I carried*
portābās, *you were carrying, you carried*
portābat, *he, she, it was carrying, he carried*, etc.

PLURAL

portābāmus, *we were carrying, we carried*
portābātis, *you were carrying, you carried*
portābant, *they were carrying, they carried*

SINGULAR

monēbam, *I was warning* or *I warned*
monēbās, *you were warning, you warned*
monēbat, *he, she, it was warning,* etc.

PLURAL

monēbāmus, *we were warning,* etc.
monēbātis, *you were warning,* etc.
monēbant, *they were warning,* etc.

CORRELATIVE USE OF *HIC* AND *ILLE*

116. The forms of **hic** and **ille** are sometimes used in the same sentence to refer to contrasted persons or things. In this use **ille** is regularly translated *the former* and **hic** *the latter*.

Puer et puella labōrant. Ille impiger, haec pigra est.

The boy and the girl are working. The former is industrious, the latter is lazy.

117. **VOCABULARY**

appropinquō, -āre, approach
castra, -ōrum, N., *pl.,* camp
maneō, -ēre, remain
moveō, -ēre, move

Rōmānus, -ī, M., a Roman
rūrsus, *adv.,* again
sine, *prep. with abl.,* without
tum, *adv.,* then, at that time

EXERCISES

118. Puer ipse saxum portābat. 2. Tum Rōmānī castra in silvā habēbant. 3. Statuam ex illō locō rūrsus movēbant. 4. Lēgātum et fīlium agricolae videō. Hic in agrō labōrat, ille in viā stat. 5. Hic vir nunc auxilium postulat quod sine amīcō est. 6. In oppidō manēbāmus quod amīcī nostrī appropinquābant.

119. 1. The Romans themselves loved Italy. 2. We feared injury because we did not have many friends. 3. The stones in the street are large and we walk with difficulty. 4. Then the sailor was living on the large island, now he is living in the town. 5. Sextus was calling together the boys again.

SUGGESTED DRILL

(1) Conjugate **appropinquō** and **moveō** in the imperfect indicative active. (2) Decline the words which mean *a large camp.* (3) Indicate the tense signs and the personal endings of the verbs of sentences 1, 2, 3, and 6, **118.** (4) Decline together **hic Rōmānus.** (5) Decline together **puer ipse.** (6) Give the third person singular in the present and the imperfect indicative active of the verbs in the vocabularies of Lessons XIV and XV.

THIRD REVIEW LESSON

120. (1) The second declension of nouns.

(2) Gender in the first and second declensions.

(3) Adjectives of the first and second declensions.

(4) The agreement of adjectives.

(5) The declension of **hic** and **ille**.

(6) The position of demonstratives.

(7) Possessive adjectives.

(8) The first conjugation, present indicative passive, imperfect indicative active.

(9) The second conjugation, present indicative, active and passive, imperfect indicative active.

(10) Apposition.

(11) The ablative of agent.

(12) The ablative of accompaniment.

(13) Terminations of the second declension.

(14) Terminations of adjectives, first and second declensions:

	SINGULAR			PLURAL		
	Masc.	*Fem.*	*Neut.*	*Masc.*	*Fem.*	*Neut.*
NOM.	-us, -er	-a	-um	-ī	-ae	-a
GEN.	-ī	-ae	-ī	-ōrum	-ārum	-ōrum
DAT.	-ō	-ae	-ō	-īs	-īs	-īs
ACC.	-um	-am	-um	-ōs	-ās	-a
ABL.	-ō	-ā	-ō	-īs	-īs	-īs

Vocative singular **-e** in **-us** masculine forms.

121. Give Latin words with which the following English words are connected in derivation:

admonition	expectation	numeral
belligerent	injury	numerous
car	Italian	probable
convocation	legation	Roman
demonstration	location	timid
domicile	move	vulnerable

LESSON XVI

THE DEMONSTRATIVE *IS*. DATIVE WITH SPECIAL VERBS

THE DEMONSTRATIVE *IS*

122. In addition to the demonstratives **hic** and **ille**, there is a third demonstrative, **is**, translated *this* or *that,* as the sense of the sentence in which it stands may require. It does not emphasize the idea that the thing to which it refers is near, as does **hic**, or that it is remote, as does **ille**. Usually it refers to something which has been recently mentioned. It is declined as follows:

	SINGULAR			PLURAL		
	Masc.	*Fem.*	*Neut.*	*Masc.*	*Fem.*	*Neut.*
Nom.	is	ea	id	eī (iī)	eae	ea
Gen.	eius	eius	eius	eōrum	eārum	eōrum
Dat.	eī	eī	eī	eīs (iīs)	eīs (iīs)	eīs (iīs)
Acc.	eum	eam	id	eōs	eās	ea
Abl.	eō	eā	eō	eīs (iīs)	eīs (iīs)	eīs (iīs)

Is ager lātus est, *this* (or *that*) *field is broad.*

Amīcī eius puerī multī sunt, *the friends of this* (or *that*) *boy are many.*

In eā īnsulā magnum oppidum est, *on this* (or *that*) *island there is a large town.*

IS AS A PRONOUN

123. The word **is** frequently serves as a personal pronoun of the third person, and is translated by a form of *he, she, it,* or (in the plural) *they,* as the meaning of the sentence requires.

Eum vidēbam, *I saw him.*

Amīcus eius benignus est, *his* (or *her*) *friend is kind.*

Eī multa dōna dās, *you give him* (or *her*) *many gifts.*

Amīcitiam eōrum dēsīderāmus, *we desire their friendship,* etc.

a. The genitives **eius** and **eōrum** (as pronouns) may either precede or follow the nouns on which they depend.

THE DATIVE WITH SPECIAL VERBS [1]

124. Some verbs, the meanings of which suggest the idea of *quality, attitude,* or *relation,* are followed by the dative, although the equivalent English verbs take a direct object.

Equus tibi placet, *the horse pleases you.*

125. The most important verbs of this class which govern the dative are those meaning to *favor, please, trust, obey, serve, resist, envy, threaten, pardon, spare,* and *persuade.*

VICTIMS FOR A ROMAN SACRIFICE

126. VOCABULARY

fortiter, *adv.,* bravely

Gallia, -ae, F., Gaul (*a name formerly given France, including part of the country on the north and northeast*)

Gallus, -ī, M., a Gaul (*an inhabitant of the country of Gaul*)

is, ea, id, this, that; *as pron.,* he, she, it

ōlim, *adv.,* formerly

persuādeō, -ēre, *with dative,* persuade

placeō, -ēre, *with dative,* please

pugnō, -āre, fight

---

[1] In the case of some of these verbs, the original meaning which made natural the use of the dative is not readily seen in translation. For example, **persuādeō,** *persuade,* meant *make attractive (to).*

EXERCISES

127. 1. Domicilium eius in Galliā est. 2. Fīlia eius virī misera est. 3. Gallī castra movēbant quod Rōmānī appropinquābant. 4. Iniūriae eōrum magnae sunt. 5. Cūr eī puellae librōs dās? 6. Ōlim hī puerī labōrābant et eōs laudābāmus. 7. Hae puellae pigrae sunt sed librī eīs placent. 8. Gallī et Rōmānī in eō proeliō fortiter pugnābant. 9. Amīcō meō nōn persuādēs.

128. 1. Their friends remained in town. 2. The girl is kind and her friends are many. 3. We ourselves often praise her. 4. The man persuaded this boy with difficulty. 5. Your plan does not please these men. 6. Why does not my plan please them?

SUGGESTED DRILL

(1) Point out those forms of **is** which are used as pronouns and those which are used as adjectives in the sentences of 127. (2) Explain the case of **eīs** in sentence 7 and of **amīcō** in sentence 9, 127. (3) Decline **is liber**. (4) Conjugate **pugnō** and **persuādeō** in the imperfect indicative active. (5) Give the genitive singular of the three demonstratives, **hic, ille,** and **is**.

LESSON XVII

IMPERFECT INDICATIVE PASSIVE, FIRST AND SECOND CONJUGATIONS: ABLATIVE OF MEANS

THE IMPERFECT INDICATIVE PASSIVE

129. The imperfect indicative passive of the first and second conjugations is formed as follows:

Singular	Singular
portābar, *I was being carried* or *I was carried*	monēbar
portābāris, -re, *you were being carried,* etc.	monēbāris, -re
portābātur, *he was being carried,* etc.	monēbātur

Plural	Plural
portābāmur, *we were being carried,* etc.	monēbāmur
portābāminī, *you were being carried,* etc.	monēbāminī
portābantur, *they were being carried,* etc.	monēbantur

a. The only difference between the active and the passive forms of this tense is in the personal endings. The ā of the tense sign becomes short before the endings **-r** and **-ntur.**

THE ABLATIVE OF MEANS

130. The means or instrument with which an act is done is expressed by the ablative without a preposition. This is called the Ablative of Means.

Gallī gladiīs pugnant, *the Gauls fight with swords.*
Puer saxō vulnerātur, *the boy is wounded by the stone.*

131. In translating the ablative of means into English, a preposition, *by* or *with,* is used. This use of the case is to be distinguished from the ablative of agent, which refers to the person by whom the act is done, and which always takes **ā** or **ab,** and from the ablative of accompaniment, which regularly takes **cum.**

132. **VOCABULARY**

augeō, -ēre, increase
gladius, -ī, M., sword
longē, *adv.*, far, at a distance
necō, -āre, kill

poena, -ae, F., punishment
sagitta, -ae, F., arrow
studeō, -ēre, *with dat.*, desire
terreō, -ēre, frighten, terrify

ROMAN SWORD AND SCABBARD

EXERCISES

133. 1. Puer equum sagittā vulnerat. 2. Eī virī gladiīs pugnant. 3. Poena ab eīs nōn timēbātur. 4. Perīculum augēbātur et ab amīcīs nōn iuvābāmur. 5. Gallī multōs Rōmānōs sagittīs necābant. 6. Puellae parvae terrēbantur et ex silvā properābant. 7. Castra ā lēgātō movēbantur quod is perīculum vidēbat. 8. Tum longē ab oppidō domicilium habēbāmus. 9. Hī puerī dōnīs multīs student.

134. 1. You (*plur.*) were often warned by him, but you did not fear. 2. Formerly Italy was praised by many. 3. The boys were fighting with stones. 4. We were helping the boys by our advice. 5. The Gauls were often wounded in battle by arrows. 6. Your plan was approved, but your friends did not give aid. 7. We do not desire war.

SUGGESTED DRILL

(1) Point out the examples of the ablative of means and also of the ablative of agent in 133. (2) Explain the case of dōnīs in sentence 9, 133. (3) In the following sentences tell what use of the ablative would be employed to translate the prepositional phrases: (a) He walked with his father. (b) He struck the horse with a stick. (4) Give the third person singular in the present indicative passive and imperfect indicative passive of necō and terreō.

LESSON XVIII

FUTURE INDICATIVE, ACTIVE AND PASSIVE, FIRST AND SECOND CONJUGATIONS

THE FUTURE TENSE

135. The future tense is formed on the present stem. In the first and second conjugations a tense sign, **bi**, is added to this stem. This tense sign becomes **bu** in the third person plural active and passive, and **be** in the second person singular passive. The **i** of the tense sign disappears before the endings **-ō** and **-or** in the first person singular.

The conjugation of **moneō** and **portō** in the future indicative, active and passive, is as follows:

learn

ACTIVE

SINGULAR	SINGULAR
portābō, *I shall carry*	monēbō, *I shall warn*
portābis, *you will carry*	monēbis, *you will warn*
portābit, *he will carry*	monēbit, *he will warn*

PLURAL	PLURAL
portābimus, *we shall carry*	monēbimus, *we shall warn*
portābitis, *you will carry*	monēbitis, *you will warn*
portābunt, *they will carry*	monēbunt, *they will warn*

PASSIVE

SINGULAR	SINGULAR
portābor, *I shall be carried*	monēbor, *I shall be warned*
portāberis, -re	monēberis, -re
portābitur	monēbitur

PLURAL	PLURAL
portābimur	monēbimur
portābiminī	monēbiminī
portābuntur	monēbuntur

136. *learned*   **VOCABULARY**

arma, -ōrum, N., *pl.,* arms, weapons

compleō, -ēre, fill, fill up

faveō, -ēre, *with dative,* favor

fossa, -ae, F., ditch

oppugnō, -āre, attack

scūtum, -ī, N., shield

superō, -āre, defeat, overcome

tamen, *adv.,* nevertheless, still

EXERCISES

ROMAN SHIELD

137. 1. Amīcī meī monēbuntur quod perīculum magnum est. 2. Hī servī arma portābunt sed nōn ipsī pugnābunt. 3. Gallī fortiter pugnant sed superābuntur. 4. Agricola fossam saxīs complēbit. 5. Illud oppidum ā Rōmānīs oppugnābitur. 6. In eō proeliō fortiter pugnābant sed tamen superābantur. 7. In oppidō multōs amīcōs vidēbimus. 8. Impigrē labōrās et laudāberis. 9. Amīcīs nostrīs semper favēmus.

138. 1. The slaves will not fight with weapons. 2. The boy will carry the shield and the sword. 3. We shall see the danger, but we shall not fear. 4. You (*sing.*) will often be praised by your friend. 5. The men will fight bravely, but nevertheless they will be defeated. 6. We shall not be frightened by the Gauls. 7. This man favored the Romans.

SUGGESTED DRILL

(1) Point out the tense signs and the personal endings in the verbs of sentences 4, 5, and 7, 137. (2) Explain the case of **amīcīs,** 9, 137. (3) Conjugate **compleō** and **superō** in the future indicative active and passive. (4) Give the third person plural active of **habeō** in the present, imperfect, and future indicative.

THIRD SUPPLEMENTARY REVIEW

VOCABULARY REVIEW

1. appropinquō, -āre
2. arma, -ōrum, N. *pl.*
3. aut, *conj.*
4. castra, -ōrum, N. *pl.*
5. concitō, -āre
6. cōnfirmō, -āre
7. dubitō, -āre
8. fortiter, *adv.*
9. habeō, -ēre
10. iniūria, -ae, F.
11. is, ea, id
12. lingua, -ae, F.
13. longē, *adv.*
14. maneō, -ēre
15. modus, -ī, M.
16. moneō, -ēre
17. moveō, -ēre
18. nāvigium, -ī, N.
19. nāvigō, -āre
20. oppugnō, -āre
21. persuādeō, -ēre
22. poena, -ae, F.
23. proelium, -ī, N.
24. pugnō, -āre
25. putō, -āre
26. sine, *prep. with abl.*
27. superō, -āre
28. tardus, -a, -um
29. timeō, -ēre
30. timidus, -a, -um
31. tum, *adv.*
32. vērō, *adv.*
33. vērus, -a, -um
34. videō, -ēre

---

1. draw near to, approach
2. arms
3. or; either . . . or
4. camp
5. arouse, excite
6. strengthen, encourage, affirm
7. doubt, hesitate
8. bravely
9. have, hold
10. wrong
11. this, that (*as adj.*); he (*as pron.*)
12. tongue, language
13. far
14. remain
15. manner
16. advise, warn
17. move
18. boat
19. sail
20. attack
21. persuade
22. penalty
23. battle
24. fight
25. think

26. without
27. overcome, excel, surpass
28. slow, late
29. fear
30. fearful

31. then
32. in truth, but
33. true
34. see

WORD STUDY

1. The diphthong **oe** as well as **ae** sometimes becomes *e* in English. This change is seen in the words derived from **poena,** which are given in the accompanying list of related English words. Another important fact to observe is that the consonant **i** of Latin words appears as *j* in English derivatives. Thus, *adjacent* is from **adiaceō.**

2. We may find two derivatives from the same source, one of which has been changed in spelling more than the other. Sometimes this is because one was taken directly from Latin into English while the other came through French. In other cases both have come through French, but one was changed in pronunciation and spelling more than the other. Thus, *lingual* and *language* both came from **lingua,** and *frail* and *fragile* both came from **fragilis.**

Most words of Latin derivation which have come through French have fewer syllables than in the original form. Usually the last syllable has disappeared, and often one or more consonants have been lost. Thus we have seen that *peril* is from **perīculum.**

3.   ### RELATED ENGLISH WORDS

armor	linguist	penitentiary	timidity
armory	mode	dubious	veracious
confirm	navigable	pugnacious	sinecure
injury	penalty	tardy	

NOTE.—For lists of Latin words for special note book work, see page 314, Section 7.

LESSON XIX

POSSESSIVES OF THE THIRD PERSON: OMISSION OF POSSESSIVES: IMPERFECT AND FUTURE INDICATIVE OF *SUM*

POSSESSIVES OF THE THIRD PERSON

139. The possessive adjective of the third person, **suus, sua, suum**, is reflexive; that is, it indicates that the subject of the sentence or clause is the possessor.

> **Puer amīcōs suōs laudat,** *the boy praises his (his own) friends.*
>
> **Puerī amīcōs suōs laudant,** *the boys praise their (their own) friends.*
>
> **Fēmina fīliam suam monet,** *the woman warns her daughter.*

a. The gender and number of the subject of the sentence or clause in which a form of **suus** stands determine whether the meaning is *his, her, its,* or *their.* For the sake of emphasis or clearness, **suus** may sometimes be translated *his own, her own, its own,* or *their own.*

b. If the possessor is some other person than the subject, *his, her,* or *its* is regularly expressed by **eius,** the genitive singular of **is,** and *their* by **eōrum** or **eārum,** the genitive plural of **is.**

> **Amīcōs eius laudant,** *they praise his friends.*
>
> **Amīcōs eōrum laudat,** *he praises their friends.*

The genitive forms of **hic** and **ille** are sometimes used instead of those of **is,** to denote possession.

THE OMISSION OF POSSESSIVES

140. The possessives are often omitted in Latin if they are not emphatic or if they are not needed for the sake of clearness. They are to be supplied in translation from Latin into English whenever the sense requires.

Fēmina fīliam amat, *the woman loves her daughter.*

141. The verb **sum** is conjugated as follows in the imperfect and future indicative:

IMPERFECT	FUTURE
	SINGULAR

eram, *I was*	erō, *I shall be*
erās, *you were*	eris, *you will be*
erat, *he, she, it was*	erit, *he, she, it will be*

PLURAL

erāmus, *we were*	erimus, *we shall be*
erātis, *you were*	eritis, *you will be*
erant, *they were*	erunt, *they will be*

142. **VOCABULARY**

inimīcus, -ī, M., enemy
īrātus, -a, -um, angry, angry at (*with dative*)
occupō, -āre, seize
populus, -ī, M., people

potentia, -ae, F., power
prīmō, *adv.,* at first
Rōmānus, -a, -um, Roman
suus, sua, suum, his, her, its, their; his own, her own, *etc.*

EXERCISES

143. 1. Prīmō illī puerī inimīcī erant. 2. Hic vir in domiciliō suō tum erat. 3. Illud oppidum ā Gallīs occupābitur. 4. Semper amīcī tuī erimus. 5. Cornēlia benigna est et amīcī eius multī sunt. 6. Patriam semper amābimus et laudābimus. 7. Hoc cōnsilium tuum bonum est. 8. Cūr hic vir fīliō suō īrātus erat? 9. Populus Rōmānus potentiam magnam habēbat. 10. Agricola equōs suōs laudat.

144. 1. The number of Gauls in the town was large 2. These gifts will be pleasing to the small boys. 3. At first the power of the Roman people was small. 4. We shall not be angry at your friend. 5. The camp was being seized by the Gauls. 6. Your daughter has her own book. 7. The woman loves her son, but she praises your daughter.

SUGGESTED DRILL

(1) Decline **suus** in full. (2) Give the possessive adjectives of the first and second persons. (3) Give the Latin equivalent for each of the possessives in the following sentences: (a) I was walking with the boy and his brother. (b) The general constructed his camp not far from the camp of the enemy. (c) I do not desire their help. (d) They cannot defend their own homes. (4) Give the third person singular and plural of **sum** in the imperfect, and future indicative.

GATE IN THE WALL OF MODERN ROME

LESSON XX

PERFECT INDICATIVE ACTIVE: MEANINGS OF PERFECT AND IMPERFECT

THE PERFECT TENSE, ACTIVE VOICE

145. The perfect tense represents an act as completed at the time of speaking or writing, or refers to a past act without giving any indication of its continuance. It is translated by the English present perfect or by the English past tense, as the sense requires.

PERFECT INDICATIVE ACTIVE OF *PORTO, MONEO,* AND *SUM*

146. The verbs **portō, moneō,** and **sum** are conjugated in the perfect indicative active as follows:

SINGULAR

portāvī, *I have carried* or *I carried*

portāvī, *I have carried, I carried*
portāvistī, *you have carried,* etc.
portāvit, *he has carried,* etc.

PLURAL

portāvimus, *we have carried,* etc.
portāvistis, *you have carried,* etc.
portāvērunt *or* portāvēre, *they have carried,* etc.

monuī, *I have warned*   **fuī,** *I have been*

SINGULAR	PLURAL	SINGULAR	PLURAL
monuī	monuimus	fuī	fuimus
monuistī	monuistis	fuistī	fuistis
monuit	monuērunt, -ēre	fuit	fuērunt, -ēre

ENDINGS OF THE PERFECT

147. The personal endings which are used in forming the perfect indicative active are different from those used in the other tenses. They are as follows:

SINGULAR	PLURAL
-ī	-imus
-istī	-istis
-it	-ērunt *or* -ēre

a. The use of the perfect endings is the same in all verbs, regular or irregular.

148. The perfect stem to which these endings are added is found by dropping the final ī of the first person singular. Thus, the perfect stem of **portō** is **portāv-**, of **moneō** is **monu-**, of **sum** is **fu-**.

149. The first person singular of the perfect indicative of all first conjugation verbs given thus far, except **iuvō**, **dō**, and **stō**, ends in -**āvī**, like the perfect of **portō**: **amāvī**, **postulāvī**, **explōrāvī**, etc. The perfect of **dō** is **dedī**, stem **ded-**; of **iuvō** is **iūvī**, stem **iūv-**; of **stō** is **stetī**, stem **stet-**.

150. Many (but not all) verbs of the second conjugation have perfects ending in -**uī**, like the perfect of **moneō**: **habuī**, **terruī**, etc.

MEANINGS OF THE IMPERFECT AND THE PERFECT

151. The perfect is distinguished from the imperfect in meaning by the fact that the imperfect represents a past act in progress or a situation in the past, while the perfect either represents an act as past, with no reference to its continuance, or brings into prominence the fact of its completion at the time of speaking or writing.

IMPF. **laudābam,** *I was praising*
PERF. **laudāvī,** *I praised* or *I have praised*

152. VOCABULARY

altus, -a, -um, high, tall, deep
cēlō, -āre, -āvī, conceal
epistula, -ae, F., letter
explōrō, -āre, -āvī, explore

expugnō, -āre, -āvī, take by
storm, capture
hodiē, *adv.*, today
invītō, -āre, -āvī, invite

EXERCISES

153. 1. Numquam fīlium tuum monuistī. 2. Nauta saepe in eō oppidō fuit. 3. Hoc saxum magnum portāvī. 4. Rōmānī ea castra expugnāvērunt. 5. Amīcōs suōs saepe invītāvērunt. 6. Hunc locum hodiē explōrāvī. 7. Multās sagittās et multōs gladiōs in eō oppidō cēlāvērunt. 8. Mūrus huius oppidī altus est. 9. Servus multās epistulās portāvit. 10. Agricola fīliō suō equum dedit.

154. 1. We have captured many towns of the Gauls. 2. My friends have not explored this island. 3. I have often invited these men. 4. This boy has always been industrious. 5. Why have you not warned these men? 6. I am expecting a long letter today. 7. I have given the boy a small gift.

SUGGESTED DRILL

(1) Indicate the personal endings of the verbs in the sentences of 153. (2) Conjugate **terreō** and **dō** in the perfect indicative active. (3) Give the third person singular, active voice, of **amō** and **habeō** in the present, imperfect, and future indicative. (4) Conjugate **invītō** in the future indicative active and passive. (5) Decline locus.

FOURTH REVIEW LESSON

155. VOCABULARY REVIEW

arma, -ōrum, N. *pl.*

bellum, -ī, N.

carrus, -ī, M.

castra, -ōrum, N. *pl.*

cōnsilium, -ī, N.

domicilium, -ī, N.

epistula, -ae, F.

fossa, -ae, F.

Gallia, -ae, F.

Gallus, -ī, M.

gladius, -ī, M.

inimīcus, -ī, M.

iniūria, -ae, F.

Ītalia, -ae, F.

lēgātus, -ī, M.

locus, -ī, M., N.

numerus, -ī, M.

populus, -ī, M.

potentia, -ae, F.

proelium, -ī, N.

Rōmānus, -ī, M.

sagitta, -ae, F.

scūtum, -ī, N.

altus, -a, -um

hic, haec, hoc

ille, illa, illud

ipse, ipsa, ipsum

īrātus, -a, -um

is, ea, id

parvus, -a, -um

Rōmānus, -a, -um

suus, sua, suum

vester, vestra, vestrum

appropinquō, -āre

augeō, -ēre

compleō, -ēre

convocō, -āre

dēmōnstrō, -āre

explōrō, -āre

expugnō, -āre

exspectō, -āre

faveō, -ēre

habeō, -ēre

invītō, -āre

iuvō, -āre

maneō, -ēre

moneō, -ēre

moveō, -ēre

necō, -āre

occupō, -āre

oppugnō, -āre

persuādeō, -ēre

placeō, -ēre

probō, -āre

properō, -āre

pugnō, -āre

studeō, -ēre

superō, -āre

terreō, -ēre

timeō, -ēre

videō, -ēre

vulnerō, -āre

fortiter

hodiē

impigrē

longē

ōlim

prīmō

rūrsus

semper

tamen

tum

vix

ā, ab

sine

156. RELATED ENGLISH WORDS

armor

augment

complete

epistle

explore

gladiator

invitation

irate

occupy

persuade

population

potential

pugnacious

student

LESSON XXI

USE OF PARTICIPLES: THE PAST PARTICIPLE

THE PARTICIPLE

157. The participle is a form of the verb which partakes of the nature of an adjective. Like the adjective, it is declined, and agrees in gender, number, and case with the word to which it belongs. The tenses of the participles of Latin verbs are present, past, and future.

THE PAST PARTICIPLE

158. English has both a past active and a past passive participle: active, *having carried;* passive, *having been carried.* Latin has the past passive participle, but no past active participle.

THE FORMS OF THE PAST PARTICIPLE

159. The past participle of **portō** is **portātus, -a, -um**, declined like **bonus**. It is translated *having been carried*, or *carried*.

> **Saxum ā puerō portātum magnum est,** *the stone carried (i. e., which was carried) by the boy is large.*

160. The past participle of **iuvō** is **iūtus, -a, -um;** of **dō, datus, -a, -um** (differing from **portātus** in having the **a** short). All other verbs of the first conjugation which have been given form their past participles like **portō: laudātus, amātus,** etc.

The past participle of **moneō** is **monitus, -a, -um;** of **videō, vīsus, -a, -um.**

> *a.* The past passive participle is used in Latin more frequently than in English. It is sometimes translated by a clause: **portātum** in the illustrative sentence above may be translated, *which was carried.*

161. **VOCABULARY**

albus, -a, -um, white

concilium, -ī, N., council

Germānī, -ōrum, M., Germans

ibi, *adv.*, there

lātē, *adv.*, widely, extensively

oppidānus, -ī, M., townsman, inhabitant of a town

pateō, -ēre, -uī, extend

perīculōsus, -a, -um, dangerous, perilous

EXERCISES

162. 1. Lēgātus concilium convocāvit, quod perīculum vidēbat. 2. Concilium ā lēgātō convocātum terrēbātur. 3. Liber ab amīcō datus puerō placet. 4. Oppidānī ā Germānīs superātī in oppidō manent. 5. Agrī Germānōrum lātē patēbant. 6. Rosa alba ā puellā portāta pulchra est. 7. Tēla ab hīs puerīs portāta perīculōsa sunt. 8. Ibi nōn manēbit, quod locus perīculōsus est.

163. 1. The inhabitants-of-the-town, having been called together, did not fear danger. 2. The gift given by your son is pleasing. 3. The town of the Germans is large and has a high wall. 4. We saw the white horses in the field. 5. The lieutenant, having been warned by the Germans, will move his camp. 6. The slaves, having been praised by Sextus, are working energetically.

SUGGESTED DRILL

(1) Give the past participles of **vītō, accūsō,** and **postulō,** with English meanings. (2) Decline the past participle of **dō** in full. (3) Conjugate **pateō** and **invītō** in the future indicative active. (4) Name the Latin nouns from which **perīculōsus** and **oppidānus** are derived. (5) Explain the case of **puerō** and of **amīcō** in sentence 3, **162.** (6) Give the gender and number of **portāta** in sentence 6 and sentence 7, 162.

LESSON XXII

PRINCIPAL PARTS: VERB STEMS

THE PRINCIPAL PARTS OF THE VERB

164. The present indicative active (first person singular), the present infinitive active, the perfect indicative active (first person singular), and the past participle, are called the Principal Parts of the verb. Any form of a verb may be made when these are known.

The principal parts of **portō** and **moneō** are as follows:

portō, portāre, portāvī, portātum
moneō, monēre, monuī, monitum

> *a.* The neuter form of the past participle is given in the principal parts, for the reason that the past participles of some verbs have no masculine or feminine forms.

THE PRINCIPAL PARTS OF FIRST CONJUGATION VERBS

165. All first conjugation verbs given thus far, except **iuvō**, **dō**, and **stō**, form their principal parts like **portō**. The principal parts of these three are as follows:

dō, dare, dedī, datum
iuvō, iuvāre, iūvī, iūtum
stō, stāre, stetī

> *a.* The fourth principal part of **stō** will be explained later; **dō** is irregular in having the **a** short in the infinitive.

THE STEMS OF THE VERB

166. A verb regularly has three stems: the present, the perfect, and the participial. The present stem is found by dropping **-re** from the present active infinitive, and the perfect stem by dropping **-ī** from the first person singular of the perfect indicative active (see Lessons V and XX). The participial stem is found by dropping **-um** from the past participle: **portātum**, stem **portāt-**; **monitum**, stem **monit-**.

USE OF THE STEMS

167. The present, the imperfect, and the future indicative, active and passive, are formed on the present stem.

The perfect stem is used only in the active voice.

Only a few forms are made on the participial stem.

168. The principal parts of the second conjugation verbs which have been given thus far are as follows:

habeō, habēre, habuī, habitum
moneō, monēre, monuī, monitum
pateō, patēre, patuī
placeō, placēre, placuī, placitum
studeō, studēre, studuī
terreō, terrēre, terruī, territum
timeō, timēre, timuī
augeō, augēre, auxī, auctum
maneō, manēre, mānsī, mānsum
persuādeō, persuādēre, persuāsī, persuāsum
compleō, complēre, complēvī, complētum
faveō, favēre, fāvī, fautum
moveō, movēre, mōvī, mōtum
videō, vidēre, vīdī, vīsum

a. The verbs of which only three principal parts are given have no past participle.

EXERCISES

169. 1. Magnum numerum equōrum in agrō vīdī. 2. Amīcī tuī tibi multōs librōs pulchrōs dedērunt. 3. Hic puer parvus in silvā mānsit. 4. Perīculum vītāvistī et laudāberis. 5. Hunc virum saepe iūvī quod impiger est. 6. Oppidānī numquam bellō fāvērunt sed fortiter pugnābunt. 7. Amīcitiae huius virī semper studuī. 8. Fīlius tuus meōs librōs ex hōc locō mōvit. 9. In multīs oppidīs habitāvī et multōs amicōs habeō. 10. In eō bellō arma Gallōrum erant gladiī et sagittae.

RUINS OF ROMAN AQUEDUCT

LESSON XXIII

PAST PERFECT AND FUTURE PERFECT INDICATIVE ACTIVE

THE PAST PERFECT INDICATIVE ACTIVE

170. The past perfect tense represents an act as completed at some specified or suggested time in the past. It is translated with the English auxiliary *had*. The tense sign is **erā**, which is added to the perfect stem. The endings are the same as those of the imperfect. The **ā** of the tense sign is shortened before the endings -m, -t, -nt.

portāveram,	**monueram,**	**fueram,**
I had carried	*I had warned*	*I had been*

SINGULAR

portāveram	monueram	fueram
portāverās	monuerās	fuerās
portāverat	monuerat	fuerat

PLURAL

portāverāmus	monuerāmus	fuerāmus
portāverātis	monuerātis	fuerātis
portāverant	monuerant	fuerant

THE FUTURE PERFECT INDICATIVE ACTIVE

171. The future perfect tense represents an act as to be completed at some specified or suggested time in the future. The tense sign is **eri**, which is added to the perfect stem.

portāverō,	**monuerō,**	**fuerō,**
I shall have carried	*I shall have warned*	*I shall have been*

SINGULAR

portāverō	monuerō	fuerō
portāveris	monueris	fueris
portāverit	monuerit	fuerit

PLURAL

portāverimus	monuerimus	fuerimus
portāveritis	monueritis	fueritis
portāverint	monuerint	fuerint

172. VOCABULARY

diū, *adv.*, long, for a long time

fuga, -ae, F., flight

hiemō, -āre, -āvī, -ātum, winter, spend the winter

hortus, -ī, M., garden

renovō, -āre, -āvī, -ātum, renew

sī, *conj.*, if

signum, -ī, N., signal

socius, -ī, M., ally

EXERCISES

173. 1. Hī puerī diū in hortō fuerint. 2. Sociī nostrī fugam Germānōrum vīderant. 3. Sī bellum renovāverint, perīculum magnum erit. 4. Signum proelī nōn vīderint. 5. Amīcī nostrī in illō oppidō hiemāverant. 6. Hōs puerōs saepe monueram. 7. Ille vir semper amīcōs iūverat. 8. Amīcīs dōna multa nōn dederat. 9. Portāvit; portāverat; portāverit; fuit; fuerat; fuerit.

174. 1. I had often warned my friend, but he did not fear. 2. Our friends will have seen many towns. 3. The flight of the allies had renewed the danger. 4. We were in the forest a long time. 5. If I see (shall have seen) the signal, I shall call together a council. 6. Why have you spent the winter in this town?

SUGGESTED DRILL

(1) Point out the past perfects and the future perfects in the sentences of 173, indicating the tense signs and the personal endings of each. (2) Give the principal parts of **renovō**, **iuvō**, and **videō**, and indicate the three stems of each. (3) Conjugate **dō** in the past perfect and the future perfect indicative active. (4) Give the third person plural of **iuvō** in the perfect, past perfect, and future perfect indicative active. (5) Give the datıve singular of the phrase meaning *that town*.

LESSON XXIV

PERFECT INDICATIVE PASSIVE: ACCUSATIVE OF DURATION OF TIME

THE PERFECT INDICATIVE PASSIVE

175. The perfect tense of any verb in the passive voice is formed by combining its past participle with the present tense of the verb **sum**.

SINGULAR

portātus sum, *I have been carried* or *I was carried*
portātus es, *you have been carried* or *you were carried*
portātus est, *he has been carried* or *he was carried*

PLURAL

portātī sumus, *we have been carried* or *we were carried*
portātī estis, *you have been carried* or *you were carried*
portātī sunt, *they have been carried* or *they were carried*

monitus sum, *I have been warned* or *I was warned*

SINGULAR	PLURAL
monitus sum	monitī sumus
monitus es	monitī estis
monitus est	monitī sunt

a. The forms of this tense are translated more frequently by the English past tense, *I was carried,* etc., than by the present perfect.

176. The participle in the forms of this tense agrees with the subject in gender as well as in number.

> **Puer laudātus est,** *the boy was praised.*
> **Puella laudāta est,** *the girl was praised.*

THE ACCUSATIVE OF DURATION OF TIME

177. A noun used to tell how long an act or a situation continues is in the accusative case.

Multās hōrās in īnsulā mānsī, *I remained on the island many hours.*

178. **VOCABULARY**

annus, -ī, M., year
circumdō, -dare, -dedī, -datum, surround
honestus, -a, -um, honorable

hōra, -ae, F., hour
quattuor, *indecl. num.,* four
schola, -ae, F., school
vīta, -ae, F., life

EXERCISES

179. 1. Multās hōrās in eō locō mānsērunt. 2. Hic amīcus saepe laudātus est, quod vīta eius honesta est. 3. Ille puer ab amīcō monitus est et nunc impigrē labōrat. 4. In hōc oppidō quattuor annōs fuerō. 5. Scholae in hōc oppidō semper bonae fuērunt. 6. Haec saxa ex illō agrō ā servō portāta sunt. 7. Lēgātus oppidum mūrō et fossā circumdedit. 8. Oppidum ā lēgātō mūrō et fossā circumdatum est.

180. 1. This boy was in school four hours. 2. The boys of this school have often been praised. 3. The Romans were in Gaul many years. 4. This man's life has always been honorable and he has many friends. 5. The camp of the Germans has not been moved. 6. For many years he had a residence in Italy.

———

SUGGESTED DRILL

(1) Point out the phrases in **180** which express duration of time. (2) Name the tense of each verb in **179**. (3) Conjugate **laudō** and **videō** in the perfect indicative passive, giving English meanings. (4) Explain the use of the ablatives in sentences 4 and 8 of **179**. (5) Give the ablative of the phrase meaning *four hours*. (6) Give the gender of **agricolā** in sentence 3 and of **fossā** in sentence 8 of 179.

FOURTH SUPPLEMENTARY REVIEW

VOCABULARY REVIEW

1. admoneō, -monēre, -monuī, -monitum
2. altus, -a, -um
3. annus, -ī, M.
4. circumdō, -dare, -dedī, -datum
5. deus, -ī, M.
6. expugnō, -āre, -āvī, -ātum
7. fuga, -ae, F.
8. multum, *adv.*
9. nē . . . quidem
10. nūntiō, -āre, -āvī, -ātum
11. occupō, -āre, -āvī, -ātum
12. permaneō, -manēre, -mānsī, -mānsūrus
13. populus, -ī, M.
14. quadringentī, -ae, -a
15. quidem, *adv.* (*postpositive*)
16. retineō, -tinēre, -tinuī, -tentum
17. sī, *conj.*
18. signum, -ī, N.
19. socius, -ī, M.
20. spatium, -ī, N.
21. spectō, -āre, -āvī, -ātum
22. suus, -a, -um
23. trecentī, -ae, -a
24. vīta, -ae, F.

1. remind
2. high, deep
3. year
4. put around, surround
5. god
6. capture by assault
7. flight
8. much
9. not even
10. announce, declare
11. seize, occupy
12. remain, hold out
13. people
14. four hundred
15. indeed, certainly, at least
16. hold back, retain
17. if
18. sign, signal, standard
19. ally, comrade
20. space, time, distance
21. look at
22. his (her, its, their) own
23. three hundred
24. life

WORD STUDY: PREFIXES AND SUFFIXES

1. New words are often formed by placing a syllable or group of syllables at the beginning or end of a word. A syllable

or group of syllables used in forming new words is called a Prefix if placed at the beginning of a word, and a Suffix if placed at the end.

LATIN PREFIXES

2. Most Latin prefixes are prepositions. For example, **ex-pugnō** is made up of **ex** and **pugnō**. There are, however, a few prefixes which are never found as separate words. The syllable **re-** of **retineō** is of this kind. Such a prefix is called an Inseparable Prefix.

CHANGES IN SPELLING

3. Often the form of a Latin prefix was changed because of the letter which immediately followed it. Thus, when **ad** was used as a prefix with **propinquō** the new word came to be **appropinquō**. This change of a consonant to the sound which follows or to a similar sound is called Assimilation.

In addition to this change in the spelling of prefixes, a vowel in the middle of a word was often changed when a prefix was joined to the original word. Thus, from **re-** and **teneō** we get **retineō**.

THE MEANING OF LATIN PREFIXES

4. Latin prepositions when used as prefixes usually have about the same meaning as when used as independent words. we shall, however, see a few differences.

The preposition **cum** has the form **com-** as a prefix, but in compounds it may appear as **col-, con-, cor-** or **co-**.[1] It most frequently means *together* or *together with*. Sometimes it means *thoroughly* or *entirely*. Occasionally a compound is found which differs scarcely at all from the original word to which the prefix was added.

The inseparable prefix **re-** means *back* or *again*.

RELATED ENGLISH WORDS

altitude	deity	popular	society	spectacle
annual	fugitive	retention	space	vital

[1] It is not necessary that pupils be required to memorize all the details of derivation here given. A careful reading of this material will, however, serve to make the relation of words more readily apparent.

LESSON XXV

PAST PERFECT AND FUTURE PERFECT INDICATIVE PASSIVE: SYNOPSIS OF VERBS

THE PAST PERFECT AND FUTURE PERFECT INDICATIVE PASSIVE

181. The past perfect in the passive voice is formed by combining the past participle with the imperfect tense of **sum**. The future perfect passive is formed by combining the past participle with the future of **sum**.

PAST PERFECT

portātus eram,   **monitus eram,**
I had been carried   *I had been warned*

SINGULAR

portātus eram, *I had been carried*   monitus eram
portātus erās, *you had been carried*   monitus erās
portātus erat, *he had been carried*   monitus erat

PLURAL

portātī erāmus, *we had been carried*   monitī erāmus
portātī erātis, *you had been carried*   monitī erātis
portātī erant, *they had been carried*   monitī erant

FUTURE PERFECT

portātus erō,   **monitus erō,**
I shall have been carried   *I shall have been warned*

SINGULAR

portātus erō, *I shall have been carried*   monitus erō
portātus eris, *you will have been carried*   monitus eris
portātus erit, *he will have been carried*   monitus erit

PLURAL

portātī erimus, *we shall have been carried*   monitī erimus
portātī eritis, *you will have been carried*   monitī eritis
portātī erunt, *they will have been carried*   monitī erunt

THE SYNOPSIS OF VERBS

182. A group of verb forms made up by taking any one person of a verb in all the tenses in one voice and number is called a Synopsis of the verb. The synopsis of **portō** in the first person singular, active voice, of the indicative mood is as follows:

Pres.	portō	Perf.	portāvī
Impf.	portābam	P. Perf.	portāveram
Fut.	portābō	F. Perf.	portāverō

183. ### VOCABULARY

anteā, *adv.*, formerly, before

dominus, -ī, M., master, owner

frūmentum, -ī, N., grain

quīnque, *indecl. numeral,* five

repudiō, -āre, -āvī, -ātum, reject

rogō, -āre, -āvī, -ātum, ask

stīpendium, -ī, N., tribute, tax

supportō, -āre, -āvī, -ātum, bring up, furnish

EXERCISES

184. 1. Hic servus ā dominō saepe monitus est. 2. Multa saxa ā puerō portāta sunt. 3. Stīpendium ā Germānīs numquam anteā datum erat. 4. Amīcitia nostra ab hīs virīs repudiāta est. 5. Auxilium tuum in proeliō rogātum est. 6. Frūmentum ā sociīs nostrīs hodiē supportātum erit. 7. In īnsulā quīnque hōrās fuerāmus. 8. Stīpendium ā Gallīs datum magnum erat. 9. Bellum ā Germānīs renovātum erat et multa oppida expugnāta erant.

185. 1. Help had been asked but had not been given. 2. Formerly the council had often been called together. 3. Grain has been furnished and we shall now move camp. 4. Why had the Germans rejected the friendship of the Romans? 5. The lieutenant remained in Gaul four years. 6. The town will have been captured by the Gauls.

(1) Give a synopsis of **portō** in the third person singular passive, and of **moneō** in the third person plural active, indicative mood. (2) Conjugate **videō** in the past perfect passive and the future perfect passive of the indicative, giving the English meanings. (3) Explain the case of **hōrās** in sentence 7, **184**. (4) Conjugate **repudiō** in the perfect passive indicative. (5) Conjugate **sum** in the past perfect and in the future perfect of the indicative. (6) Give the vocative singular of **dominus**.

FIFTH REVIEW LESSON

186. (1) The declension of **is**.

(2) Possessives of the third person.

(3) The imperfect indicative passive of the first and second conjugations.

(4) The future indicative active and passive of the first and second conjugations.

(5) The perfect indicative active.

(6) The past perfect indicative active.

(7) The future perfect indicative active.

(8) The perfect, past perfect, and future perfect passive.

(9) The past participle.

(10) The principal parts of verbs.

(11) The dative with special verbs.

(12) The accusative of duration.

(13) The ablative of means.

187. Give Latin words with which the following English words are connected in derivation:

annual	renovate	social
council	repudiate	support
dominate	scholastic	stipend
horticulture	signal	vital

LESSON XXVI

FUTURE ACTIVE PARTICIPLE: PREPOSITIONS WITH ACCUSATIVE

THE FUTURE ACTIVE PARTICIPLE

188. Latin verbs have a future active participle formed on the participial stem. It is declined like the past passive participle, from which it is to be distinguished by **-ūr**, preceding the case ending.

> **portātūrus, -a, -um,** *about to carry,* or *going to carry.*
> **monitūrus, -a, -um,** *about to warn,* or *going to warn.*

> *a.* Some verbs which have no past participle have a future active participle. The future active participle of such verbs is given as the fourth principal part.

The future participle of **sum** is **futūrus.** The principal parts of **sum** are **sum, esse, fuī, futūrus.** The fourth of the principal parts of **stō** is **stātūrus.**

189. The future participle is often combined with the forms of **sum** to refer to something which some one intends to do or is about to do.

> **Mānsūrus eram,** *I was about to remain, I intended to remain.*
> **Laudātūrus est,** *he is about to praise, he intends to praise.*

PREPOSITIONS WITH THE ACCUSATIVE

190. A number of prepositions have their objects in the accusative case. With some of these the object is used to name the place toward which motion is directed. Others express ideas of relation in situation, like the English *beyond, in front of, behind, around.* A few express abstract relations, such as *on account of, against, about.*

191. <center>VOCABULARY</center>

ad, *prep. with accusative,* to, toward

adversus, -a, -um, unfavorable, opposed

in, *prep. w. acc.,* into

mora, -ae, F., delay

post, *prep. w. acc.,* behind, after

propter, *prep. w. acc.,* on account of

sex, *indecl. num.,* six

trāns, *prep. w. acc.,* across, beyond

a. The ablative with **in** tells where an act takes place or where something exists. The accusative with **in** names the place to which an act is directed.

EXERCISES

192. 1. Propter adversum proelium sociī nostrī in oppidō mānsērunt. 2. Ad hunc locum sine morā Rōmānī castra mōvērunt. 3. Tibi multa dōna datūrus sum. 4. Fēmina fīliam suam in hortum vocāvit. 5. Castra Germānōrum trāns eam silvam erant. 6. Fossa alta post oppidum est. 7. Sex virī in viā ambulant. 8. Hunc puerum monitūrus erās. 9. Concilium sine morā convocāvī et perīculum dēmōnstrāvī. 10. Nōn diū in hōc locō mānsūrī sumus.

193. 1. On account of the great danger there will be delay. 2. The lieutenant invited the Germans to the camp. 3. The slaves carried the weapons and the grain into the town. 4. The horses and carts are behind the forest. 5. The master of the slaves lives beyond those fields. 6. You (*plur.*) have been defeated because you did not ask aid.

SUGGESTED DRILL

(1) Give the future active participles of **augeō, moneō,** and **dō.** (2) Mention some of the prepositions which take the ablative. (3) Conjugate **dēmōnstrō** in the perfect indicative active and passive. (4) Explain the case of **hortum,** in sentence 4, and of **viā,** in sentence 7, 192. (5) Give the principal parts of **moveō.** (6) Give a synopsis of **vocō** in the first person plural of the indicative passive.

LESSON XXVII

THIRD CONJUGATION, $\bar{o}$ VERBS, PRESENT INDICATIVE: DATIVE OF PURPOSE

THE THIRD CONJUGATION, $\bar{o}$ VERBS

194. The present active infinitive of the third conjugation ends in **-ere**. The stem ending **-e** is replaced in most forms of the present indicative by **-i** or **-u**.

195. Verbs which have all their forms in the third conjugation are conjugated as follows in the present indicative:

dūcō, *I lead*

ACTIVE	PASSIVE
	SINGULAR
dūcō, *I lead*	dūcor, *I am led*
dūcis, *you lead*	dūceris *or* dūcere, *you are led*
dūcit, *he leads*	dūcitur, *he is led*
	PLURAL
dūcimus, *we lead*	dūcimur, *we are led*
dūcitis, *you lead*	dūciminī, *you are led*
dūcunt, *they lead*	dūcuntur, *they are led*

THE DATIVE OF PURPOSE

196. The purpose or end which something serves or is intended to serve is sometimes expressed by the dative.

Cōpiās subsidiō mīsit, *he sent the troops as reinforcements (to serve as reinforcements).*

a. The dative of purpose is often used where the English idiom would require a predicate nominative.

Amīcitia tua semper mihi auxiliō fuit, *your friendship has always been a help to me (for a help to me).*

197. VOCABULARY

ante, *prep. w. acc.*, before, in front of; *adv.*, previously

cōpia, -ae, F., supply; *pl.*, forces

dūcō, -ere, dūxī, ductum, lead

impedīmentum, -ī, N., hindrance; *pl.*, baggage

mittō, -ere, mīsī, missum, send

relinquō, -ere, relīquī, relictum, leave

septem, *indecl. num.*, seven

subsidium, -ī, N., reinforcements, reserves

EXERCISES

198. 1. Lēgātus magnās cōpiās ad proelium dūcit. 2. Multās epistulās ad amīcōs mittimus. 3. Septem Gallī in proeliō necātī sunt. 4. Hic mūrus magnō impedīmentō fuit. 5. Servus ad oppidum mittitur. 6. Multī virī subsidiō mittuntur. 7. Puella librōs in viā relinquit. 8. Librī ante portam in viā ā puellā relinquuntur.

199. 1. The forces of the Romans are again sent into Gaul. 2. He gave me the book as a gift (for a gift). 3. I am sending these men as reinforcements. 4. There was a large forest in front of the town. 5. The slave leaves the weapons in the street. 6. On account of the delay we shall call together a council.

SUGGESTED DRILL

(1) Conjugate mittō and relinquō in the present indicative, active and passive. (2) Name the prepositions which have been used thus far with the accusative. (3) Give the future active participles of dūcō and mittō. (4) Explain the case of subsidiō in sentence 6, and of puellā in sentence 8, 198. (5) Give the principal parts of the verb necō. (6) Give the terminations of the present active infinitive in the first, second, and third conjugations.

LESSON XXVIII

FOURTH CONJUGATION, PRESENT INDICATIVE: SUBSTANTIVE USE OF ADJECTIVES

THE FOURTH CONJUGATION

200. The present active infinitive of the fourth conjugation ends in -īre. The present indicative is as follows:

audiō, *I hear*

ACTIVE	PASSIVE
	SINGULAR
audiō, *I hear*	audior, *I am heard*
audīs, *you hear*	audīris *or* audīre, *you are heard*
audit, *he hears*	audītur, *he is heard*
	PLURAL
audīmus, *we hear*	audīmur, *we are heard*
audītis, *you hear*	audīminī, *you are heard*
audiunt, *they hear*	audiuntur, *they are heard*

THE SUBSTANTIVE USE OF ADJECTIVES

201. Adjectives are often used as nouns, especially in the masculine plural and in the neuter plural: **multī** is translated *many men*, or *many;* **multa** is translated *many things.* In military language **nostrī** means *our men* or *our soldiers.*

Multī perīculum vīdērunt, *many saw the danger.*

202.   **VOCABULARY**

audiō, -īre, audīvī, audītum, hear

gerō, gerere, gessī, gestum, carry, carry on; **bellum gerere,** wage war

inter, *prep. w. acc.,* among, between

mūniō, -īre, mūnīvī, mūnītum, fortify

octō, *indecl. num.,* eight

sonus, -ī, M., sound

tuba, -ae, F., trumpet

veniō, -īre, vēnī, ventum, come

EXERCISES

203. 1. Sonum tubārum audiō. 2. Germānī castra hodiē
mūniunt. 3. Lēgātus cum sociīs venit. 4. Nōn saepe bellum
gerimus. 5. Castra inter silvam et oppidum ā nostrīs mūni-
untur. 6. Octō equōs in agrō vidēmus. 7. Sonus tubae ā
nostrīs audītur. 8. Ab hīs puerīs audīmur sed nōn vidēmur.
9. Virī sonum proelī audiunt et timent. 10. Venīs quod
vocātus es. 11. Rōmānī in Galliā bellum gestūrī erant.

FRAGMENT OF PAPYRUS ROLL FROM HERCULANEUM

204. 1. Our men are fortifying this town. 2. War is
being waged with the Gauls. 3. This field is between the
road and the forest. 4. That town had seven gates. 5.
Many are coming with their weapons as reinforcements
(for reinforcement). 6. We hear the sound of carts and
horses in the street.

———

SUGGESTED DRILL

(1) Indicate the stem and the ending of **audītur** in sentence 7, **203.**
(2) Point out the difference between the formation of the first person
plurals of **gerō** and of **audiō**. (3) Conjugate **veniō** in the present
indicative active, and **mūniō** in the present indicative active and
passive. (4) Give the third person plural of **rogō, videō,** and **audiō**
in the present indicative, active and passive. (5) Give the future
active participles of **audiō** and **gerō**. (6) Explain the use of **nostrīs**
in sentence 5, **203.**

LESSON XXIX

IMPERFECT INDICATIVE OF THIRD AND FOURTH CONJUGATIONS: CONSTRUCTION WITH *IUBEŌ*

THE IMPERFECT INDICATIVE OF THE THIRD AND FOURTH CONJUGATIONS

205. The imperfect tense of third conjugation verbs which are conjugated like **dūcō** is formed in exactly the same manner as the past tense of second conjugation verbs. Fourth conjugation verbs have **iē** before the tense sign.

dūcēbam, *I was leading*	audiēbam, *I was hearing*
dūcēbar, *I was being led*	audiēbar, *I was being heard*

ACTIVE	PASSIVE	ACTIVE	PASSIVE
	SINGULAR		
dūcēbam	dūcēbar	audiēbam	audiēbar
dūcēbās	dūcēbāris, -re	audiēbās	audiēbāris, -re
dūcēbat	dūcēbātur	audiēbat	audiēbātur
	PLURAL		
dūcēbāmus	dūcēbāmur	audiēbāmus	audiēbāmur
dūcēbātis	dūcēbāminī	audiēbātis	audiēbāminī
dūcēbant	dūcēbantur	audiēbant	audiēbantur

CONSTRUCTION WITH *IUBEŌ*

206. The verb **iubeō** may take as an object an infinitive with subject accusative.

Eum manēre iubēmus, *we order him to remain.*

207.   **VOCABULARY**

Helvētiī, -ōrum, M. *pl.,* the Helvetians, *an important Gallic tribe*

iubeō, -ēre, iussī, iussum, order, command

prōvincia, -ae, F., province, the Province, *the south-eastern part of Gaul*

reperiō, -īre, repperī, repertum, find, find out

statim, *adv.*, at once

trādō, -ere, trādidī, trāditum, surrender (*transitive*)

tūtus, -a, -um, safe

vincō, -ere, vīcī, victum, conquer, defeat

EXERCISES

208. 1. Helvētiī cōpiās ex castrīs dūcēbant. 2. Cūr huic virō arma tua nōn trādis? 3. Gallōs vincēbāmus quod arma bona habēbāmus. 4. Hunc puerum statim venīre iussī. 5. Nostrī auxiliō tum veniēbant. 6. Tēla ā lēgātō in hōc domiciliō reperta sunt. 7. Rōmānī bellum in Galliā gerēbant, et multa oppida Gallōrum expugnāverant. 8. Hic locus numquam tūtus fuit. 9. Bellum ā Gallīs in prōvinciā gerēbātur.

209. 1. The lieutenant orders the Helvetians to find the weapons at once. 2. The townspeople were surrendering their arms to the lieutenant. 3. The province is now safe. 4. We were sending many books and letters. 5. The boys and girls were coming from the town.

ROMAN CENTURION

SUGGESTED DRILL

(1) Indicate the tense signs and the personal endings in the verbs of sentences 1, 3, and 9, 208. (2) Conjugate **trādō** and **reperiō** in the present active indicative and the imperfect active indicative. (3) Explain the use of the infinitive **venīre** in sentence 4, 208. (4) Point out an adjective used as a noun in the sentences of 208. (5) Explain the case of **Galliā** in sentence 7, 208. (6) Conjugate **iubeō** in the perfect indicative active.

LESSON XXX

FUTURE INDICATIVE OF THIRD AND FOURTH CONJUGATIONS: ABLATIVE OF TIME

THE FUTURE INDICATIVE OF THE THIRD AND FOURTH CONJUGATIONS

210. The tense sign of the future in the third and fourth conjugations is **ē**, except in the first person singular, where it appears as **a**. In the fourth conjugation the tense sign is preceded by **i**. In third conjugation verbs like **dūcō**, the tense sign replaces the vowel in which the present stem ends.

ACTIVE

SINGULAR

dūcam, *I shall lead*	audiam, *I shall hear*
dūcēs, *you will lead*	audiēs, *you will hear*
dūcet, *he will lead*	audiet, *he will hear*

PLURAL

dūcēmus, *we shall lead*	audiēmus, *we shall hear*
dūcētis, *you will lead*	audiētis, *you will hear*
dūcent, *they will lead*	audient, *they will hear*

PASSIVE

dūcar, *I shall be led*   **audiar,** *I shall be heard*

SINGULAR	PLURAL	SINGULAR	PLURAL
dūcar	dūcēmur	audiar	audiēmur
dūcēris, -re	dūcēminī	audiēris, -re	audiēminī
dūcētur	dūcentur	audiētur	audientur

THE ABLATIVE OF TIME

211. The ablative without a preposition is used to indicate the time at which or within which an act is done or a situation exists. It is commonly translated with the English prepositions *in* or *at*.

Eō annō concilium convocātum est, *the council was called together in that year.*

212. **VOCABULARY**

āmittō, -ere, āmīsī, āmissum, lose

celeriter, *adv.*, swiftly, rapidly

contendō, -ere, contendī, contentum, contend; hasten

decem, *indecl. num.*, ten

excēdō, -ere, excessī, excessum, withdraw

nātūra, -ae, F., nature

novus, -a, -um, new

prīmus, -a, -um, first

EXERCISES

213. 1. Propter nātūram locī magnās cōpiās nōn dūcēbāmus. 2. Gallī eō annō multa oppida āmīsērunt. 3. Germānī cum cōpiīs nostrīs saepe ante castra contendunt. 4. Helvētiī eō bellō vincentur. 5. Hī virī decem hōrās labōrāvērunt. 6. Prīmā hōrā oppidum occupābitur. 7. Sī perīculum erit, celeriter veniam. 8. Puerōs fossam complēre iubēbit. 9. Cōpiae nostrae ex castrīs nōn excēdent. 10. Nostrī cum Germānīs ante castra contendent.

214. 1. We shall hasten from the camp at the first hour. 2. The slave will find out the nature of the place. 3. The sound of weapons will be heard by the women. 4. The men are withdrawing from the towns to the forests. 5. The forces of the Germans are coming swiftly.

SUGGESTED DRILL

(1) Give the third person singular of **dūcō** and **audiō** in the present, imperfect, and future tenses of the indicative active. (2) Give the third person plural of **mittō** and **moneō** in these three tenses of the indicative passive. (3) Conjugate **vincō** and **mūniō** in the future indicative active and passive. (4) Explain the difference between the idea of time which is expressed by the ablative and that which is expressed by the accusative (177, 211). (5) Point out the examples of the ablative of time in the sentences of **213**.

SIXTH REVIEW LESSON

215.

VOCABULARY REVIEW

annus, -ī, M.
concilium, -ī, N.
cōpia, -ae, F.
dominus, -ī, M.
frūmentum, -ī, N.
fuga, -ae, F.
hortus, -ī, M.
mora, -ae, F.
nātūra, -ae, F.
oppidānus, -ī, M.
prōvincia, -ae, F.
schola, -ae, F.
signum, -ī, N.
socius, -ī, M.
sonus, -ī, M.
stīpendium, -ī, N.
tuba, -ae, F.
vīta, -ae, F.

audiō, -īre, -īvī, -ītum
circumdō, -dare, -dedī, -datum
contendō, -tendere, -tendī, -tentum
dūcō, -ere, dūxī, ductum
gerō, -ere, gessī, gestum
hiemō, -āre, -āvī, -ātum
iubeō, -ēre, iussī, iussum
mittō, -ere, mīsī, missum
mūniō, -īre, -īvī, -ītum
pateō, -ēre, -uī
relinquō, -ere, relīquī, relictum
reperiō, -īre, repperī, repertum
repudiō, -āre, -āvī, -ātum
rogō, -āre, -āvī, -ātum
supportō, -āre, -āvī, -ātum
trādō, -dere, -didī, -ditum
veniō, -īre, vēnī, ventum
vincō, -ere, vīcī, victum

adversus, -a, -um
albus, -a, -um
honestus, -a, -um
perīculōsus, -a, -um
prīmus, -a, -um
tūtus, -a, -um

anteā
celeriter
diū
ibi
lātē
statim

ad
ante
inter
post
propter
trāns

216.

RELATED ENGLISH WORDS

adverse
audible
contention
copious
decimal

interstate
missive
natural
novelty
postpone

primary
provincial
relinquish
sonorous
transport

LESSON XXXI

VERBS OF THE THIRD CONJUGATION ENDING IN *-iō*

217. There are two classes of verbs in the third conjugation, commonly distinguished as ō verbs and iō verbs. The ō verbs are those which are conjugated like **dūcō**. The iō verbs are conjugated in the present indicative partly like **dūcō** and partly like verbs of the fourth conjugation. In the imperfect indicative and the future indicative they are conjugated exactly like verbs of the fourth conjugation.

capiō, *I take*

PRESENT

| | ACTIVE | | PASSIVE | |
SINGULAR	PLURAL		SINGULAR	PLURAL
capiō	capimus		capior	capimur
capis	capitis		caperis, -re	capiminī
capit	capiunt		capitur	capiuntur

IMPERFECT

SINGULAR	PLURAL		SINGULAR	PLURAL
capiēbam	capiēbāmus		capiēbar	capiēbāmur
capiēbās	capiēbātis		capiēbāris, -re	capiēbāminī
capiēbat	capiēbant		capiēbātur	capiēbantur

FUTURE

SINGULAR	PLURAL		SINGULAR	PLURAL
capiam	capiēmus		capiar	capiēmur
capiēs	capiētis		capiēris, -re	capiēminī
capiet	capient		capiētur	capientur

a. In the first person plural and the second person plural of both voices, and in the second person singular of the active voice in the present tense, the forms of the verbs of this class are to be distinguished from the corresponding forms of the fourth conjugation by the fact that the connecting vowel, **i**, is short. In the second person singular of the passive in the present tense the connecting vowel is **e**, while in the corresponding form of the fourth conjugation it is **ī**.

218. **VOCABULARY**

capiō, -ere, cēpī, captum,
  take, capture
faciō, -ere, fēcī, factum,
  make, do
fugiō, -ere, fūgī, fugitūrus,
  flee

iaciō, -ere, iēcī, iactum, throw
incognitus, -a, -um, unknown
nihil, *indecl.,* N., nothing
nūntius, -ī, M., messenger
pōnō, -ere, posuī, positum,
  place

EXERCISES

219. 1. Nūntius in oppidō capiētur et necābitur. 2. Puer carrum parvum facit. 3. Tēla ā Germānīs et Gallīs iaciuntur. 4. Nostrī in eō oppidō multum frūmentum capiēbant. 5. Sī oppidum capiētur, fugiēmus. 6. Rōmānī castra ante silvam pōnent. 7. Is locus incognitus erat sed nōn timēbāmus. 8. Ille vir multās iniūriās faciēbat. 9. Puerī fugiēbant quod perīculum vidēbant. 10. Multī in (*at*) mūrum tēla iaciēbant.

220. 1. The boy takes the sword and shield. 2. The slave will throw a weapon over (across) the wall. 3. Why were you fleeing from the camp? 4. We were making a large number of shields. 5. The town will be taken by the Germans.

SUGGESTED DRILL

(1) Conjugate **iaciō** and **reperiō** in the present indicative passive. (2) Conjugate **pōnō** and **faciō** in the imperfect indicative active. (3) Give the tense sign of the future in the first and second conjugations. (4) Conjugate **videō** and **faciō** in the future indicative active. (5) Indicate the stem, tense sign, and personal ending of **timēbāmus,** in sentence 7, **219.**

LESSON XXXII

REVIEW OF THE FOUR CONJUGATIONS IN THE PRESENT SYSTEM, INDICATIVE MOOD

221.

PRESENT INFINITIVE

		TERMINATIONS	STEM
I.	portāre	-āre	portā-
II.	monēre	-ēre	monē-
III.	{ dūcere	-ere	dūce- }
	{ capere		cape- }
IV.	audīre	-īre	audī-

THE PRESENT INDICATIVE

222. The present tense is formed by adding the personal endings to the present stem. In the first person singular of the first conjugation and of the ō verbs of the third conjugation the stem vowel disappears. In the third conjugation the vowel of the stem ending becomes **u** before **-nt** and **-ntur**. It becomes **i** before all other endings except **-ris**. In all **iō** verbs **-nt** and **-ntur** are preceded by **iu**.

ACTIVE

SINGULAR

I.	II.	III.		IV.
portō	moneō	dūcō	capiō	audiō
portās	monēs	dūcis	capis	audīs
portat	monet	dūcit	capit	audit

PLURAL

portāmus	monēmus	dūcimus	capimus	audīmus
portātis	monētis	dūcitis	capitis	audītis
portant	monent	dūcunt	capiunt	audiunt

PASSIVE

SINGULAR

portor	moneor	dūcor	capior	audior
portāris, -re	monēris, -re	dūceris, -re	caperis, -re	audīris, -re
portātur	monētur	dūcitur	capitur	audītur

PLURAL

portāmur	monēmur	dūcimur	capimur	audīmur
portāminī	monēminī	dūciminī	capiminī	audīminī
portantur	monentur	dūcuntur	capiuntur	audiuntur

THE IMPERFECT INDICATIVE

223. The sign of the imperfect tense, **bā**, appears in all four conjugations. In third conjugation **ō** verbs the short **e** of the stem becomes long before **bā**, making their imperfect tense identical with that of the second conjugation. Third conjugation verbs in **iō** and all fourth conjugation verbs have the tense sign preceded by **iē**.

ACTIVE

SINGULAR

I.	II.	III.		IV.
portābam	monēbam	dūcēbam	capiēbam	audiēbam
portābās	monēbās	dūcēbās	capiēbās	audiēbās
portābat	monēbat	dūcēbat	capiēbat	audiēbat

PLURAL

portābāmus	monēbāmus	dūcēbāmus	capiēbāmus	audiēbāmus
portābātis	monēbātis	dūcēbātis	capiēbātis	audiēbātis
portābant	monēbant	dūcēbant	capiēbant	audiēbant

PASSIVE

SINGULAR

portābar	monēbar	dūcēbar	capiēbar	audiēbar
portābāris, -re	monēbāris, -re	dūcēbāris, -re	capiēbāris, -re	audiēbāris, -re
portābātur	monēbātur	dūcēbātur	capiēbātur	audiēbātur

PLURAL

portābāmur	monēbāmur	dūcēbāmur	capiēbāmur	audiēbāmur
portābāminī	monēbāminī	dūcēbāminī	capiēbāminī	audiēbāminī
portābantur	monēbantur	dūcēbantur	capiēbantur	audiēbantur

THE FUTURE INDICATIVE

224. In the first and second conjugations the tense sign is **bi** except in the third person plural, in which it appears as **bu**, and in the second person singular of the passive, where it becomes **be.** The **i** disappears before -**ō** and -**or.** In the third and fourth conjugations the tense sign is **ē** (in the first person singular, **a**). The **i** of the **iō** verbs of the third conjugation and of the verbs of the fourth conjugation is retained.

ACTIVE

SINGULAR

I.	II.	III.		IV.
portābō	monēbō	dūcam	capiam	audiam
portābis	monēbis	dūcēs	capiēs	audiēs
portābit	monēbit	dūcet	capiet	audiet

PLURAL

portābimus	monēbimus	dūcēmus	capiēmus	audiēmus
portābitis	monēbitis	dūcētis	capiētis	audiētis
portābunt	monēbunt	dūcent	capient	audient

PASSIVE

SINGULAR

portābor	monēbor	dūcar	capiar	audiar
portāberis, -re	monēberis, -re	dūcēris, -re	capiēris, -re	audiēris, -re
portābitur	monēbitur	dūcētur	capiētur	audiētur

PLURAL

portābimur	monēbimur	dūcēmur	capiēmur	audiēmur
portābiminī	monēbiminī	dūcēminī	capiēminī	audiēminī
portābuntur	monēbuntur	dūcentur	capientur	audientur

225.   **VOCABULARY**

captīvus, -ī, M., prisoner
castellum, -ī, N., fort, redoubt
cōnficiō, -ere, cōnfēcī, cōnfec-
    tum, finish, complete
iterum, *adv.*, again

lūna, -ae, F., moon
magnopere, *adv.*, greatly
pācō, -āre, -āvī, -ātum, sub-
    due, make peaceful
victōria, -ae, F., victory

BRIDGE OVER THE TIBER

EXERCISES

226. 1. In castrīs multī captīvī et servī erant. 2. Gallī
castella Rōmānōrum oppugnābunt sed nōn capient. 3. Germānī ante novam lūnam nōn contendent. 4. Tum castella
faciēbāmus quod magnopere perīculum timēbāmus. 5. Quod
Gallia pācāta erat, bellum nōn timēbātur. 6. Hoc bellum
nōn celeriter cōnficiētur. 7. Ea victōria magna fuit et
multa oppida capta sunt. 8. Auxilium tuum, mī amīce,
iterum postulō.

227. 1. We saw many prisoners in the camp. 2. The
Germans will not again attack this fort, but they will capture the camp. 3. Ireland was never subdued by the Romans.
4. This victory will frighten the Gauls greatly and they
will flee from their towns.

FIFTH SUPPLEMENTARY REVIEW
VOCABULARY REVIEW

1. ad, *prep, with acc.*
2. addūcō, -dūcere, -dūxī, -ductum
3. adiciō, -icere, -iēcī, -iectum
4. āmittō, -mittere, -mīsī, -missum
5. ante, *prep. (with acc.), and adv.*
6. anteā, *adv.*
7. audiō, -īre, -īvī, -ītum
8. capiō, -ere, cēpī, captum
9. celeriter, *adv.*
10. cōnficiō, -ficere, -fēcī, -fectum
11. coniciō, -icere, -iēcī, -iectum
12. contendō, -tendere, -tendī, -tentum
13. cōpia, -ae, F.
14. dūcō, -ere, dūxī, ductum
15. ēiciō, -ere, ēiēcī, ēiectum
16. excēdō, -cēdere, -cessī, -cessum
17. excipiō, -cipere, -cēpī, -ceptum
18. faciō, -ere, fēcī, factum
19. frūmentum, -ī, N.
20. gerō, -ere, gessī, gestum
21. iaciō, -ere, iēcī, iactum
22. impedīmentum, -ī, N.
23. in, *prep. with abl. and acc.*
24. indūcō, -dūcere, -dūxī, -ductum
25. inter, *prep. with acc.*
26. intercipiō, -cipere, -cēpī, -ceptum
27. invideō, -vidēre, -vīdī, -vīsum
28. iubeō, -ēre, iussī, iussum
29. magnopere, *adv.*
30. mittō, -ere, mīsī, missum
31. mūniō, -īre, -īvī, -ītum
32. nātūra, -ae, F.
33. novus, -a, -um
34. pācō, -āre, -āvī, -ātum
35. perdūcō, -dūcere, -dūxī -ductum
36. pōnō, -ere, posuī, positum
37. post, *prep. with acc.*
38. prōdūcō, -dūcere, -dūxī, -ductum
39. propter, *prep. with acc.*
40. prōvideō, -vidēre, -vīdī, -vīsum
41. relinquō, -linquere, -līquī, -lictum
42. satisfaciō, -facere, -fēcī, -factum
43. suscipiō, -cipere, -cēpī, -ceptum
44. trādō, -dere, -didī, -ditum
45. trāns, *prep. with acc.*
46. veniō, -īre, vēnī, ventum
47. victōria, -ae, F.
48. vincō, -ere, vīcī, victum

1. to
2. lead to, influence
3. throw to, add
4. send away, lose
5. before
6. before
7. hear
8. take
9. swiftly, quickly
10. finish, exhaust
11. hurl
12. struggle, hasten
13. supply; *pl.* forces
14. lead
15. throw out
16. go out
17. take, accept
18. do, make
19. grain
20. carry, accomplish
21. throw, hurl
22. hindrance; *pl.* baggage
23. in, on (*with abl.*); into (*with acc.*)
24. lead in, induce
25. between, among
26. intercept, cut off
27. envy
28. order
29. greatly
30. send
31. fortify
32. nature
33. new
34. pacify
35. lead through, extend
36. put, place
37. after, behind
38. lead forward
39. on account of
40. foresee
41. leave behind, abandon
42. satisfy
43. undertake
44. hand over
45. across
46. come
47. victory
48. conquer.

WORD STUDY

1. The prepositions **ad** and **in** are among the most commonly used prefixes. By assimilation **ad** becomes **ac-, ag-, af-, ap-, ar-, as-, at-,** and sometimes **a-**. In English derivatives and in the spelling of some Latin books it also becomes **al-** and **an-**.

Similarly, **in-** becomes **il-, im-,** and **ir-**.

LATIN COMPOUND VERBS

2. In the vocabulary of this lesson the following compounds may be noted:

addūcō (ad + dūcō)
adiciō (ad + iaciō)
āmittō (ā + mittō)
cōnficiō (com + faciō)
coniciō (com + iaciō)
contendō (com + tendō)

ēiciō (ē + iaciō)
excēdō (ex + cēdō)
excipiō (ex + capiō)
indūcō (in + dūcō)
intercipiō (inter + capiō)

LESSON XXXIII

REVIEW OF THE PERFECT SYSTEM, INDICATIVE MOOD: WORD ORDER

REVIEW OF THE PERFECT SYSTEM IN THE ACTIVE VOICE

228. (1) The formation of the perfect system is the same in all four conjugations. The perfect stem (which is used only in the active voice) is found by dropping the ī of the perfect active indicative, the third of the principal parts. The endings of the perfect indicative active are the same for all verbs.

SINGULAR

I.	II.	III.		IV.	TERMINATIONS
portāvī	monuī	dūxī	cēpī	audīvī	-ī
portāvistī	monuistī	dūxistī	cēpistī	audīvistī	-istī
portāvit	monuit	dūxit	cēpit	audīvit	-it

PLURAL

portāvimus	monuimus	dūximus	cēpimus	audīvimus	-imus
portāvistis	monuistis	dūxistis	cēpistis	audīvistis	-istis
portāvērunt	monuērunt	dūxērunt	cēpērunt	audīvērunt	-ērunt
or -ēre	*or* -ēre	*or* -ēre	*or* -ēre	*or* -ēre	*or* -ēre

(2) The sign of the past perfect indicative is **erā**, which is added to the perfect stem. The endings are those used in the imperfect active.

I.	II.	III.		IV.
portāveram	monueram	dūxeram	cēperam	audīveram
portāverās,	monuerās,	dūxerās,	cēperās,	audīverās,
etc.	*etc.*	*etc.*	*etc.*	*etc.*

(3) The sign of the future perfect is **eri**, which is added to the perfect stem. Before ō the i of the tense sign disappears.

portāverō	monuerō	dūxerō	cēperō	audīverō
portāveris,	monueris,	dūxeris,	cēperis,	audīveris,
etc.	*etc.*	*etc.*	*etc.*	*etc.*

REVIEW OF THE PERFECT SYSTEM IN THE PASSIVE VOICE

229. The formation of the perfect system in the passive is the same in all four conjugations. The perfect is made up of the past passive participle and the present tense of **sum**; the past perfect of the past passive participle and the imperfect tense of **sum**; and the future perfect of the past passive participle and the future tense of **sum**.

PERFECT	PAST PERFECT	FUTURE PERFECT
portātus sum	portātus eram	portātus erō
monitus sum,	monitus eram,	monitus erō,
etc.	*etc.*	*etc.*

VARIATION FROM THE NORMAL WORD ORDER

230. The normal order of a Latin sentence requires that the subject, with its modifiers, stand first, and that the verb, preceded by its modifiers, stand last. But there are many requirements of emphasis which may change this order. Any word which is to be emphasized may stand in a different position in the sentence from that in which it would normally be placed. The fact that the form of a Latin word shows what its relation is to other words, makes possible a much freer arrangement in Latin than in English. If the subject is to be made emphatic, it may be placed last instead of first. But the fact that any word is put in an unusual position means that one or more of the other words in the sentence will be crowded out of the normal position. Sometimes the normal order is changed merely for the sake of variety.

231. **VOCABULARY**

animus, -ī, M., mind, courage, spirit
cārus, -a, -um, dear
iūstitia, -ae, F., justice
Labiēnus, -ī, M., Labienus, *an officer in Caesar's army*
nōndum, *adv.*, not yet

perveniō, -īre, pervēnī, perventum, arrive
recipiō, -ere, recēpī, receptum, receive, take back
rēgnum, -ī, N., royal authority, kingdom
trīduum, -ī, N., three days

EXERCISES

232. 1. Rōmānīs cāra fuit patria. 2. Ibi trīduum mānsī sed audīvī nihil. 3. Hic vir propter iūstitiam laudātus est. 4. Labiēnus trīduō cum cōpiīs suīs in hoc oppidum pervēnit. 5. Nōndum āmissus est animus. 6. Multōs Gallōs ad castellum dūxerat. 7. Eī virī in oppidum receptī sunt. 8. Tum rēgnum occupāvit et multōs necāvit. 9. Captīvī poenam timēbant et ex castrīs fūgērunt. 10. Ā Labiēnō saepe Gallōrum cōpiae victae erant. 11. Dūxistis; cēpistis; audīvērunt; cēpit; cēperat; cēperit. 12. Audītus est; audītus erat; audītus erit; captī sunt; captī erant; captī erunt.

THE ROMAN FORUM IN ITS PRESENT CONDITION

233. 1. In three days I shall have arrived in Gaul. 2. Our allies had placed large stones on the wall. 3. The royal authority has been seized and the towns have been captured. 4. We had fortified the camp and were awaiting the forces of the Germans. 5. I came, I saw, I conquered.

LESSON XXXIV

ADJECTIVES WITH THE GENITIVE IN -ĪUS

234. There are nine adjectives which have the genitive singular ending in -īus and the dative singular ending in -ī. In the other cases of the singular and in all the cases of the plural they have the same endings as adjectives of the first and second declensions. The vocative is lacking except in rare uses of **ūnus** and **sōlus**. Most of these words are used also as pronouns. They are as follows:

alius, alia, aliud, another	**ūnus, -a, -um,** one
sōlus, -a, -um, alone, only	**tōtus, -a, -um,** whole
ūllus, -a, -um, any	**nūllus, -a, -um,** no

alter, altera, alterum, the other (*of two*)
neuter, neutra, neutrum, neither
uter, utra, utrum, which (*of two*)

235. These adjectives are declined as follows:

SINGULAR

Masc.	Fem.	Neut.	Masc.	Fem.	Neut.
sōlus	sōla	sōlum	alter	altera	alterum
sōlīus	sōlīus	sōlīus	alterīus	alterīus	alterīus
sōlī	sōlī	sōlī	alterī	alterī	alterī
sōlum	sōlam	sōlum	alterum	alteram	alterum
sōlō	sōlā	sōlō	alterō	alterā	alterō

PLURAL

sōlī	sōlae	sōla, *etc.*	alterī	alterae	altera, *etc.*

a. **Alius** has the neuter **aliud.** Otherwise it is declined like the remaining words of the group. The ī of the genitive ending of **alter** is sometimes short (**alterius**).

b. These words are sometimes used in pairs (correlatives) as follows:

alius..... alius = *one .... another.*
alii...... alii = *some .... others.*
alter..... alter = *one .... the other.*
alteri.... alteri = *the one party.... the other party.*

Alius fugit, alius manet in castrīs, *one flees, another remains in the camp.*

EXERCISES

236. 1. Ūnum virum et decem puerōs vīdimus. 2. Alter fūgit, alter captus est. 3. Aliī statim vēnērunt, aliī in oppidō mānsērunt. 4. Alius gladium gerēbat, alius nūlla arma habēbat. 5. Gladius meus mihi auxiliō fuit. 6. Mūrus neutrīus oppidī altus est. 7. Utrī puellae dōnum dedistī? 8. Amīcitiam tōtīus Ītaliae repudiāvit. 9. Alterī in castrīs mānsērunt, alterī ad silvam fūgērunt. 10. Nūllīus īnsulae; Labiēnō sōlī; ūllīus morae; alterīus locī.

237. 1. The nature of the whole place was unknown. 2. The one was a Gaul, the other was a German. 3. He will give the letter to the messenger alone. 4. Some fight bravely, others hasten from the camp. 5. One demands aid, another avoids danger. 6. This boy has no book. 7. The danger of neither is great.

SUGGESTED DRILL

(1) Explain the case of **auxiliō** in sentence 5, **236.** (2) Decline together **neuter liber.** (3) Decline together **ūnum oppidum.** (4) Give a synopsis of **āmittō** in the third singular active of the indicative. (5) Conjugate **trādō** in the perfect passive indicative and the past perfect passive indicative. (6) Conjugate **recipiō** in the future perfect, active and passive.

LESSON XXXV

THE THIRD DECLENSION

238. The third declension has three classes of nouns, known as Consonant Stems, i-Stems, and Mixed Stems. The genitive ending is -is.

a. Some masculine and feminine nouns have a nominative ending -s. If the stem ends in -c or -g the combination of the final -c or -g of the stem with -s gives -x: **dux**, nominative from the stem **duc-**; **lēx** nominative from the stem **lēg-**. If the stem ends in -d or -t the final consonant is dropped before -s: **laus**, nominative from the stem **laud-**. If the vowel i stands before the final consonant of the stem it is frequently changed to **e** in the nominative: **prīnceps**, nominative from the stem **prīncip-**, **mīles**, nominative from the stem **mīlit-**.

Consonant stems are declined as follows:

lēx, F., *law*　　　　　　**mīles**, M., *soldier*
BASE, **lēg-**　　　　　　　BASE, **mīlit-**

					TERMI-NATIONS
		SINGULAR			
NOM.	lēx	NOM.	mīles		-s
GEN.	lēgis	GEN.	mīlitis		-is
DAT.	lēgī	DAT.	mīlitī		-ī
ACC.	lēgem	ACC.	mīlitem		-em
ABL.	lēge	ABL.	mīlite		-e
		PLURAL			
NOM.	lēgēs	NOM.	mīlitēs		-ēs
GEN.	lēgum	GEN.	mīlitum		-um
DAT.	lēgibus	DAT.	mīlitibus		-ibus
ACC.	lēgēs	ACC.	mīlitēs		-ēs
ABL.	lēgibus	ABL.	mīlitibus		-ibus

b. Nouns with stems ending in **-tr** have the nominative ending in **-ter**: **frāter** from the stem **frātr-**.

c. Nouns with stems ending in **-din** and **-gin** replace **-in** of the stem by **-ō** in the nominative: **virgō** from the stem **virgin-**, **multitūdō** from the stem **multitūdin-**. The nominative **homō** is formed by replacing **-in** of the stem in the same manner.

frāter, M., *brother*
BASE, **frātr-**

homō, *man*
BASE, **homin-**

			TERMI-NATIONS
		SINGULAR	
NOM.	frāter	NOM. homō	—
GEN.	frātris	GEN. hominis	-is
DAT.	frātrī	DAT. hominī	-ī
ACC.	frātrem	ACC. hominem	-em
ABL.	frātre	ABL. homine	-e
		PLURAL	
NOM.	frātrēs	NOM. hominēs	-ēs
GEN.	frātrum	GEN. hominum	-um
DAT.	frātribus	DAT. hominibus	-ibus
ACC.	frātrēs	ACC. hominēs	-ēs
ABL.	frātribus	ABL. hominibus	-ibus

d. Nouns with stems ending in **-ōn** form the nominative by dropping **n**: **legiō** from the stem **legiōn-**.

e. Most nouns with stems ending in **-l** or **-r** have the nominative identical with the stem. A long vowel of the stem is shortened before a final **l** or **r** of the nominative.

f. The base is identical with the stem in nouns with consonant stems. Since the base can always be found by dropping the genitive ending, any noun of this class can be declined according to the models given above when its genitive is known.

239. VOCABULARY

condūcō, -ere, condūxī, con-
   ductum, bring together,
   collect
frāter, frātris, M., brother
homō, hominis, M., man,
   human being

interficiō, -ere, interfēcī,
   interfectum, kill
item, adv., also, likewise
lēx, lēgis, F., law
mīles, mīlitis, M., soldier
rēx, rēgis, M., king

EXERCISES

240. 1. Rēx multōs mīlitēs habuit. 2. Frāter meus item mīles fuit et in bellō vulnerātus est. 3. Hanc lēgem probāmus et laudāmus. 4. Ad eum locum magnum numerum mīlitum condūxit. 5. Rēx ab inimīcō interfectus est. 6. Hī hominēs lēgēs nōn timent. 7. Aliī gladiōs trādidērunt, aliī interfectī sunt. 8. Is vir potentiam nūllīus rēgis timet. 9. Hōrum hominum alter amīcus (est), alter incognitus est.

241. 1. This law is good, but it was then unknown. 2. The king had brought together into the town a large number of men. 3. Your brother also saw the soldiers in the forest. 4. Many Gauls were killed in flight by the soldiers. 5. This man has lost his brother and his son. 6. The slave is alone in the field.

SUGGESTED DRILL

(1) Decline together lēx bona. (2) Decline together frāter meus. (3) Give the accusative plural of sagitta, ager, and frāter. (4) Give the genitive singular of the words meaning one soldier. (5) Give the principal parts of trādidērunt. (6) Give the base of the noun rēx.

SEVENTH REVIEW LESSON

242. (1) The third declension of nouns, consonant stems.

(2) Adjectives with the genitive in -īus.

(3) The present indicative of the third conjugation, ō verbs.

(4) The present indicative of the fourth conjugation.

(5) The imperfect indicative of the third and fourth conjugations.

(6) The future indicative of the third and fourth conjugations.

(7) The present, imperfect, and future of iō verbs of the third conjugation.

(8) The future active participle.

(9) The substantive use of adjectives.

(10) The dative of purpose.

(11) The accusative with prepositions.

(12) The ablative of time.

243. Give Latin words with which the following English words are connected in derivation:

animated	impediment	nullify
alternate	item	reception
captive	justice	regal
castle	legal	sole
conduct	lunar	subsidy
fact	military	total
fraternal	neutral	union
fugitive	nihilist	victory

LESSON XXXVI

THE THIRD DECLENSION, CONSONANT STEMS (Continued): DATIVE OF REFERENCE

NEUTER CONSONANT STEMS

244. There are many neuter nouns among the consonant stems of the third declension. These, like the masculine and feminine nouns, form the nominative in different ways.

a. Nouns which have **-in** as the stem ending change **i** of the stem to **e** in the nominative: **flūmen** from the stem **flūmin-.** A few other nouns likewise change the vowel before the final consonant of the stem in forming the nominative: **caput** from the stem **capit-.**

flūmen, N., *river*   **caput,** N., *head*
BASE, **flūmin-**   BASE, **capit-**

	SINGULAR			TERMINATIONS
Nom.	flūmen	Nom.	caput	—
Gen.	flūminis	Gen.	capitis	-is
Dat.	flūminī	Dat.	capitī	-ī
Acc.	flūmen	Acc.	caput	—
Abl.	flūmine	Abl.	capite	-e
	PLURAL			
Nom.	flūmina	Nom.	capita	-a
Gen.	flūminum	Gen.	capitum	-um
Dat.	flūminibus	Dat.	capitibus	-ibus
Acc.	flūmina	Acc.	capita	-a
Abl.	flūminibus	Abl.	capitibus	-ibus

b. Neuter nouns with stems ending in **-er** or **-or** regularly have the nominative in **-us**: **genus** from the stem **gener-, corpus** from the stem **corpor-.**[1] The nominative **iter** used with the stem **itiner-** is somewhat irregular.

---

[1] In these words the stem ending was originally **-s.**

corpus, N., *body*   **iter,** N., *journey, road*
BASE, **corpor-**   BASE, **itiner-**

	SINGULAR			TERMI-NATIONS
NOM.	corpus	NOM.	iter	—
GEN.	corporis	GEN.	itineris	**-is**
DAT.	corporī	DAT.	itinerī	**-ī**
ACC.	corpus	ACC.	iter	—
ABL.	corpore	ABL.	itinere	**-e**

	PLURAL			
NOM.	corpora	NOM.	itinera	**-a**
GEN.	corporum	GEN.	itinerum	**-um**
DAT.	corporibus	DAT.	itineribus	**-ibus**
ACC.	corpora	ACC.	itinera	**-a**
ABL.	corporibus	ABL.	itineribus	**-ibus**

THE DATIVE OF REFERENCE

245. The dative is often used to refer to a person who is likely to be affected favorably or unfavorably by an act or situation, or with reference to whom an act is said to be done or a situation to exist. This is called the Dative of Reference.

> **Librum amīcō ēmī,** *I bought a book for a friend.*

a. This use of the dative is sometimes found with words denoting things.

b. The dative of reference is often used in connection with a dative of purpose.

> **Mīlitēs oppidānīs auxiliō erant,** *the soldiers were a help (for a help) to the townspeople.*

> **Vir amīcō auxiliō vēnit,** *the man came to help (as a help for) his friend.*

246. VOCABULARY

armātus, -a, -um, armed
caput, capitis, N., head
corpus, corporis, N., body
dēfessus, -a, -um, tired out,
　exhausted
emō, -ere, ēmī, ēmptum, buy

flūmen, flūminis, N., river
iter, itineris, N., march, jour-
　ney, road
nēmō, *dat.* nēminī, *acc.* nē-
　minem (*no genitive or abl.*),[1]
　no one.

EXERCISES

247. 1. Id flūmen lātum et altum est. 2. Hī hominēs magna corpora habent, sed nōn mīlitēs bonī erunt. 3. Frāter tuus iter longum fēcerat et dēfessus erat. 4. Hic equus pulcher caput parvum habet. 5. Tum lēgātus mīlitēs suōs celeriter condūxit quod Germānī appropinquābant. 6. Anteā nēmō in eō oppidō armātus erat, nunc multī arma habent. 7. Hic homō equum fīliō suō ēmit. 8. Gallī magnō auxiliō Rōmānīs in eō bellō erant.

248. 1. The head of that statue is beautiful. 2. The Gauls fought in the river and many were killed. 3. I saw no one on that journey. 4. The soldiers were a great help to our friends in danger. 5. The boys have worked industriously and are tired out. 6. I bought these books for my brother.

SUGGESTED DRILL

(1) Conjugate **emō** in the present and future indicative, active and passive. (2) Give a synopsis of **videō** in the third person singular, indicative passive. (3) Give a synopsis of **emō** in the third person plural, indicative active. (4) Decline together the words which mean *a beautiful river.* (5) Explain the case of **auxiliō** and of **Rōmānīs,** in sentence 8, 247.

---

[1] The missing genitive and ablative forms of this word are supplied by the genitive and ablative forms of **nūllus.**

LESSON XXXVII

THE THIRD DECLENSION, *I*-STEMS AND MIXED STEMS

GENITIVE AND ACCUSATIVE PLURAL FORMS

249. Nouns with **i**-stems and mixed stems have the genitive plural ending in **-ium**. Masculine and feminine nouns of these classes may have either **-ēs** or **-īs** as the ending of the accusative plural. In the singular they are usually declined like consonant stems.

MASCULINE AND FEMININE *I*-STEMS AND MIXED STEMS

250. (1) Nouns which have the nominative ending in **-is** or **-ēs**, and which have the same number of syllables in the genitive as in the nominative, are **i**-stem nouns.

(2) The most important mixed stems are:

- *a.* Monosyllables ending in **-s** or **-x** following a consonant: **mōns, arx.**
- *b.* Words of more than one syllable ending in **-ns** or **-rs**; **cliēns, cohors.**
- *c.* The noun **nox.**

Nouns with **i**-stems and mixed stems are indicated in the vocabulary by the ending of the genitive plural, **-ium,** printed after that of the genitive singular.

MANNER OF WEARING THE TOGA

Masculine and feminine **i**-stems are declined thus:

hostis, M., *enemy*
Base, **host-**

caedēs, F., *slaughter*
Base, **caed-**

				TERMI-NATIONS
		SINGULAR		
Nom.	hostis	Nom.	caedēs	-s
Gen.	hostis	Gen.	caedis	-is
Dat.	hostī	Dat.	caedī	-ī
Acc.	hostem	Acc.	caedem	-em
Abl.	hoste	Abl.	caede	-e
		PLURAL		
Nom.	hostēs	Nom.	caedēs	-ēs
Gen.	hostium	Gen.	caedium	-ium
Dat.	hostibus	Dat.	caedibus	-ibus
Acc.	hostīs, -ēs	Acc.	caedīs, -ēs	-īs, -ēs
Abl.	hostibus	Abl.	caedibus	-ibus

The declension of mixed stems is as follows:

urbs, F., *city*
Base, **urb-**

gēns, F., *nation, race*
Base, **gent-**

				TERMI-NATIONS
		SINGULAR		
Nom.	urbs	Nom.	gēns	-s
Gen.	urbis	Gen.	gentis	-is
Dat.	urbī	Dat.	gentī	-ī
Acc.	urbem	Acc.	gentem	-em
Abl.	urbe	Abl.	gente	-e
		PLURAL		
Nom.	urbēs	Nom.	gentēs	-ēs
Gen.	urbium	Gen.	gentium	-ium
Dat.	urbibus	Dat.	gentibus	-ibus
Acc.	urbēs, -īs	Acc.	gentēs, -īs	-ēs, -īs
Abl.	urbibus	Abl.	gentibus	-ibus

251. VOCABULARY

caedēs, caedis, -ium, F., slaughter, massacre

dēleō, -ēre, -ēvī, -ētum, destroy

dēserō, -ere, dēseruī, dēsertum, desert

fīnis, fīnis, -ium, M., end, limit; *pl.*, country

gēns, gentis, -ium, F., nation race

hostis, hostis, -ium, M., enemy (*of the state*)

incendō, -ere, incendī, incēnsum, set on fire, burn

urbs, urbis, -ium, F., city

EXERCISES

252. 1. Gallī fīnīs lātōs habēbant. 2. In fīnibus eōrum multae urbēs erant. 3. Gentēs Germānōrum cum eīs bellum ōlim gerēbant. 4. Multās urbēs et oppida Gallōrum expugnāvērunt et incendērunt. 5. Hī saepe oppida dēseruērunt quod hostīs timēbant. 6. Ā Germānīs magna caedēs facta est et multa oppida dēlēta sunt. 7. Sed Rōmānī in Galliam vēnērunt et Germānōs vīcērunt. 8. Gallōs quoque (*also*) superāvērunt et Galliam prōvinciam Rōmānam fēcērunt.

253. 1. This nation has large cities in its territories. 2. No one fears danger and no one deserts his place. 3. This road is unknown to the enemy. 4. Our soldiers made a great slaughter of the enemy and destroyed many towns. 5. This book has been a great help (for a great help) to your son.

SUGGESTED DRILL

(1) Give the nominative singular of each noun in 252. (2) Indicate the stem of each verb in the sentences of 252; and state whether it is the present, perfect, or participial stem. (3) Point out a phrase in the sentences of 253 which is translated by the dative of reference. (4) Decline fīnis. (5) Decline together the words for *an exhausted enemy*. (6) Name the nine adjectives which have the genitive ending -īus.

vendo vendere vendidi venditu... (handwritten)

LESSON XXXVIII

THE THIRD DECLENSION (Continued), NEUTER *I*-STEMS: GENDER IN THIRD DECLENSION

THE THIRD DECLENSION, NEUTER *I*-STEMS

254. Nouns of the third declension which end in -e, -al, or -ar are i-stems and are neuter in gender. They have the ablative singular ending in -ī, the nominative and accusative plural in -ia, and the genitive plural in -ium.

	īnsigne, N., *badge, decoration* BASE, **īnsign-**	**calcar**, N., *spur* BASE, **calcār-**	**animal**, N., *animal* BASE, **animāl-**	
		SINGULAR		TERMINATIONS
NOM.	īnsigne	calcar	animal	—
GEN.	īnsignis	calcāris	animālis	-is
DAT.	īnsignī	calcārī	animālī	-ī
ACC.	īnsigne	calcar	animal	—
ABL.	īnsignī	calcārī	animālī	-ī
		PLURAL		
NOM.	īnsignia	calcāria	animālia	-ia
GEN.	īnsignium	calcārium	animālium	-ium
DAT.	īnsignibus	calcāribus	animālibus	-ibus
ACC.	īnsignia	calcāria	animālia	-ia
ABL.	īnsignibus	calcāribus	animālibus	-ibus

GENDER IN THE THIRD DECLENSION

255. Nouns ending in -tās and -tūs, and most nouns ending in -gō and -iō, are feminine.

Nouns ending in -tor are masculine.

Nouns ending in -e, -al, -ar, -n, and -t are neuter.

256.   VOCABULARY

aedificō, -āre, -āvī, -ātum,
  build
animal, animālis, -ium, N.,
  animal
calcar, calcāris, -ium, N., spur
certē, *adv.*, certainly, at least

īnsigne, īnsignis, -ium, N.,
  badge, decoration
legiō, legiōnis, F., legion
nāvis, nāvis, -ium, F., ship
vēndō, -ere, vēndidī, vēnditum, sell

EXERCISES

257. 1. In hīs locīs multa animālia interfecta sunt. 2.
Equus meus calcar magnopere timet. 3. Hī mīlitēs īnsignia
habent quod fortiter in bellō pugnāvērunt. 4. Labiēnus
multās nāvēs aedificāvit et oppidum mūnīvit. 5. Ūna legiō
ab hostibus dēlēta est. 6. Lēgātus urbem expugnāvit et
multōs servōs vēndidit. 7. Hic homō certē hostis patriae
fuit, sed nōn interfectus est. 8. Ōlim multae nāvēs in
flūminibus patriae nostrae vīsae sunt.

258. 1. This small animal has a large head. 2. The boy
wounded the horse with the spur. 3. Many ships were built
by the lieutenant and the town was fortified. 4. We saw
the badges and the weapons of the Gauls. 5. The soldiers
were a help (for a help) to the sailors.

SUGGESTED DRILL

(1) Decline **nāvis longa**. (2) Decline **animal magnum**. (3) Give
the principal parts of the verbs in sentences 6, 7, and 8, 257. (4) Point
out the differences between the case endings of **corpus** and of **calcar**.
(5) Conjugate **vēndō** in the past perfect active indicative. (6) Explain
the case use of **hostibus** in sentence 5, 257.

LESSON XXXIX

THE THIRD DECLENSION, IRREGULAR AND EXCEPTIONAL NOUNS

DECLENSION OF *vīs*

259. A few nouns of the third declension are somewhat irregular. The noun **vīs** has a different stem in the plural from that used in the singular.

vīs, *force, violence;* pl., *strength*
BASES, **vī-, vīr-**

	SINGULAR	PLURAL
NOM.	vīs	vīrēs
GEN.	—	vīrium
DAT.	—	vīribus
ACC.	vim	vīrīs *or* vīrēs
ABL.	vī	vīribus

a. The accusative plural of **vīs** is to be distinguished from the dative and ablative plural of **vir** by the long **ī** of the first syllable.

DECLENSION OF *IGNIS* AND *TURRIS*

260. There are a few **i**-stems which show variations from the declension of consonant stems in the singular as well as in the plural.

ignis, M., *fire*
BASE, **ign-**

turris, F., *tower*
BASE, **turr-**

	SINGULAR	PLURAL	SINGULAR	PLURAL
NOM.	ignis	ignēs	turris	turrēs
GEN.	ignis	ignium	turris	turrium
DAT.	ignī	ignibus	turrī	turribus
ACC.	ignem	ignīs, -ēs	turrim, -em	turrīs, -ēs
ABL.	ignī, igne	ignibus	turrī, turre	turribus

261.   VOCABULARY

bōs,[1] bovis, M., F., OX, COW;
  pl., cattle
ignis, ignis, -ium, M., fire
impediō, -īre, impedīvī, im-
  pedītum, hinder
mōns, montis, -ium, M.,
  mountain

neque, *conj.*, nor; neque . . .
  neque, neither . . . nor
nōn numquam, *adv.*, sometimes
turris, turris, -ium, F., tower
vīs, *see* 259, F., force, violence;
  pl., strength

EXERCISES

262. 1. Hostēs urbem ignī dēlēvērunt. 2. Vim hostium nōn timēbāmus neque eōs vītābāmus. 3. In eō monte turrim altam vīdimus. 4. Gallī iter nostrōrum impedīvērunt et multōs mīlitēs interfēcērunt. 5. Puer territus est quod bovēs in agrō vīderat. 6. Neque rēx neque frāter eius tum in urbe erat. 7. Nōn numquam nāvēs ex hāc turrī videntur. 8. Lēgātus quattuor legiōnēs ad montem dūxit et ibi castra mūnīvit.

263. 1. The Gauls destroyed the tower with fire. 2. The violence of the soldiers frightened the townspeople and many fled from the town. 3. The boy had wandered in the mountains five hours. 4. We saw horses and cattle on the islands, but we saw no men. 5. Sometimes the march of the legions was hindered by the deep rivers and the forests. 6. In that city there was neither slave nor master.

SUGGESTED DRILL

(1) Name the three classes of nouns in the third declension. (2) Give the case endings of masculine and feminine consonant stems. (3) Give the case endings of masculine and feminine i-stems and mixed stems. (4) Give the rules for gender in the third declension. (5) Decline together **vīs magna.**

---

[1] The genitive, dative, and ablative of the plural of bōs are somewhat irregular. These forms do not occur in the exercises of this book.
They may be found in the Appendix, section 3, D.

LESSON XL

ĪDEM: GENITIVE OF THE WHOLE

DECLENSION OF *ĪDEM*

264. The declension of **īdem**, *same*, is as follows:

SINGULAR

	Masc.	Fem.	Neut.
NOM.	īdem	eadem	idem
GEN.	eiusdem	eiusdem	eiusdem
DAT.	eīdem	eīdem	eīdem
ACC.	eundem	eandem	idem
ABL.	eōdem	eādem	eōdem

PLURAL

NOM.	īdem *or* eīdem	eaedem	eadem
GEN.	eōrundem	eārundem	eōrundem
DAT.	eīsdem *or* īsdem	eīsdem *or* īsdem	eīsdem *or* īsdem
ACC.	eōsdem	eāsdem	eadem
ABL.	eīsdem *or* īsdem	eīsdem *or* īsdem	eīsdem *or* īsdem

THE GENITIVE OF THE WHOLE (PARTITIVE GENITIVE)

265. The genitive is sometimes used to designate the whole of something of which a part is denoted by the word on which the genitive depends. This use of the genitive is called the Genitive of the Whole.

Multī nostrōrum fūgērunt, *many of our men fled.*

a. The Latin uses the genitive of the whole in certain phrases where the English employs an adjective in agreement.

Nihil novī, *nothing new (nothing of that which is new).*

266. VOCABULARY

absum, abesse, āfuī, āfutūrus,
  be absent, be distant
aestās, aestātis, F., summer
apud, *prep. w. acc.,* among,
  with, at the house of
dē, *prep. w. abl.,* from; about
dux, ducis, M., leader

eques, equitis, M., horseman;
  pl., cavalry
īdem, eadem, idem, same, the
  same
pars, partis, -ium, F., part
vexō, -āre, -āvī, -ātum, overrun, plunder

EXERCISES

267. 1. Pars equitum statim fūgit et multī interfectī sunt.
2. Hī hominēs numquam amīcōs dēseruērunt. 3. Apud Rōmānōs iūstitia semper laudāta est. 4. Īdem dux ad castra
iterum cum eīsdem mīlitibus veniet. 5. Silva nōn longē ab
eō flūmine abest. 6. Eam aestātem in Ītaliā cum amīcīs
mānsī. 7. Germānī eandem partem Ītaliae anteā vexāve-
rant. 8. Gallī turrim ignī dēlēvērunt sed oppidum nōn
expugnāvērunt. 9. Nihil novī dē bellō audīvī, quod nōn in
urbe fuī.

268. 1. Part of the men were absent from the town because
the lieutenant feared no danger from (**ab**) the enemy. 2. We
shall send the same leader and the same soldiers. 3. We remained in Italy one summer and saw many beautiful cities.
4. The Gauls overran part of Britain and destroyed many
towns. 5. Among the soldiers, these arms are praised. 6.
We saw the horsemen in the river and we fled.

———

SUGGESTED DRILL

(1) Decline together **īdem dux.** (2) Decline together **eadem pars.**
(3) Point out three examples of the use of the genitive of the whole
in the sentences of 267. (4) Conjugate **absum** in the present indicative
and the future indicative. (5) Give a synopsis of **fugiō** in the third
person singular indicative active. (6) Explain the case of **aestātem,**
in sentence 6, 267.

EIGHTH REVIEW LESSON

269.   VOCABULARY REVIEW

aestās, -tātis, F.

animal, animālis, N.

animus, -ī, M.

bōs, bovis, M., F.

caedēs, caedis, F.

calcar, calcāris, N.

captīvus, -ī, M.

caput, capitis, N.

castellum, -ī, N.

corpus, corporis, N.

dux, ducis, M.

eques, equitis, M.

fīnis, fīnis, M.

flūmen, flūminis, N.

frāter, frātris, M.

gēns, gentis, F.

homō, hominis, M.

hostis, hostis, M.

ignis, ignis, M.

impedīmentum, -ī, N.

īnsigne, īnsignis, N.

iter, itineris, N.

iūstitia, -ae, F.

legiō, legiōnis, F.

lēx, lēgis, F.

lūna, -ae, F.

mīles, mīlitis, M.

mōns, montis, M.

nāvis, nāvis, F.

nēmō, *dat.* nēminī, M., F.

nihil, *indeclinable*, N.

alius, alia, aliud

alter, altera, alterum

armatus, -a, -um

cārus, -a, -um

dēfessus, -a, -um

īdem, eadem, idem

incognitus, -a, -um

neuter, neutra, neutrum

nūllus, nūlla, nūllum

sōlus, sōla, sōlum

tōtus, tōta, tōtum

ūllus, ūlla, ūllum

ūnus, ūna, ūnum

uter, utra, utrum

absum, abesse, āfuī, āfutūrus

aedificō, -āre, -āvī, -ātum

āmittō, -ere, āmīsī, āmissum

condūcō, -dūcere, -dūxī, -ductum

dēleō, -ēre, -ēvī, -ētum

dēserō, -ere, -uī, -tum

emō, -ere, ēmī, ēmptum

excēdō, -cēdere, -cessī, -cessum

faciō, -ere, fēcī, factum

fugiō, -ere, fūgī, fugitūrus

iaciō, -ere, iēcī, iactum

impediō, -īre, -īvī, -ītum

incendō, -ere, incendī, incēnsum

interficiō, -ficere, -fēcī, -fectum

pācō, -āre, -āvī, -ātum

perveniō, -venīre, -vēnī, -ventum

recipiō, -cipere, -cēpī, -ceptum

nūntius, -ī, M.

pars, partis, F.

rēgnum, -ī, N.

rēx, rēgis, M.

subsĭdium, -ī, N.

trīduum, -ī, N.

turris, turris, F.

urbs, urbis, F.

victōria, -ae, F.

vīs, F.

vēndō, -dere, -didī, -ditum

vexō, -āre, -āvī, -ātum

certē

item

iterum

magnopere

nōndum

nōn numquam

dē

neque

270. RELATED ENGLISH WORDS

absent	hostile
animal	ignite
army	impede
bovine	incendiary
capital	legion
corporal	naval
desert	part
duke	turret
edifice	urban
ensign	vendor
final	vex

DRAWING ON THE OUTER WALL OF A HOUSE IN POMPEII

LESSON XLI

PRESENT PASSIVE INFINITIVE OF REGULAR VERBS: USE OF INFINITIVE

THE PRESENT PASSIVE INFINITIVE

271. The terminations of the present passive infinitive in the four conjugations are as follows.

I.	II.	III.	IV.
-ārī	-ērī	-ī	-īrī

The following table shows the formation and translation of the present infinitives, active and passive, of the four conjugations:

	ACTIVE	PASSIVE
I.	portāre, *to carry*	portārī, *to be carried*
II.	monēre, *to warn*	monērī, *to be warned*
III.	dūcere, *to lead*	dūcī, *to be led*
	capere, *to take*	capī, *to be taken*
IV.	audīre, *to hear*	audīrī, *to be heard*

THE INFINITIVE AS MODIFIER OF A VERB (COMPLEMENTARY INFINITIVE)

272. The infinitive is frequently used in direct dependence on a verb, as an object, or as an adverbial modifier. When thus used, it may be said to complete the meaning of the verb on which it depends.

Mātūrat venīre, *he hastens to come.*

a. A dependent English infinitive expressing purpose in such phrases as, *We came to help you,* represents a different usage, and cannot be translated by a Latin infinitive.

273. <center>VOCABULARY</center>

conveniō, -īre, convēnī, con-
  ventum, come together,
  assemble
cupiō, -ere, cupīvī, cupītum,
  wish, desire
ferus, -a, -um, fierce
praemium, -ī, N., reward

incipiō, -ere, incēpī, incep-
  tum, begin
invītus, -a, -um, unwilling
mātūrō, -āre, -āvī, -ātum,
  hasten
possideō, -ēre, possēdī, pos-
  sessum, possess

EXERCISES

274. 1. Hic puer laudārī semper cupit. 2. Hostēs convenīre nōn mātūrāvērunt quod invītī erant. 3. Eī hominēs
ferī fīnēs lātōs possident. 4. Lēgātus mīlitēs ad castra hostium dūcī iubet. 5. Sonus armōrum audīrī incipit et oppidānī terrentur. 6. Urbs nostra longē ā monte abest. 7.
Praemium eī nōn dabitur quod nōn honestus est. 8. Magna
pars eius īnsulae Gallīs incognita erat sed Rōmānī ibi multa
oppida reppērerunt.

275. 1. The lieutenant wishes to be sent to Gaul. 2. You
do not wish to be warned because you do not see the danger.
3. This reward was given by the king to his brother. 4. The
soldiers are beginning to assemble, but the leader is absent.
5. Many hastened to flee from the city, but this man remained.
6. There are many fierce animals in the forests of that island.

SUGGESTED DRILL

(1) Give the present active and passive infinitives of all the verbs
of the vocabulary of this lesson. (2) Explain the use of the infinitives
in sentences 1 and 2, 274. (3) Explain the case of **īnsulae,** 8, 274.
(4) Give the genitive and the dative singular of the phrase which
means *the same reward.* (5) Give the accusative singular and plural
of **vīs.**

LESSON XLII

ADJECTIVES OF THE THIRD DECLENSION: ABLATIVE OF MANNER

ADJECTIVES OF THE THIRD DECLENSION

276. Some adjectives of the third declension have only one form for the three genders in the nominative singular, others have two forms, one for the masculine and feminine and one for the neuter, and others have three forms, one for each gender. They are accordingly known as adjectives of one, two, or three endings.

Those of three endings and two endings are **i**-stems. They are declined as follows:

ADJECTIVES OF THREE ENDINGS

ācer, *bold*

	SINGULAR			PLURAL		
	Masc.	*Fem.*	*Neut.*	*Masc.*	*Fem.*	*Neut.*
Nom.	ācer	ācris	ācre	ācrēs	ācrēs	ācria
Gen.	ācris	ācris	ācris	ācrium	ācrium	ācrium
Dat.	ācrī	ācrī	ācrī	ācribus	ācribus	ācribus
Acc.	ācrem	ācrem	ācre	ācrēs, -īs	ācrēs, -īs	ācria
Abl.	ācrī	ācrī	ācrī	ācribus	ācribus	ācribus

ADJECTIVES OF TWO ENDINGS

omnis, *all*

	SINGULAR		PLURAL	
	Masc. and Fem.	*Neut.*	*Masc. and Fem.*	*Neut.*
Nom.	omnis	omne	omnēs	omnia
Gen.	omnis	omnis	omnium	omnium
Dat.	omnī	omnī	omnibus	omnibus
Acc.	omnem	omne	omnēs, -īs	omnia
Abl.	omnī	omnī	omnibus	omnibus

THE ABLATIVE OF MANNER

277. The manner in which an act is done may be expressed by the ablative with **cum**. But **cum** may be omitted if the noun is modified by an adjective. This use of the ablative is called the Ablative of Manner.

Cum virtūte pugnant, *they fight with courage.*

Cum magnā virtūte pugnant, or virtūte magnā pugnant,
they fight with great courage.

278. **VOCABULARY**

ācer, ācris, ācre, spirited, bold, sharp

Caesar, Caesaris, M., Caesar, (*Gaius Julius Caesar, a famous Roman general and statesman*)

celeritās, -tātis, F., speed

fortis, forte, brave

omnis, omne, all, every

pedester, pedestris, pedestre, on foot; **cōpiae pedestrēs,** infantry

vīcus, -ī, M., village

virtūs, virtūtis, F., courage

EXERCISES

279. 1. Cōpiae pedestrēs (cum) magnā celeritāte appropinquāvērunt. 2. Nūllum bellum in omnī Ītaliā eō annō erat. 3. Ille puer equum ācrem habet. 4. Gallī fortēs erant et bellum cum virtūte gerēbant. 5. Hostēs omnēs vīcōs incendērunt et agrōs vexāvērunt. 6. Omnēs convenīre iussī erant sed multī invītī erant. 7. Inter montem et flūmen urbs magna erat. 8. Caesar saepe virtūtem mīlitum suōrum laudat. 9. In omnibus locīs ignēs vidēbantur et multī fugiēbant.

280. 1. The Germans attacked the city with great courage and many of them were killed. 2. Part of the village was burned by the enemy. 3. The lieutenant sent the infantry with great speed, but the horsemen had fled. 4. The danger begins to be seen by all. 5. You demand the aid of all your friends, but you never help them.

---

(1) Decline together **mīles ācer**. (2) Decline together **vir fortis**. (3) Give the genitive plural of **mōns** and **flūmen**. (4) Decline **pedester** in full. (5) Explain the case of **virtūte** in sentence 4 and of **flūmen** in sentence 7, 279. (6) Give the principal parts of the verbs **gerō** and **iubeō**.

LESSON XLIII

THIRD DECLENSION ADJECTIVES (Continued): ORDER OF WORDS IN PREPOSITIONAL PHRASES

THIRD DECLENSION ADJECTIVES OF ONE ENDING

281. Most third declension adjectives of one ending are **i**-stems. The ablative singular sometimes ends in **-e**.

fēlīx, *fortunate*   **potēns**, *powerful*

SINGULAR

	Masc. and Fem.	*Neut.*	*Masc. and Fem.*	*Neut.*
NOM.	fēlīx	fēlīx	potēns	potēns
GEN.	fēlīcis	fēlīcis	potentis	potentis
DAT.	fēlīcī	fēlīcī	potentī	potentī
ACC.	fēlīcem	fēlīx	potentem	potēns
ABL.	fēlīcī	fēlīcī	potentī, -e	potentī, -e

PLURAL

	Masc. and Fem.	*Neut.*	*Masc. and Fem.*	*Neut.*
NOM.	fēlīcēs	fēlīcia	potentēs	potentia
GEN.	fēlīcium	fēlīcium	potentium	potentium
DAT.	fēlīcibus	fēlīcibus	potentibus	potentibus
ACC.	fēlīcēs, -īs	fēlīcia	potentēs, -īs	potentia
ABL.	fēlīcibus	fēlīcibus	potentibus	potentibus

282. **Vetus,** *old,* is a consonant stem, and is declined as follows:

| | SINGULAR | | PLURAL | |
	Masc. and Fem.	*Neut.*	*Masc. and Fem.*	*Neut.*
NOM.	vetus	vetus	veterēs	vetera
GEN.	veteris	veteris	veterum	veterum
DAT.	veterī	veterī	veteribus	veteribus
ACC.	veterem	vetus	veterēs	vetera
ABL.	vetere	vetere	veteribus	veteribus

ORDER OF WORDS IN PREPOSITIONAL PHRASES

283. Phrases consisting of a monosyllabic preposition and a noun modified by an adjective sometimes have the adjective first and the preposition between the adjective and the noun.

> **Magnā cum virtūte,** *with great courage.*
> **Hīs dē causīs,** *from these causes (for these reasons).*

284. **VOCABULARY**

accipiō, -ere, accēpī, acceptum, accept, receive

centum, *indecl. num.,* one hundred

dē, *prep. with abl.,* from, down from; about, concerning

dēbeō, -ēre, -uī, -itum, owe, ought

fēlīx, *genitive* **fēlīcis,** happy, fortunate

pāx, pācis, F., peace

potēns, *genitive* **potentis,** powerful

vetus, *genitive* **veteris,** old; former, of long standing

EXERCISES

285. 1. Nihil dē frātre tuō audīvimus. 2. Hic puer praemia magna in scholā accēpit et ab amīcō tuō laudātur. 3. Epistulam hodiē ad eum hominem mittere dēbēmus. 4. Virī bonī semper pācem cupiunt. 5. Omnēs eum propter iūstitiam et virtūtem eius laudant. 6. Hic rēx fēlīx et potēns erat et multōs sociōs habēbat. 7. In eō locō eōsdem virōs saepe vīderāmus. 8 Magnā cum celeritāte centum virī ex agrīs convēnērunt.   9. Hae iniūriae veterēs sunt sed tamen in animō manent.

ARCH OVER ROMAN ROAD

286. 1. You (*singular*) ought to invite all your friends. 2. This powerful king had many soldiers and he waged many wars. 3. We are happy because we have received a letter today. 4. These soldiers were far distant from the battle. 5. This man is working, and we ought to help him. 6. Our old friends are now in the city.

SUGGESTED DRILL

(1) Give the Latin equivalent for the phrase *with great speed*. (2) Explain the use of the infinitive **mittere**, in sentence 3, **285**. (3) Mention adjectives illustrating each of the three classes of third declension adjectives. (4) Give the ablative singular and the genitive plural of **fortis** and **vetus**. (5) Give a synopsis of **accipiō** in the third person singular, active, and the third person plural, passive, indicative.

SIXTH SUPPLEMENTARY REVIEW

VOCABULARY REVIEW

1. abdō, -dere, -didī, -ditum
2. absum, -esse, āfuī, āfutūrus
3. accipiō, -cipere, -cēpī, -ceptum
4. ācer, -cris, -cre
5. addō, -dere, -didī, -ditum
6. aestās, -tātis, F.
7. animus, -ī, M.
8. apud, *prep. with acc.*
9. caput, capitis, N.
10. celeritās, -tātis, F.
11. centum
12. certē, *adv.*
13. conveniō, -venīre, -vēnī, -ventum
14. corpus, corporis, N.
15. cupiō, -ere, cupīvī, cupītum
16. dē, *prep. with abl.*
17. dēbeō, -ēre, -uī, -itum
18. dēsum, -esse, -fuī
19. dux, ducis, M.
20. ēgregius, -a, -um
21. eques, equitis, M.
22. fīnis, fīnis, M.
23. flūmen, flūminis, N.
24. fortis, forte
25. frāter, frātris, M.
26. genus, generis, N.
27. homō, hominis, M.
28. hostis, hostis, M.

29. īdem, eadem, idem
30. impediō, -īre, -īvī, -ītum
31. incendō, -cendere, -cendī, -cēnsum
32. incipiō, -cipere, -cēpī, -ceptum
33. interficiō, -ficere, -fēcī, -fectum
34. iter, itineris, N.
35. lēx, lēgis, F.
36. mīles, mīlitis, M.
37. mōns, montis, M.
38. nāvis, nāvis, F.
39. nec *or* neque, *conj.*
40. negōtium, -ī, N.
41. neque . . . neque *or* nec . . . nec
42. nōbilis, -e
43. ōmnis, -e
44. pars, partis, F.
45. pāx, pācis, F.
46. pedester, -tris, -tre
47. perveniō, -venīre, -vēnī, -ventum
48. praemium, -ī, N.
49. recipiō, -cipere, -cēpī, -ceptum
50. rēgnum, -ī, N.
51. rēx, rēgis, M.
52. servō, -āre, -āvī, -ātum
53. terra, -ae, F.
54. trahō, -ere, trāxī, tractum

55. turris, turris, F.
56. urbs, urbis, F.
57. virtūs, virtūtis, F.
58. vīs (*see 259*) F.

---

1. put away, hide
2. be away
3. accept, receive
4. sharp, keen
5. add
6. summer
7. spirit, life, soul
8. among, at the home of
9. head
10. speed, swiftness
11. one hundred
12. certainly, at least
13. come together
14. body
15. desire
16. down from, concerning
17. owe, ought
18. be lacking
19. leader
20. eminent, unusual
21. horseman

22. end; *pl.* boundaries, territory
23. river
24. brave
25. brother
26. race, kind
27. man
28. enemy (of the state)
29. the same
30. hinder
31. set on fire
32. begin, undertake
33. kill
34. journey, road
35. law
36. soldier
37. mountain
38. ship
39. and not, nor
40. business, trouble
41. neither, neither . . . nor

42. (knowable), noble, famous
43. every; *pl.* all
44. part
45. peace
46. infantry (*adj.*)
47. come through, arrive
48. reward
49. take back; receive; *with sē,* withdraw
50. kingdom
51. king
52. save, protect
53. land, earth
54. drag
55. tower
56. city
57. manliness, courage
58. force, violence; *pl.* strength

WORD STUDY

1. Explain the formation of **accipiō, addō, absum.**
2. Find Latin words to which the following are related:

capital	final	incendiary	military
convention	fraternal	itinerary	pedestrian
duke	impede	legal	reception

LESSON XLIV

THE RELATIVE PRONOUN

THE DECLENSION OF THE RELATIVE PRONOUN

287. The relative pronoun is declined as follows:

	SINGULAR			PLURAL		
	Masc.	*Fem.*	*Neut.*	*Masc.*	*Fem.*	*Neut.*
NOM.	quī	quae	quod	quī	quae	quae
GEN.	cuius	cuius	cuius	quōrum	quārum	quōrum
DAT.	cui	cui	cui	quibus	quibus	quibus
ACC.	quem	quam	quod	quōs	quās	quae
ABL.	quō	quā	quō	quibus	quibus	quibus

AGREEMENT OF RELATIVE PRONOUN

288. The relative pronoun agrees with its antecedent in gender and number, but its case depends on its use in its own clause.

Homō quem vidēs amīcus meus est, *the man whom you see is my friend.*

289. VOCABULARY

causa, -ae, F., cause
dēfendō, -ere, dēfendī, dēfēn-
    sum, defend
mare, maris, N., sea
māter, mātris, F., mother
pater, patris, M., father

quī, quae, quod, who, which,
    that
resistō, -ere, restitī, (*with
    dative*), resist
tempus, temporis, N., time,
    occasion

EXERCISES

290. 1. Praemia lēgātō quī oppidum dēfendit dabuntur. 2. Haec urbs cuius mūrum eō tempore vidēbās magna est. 3. Pater puerī cui praemia data sunt fēlīx est. 4. Fēmina quam vidēs est māter huius puerī. 5. Multae erant causae eius bellī veteris. 6. Hoc mare lātum et altum est. 7. Oppidānī

mīlitibus resistēbant ā quibus oppidum oppugnātum erat.
8. Gallī magnā cum virtūte patriam suam dēfendēbant. 9.
Multī erant vīcī quōs mīlitēs incendērunt.

291. 1. The cause of the war which was being waged is
unknown. 2. At that time there was peace among the Gauls.
3. The father of this king resisted the enemies who wished
to destroy his city. 4. The legion which had been sent,
attacked the camp with great courage. 5. You feared the
violence of these soldiers, but they have defended your city.

SUGGESTED DRILL

(1) Explain what is meant by "simple sentence," "complex sentence," and "compound sentence." (2) State to which of these
classes each of the sentences of 291 belongs. (3) Point out the subordinate clauses of the complex sentences in 291. (4) Name the
antecedents of the relative pronouns in these complex sentences.
(5) Explain the cases of the relative pronouns in 290.

LESSON XLV

THE FOURTH DECLENSION

292. In the fourth declension the nominative ends in -**us**
for the masculine and feminine and in -**ū** for the neuter.
Most nouns ending in -**us** are masculine.

exercitus, M., *army*　　　　　　**cornū**, N., *horn*
　BASE, **exercit-**　　　　　　　　　BASE, **corn-**

SINGULAR

		TERMI-NATIONS				TERMI-NATIONS
NOM.	exercitus	-us		NOM.	cornū	-ū
GEN.	exercitūs	-ūs		GEN.	cornūs	-ūs
DAT.	exercituī, -ū	-uī, -ū		DAT.	cornū	-ū
ACC.	exercitum	-um		ACC.	cornū	-ū
ABL.	exercitū	-ū		ABL.	cornū	-ū

PLURAL

Nom.	exercitūs	-ūs		Nom.	cornua	-ua
Gen.	exercituum	-uum		Gen.	cornuum	-uum
Dat.	exercitibus	-ibus		Dat.	cornibus	-ibus
Acc.	exercitūs	-ūs		Acc.	cornua	-ua
Abl.	exercitibus	-ibus		Abl.	cornibus	-ibus

a. The dative and ablative plurals of a few masculine
and feminine nouns of the fourth declension end in
-ūbus.

293.   **VOCABULARY**

circumveniō, -venīre, -vēnī,
-ventum, surround

cornū, cornūs, n., horn; wing
(*of an army*)

exercitus, -ūs, m., army, body
of trained men

flūctus, -ūs, m., wave

manus, -ūs, f., hand; band
(*of men*)

petō, -ere, petīvī *or* petiī, petītum, beg for, seek

tendō, -ere, tetendī, tentum,
hold out

vōx, vōcis, f., voice

EXERCISES

294. 1. Flūctūs maris altī erant et nāvis in perīculō erat.
2. Castra in quibus exercitus est circumventa sunt. 3. Gallī
ad Caesarem manūs tendēbant et pācem petēbant. 4. Vōcēs
Gallōrum quās mīlitēs audīvērunt eōs terruērunt. 5. Id
cornū superātum est. 6. Exercitus quem Gallī condūxerant
parvus erat. 7. Legiō quam Labiēnus in castrīs relīquit ab
hostibus oppugnāta est. 8. Fēlīx es quod patria tua pācem
habet.

295. 1. The Germans will surround the town which the
army is defending. 2. We heard the sound of the waves at
that time. 3. The Gauls resisted the army of the Romans and
fought bravely. 4. The enemy will hold out their hands and
beg for peace. 5. You did not receive the letter which I sent.

(1) Decline together the words which mean *a small hand*. (2) Explain the gender and number of the relative pronouns in the sentences of 294. (3) Point out the complex sentences in 295. (4) Point out the subjects of the subordinate clauses in these complex sentences. (5) Indicate the personal endings, tense signs, and stems of the forms **tendēbant** and **condūxerant**. (6) Conjugate **petō** in the future indicative active.

NINTH REVIEW LESSON

296. (1) The third declension of **i**-stem nouns.
(2) The third declension of adjectives.
(3) The fourth declension of nouns.
(4) The declension of **īdem.**
(5) The relative pronoun.
(6) The present infinitive of the four conjugations.
(7) Gender in the third declension.
(8) The genitive of the whole.
(9) The ablative of manner.

297. Give Latin words with which the following English words are connected in derivation.

accept	fortitude	pedestrian
celerity	inception	possession
century	manual	premium
convene	marine	resist
convention	maternal	temporary
defend	omnipresent	veteran
felicity	pacify	virtue
fluctuate	paternal	vocal

LESSON XLVI

DECLENSION OF *DOMUS*: LOCATIVE CASE

DECLENSION OF *DOMUS*

298. The noun **domus**, *home*, is irregular in that some of its cases have forms both of the second and of the fourth declensions.

	SINGULAR	PLURAL
Nom.	domus	domūs
Gen.	domūs, domī	domuum, domōrum
Dat.	domuī, domō	domibus
Acc.	domum	domōs, domūs
Abl.	domō, domū	domibus

THE LOCATIVE CASE

299. With names of towns and small islands, also with **domus**, the place where some act is done or something exists is expressed by a form called the Locative Case. This has the same form as the genitive in the singular of nouns of the first and second declensions; elsewhere it has the same form as the ablative: **Rōmae**, *at Rome*. **Ocelī**, *at Ocelum*.

The locative of **domus** is **domī**.

a. The ablative of the noun **locus** (and occasionally of a few other nouns of similar meaning) is commonly used without a preposition to denote Place Where, if modified by an adjective: **hīs locīs**, *in these places*.

300. VOCABULARY

clārus, -a, -um, distinguished, famous

cōnscrībō, -ere, cōnscrīpsī, cōnscrīptum, enroll

domus, -ūs, (-ī), F., home, house

inīquus -a, -um, unfavorable, unjust

laus, laudis, F., praise

nōmen, nōminis, N., name

Ocelum, -ī, N., Ocelum (*a town*)

Rōma, -ae, F., Rome

EXERCISES

301. 1. Saepe nōmen huius virī audīvistī. 2. Nōn omnēs quī fortēs sunt laudem cupiunt. 3. Hic homō clārus Rōmae domicilium habēbat. 4. Cūr hae legiōnēs nōn Ocelī hiemābant? 5. Exercitus castra in locō inīquō posuit. 6. Caesar quattuor legiōnēs novās cōnscrīpsit. 7. Multōs annōs domī mānsimus. 8. Hic puer labōrat quod praemium petit. 9. Id cornū exercitūs locum dēseruit et ad montem fūgit.

ROMAN OIL VAULT

302. 1. The names of these nations are unknown to Caesar. 2. The soldiers who fought bravely in an unfavorable place received praise. 3. The son of this distinguished German is in Rome. 4. At home you (*sing.*) were often unhappy. 5. The town in which the soldier's father lives is small. 6. We do not desire war, but we shall defend our homes.

SUGGESTED DRILL

(1) Give the endings of the fourth declension. (2) Decline together **flūctus altus**. (3) Decline the relative pronoun in full. (4) Give a synopsis of **cōnscrībō** in the third person singular, active voice, indicative. (5) Explain the case of **Rōmae** in sentence 3, 301.

The Conquest of Gaul

The greater part of the region known as Gaul was conquered by the Romans in a series of campaigns lasting from 58 to 50 B. C. The Roman army was under the command of Gaius Julius Caesar, who was governor of the Roman province lying to the south of independent Gaul. The province had been conquered and brought under Roman authority some years earlier. The extension of Roman influence over the whole of Gaul brought about the adoption of the Latin language and of Roman customs in this important part of Europe, a result which has affected all the later history of France and of the whole civilized world.

The successes of Caesar in this war made it possible for him to become the ruler of Rome a little later, and to change the form of its government from a republic to a monarchy.

The main events of the first two years of the war are told in connection with the lessons which follow.

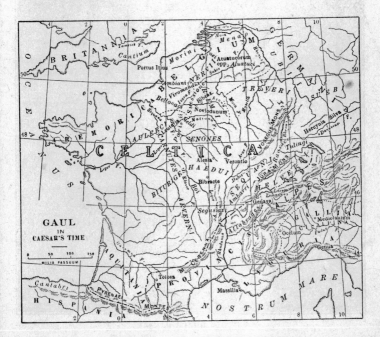

GAUL
IN
CAESAR'S TIME

GAIUS JULIUS CAESAR

LESSON XLVII

NUMERALS: DECLENSION OF *DUO* AND *TRĒS*

CARDINAL NUMERALS

303. The cardinal numerals from one to twenty are as follows:

ūnus, -a, -um,	*one*	ūndecim,	*eleven*
duo, duae, duo,	*two*	duodecim,	*twelve*
trēs, tria,	*three*	tredecim,	*thirteen*
quattuor,	*four*	quattuordecim,	*fourteen*
quīnque,	*five*	quīndecim,	*fifteen*
sex,	*six*	sēdecim,	*sixteen*
septem,	*seven*	septendecim,	*seventeen*
octō,	*eight*	duodēvīgintī,	*eighteen*
novem,	*nine*	ūndēvīgintī,	*nineteen*
decem,	*ten*	vīgintī,	*twenty*

DECLENSION OF *DUO* AND *TRĒS*

304. **Duo** and **trēs** are declined as follows:

	Masc.	Fem.	Neut.	Masc. and Fem.	Neut.
Nom.	duo	duae	duo	trēs	tria
Gen.	duōrum	duārum	duōrum	trium	trium
Dat.	duōbus	duābus	duōbus	tribus	tribus
Acc.	duōs, duo	duās	duo	trēs	tria
Abl.	duōbus	duābus	duōbus	tribus	tribus

a. The declension of **ūnus** has been explained in **234**. With the exception of **duo** and **trēs**, the other numerals given above are not declined. The remaining numerals from twenty-one to one thousand may be found in the Appendix, section 14.

305. **VOCABULARY**

Aquītānī, -ōrum, M. *pl.*, the Aquitanians

Belgae, -ārum, M. *pl.*, the Belgians

Celtae, -ārum, M. *pl.*, the Celts

dīvidō, -ere, dīvīsī, dīvīsum, divide, separate

dīvīsus, -a, -um (*participle as adjective*), divided

fortissimus, -a, -um (*superlative of* **fortis**), bravest

incolō, -ere, incoluī, inhabit

quoque,[1] *adv.*, also

tertius, -a, -um, third

EXERCISES

Gaul and Its Inhabitants

306. Gallia est omnis dīvīsa in partēs trēs. Ūnam hārum partium incolunt Belgae, aliam Aquītānī. Tertiam pártem incolunt Celtae. Hōrum omnium fortissimī sunt Belgae quī longē ā prōvinciā nostrā absunt et saepe cum Germānīs bellum gerunt. Helvētiī sunt gēns Celtārum. Hī quoque cum Germānīs bellum gerunt et fortissimī Celtārum sunt.

307. 1. There are three parts of Gaul. 2. The province is far distant from the Belgians. 3. One part is inhabited by brave men. 4. War is often waged with the Germans, who have good weapons and do not fear the Gauls. 5. The third part is inhabited by the Celts.

———

SUGGESTED DRILL

(1) Decline **ūnus.** (2) Give the accusative of the phrase meaning *three Aquitanians.* (3) Give the present passive infinitive of **dīvidō.** (4) Explain the case of **Celtārum** in the last sentence of 306. (5) Decline **omnis.** (6) Conjugate **incolō** in the perfect indicative active.

———

[1] The adverb **quoque** always stands after the word which it emphasizes.

LESSON XLVIII
THE FIFTH DECLENSION ∨

308. The genitive singular of the fifth declension ends in -ēī (after a consonant, -eī). The nominative singular ends in -ēs.

diēs, *day*—BASE, di-
rēs, *thing*—BASE, r-

	SINGULAR		TERMI-NATIONS	PLURAL		TERMI-NATIONS
NOM.	diēs	rēs	-ēs	diēs	rēs	-ēs
GEN.	diēī	reī	-ēī (-eī)	diērum	rērum	-ērum
DAT.	diēī	reī	-ēī (-eī)	diēbus	rēbus	-ēbus
ACC.	diem	rem	-em	diēs	rēs	-ēs
ABL.	diē	rē	-ē	diēbus	rēbus	-ēbus

a. **Diēs** is sometimes masculine and sometimes feminine in the singular, but always masculine in the plural. The other nouns of this declension are feminine (except one compound of **diēs**).

b. Only **diēs** and **rēs** are declined in full. Other nouns of this declension lack some or all of the plural forms.

309.   VOCABULARY

cīvitās, -tātis, F., state

diēs, -ēī, M., F., day

ducentī,[1] -ae, -a, *num. adj.*, two hundred

ēnūntiō, -āre, -āvī, -ātum, make known, report, disclose

fīnitimus, -a, -um, neighboring; M. *pl.*, neighbors

indicium, -ī, N., disclosure, information; per indicium, through informers

Orgetorīx, Orgetorīgis, M., Orgetorix, *a Helvetian chief*

per, *prep. w. acc.*, through, by means of

rēs, reī, F., thing, affair

---

[1] The numerals for two hundred, three hundred, etc., are declined like the plural of **bonus**. **Centum** is not declined.

EXERCISES

310. 1. Multōs diēs; eō diē; hīs diēbus; omnium rērum; ad eās rēs. 2. Caesar ducentōs mīlitēs in castrīs relīquit.

THE PLOT OF ORGETORIX

Ōlim fuit dux apud Helvētiōs cuius nōmen erat Orgetorīx. Is rēgnum in cīvitāte occupāre cupiēbat, et auxilium ab duōbus ducibus cīvitātum fīnitimārum postulāvit. Sed ea rēs Helvētiīs per indicium ēnūntiāta est, quī cōnsiliis Orgetorīgis restitērunt.

311. 1. Orgetorix, who wished to seize royal power, had large forces. 2. For many days this man worked industriously. 3. On that day two famous men were killed. 4. Our friends remained in Rome three days. 5. The Romans sent two armies into Gaul. 6. A reward was given to the slave who disclosed this fact (thing).

———

SUGGESTED DRILL

(1) Decline the phrase meaning *three days*. (2) Decline **domus**. (3) Give the rule for the locative case (299). (4) Conjugate **ēnūntiō** in the present indicative active. (5) Give the genitive plural of **hōra, animus,** and **diēs**. (6) Explain the case of **Helvētiīs** in the last sentence of 310.

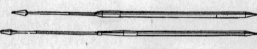

ROMAN JAVELINS

LESSON XLIX

ACCUSATIVE OF EXTENT: ACCUSATIVE OF PLACE TO WHICH

THE ACCUSATIVE OF EXTENT

312. The accusative is used to express extent in space.

Fossa duo mīlia passuum patēbat, *the ditch extended two miles.*

THE ACCUSATIVE OF PLACE TO WHICH

313. With names of towns and small islands, also with **domus,** the accusative without a preposition is used to name the place to which motion is directed. With other words a preposition, **ad** or **in,** is used.

Legiōnēs Ocelum venient, *the legions will come to Ocelum.*
Legiōnēs ad urbem venient, *the legions will come to the city.*

314. **VOCABULARY**

atque, *conj.,* and
contentus, -a, -um, contented, satisfied
itaque, *adv.,* and so, accordingly
lātitūdō, lātitūdinis, F., width
longitūdō, longitūdinis, F., length

mīlle, *indecl. num.,* thousand, one thousand
octōgintā, *indecl. num.,* eighty
passus, -ūs, M., pace; **mīlle passūs** (*or* **passuum**), a (Roman) mile
quadrāgintā, *indecl. num.,* forty

a. **Mīlle** in the singular is not declined and is generally used as an adjective. In the plural it is a third declension neuter noun with the forms **mīlia, mīlium, mīlibus,** etc. The Latin form of expression is always *two thousands of soldiers,* **duo mīlia mīlitum,** etc. The genitive used in these phrases is the genitive of the whole.

EXERCISES

315. 1. Nūntius Rōmam nōndum pervēnit. 2. Pater puellae domum veniet. 3. Puerī librōs suōs domum portāvērunt. 4. Exercitus per magnam silvam iter fēcerat.

The Helvetian Emigration

Helvētiī fīnēs lātōs et agrōs bonōs possidēbant. Fīnēs eōrum ducenta quadrāgintā mīlia passuum in longitūdinem, centum octōgintā in lātitūdinem patēbant. Helvētiī nōn contentī erant quod bellum gerere semper cupiēbant et multīs locīs flūmina et montēs altī ā gentibus fīnitimīs eōs dīvidēbant. Itaque vīcōs incendērunt atque ē patriā suā excessērunt.

316. 1. The territories of the Helvetians extended many miles. 2. The sailor has not yet arrived at Rome. 3. We shall come home within ten days. 4. The army which was sent to Ocelum was small. 5. The legions marched (made a march) through the mountains for many days (**177**). 6. The Helvetians collected an army and resisted the friends of Orgetorix.

SUGGESTED DRILL

(1) Explain the case of **Rōmam** in sentence 1, **315**. (2) Decline **passus**. (3) Explain the case of **gentibus** in line 8, **315**. (4) Indicate the personal endings in the last three verbs of **315**. (5) Give the cardinal numerals from one to twenty. (6) Point out a phrase in **316** which expresses duration of time and one which expresses time within which, and name the Latin case required by each.

ROMAN COINS

LESSON L

CONJUGATION OF *EŌ*: ABLATIVE OF ROUTE

THE CONJUGATION OF *EŌ*

317. The irregular verb **eō**, *go*, is conjugated in the present system in the indicative as follows:

PRESENT	IMPERFECT	FUTURE
	SINGULAR	
eō	ībam	ībō
īs	ībās	ībis
it	ībat	ībit
	PLURAL	
īmus	ībāmus	ībimus
ītis	ībātis	ībitis
eunt	ībant	ībunt

The perfect system is regularly formed with the stem **i-**.

PERFECT	PAST PERFECT	FUTURE PERFECT
	SINGULAR	
iī	ieram	ierō
īstī *or* iistī	ierās	ieris
iit *or* īt	ierat	ierit
	PLURAL	
iimus	ierāmus	ierimus
īstis *or* iistis	ierātis	ieritis
iērunt *or* iēre	ierant	ierint

a. Occasionally forms are found in the perfect system with the stem **īv-**: **īvit**, **īverat**, etc.

b. The compounds **exeō**, *go out*, **trānseō**, *go across*, **redeō**, *return*, etc., are conjugated like **eō**.

THE ABLATIVE OF ROUTE

318. The way or route by which one goes may be expressed by the ablative without a preposition.

Hāc viā ībimus, *we shall go by this road.*

319.　　　　　**VOCABULARY**

Cassius, -ī, M., Cassius, *a Roman name (Lucius Cassius, a Roman consul killed in battle with the Helvetians)*

eō, īre, iī (īvī), itum, go

exeō, -īre, exiī, exitum, go out, go forth (from), go from

iugum, -ī, N., yoke; ridge (*of hills or mountains*)

L., *abbreviation for* **Lūcius,** *a Roman first name*

profectiō, -ōnis, F., setting out, departure

proximus, -a, -um, nearest, next to

sub, *prep. with acc. or abl.,* under (*takes acc. to denote place toward which motion is directed, and abl. to denote place where something exists or occurs*)

trānseō, -īre, trānsiī, trānsitum, cross

EXERCISES

320. 1. Exeunt; exībant; exībunt; trānsit; trānsībit; it; ībit. 2. Omnēs eōdem itinere ībant. 3. Ex urbe cum omnibus amīcīs suīs exiit. 4. Eō diē legiōnēs vīgintī mīlia passuum ierant.

THE HELVETIANS AND THE ROMANS

Helvētiī hostēs populī Rōmānī erant et anteā exercitum Rōmānum vīcerant. L. Cassium, ducem eius exercitūs, interfēcerant et exercitum sub iugum mīserant. Itaque profectiō eōrum perīculōsa populō Rōmānō erat quod prōvincia Rōmāna proxima fīnibus Helvētiōrum erat.

321. 1. A Roman army had been defeated by the Helvetians. 2. Their territories were next to the Roman province. 3. Lucius Cassius had led an army into Gaul, but the Gauls had defeated him. 4. They were crossing the river with all their forces. 5. The soldiers who had been enrolled in Italy were led into Gaul by this route.

SUGGESTED DRILL

(1) Give a synopsis of **trānseō** in the third person singular, of the indicative. (2) Explain the cases of **ducem** and **fīnibus** in lines 6 and 9, 320. (3) Give the case endings of the fifth declension. (4) Give rules for gender in the fourth and fifth declensions. (5) Point out an example of the ablative of route in the sentences of 320. (6) Give the rule for the expression of place to which.

TENTH REVIEW LESSON

322.   VOCABULARY REVIEW

causa, -ae, F.

celeritās, -tātis, F.

cīvitās, -tātis, F.

cornū, -ūs, N.

diēs, diēī, M. *and* F.

domus, -ūs (-ī), F.

exercitus, -ūs, M.

flūctus, -ūs, M.

grātia, -ae, F.

indicium, -ī, N.

iugum, -ī, N.

lātitūdō, -dinis, F.

laus, laudis, F.

longitūdō, -dinis, F.

manus, -ūs, F.

mare, maris, N.

māter, mātris, F.

fortis, forte

inīquus, -a, -um

invītus, -a, -um

mīlle

octōgintā (*indeclinable*)

omnis, omne

pedester, -tris, -tre

potēns, *gen.* potentis

proximus, -a, -um

quadrāgintā (*indeclinable*)

tertius, -a, -um

vetus, *gen.* veteris

accipiō, -cipere, -cēpī, -ceptum

circumveniō, -venīre, -vēnī, -ventum

cōnscrībō, -scrībere, -scrīpsī, -scrīptum

conveniō, -venīre, -vēnī, -ventum

cupiō, -ere, cupī ī, cupītum

nōmen, nōminis, N.	dēbeō, -ēre, -uī, -itum
passus, -ūs, M.	dēfendō, -ere, dēfendī, dēfēnsum
pater, patris, M.	dīvidō, -ere, dīvīsī, dīvīsum
pāx, pācis, F.	ēnūntiō, -āre, -āvī, -ātum
praemium, -ī, N.	eō, īre, iī *or* īvī, itum
profectiō, -ōnis, F.	exeō, -īre, -iī *or* -īvī, -itum
rēs, reī, F.	incipiō, -cipere, -cēpī, -ceptum
tempus, temporis, N.	incolō, -ere, -uī
vīcus, -ī, M.	petō, -ere, -īvī, -ītum
virtūs, virtūtis, F.	possideō, -ēre, possēdī, possessum
vōx, vōcis, F.	resistō, -ere, restitī
quī, quae, quod	tendō, -ere, tetendī, tentum
ācer, ācris, ācre	trānseō, -īre, -iī *or* -īvī, -itum
centum (*indeclinable*)	quoque
clārus, -a, -um	dē
contentus, -a, -um	per
ducentī, -ae, -a	sub
fēlīx, *gen.* fēlīcis	atque
fīnitimus, -a, -um	

323. RELATED ENGLISH WORDS

approximate	enunciate	longitude
city	exit	nominate
contented	iniquity	octogenarian
divide	latitude	subnormal
division	laudable	transition

LESSON LI

DATIVE WITH COMPOUNDS: DATIVE OF POSSESSION

THE DATIVE WITH COMPOUNDS

324. Frequently with verbs compounded with **ante, ob, prae,** and **sub,** the noun or pronoun connected in sense with the preposition is put in the dative.[1]

Prōvinciae praeest, *he is in command of the province.*

a. The dative may also be used in the same manner with compounds of **ad** and **in** when motion is not expressed.

Bellum Gallīs īnferunt, *they make war on the Gauls.*

b. If the simple verb is transitive, the compound may take an accusative and a dative.

Labiēnum castrīs praefēcit, *he placed Labienus in command of the camp.*

c. Often the dative with a compound is merely an indirect object or a dative of reference, or is to be explained by the rule of Lesson XVI.

THE DATIVE OF POSSESSION

325. The possessor of something may be denoted by a noun or pronoun in the dative case, with the thing possessed in the nominative as the subject of a form of the verb meaning *to be.*

Puerō[2] gladius est, *the boy has a sword.*

---

[1] Other prepositions whose compounds sometimes take a dependent dative are **circum, con, inter, post, prō, super.**

[2] The exact force of the case in this construction cannot be rendered in idiomatic English.

326. VOCABULARY

ācriter, *adv.*, fiercely, spiritedly

cōnstituō, -stituere, -stituī, -stitūtum, determine, decide; draw up (*troops, an army*, etc.)

dīcō, -ere, dīxī, dictum, say

inimīcus, -a, -um, unfriendly

nox, noctis, -ium, F., night

omnīnō, *adv.*, only

praesum, -esse, -fuī, -futūrus, be in command of, be in charge of

prohibeō, -ēre, -uī, -itum, prevent, restrain, keep back

ut, *adv.*, as

EXERCISES

327. 1. Labiēnus nōn tōtī exercituī praefuit. 2. Huic hominī multī amīcī sunt. 3. In Britanniā noctēs aestāte nōn longae sunt. 4. In eō locō Gallī et Germānī ācriter contendēbant.

CAESAR INTERFERES

Eō tempore Caesar prōvinciae praeerat. Is Helvētiōs prohibēre cōnstituit quod inimīcī populō Rōmānō erant, ut ante dīximus. Erat omnīnō legiō ūna in eā parte Galliae, et Helvētiīs (325) magnae cōpiae erant. Sociōs (*as allies*) habēbant trēs aliās gentēs quae domōs suās relinquēbant et cum Helvētiīs ē fīnibus suīs exībant.

328. 1. Caesar had one legion. 2. A brave man is-in-command-of the town. 3. The Helvetians and their allies will not wage war long. 4. We shall go home and remain there two days. 5. The soldier who stands before the gate has a shield. 6. Labienus was-in-command-of the legions which were left in Gaul. 7. The enemy attacked the town fiercely that night.

SUGGESTED DRILL

(1) Explain the case of **exercituī** in sentence 1, and **hominī** in sentence 2, 327. (2) Conjugate **exeō** in the future indicative, and **trānseō** in the imperfect indicative. (3) Decline **eadem nox**. (4) Conjugate **dīcō** in the perfect indicative, active and passive. (5) Give a synopsis of **praesum** in the third person plural. (6) Decline **duo**.

SEVENTH SUPPLEMENTARY REVIEW
VOCABULARY REVIEW

1. ac *or* atque, *conj.*
2. ācriter, *adv.*
3. circumveniō, -venīre, -vēnī, -ventum
4. cīvitās, -tātis, F.
5. cōnscrībō, -scrībere, -scrīpsī, -scrīptum
6. cōnsul, cōnsulis, M.
7. cornū, -ūs, N.
8. dēfendō, -fendere, -fendī, -fēnsum
9. dīcō, -ere, dīxī, dictum
10. diēs, diēī, M., F.
11. domus, -ūs (-ī), F.
12. ducentī, -ae, -a
13. equester, -tris, -tre
14. exercitus, -ūs, M.
15. fīnitimus, -a, -um
16. hiems, hiemis, F.
17. immortālis, -e
18. inimīcus, -a, -um
19. inīquus, -a, -um
20. inveniō, -venīre, -vēnī, -ventum
21. iūdex, -dicis, M.
22. iūdicium, N.
23. laus, laudis, F.
24. mīlle (*pl.* mīlia)
25. manus, -ūs, F.
26. mare, maris, N.
27. māter, -tris, F.
28. nōmen, nōminis, N.
29. nox, noctis, F.
30. ōrātiō, -ōnis, F.
31. passus, -ūs, M.
32. pater, patris, M.
33. per, *prep. with acc.*
34. petō, -ere, -īvī, -ītum
35. praesēns, -entis
36. praesum, -esse, -fuī
37. prohibeō, -ēre, -uī, -itum
38. pūblicus, -a, -um
39. quī, quae, quod
40. recēns, recentis
41. rēs, reī, F.
42. rēs pūblica, reī pūblicae
43. resistō, -sistere, -stitī
44. scrībō, -ere, scrīpsī, scrīptum
45. singulāris, -e
46. soror, sorōris, F.
47. tempus, temporis, N.
48. ūnus . . . decem
49. ūndecim . . . vīgintī
50. vōx, vōcis, F.

---

1. and also, and
2. sharply, fiercely
3. come around, surround
4. citizenship, state
5. enrol
6. consul

7. horn, wing (*of an army*)
8. defend
9. say
10. day
11. home, house
12. two hundred
13. cavalry (*adj.*)
14. army
15. neighboring
16. winter
17. without death, immortal
18. hostile; *as noun*, enemy
19. uneven, unfavorable, unjust
20. come upon, find
21. judge, juror
22. trial, judgment
23. praise
24. one thousand
25. hand, group, force
26. sea
27. mother
28. name
29. night
30. speaking, speech
31. pace (*about five feet*)
32. father
33. through
34. seek
35. present in person
36. be in command of
37. prohibit, prevent
38. belonging to the state, official, public
39. who
40. fresh, new, recent
41. thing
42. commonwealth, government
43. resist
44. write

45. single, unusual
46. sister
47. time
48. one . . . ten
49. eleven . . . twenty
50. voice, speech, remark

WORD STUDY

As a prefix **per** means *through, thoroughly,* or *very.*

1. Find compounds of **per** in the vocabularies of Supplementary Reviews V and VI.

2. Find four compounds of **veniō** in this and preceding Supplementary Reviews.

3. Point out Latin words in the vocabulary of this lesson to which the following are related.

defense	inimical	manual	prohibition	unit
dictionary	judicial	maternal	temporal	

LESSON LII

ABLATIVE OF SEPARATION: ABLATIVE OF PLACE FROM WHICH

THE ABLATIVE OF SEPARATION

329. Verbs meaning to *separate, remove, deprive of, lack, be absent,* and the like, take the Ablative of Separation, often with the prepositions **ab** or **ex**.

Haec flūmina Gallōs ā Belgīs dīvidunt, *these rivers separate the Gauls from the Belgians.*

THE ABLATIVE OF PLACE FROM WHICH

330. With names of towns and small islands, and with **domus**, the ablative without a preposition is used to express the idea of Place from Which. With other words a preposition (**ab**, **ex**, or **dē**) is used.

Helvētiī domō excessērunt, *the Helvetians departed from home.*

Helvētiī ex urbe excessērunt, *the Helvetians departed from the city.*

331.   **VOCABULARY**

facile, *adv.*, easily

Genava, -ae, F., Geneva

parō, -āre, -āvī, -ātum, prepare

pertineō, -ēre, -uī, extend, pertain

repellō, -ere, reppulī, repulsum, drive back, repulse, repel

Rhodanus, -ī, M., the Rhone, *a river of Gaul*

ventus, -ī, M., wind

EXERCISES

332. 1. Prōvincia nostra ā marī ad montēs pertinet. 2. Propter magnam vim ventī nāvēs nostrae magnō in perīculō erant. 3. Tum pars exercitūs Genavae erat. 4. Lēgātus nōndum Rōmā exiit.

The Helvetians Repulsed

Caesar statim mīlitēs in prōvinciā cōnscrīpsit et bellum
cum Helvētiīs gerere parāvit. Iter quō (**318**) exīre parābant
per prōvinciam Rōmānam erat. Flūmen Rhodanus prōvinciam ā finibus Helvētiōrum dīvidit sed id flūmen facile
multis locīs (**299**, *a*) trānsītur. Hīs locīs Caesar mūrō et fossā
(**130**) Helvētiōs prohibuit. Tum mīlitēs Rōmānī tēla iēcē-
runt et hostēs reppulērunt.

ROMAN DRINKING CUPS

333. 1. Many soldiers came from Ocelum. 2. These three
nations have gone forth from home. 3. The mountains
which you see separate the Helvetians from the neighboring
state. 4. The Gauls will go by this road because they have
no other road. 5. A river separates the Belgians from the
Germans. 6. Your brother and my friend were in Geneva
the same summer.

SUGGESTED DRILL

(1) Explain the case of **exercitūs** and **Genavae** in sentence 3, 332.
(2) Name the simple verb from which the compound **pertineō** is
derived, and give principal parts of both. (3) Mention two English
words derived from **repellō** and state from which stem of the verb each
is derived. (4) Explain the case of **Rōmā** in sentence 4, 332. (5)
Name some prepositions whose compounds may govern the dative.

LESSON LIII

COMPARISON OF ADJECTIVES: DECLENSION OF COMPARATIVES

THE COMPARISON OF ADJECTIVES

334. (1) The comparative degree of an adjective is formed by replacing the genitive ending of the positive with **-ior** for the masculine and feminine and with **-ius** for the neuter.

The superlative is regularly formed by replacing the genitive ending of the positive with **-issimus (-a, -um)**.

Positive	Comparative	Superlative
altus, *high*	**altior, altius,** *higher*	**altissimus, -a, -um,** *highest*
fortis, *brave*	**fortior, fortius,** *braver*	**fortissimus, -a, -um,** *bravest*

(2) The comparatives are third declension adjectives of two endings and are declined as follows:

	SINGULAR		PLURAL	
	Masc. and Fem.	*Neut.*	*Masc. and Fem.*	*Neut.*
Nom.	lātior	lātius	lātiōrēs	lātiōra
Gen.	lātiōris	lātiōris	lātiōrum	lātiōrum
Dat.	lātiōrī	lātiōrī	lātiōribus	lātiōribus
Acc.	lātiōrem	lātius	lātiōrēs, (-īs)	lātiōra
Abl.	lātiōre	lātiōre	lātiōribus	lātiōribus

a. The superlative is declined like **bonus.**

b. The comparative is often translated with the adverb *rather* or *too,* and the superlative with *very.*

Flūmen lātius erat, *the river was rather wide.*

Montem altissimum vīdimus, *we saw a very high mountain.*

335.   VOCABULARY

angustus, -a, -um, narrow

autem, but, however (*never stands first in its clause*)

dēiciō, -ere, dēiēcī, dēiectum, dislodge; disappoint

Haeduus, -ī, M., a Haeduan; *pl.*, the Haeduans

impendeō, -ēre, overhang, impend

Sēquanī, -ōrum, M. *pl.*, the Sequani

spēs, speī, F., hope

vāstō, -āre, -āvī, -ātum, lay waste

EXERCISES

336. 1. Flūmen lātissimum; mōns altior; vir clārissimus; mīlitem fortissimum; iter angustius. 2. Germānī in Galliam trānsierant et agrōs Gallōrum vāstābant. 3. Itinere angustiōre exiērunt. 4. Montēs altiōrēs numquam vīdī.

ANOTHER ROUTE FOUND.

Itaque Helvētiī dē eā spē dēiectī sunt. Sed aliud iter erat per fīnēs Sēquanōrum. Id angustum erat et mōns altissimus impendēbat. Sēquanī autem nōn restitērunt et Helvētiī omnēs cōpiās suās hāc viā dūxērunt. Per fīnēs Sēquanōrum sine iniūriā iērunt et in fīnēs Haeduōrum pervēnērunt, quōrum agrōs vāstāvērunt.

337. 1. The Helvetians had great hopes of victory. 2. This mountain was higher and this road was narrower. 3. These boys are very brave. 4. These gifts are the most pleasing of all. 5. The most famous city of Italy was set on fire. 6. Our fields have been laid waste by our enemies and we fear their power (violence). 7. No one has kinder friends.

––––––

SUGGESTED DRILL

(1) Compare (i. e., give the positive, comparative, and superlative of) the adjectives **angustus, cārus, benignus,** and **longus.** (2) Decline the comparative of **tūtus.** (3) Explain the case of **itinere** in sentence 3, **336.** (4) Give the genitive of the phrase **vir clārior.** (5) Decline together **diēs longior.** (6) Point out the compound sentences in **337.**

LESSON LIV

COMPARISON OF ADJECTIVES (Continued): ABLATIVE OF COMPARISON

COMPARISON OF ADJECTIVES (Continued)

338. Adjectives ending in **-er** form the superlative by adding **-rimus (-a, -um)** to the nominative singular masculine of the positive.

POSITIVE	COMPARATIVE	SUPERLATIVE
miser	miserior, miserius	miserrimus, -a, -um
ācer	ācrior, ācrius	ācerrimus, -a, -um

    a. The comparative is formed like that of other adjectives.

339. The following adjectives ending in -lis form the superlative by replacing the genitive ending of the positive with **-limus**: **facilis, difficilis, similis, dissimilis, humilis.** *learn.*

POSITIVE	COMPARATIVE	SUPERLATIVE
facilis	facilior, -ius	facillimus, -a, -um
similis	similior, -ius	simillimus, -a, -um

    a. Other adjectives ending in -lis form the superlative regularly with -issimus.[1]

THE ABLATIVE OF COMPARISON

340. With a comparative, if **quam,** *than,* is omitted, the noun or pronoun denoting the person or thing with which comparison is made, is put in the ablative.

    Ille puer fortior frātre est, *that boy is braver than his brother.*

---

[1] **gracilis,** *slender,* is sometimes given in this list of adjectives, but its superlative is so rare as to make it of little importance.

a. If **quam** is used, the word denoting the person or thing with which comparison is made stands in the same case as the thing compared.

Ille puer fortior quam frāter est, *that boy is braver than his brother.*

b. If the word denoting the person or thing compared stands in any other case than the nominative or accusative, **quam** must be used.

341. VOCABULARY

Alpēs, -ium, F. *pl.*, the Alps
difficilis, -e, difficult
facilis, -e, easy
intereā, *adv.*, meanwhile, in the meantime

perterreō, -terrēre, -terruī, -territum, frighten thoroughly
quam, *adv.*, than, how, as
similis, -e, like
ūtilis, -e, useful

EXERCISES

342. 1. Rēs difficillima; iter facillimum; ager simillimus; in locō difficillimō. 2. Is homō miserrimus omnium erat. 3. Nostrī hostēs ācerrimī superātī sunt. 4. Mihi amīcus ūtilissimus fuistī. 5. Nēmō honestior hōc homine est. 6. Nēmō honestior quam hic homō est.

THE HAEDUANS ASK AID

Haeduī quī erant amīcī et sociī populī Rōmānī statim ad Caesarem nūntiōs mīsērunt et auxilium petiērunt. Perterritī sunt, et vim hostium vix ab oppidīs prohibēbant. Caesar intereā quīnque legiōnēs ex aliā parte prōvinciae per Alpēs dūxerat et cum omnibus cōpiīs ad hostēs contendēbat.

343. 1. Meanwhile the fields of the Haeduans were being laid waste. 2. The road by which the Helvetians went forth was very difficult. 3. The Germans were braver than the Haeduans. 4. This man is taller than his brother. 5. This girl is the unhappiest of all.   6. At that time flight was very easy.   7. The cart was very useful on (in) the journey.

---

(1) Compare **difficilis, ūtilis, pulcher,** and **līber.**   (2) Give the rule for expressions of place from which.   (3) Give the rule for the dative of possession.   (4) Give the rule for expressions of extent in space. (5) Give the present infinitives, active and passive, of **petō, prohibeō,** and **oppugnō.**

LESSON LV

COMPARISON OF ADJECTIVES (Continued): ABLATIVE OF DEGREE OF DIFFERENCE

ADJECTIVES COMPARED IRREGULARLY

344. There are a few adjectives which form their comparatives and superlatives irregularly. The most important are the following:

POSITIVE	COMPARATIVE	SUPERLATIVE
bonus, -a, -um	melior, -ius	optimus, -a, -um
malus, -a, -um	peior, -ius	pessimus, -a, -um
magnus, -a, -um	maior, maius	maximus, -a, -um
multus, -a, -um	——, plūs	plūrimus, -a, -um
parvus, -a, -um	minor, minus	minimus, -a, -um

DECLENSION OF *PLŪS*

345. **Plūs** is an adjective in the plural, but in the singular it is a neuter noun. It is declined as follows:

	SINGULAR Neut.	PLURAL Masc. and Fem.	Neut.
NOM.	plūs	plūrēs	plūra
GEN.	plūris	plūrium	plūrium
DAT.	——	plūribus	plūribus
ACC.	plūs	plūrēs *or* -īs	plūra
ABL.	plūre	plūribus	plūribus

a. **Complūrēs,** *several,* is declined like the plural of plūs except that the neuter may have either -**ia** or -**a** in the nominative and accusative.

b. **Citerior, ulterior,** and a few other comparatives have no positive. The comparison of **superus** and **īnferus** is as follows:

POSITIVE	COMPARATIVE	SUPERLATIVE
superus	superior	suprēmus *or* summus
īnferus	īnferior	īnfimus *or* īmus

THE ABLATIVE OF DEGREE OF DIFFERENCE

346. The ablative is used to express the degree or measure of difference between two objects or persons compared.

Turris duōbus pedibus altior quam mūrus est, *the tower is two feet higher than the wall (higher by two feet).*

a. A frequent use of this construction is to be seen in **multō,** the ablative of the neuter **multum,** used as a noun: **multō clārior,** *much more distinguished (more distinguished by much).*

347. **VOCABULARY**

Arar, Araris, M., the Saône, *a river of Gaul*
citrā, *prep. w. acc.,* on this side of
concīdō, -ere, concīdī, concī-sum, cut to pieces, kill
impedītus, -a, -um, impeded, hindered

impetus, -ūs, M., attack
imprōvīsō, *adv.,* unexpectedly
pēs, pedis, M., foot
reliquus, -a, -um, remaining, rest of; M. *pl. as noun,* the rest
trādūcō, -dūcere, -dūxī, -duc-tum, lead across

EXERCISES

348. 1. Haec urbs multō maior eō oppidō est. 2. Ea fēmina ūnō pede altior quam fīlia est. 3. Gallī nōn for-tiōrēs Germānīs erant. 4. Lēgātus reliquīs legiōnibus praeerat quae citrā flūmen relictae erant. 5. Maxima pars; maior ager; minor exercitus.

THE HELVETIAN DISASTER AT THE SAÔNE

Hī tum flūmen Ararim[1] trānsībant et trēs partēs cōpiārum trādūxerant. Caesar imprōvīsō impetum in eam partem fēcit quae citrā flūmen erat. Magnam partem eōrum impedītōrum concīdit. Reliquī in silvās proximās fūgērunt.

ROMAN SOLDIERS STORMING A TOWN

349. 1. The larger part remained on this side of the river. 2. The river is much wider than the ditch. 3. This route is many miles longer. 4. This school is the best but not the largest. 5. We saw a better place in the forest. 6. The Gauls made an attack unexpectedly on the legion which was crossing the river. 7. The tower is ten feet higher than the wall.

SUGGESTED DRILL

(1) Decline the comparatives of **magnus** and **parvus**. (2) Point out examples of the ablative of degree of difference in **348**. (3) Explain the case of **Germānīs** in sentence 3, and of **legiōnibus** in sentence 4, **348**. (4) Decline together **impetus ācrior** in the singular. (5) Give a synopsis of **trānseō** and of **trādūcō** in the third person singular, active voice, in the indicative mood, giving English meanings throughout.

---

[1] A few i-stem proper nouns have the accusative singular in **-Im**.

ELEVENTH REVIEW LESSON

350. (1) The fifth declension of nouns.
(2) The comparison of adjectives.
(3) The conjugation of **eō**.
(4) Numerals.
(5) The dative with compounds.
(6) The dative of possession.
(7) The accusative of extent.
(8) The accusative of place to which.
(9) The ablative of comparison.
(10) The ablative of degree of difference.
(11) The ablative of place from which.
(12) The ablative of route.
(13) The ablative of separation.
(14) The locative case.

351. Give Latin words with which the following English words are connected in derivation:

constitution	impetuous	relic
dejected	inimical	repel
dictionary	nocturnal	repulse
difficult	pedal	similar
facility	pertinent	utility
impending	prohibition	ventilation

ROMAN SPOONS AND BOWL

LESSON LVI

GENITIVE OF DESCRIPTION: ABLATIVE OF DESCRIPTION

THE GENITIVE OF DESCRIPTION

352. The genitive modified by an adjective may be used to describe a person or thing.

> **Homō magnae virtūtis,** *a man of great courage.*

a. The genitive is often employed in this construction to express measure.

> **Mūrus trium pedum,** *a three-foot wall* (*a wall of three feet*).

THE ABLATIVE OF DESCRIPTION

353. The ablative modified by an adjective may be used to describe a person or thing.

> **Homō magnā virtūte,** *a man of great courage,* i. e., *a man with great courage.*

a. In many phrases such as the example above, either the genitive or the ablative may be used, but physical characteristics are usually expressed by the ablative, and measure always by the genitive.

354.   VOCABULARY

altitūdō, altitūdinis, F., height, depth

auctōritās, -tātis, F., influence, authority

calamitās, -tātis, F., disaster

commemorō, -āre, -āvī, -ātum, mention

pōns, pontis, M., bridge

praedicō, -āre, -āvī, -ātum, announce, boast

respōnsum, -ī, N., reply, answer

trānsportō, -āre, -āvī, -ātum, convey across

EXERCISES

355. 1. Orgetorīx magnā auctōritāte apud Helvētiōs fuerat.
2. Lēgātī Gallōrum hoc respōnsum dedērunt neque vim Rōmānōrum timēbant. 3. Mūrus magnā altitūdine erat. 4.
Mīlitēs iter sex diērum fēcērunt. 5. Exercitus magnī animī
est quod saepe hī hostēs victī sunt.

CAESAR CROSSES THE SAÔNE

Post id proelium Caesar pontem fēcit et exercitum trā-
dūxit. Helvētiī flūmen vīgintī diēbus trānsierant sed Caesar
ūnō diē omnem exercitum trānsportāvit. Tum Helvētiī lēgātōs mīsērunt et pācem petiērunt. Lēgātī autem multa (*much*)
praedicāvērunt dē virtūte suae gentis et calamitātem veterem
populī Rōmānī commemorāvērunt.

356. 1. The river was of great width. 2. The soldiers
were of great courage and defended the camp bravely. 3.
A journey of five days was made by the army. 4. The
soldier whom you see is much braver than his brother. 5.
The men went by the most difficult road. 6. He is not a
boy of great strength, but he works energetically. 7. You
ask for peace, and this is my answer.

SUGGESTED DRILL

(1) Mention some English words derived from the words in the
vocabulary of this lesson. (2) Give the Latin adjective from which
the noun **altitūdō** is derived. (3) Explain the derivation of **trānsportō**.
(4) Explain the case of **altitūdine** in sentence 3, and of **diērum** in sentence, 4, 355. (5) Explain the gender of **multa**, line 9, 355. (6) Give
the genitive of the phrase which means *one day*.

LESSON LVII

THE FORMATION OF ADVERBS

357. Most adverbs are formed from adjectives by the use of certain adverbial endings. Those derived from adjectives of the first and second declension regularly take -ē in place of the genitive ending of the adjective. Those derived from third declension adjectives regularly have -ter or -iter (-er only, if the genitive ending follows -nt), in place of the genitive ending.

lātus, *wide*	lātē, *widely*
fortis, *brave*	fortiter, *bravely*
audāx, *bold*	audācter, *boldly*
prūdēns, *prudent*	prūdenter, *prudently*

a. The neuter accusative singular of some adjectives is used as an adverb: **facile**, *easily;* **multum**, *much.*

b. The adverb of **magnus** is **magnopere;** of **bonus**, **bene.** Some adverbs do not have a corresponding adjective: e. g., **saepe**, *often.*

358.   **VOCABULARY**

complūrēs, -a, (-ia), several, some

condiciō, -ōnis, F., terms, condition

fidēs, fideī, F., confidence; **fidem habēre,** trust (*with dative*)

obses, obsidis, M., hostage

paucī, -ae, -a (*singular not often used*), few; *masculine as noun*, a few

poscō, -ere, poposcī, demand

prōcēdō, -ere, prōcessī, prō-cessum, advance

EXERCISES

359. 1. Helvētiī quī in fīnēs Haeduōrum pervēnerant agrōs lātē vāstābant. 2. Exercitus noster celeriter flūmen trānsiit sed hostēs fūgerant.

MARCHING AND FIGHTING

Caesar quod eīs fidem nōn habēbat obsidēs poposcit. Hī autem eam condiciōnem nōn accēpērunt neque pāx est facta. Tum Helvētiī castra mōvērunt et ex eō locō prōcessērunt. Caesar item castra mōvit et iter paucīs mīlibus passuum post eōs fēcit. Complūrēs diēs idem factum est. Hīs diēbus equitēs Rōmānī in hostēs impetum fēcērunt sed repulsī sunt et paucī sunt interfectī.

ROMAN TEMPLE AT CORI

360. 1. The enemy fiercely made an attack on our horsemen. 2. The fields of the Haeduans, who were allies of the Romans, were laid waste widely. 3. Several men advanced toward (**ad**) Caesar. 4. These men who were killed in war certainly loved their country. 5. The hostages greatly desired to see their friends.

SUGGESTED DRILL

(1) Form adverbs from the adjectives **altus, grātus,** and **honestus.**
(2) Explain the derivation of **ācriter** and **fēlīciter.** (3) Explain the meaning of the phrase *bona fide.* (4) Explain the derivation of **the** words *transportation* and *procession.* (5) Decline **complūrēs.**

LESSON LVIII

THE COMPARISON OF ADVERBS

361. The comparative of an adverb is the same as the accusative singular neuter form of the comparative of the adjective from which the adverb is derived. The superlative is formed by changing the ending **-us** of the superlative of the corresponding adjective to **-ē**.

	POSITIVE	COMPARATIVE	SUPERLATIVE
ADJ.	lātus	lātior	lātissimus
ADV.	lātē	lātius	lātissimē
ADJ.	ācer	ācrior	ācerrimus
ADV.	ācriter	ācrius	ācerrimē
ADJ.	facilis	facilior	facillimus
ADV.	facile	facilius	facillimē

a. The following are irregular:

POSITIVE		COMPARATIVE	SUPERLATIVE
bene,	*well*	melius	optimē
male,	*badly*	peius	pessimē
magnopere,	*greatly*	magis	maximē
multum,	*much*	magis	maximē
multum,	*much*	plūs	plūrimum
parum,	*little*	minus	minimē
prope,	*near*	propius	proximē
saepe,	*often*	saepius	saepissimē
diū,	*long*	diūtius	diūtissimē

b. Occasionally adverbs (and also adjectives) are compared with **magis**, *more*, and **maximē**, *most*.

362. VOCABULARY

dēterreō, -ēre, dēterruī, dē-
territum, hinder, prevent

Dumnorīx, Dumnorīgis, M.,
Dumnorix, *a Gaul*

imperium, -ī, N., power, supreme power, authority

magis, *adv.*, more

prīnceps, prīncipis, M., leader,
chief

prōmittō, -ere, prōmīsī, prō-
missum, promise

satis, *adv.*, enough

summus, -a, -um, highest, supreme, highest part of

EXERCISES

363. 1. Belgae longissimē absunt. 2. Facilius eīs persuāsit.
3. Tum ācerrimē bellum gerēbant. 4. Ea loca lātius explō-
rābimus sī id cupis. 5. Nōn magnopere impetum hostium
timēmus quod arma meliōra habēmus.

FAILURE OF SUPPLIES

Caesarī erat impedīmentō (**196**) quod[1] exercitus eius satis
frūmentī nōn habēbat. Haeduī frūmentum prōmīserant sed
nōn dabant. Erant multī inter eōs quī Rōmānīs inimīcī
erant et aliōs dēterrēbant. Prīnceps hōrum erat Dumnorīx.
Is amīcus Orgetorīgis, ducis Helvētiōrum, fuerat et in cīvitāte
Haeduōrum summō imperiō studēbat.

364. 1. Caesar desired supreme power. 2. We have not
enough grain, but we are expecting aid from Italy. 3. The
enemy were more often driven back. 4. The Romans crossed
very easily because they had many boats (**nāvēs**). 5. Nothing
pleases the Gauls more than war. 6. This wing of the army
which had made an attack, drove back the horsemen.

SUGGESTED DRILL

(1) Compare the adverbs **fortiter** and **certē**. (2) Give the endings
which are regularly used in the formation of adverbs. (3) Point out
the irregularity in the formation of the adverb **male**. (4) Explain the
comparison of the adverb **parum**. (5) Give the rules for the ablative
of comparison and the ablative of degree of difference.

-----

[1] Translate *that* or *the fact that*.

EIGHTH SUPPLEMENTARY REVIEW

VOCABULARY REVIEW

1. altitūdō, -dinis, F.
2. auctōritās, -tātis, F.
3. autem, *conj.* (*post-positive*)
4. commoveō, -movēre, -mōvī, -mōtum
5. commūnis, -e
6. condiciō, -ōnis, F.
7. cōnsulō, -ere, -uī, -tum
8. dēiciō, -icere, -iēcī, -iectum
9. difficilis, -e
10. exclūdō, -clūdere, -clūsī, -clūsum
11. facile, *adv.*
12. facilis, -e
13. familiāris, -e
14. fidēs, -eī, F.
15. imperium, -ī, N.
16. inopia, -ae, F.
17. integer, -gra, -grum
18. pār, *gen.* paris
19. parō, -āre, -āvī, -ātum
20. paucī, -ae, -a
21. permittō, -mittere, -mīsī, -missum
22. permoveō, -movēre, -mōvī, -mōtum
23. perterreō, -ēre, -uī, -itum
24. pertineō, -ēre, -uī
25. prīnceps, prīncipis, M.
26. pōns, pontis, M.
27. prōcēdō, -cēdere, -cessī
28. quam, *adv.*
29. reliquus, -a, -um
30. remittō, -mittere, -mīsī, -missum
31. removeō, -movēre, -mōvī, -mōtum
32. repellō, -ere, reppulī, repulsum
33. satis, *adv.*
34. sescentī, -ae, -a
35. similis, -e
36. spēs, speī, F.
37. submittō, -mittere, -mīsī, -missum
38. trādūcō, -dūcere, -dūxī, -ductum

1. height, depth
2. influence
3. moreover, on the other hand
4. alarm, excite
5. common
6. condition, terms
7. consult
8. throw down
9. difficult

10. shut out
11. easily
12. easy
13. of the household, intimate
14. good faith, protection
15. command, power
16. need, lack
17. whole, unimpaired
18. equal
19. get ready, prepare for
20. few
21. permit, grant, entrust
22. arouse, disturb
23. alarm
24. reach, extend, pertain
25. leader, chief man
26. bridge
27. go forward, advance
28. than, how
29. the rest, remaining, remainder of
30. send back
31. move back, remove
32. drive back, repulse
33. enough, quite
34. six hundred
35. like
36. hope
37. send to the assistance of, yield to
38. lead across

WORD STUDY

1. In addition to the preposition **in**, which has already been seen as a prefix, there is an inseparable prefix **in-** meaning *not* or *un-* (as English prefix). It takes by assimilation the forms **il-, im-, ir-**. Examples of its use in preceding Supplementary Review vocabularies are the following:

iniūria (in + iūs, *right*)

immortālis (in + mortālis, *mortal*)

inīquus (in + aequus)

NOTE—In Latin compounds **ae** becomes **ī** except when it stands in the first syllable of the compound.

2. Indicate the compounds of **per** and **re-** in the vocabulary of this lesson.

3. What form does **trāns** take as a prefix in this lesson?

4. Find a compound of **satis** in Supplementary Review V.

5. Give English words which are related in derivation to the following Latin words:

commoveō   exclūdō   familiāris   permittō   removeō   similis
cōnsulō   facilis   fidēs   prōcēdō   repellō   submittō

LESSON LIX *learn*

PRESENT PARTICIPLE: ABLATIVE OF RESPECT

THE PRESENT PARTICIPLE

365. The present active participle of a Latin verb ends in **-ns**, and is formed on the present stem. Its formation in the regular verbs of the four conjugations is as follows:

I.	II.	III.		IV.
portō	moneō	dūcō	capiō	audiō
portāns,	monēns,	dūcēns,	capiēns,	audiēns,
carrying	*warning*	*leading*	*taking*	*hearing*

a. Like the other participles, the present participle agrees in gender, number, and case with the noun or pronoun to which it belongs. It is declined as an adjective of the third declension with the stem ending in **-nt**.

adds to the Character vowel

SINGULAR

	Masc. and Fem.	*Neut.*
NOM.	portāns	portāns
GEN.	portantis	portantis
DAT.	portantī	portantī
ACC.	portantem	portāns
ABL.	portante (-ī)	portante (-ī)

PLURAL

NOM.	portantēs	portantia
GEN.	portantium	portantium
DAT.	portantibus	portantibus
ACC.	portantēs (-īs)	portantia
ABL.	portantibus	portantibus

b. The present active participle is used in Latin less frequently than in English. There is no present passive participle in Latin.

THE ABLATIVE OF RESPECT

366. The ablative without a preposition is used to indicate in what respect a statement is true.

Mīles Gallōs virtūte praecēdēbat, *the soldier surpassed the Gauls in courage.*

367.　　　　　VOCABULARY

adhibeō, -ēre, -uī, -itum, summon

condōnō, -āre, -āvī, -ātum, pardon

Dīviciācus, -ī, m., Diviciacus, *a Gaul*

graviter, *adv.,* heavily, severely

implōrō, -āre, -āvī, -ātum, entreat, ask, ask for, implore

noceō, -ēre, -uī, -itum (*with dative*), injure

praecēdō, -cēdere, -cessī, -cessum, surpass

prō, *prep. w. abl.,* for, on behalf of

EXERCISES

368. 1. Accūsāns; implōrāns; mūnientēs; iacientēs; dūcentēs. 2. Vōcēs captīvōrum auxilium implōrantium audiēbantur. 3. Puerō impigrē labōrantī favēmus. 4. Ille vir melior cōnsiliō (*judgment*) est. 5. Frātrem meum cōnsiliō nōn praecēdis. 6. Nūllī mīlitēs fortiōrēs animō sunt. 7. Hic homō frātrī suō nocēre cupit.

DUMNORIX CENSURED BY CAESAR

Dumnorīgī (**325**) erat frāter nōmine[1] Dīviciācus quī amīcus populī Rōmānī erat. Is frūmentum supportāre cupiēbat sed Dumnorīx maiōrem potentiam in cīvitāte habēbat. Caesar hōs duōs frātrēs adhibuit atque Dumnorīgem graviter accūsāvit. Quod Dīviciācus prō frātre Caesarem implōrāvit, Caesar eam rem condōnāvit.

369. 1. Caesar's army surpassed the Germans in courage. 2. They are few in number, but brave in spirit. 3. The man

---

[1] nōmine, *by name,* is here an ablative of respect.

imploring help was heard by all. 4. The mountain over-hanging is very high. 5. An arrow wounded the fleeing soldier. 6. The fire had injured the tower and the bridge.

---

(1) Give the present active participles of **adhibeō, veniō, tendō,** and **aedificō,** with the English meanings. (2) Decline the present parti-ciples of **mūniō, accūsō,** and **dūcō.** (3) Explain the case of **cōnsiliō** in sentence 4, and of **animō** in sentence 6, 368. (4) Explain the case of **frātrī,** in sentence 7, 368. (5) Compare the adverb **graviter** (*from the adjective* **gravis**).

LESSON LX

THE ABLATIVE ABSOLUTE

370. A noun or pronoun in the ablative case, together with a participle, an adjective, or another noun in agree-ment, may be used to refer to some circumstance or event loosely connected with the rest of the sentence.

Monte occupātō mīlitēs exspectābant, *the mountain hav-ing been seized (after seizing the mountain), the soldiers waited.*

Nūllō prohibente iter fēcērunt, *no one preventing, they made their march.*

Helvētiīs invītīs Orgetorīx haec fēcit, *the Helvetians being unwilling, Orgetorix did these things.*

Labiēnō duce montem ascendērunt, *Labienus being leader, they ascended the mountain.*

a. The original force of the case may be seen if these phrases are translated with the English preposition *with.*

> *with* the mountain seized
> *with* no one preventing
> *with* the Helvetians unwilling
> *with* Labienus (as) leader

b. The participle *being,* which is often employed in translating the ablative absolute, has no equivalent in Latin.

371. Often the ablative absolute is best translated by a clause introduced by *when, after, if, since,* or *although,* as the sense of the main clause may suggest.

Monte occupātō, *when the mountain had been seized.*

a. Various prepositional phrases, also, may be employed in translating this ablative.

Sēquanīs invītīs, *against the will of the Sequani.*
Caesare cōnsule, *in the consulship of Caesar.*

372. VOCABULARY

ascendō, -ere, ascendī, ascēnsum, ascend

cognōscō, -ere, cognōvī, cognitum, find out; *perf.,* know

dēcertō, -āre, -āvī, -ātum, fight to a finish; **proeliō dēcertāre,** fight a decisive battle

explōrātor, -tōris, M., scout

lūx, lūcis, F., light; **prīma lūx,** daybreak

praemittō, -ere, praemīsī, praemissum, send ahead

teneō, -ēre, -uī, hold

Cōnsidius, -ī, M., Considius, *an officer in Caesar's army*

EXERCISES

373. 1. Legiōne cōnscrīptā, Caesar bellum gerere parābat. 2. Duce interfectō, mīlitēs repulsī sunt. 3. Hīs rēbus cognitīs, explōrātōrēs in eō locō mānsērunt.

CAESAR PLANS AN ATTACK

Eōdem diē Helvētiī sub monte castra posuērunt octō mīlia passuum ā castrīs Rōmānōrum. Hāc rē cognitā, Caesar quī proeliō dēcertāre cupiēbat Labiēnum cum duābus legiōnibus montem ascendere iussit. Prīmā lūce summus mōns[1] ā Labiēnō tenēbātur et Caesar cum cōpiīs suīs nōn longē aberat.

---

[1] *The mountain top.*

ELEMENTARY LATIN 157

Tum Caesar hominem nōmine Cōnsidium cum explōrātōribus praemīsit. Is multōs annōs in exercitū fuerat atque
Caesar eī fidem habēbat.

374. 1. After Considius had been sent ahead (*abl. abs.*)
Caesar advanced at daybreak. 2. With Caesar as leader the
soldiers fought bravely. 3. When the king had been killed
the army fled. 4. If the legion is defeated the town will be
captured. 5. The Germans do not surpass our soldiers in
courage. 6. When this was known, scouts were sent ahead.

SUGGESTED DRILL

(1) Translate the examples of the ablative absolute in 373 literally,
then suggest clauses which are equivalent to these phrases. (2) State
which of the original uses of the ablative (33) is seen in the ablative
absolute. (3) Give English phrases which are equivalent to the subordinate clauses of the sentences of 374 in the form (literal equivalents) of the ablative absolute. (4) Give the present active participles
of ascendō and teneō.

TWELFTH REVIEW LESSON

375. VOCABULARY REVIEW

altitūdō, -dinis, F.
auctōritās, -tātis, F.
calamitās, -tātis, F.
condiciō, -ōnis, F.
explōrātor, -tōris, M.
fidēs, -eī, F.
imperium, -ī, N.
impetus, -ūs, M.
lūx, lūcis, F.
nox, noctis, F.
pōns, pontis, M.
prīnceps, prīncipis, M.

respōnsum, -ī, N.
ventus, -ī, M.
angustus, -a, -um
complūrēs, -a *or* -ia
difficilis, -e
facilis, -e
impedītus, -a, -um
inimīcus, -a, -um
paucī, -ae, -a
reliquus, -a, -um
similis, -e
summus, -a, -um

ūtilis, -e
ācriter
facile
graviter
imprōvīsō
intereā
quam
satis
ut
citrā
prō
autem

adhibeō, -ēre, -uī, -itum
ascendō, -ere, ascendī, ascēnsum
cognōscō, -ere, cognōvī, cognitum
commemorō, -āre, -āvī, -ātum
concīdō, -ere, concīdī, concīsum
condōnō, -āre, -āvī, -ātum
cōnstituō, -stituere, -stituī, -stitūtum
dēcertō, -āre, -āvī, -ātum
dēiciō, -ere, dēiēcī, dēiectum
dēterreō, -ēre, -uī, -itum
dīcō, -ere, dīxī, dictum
impendeō, -ēre
noceō, -ēre, -uī, -itum
parō, -āre, -āvī, -ātum
perterreō, -ēre, -uī, -itum
pertineō, -ēre, -uī
poscō, -ere, poposcī
praedicō, -āre, -āvī, -ātum
praemittō, -mittere, -mīsī, -missum
praesum, -esse, -fuī, -futūrus
prōcēdō, -cēdere, -cessī, -cessum
prohibeō, -ēre, -uī, -itum
repellō, -ere, reppulī, repulsum
teneō, -ēre, -uī
trādūcō, -dūcere, -dūxī, -ductum
trānsportō, -āre, -āvī, -ātum
vāstō, -āre, -āvī, -ātum

RELATED ENGLISH WORDS

altitude	deter	proceed
ascend	fidelity	procession
ascension	imperial	pro-slavery
calamity	implore	response
commemorate	lucid	tenant
condone	principal	transportation

LESSON LXI

THE CONJUGATION OF *POSSUM*

376. The verb **possum** is a compound of the verb **sum** and the adjective **potis**, *able*. The present system in the indicative mood is as follows:

PRESENT

SINGULAR	PLURAL
possum, *I am able* or *I can*	possumus, *we are able*, etc.
potes, *you are able, you can*	potestis, *you are able*, etc.
potest, *he is able, he can*	possunt, *they are able*, etc.

IMPERFECT

SINGULAR	PLURAL
poteram, *I was able, I could*	poterāmus, *we were able*, etc.
poterās, *you were able*, etc.	poterātis, *you were able*, etc.
poterat, *he was able*, etc.	poterant, *they were able*, etc.

FUTURE

SINGULAR	PLURAL
poterō, *I shall be able*	poterimus, *we shall be able*
poteris, *you will be able*	poteritis, *you will be able*
poterit, *he will be able*	poterunt, *they will be able*

377. **VOCABULARY**

aciēs, -ēī, F., line of battle

collis, collis, -ium, M., hill

cōnspiciō, -ere, cōnspexī, cōnspectum, catch sight of, see

īnstruō, -ere, īnstrūxī, īnstrūctum, draw up, arrange

metus, -ūs, M., fear

possum, posse, potuī, be able, can

redeō,[1] -īre, -iī, -itum, return

subdūcō, -ere, subdūxī, subductum, withdraw

EXERCISES

378. 1. Mīlitēs quōs dūcis oppidum capere possunt. 2. Eum vidēre poteram quod in colle erat. 3. In patriam suam redīre poterit. 4. Fluctūs audīre potes. 5. Mōns ex urbe cōnspicī potest. 6. Propter metum silvās nōn explorāvī.

---

[1] A compound of **eō**.

THE BLUNDER OF CONSIDIUS

Cōnsidius, hominibus in summō monte cōnspectīs, perterritus est. Eōs Rōmānōs esse nōn cognōvit et ad Caesarem magnā celeritāte rediit. Caesar impetum timēns suōs in collem proximum subdūxit. Aciē īnstrūctā Helvētiōs exspectābat. Hominēs autem quōs Cōnsidius vīderat mīlitēs Caesaris erant quī montem cum Labiēnō ascenderant.

379. 1. After drawing up the line of battle (*abl. abs.*) Labienus will wait for Caesar. 2. The legions can repulse the enemy. 3. We could not help our friends. 4. Grain cannot be sent. 5. The enemy having been repulsed, we can advance. 6. You can see the statue which stands on a hill.

SUGGESTED DRILL

(1) Explain the use of the ablatives **celeritāte**, line 7, and **aciē**, line 8, 378. (2) Conjugate **redeō** in the imperfect and future tenses of the indicative active. (3) Give a synopsis of **īnstruō** in the third person singular, active and passive. (4) Decline **collis**. (5) Decline the phrase **aciēs longa** in the singular. (6) Explain the derivation of **subdūcō**.

THE CAPITOLINE HILL (RESTORATION)

LESSON LXII

PERSONAL PRONOUNS: OBJECTIVE GENITIVE

THE PERSONAL PRONOUNS

380. As has been seen, the personal pronouns as subjects may, if not emphatic, be indicated by the endings of the verb. The nominative forms are used, however, when they are needed for emphasis or contrast.

The personal pronouns of the first and second persons are declined as follows:

	SINGULAR	PLURAL	SINGULAR	PLURAL
Nom.	ego	nōs	tū	vōs
Gen.	meī	nostrum, nostrī	tuī	vestrum, vestrī
Dat.	mihi	nōbīs	tibi	vōbīs
Acc.	mē	nōs	tē	vōs
Abl.	mē	nōbīs	tē	vōbīs

a. As a pronoun of the third person, the forms of **is** are commonly employed.

THE OBJECTIVE GENITIVE

381. Certain nouns and adjectives which express action or feeling sometimes take a dependent genitive in a relation similar to that of the direct object to the verb on which it depends. This is called the Objective Genitive

Metus perīculī, *fear of danger.*

a. The forms **meī, tuī, nostrī, vestrī,** are used as objective genitives and seldom in any other way. Possession is expressed in the first and second persons by the possessive adjectives **meus, tuus, noster, vester,** as explained in **80.**

b. The forms **nostrum** and **vestrum** are used as genitives of the whole.

382. VOCABULARY

āvertō, -ere, āvertī, āversum, turn away

Bibracte, -tis, N., Bibracte, *a town of the Haeduans*

convertō, -ere, convertī, conversum, turn, change; signa convertere, wheel about

dēnique, *adv.*, finally

ego, meī, I

lacessō, -ere, -īvī, -ītum, harass, attack

posterus, -a, -um, following, the following, next

renūntiō, -āre, -āvī, -ātum, bring back word, report

tū, tuī, you

EXERCISES

383. 1. Ego in urbe, tū in oppidō habitās. 2. Apud Germānōs est metus tuī. 3. Frāter meus mihi hunc gladium dedit. 4. Vōs semper amāvimus. 5. Ā mē laudātus es. 6. Exercitus eō diē Genavam pervenīre nōn poterat.

CAESAR CHANGES HIS COURSE

Dēnique Labiēnus et legiōnēs ab explōrātōribus vīsī sunt. Celeriter Caesarī renūntiātum est. Sed Helvētiī castra mōverant neque proelium factum est. Posterō diē Caesar iter ab Helvētiīs āvertit et Bibracte īre contendit quod erat in eō oppidō cōpia frūmentī. Tum Helvētiī itinere conversō exercitum Rōmānum lacessīvērunt.

384. 1. Fear of you (*sing.*) did not hinder the enemy. 2. We have no hope of peace. 3. I gave you the book which you have. 4. I shall not go to Rome against your will (*abl. abs.*, you unwilling). 5. They were defended by us. 6. I cannot see you, but I hear your voice.

SUGGESTED DRILL

(1) Explain the reason for the use of the personal pronouns in sentence 1, 383. (2) Point out an example of the use of the objective genitive in 383. (3) Point out two phrases in 384 which will be translated by the objective genitive. (4) Give a synopsis of **redeō** in the third person, singular and plural, active voice. (5) Conjugate **possum** in the present tense.

LESSON LXIII

REFLEXIVES: *CUM* AS ENCLITIC

THE REFLEXIVE PRONOUN

385. The reflexive pronoun is used in the genitive, dative, accusative, or ablative to refer back to the subject.

> **Nōn mē laudō,** *I do not praise myself.*
> **Tibi placēs,** *you please yourself.*
> **Sē dēfendit,** *he defends himself.*

a. The reflexive must be distinguished from the intensive **ipse,** which merely emphasizes the word with which it agrees. The reflexive denotes the same person or thing as the subject, but its case depends on some other element of the sentence.

> **Vir ipse amīcum accūsat** (intensive), *the man himself accuses his friend.*
> **Vir sē accūsat** (reflexive), *the man accuses himself.*

386. In the first and second persons the forms of **ego** and **tū** (excluding, of course, the nominative) serve as reflexives. In the third person there is a reflexive pronoun which has no other uses. It is translated *himself, herself, itself,* or *themselves,* as the gender and number of the subject may require.

	Singular	Plural
Gen.	suī	suī
Dat.	sibi	sibi
Acc.	sē *or* sēsē	sē *or* sēsē
Abl.	sē *or* sēsē	sē *or* sēsē

THE ENCLITIC USE OF *CUM*

387. With the ablatives **mē, tē, sē, nōbīs, vōbīs,** and regularly **quibus,** the preposition **cum** is used as an enclitic. That is, it is added to the word as a final syllable.

> **mēcum,** *with me.*   **tēcum,** *with you,* etc.

388.
VOCABULARY

collocō, -āre, -āvī, -ātum, place, station

comparō, -āre, -āvī, -ātum, prepare

equitātus, -ūs, M., cavalry (a collective noun)

interim, adv., meanwhile

medius, -a, -um, the middle of, middle

proximē, adv. (superlative of prope), last

suī, of himself, herself, itself, themselves

veterānus, -a, -um, veteran

EXERCISES

389. 1. Cūr nōn tē in hīs perīculīs dēfendis? 2. Ego mē laudō, tū nōn mē laudās. 3. Equitātū praemissō lēgātus cum paucīs mīlitibus in colle manēbat. 4. Sē fortiter dēfendit. 5. Sibi semper fāvit, sed aliōs amīcōs habet nūllōs. 6. Cūr nōn mēcum manēbis? 7. Mīlitēs sē dēfendunt.

PREPARATIONS FOR BATTLE

Caesar iterum aciem īnstrūxit et omnia comparāvit ad proelium. Equitātus interim cum hostibus contendēbat. Quattuor legiōnēs veterānās Caesar in colle mediō collocāvit. Eae legiōnēs quās proximē cōnscrīpserat in summō iugō īnstrūctae sunt. Omnia impedīmenta ad eundem locum missa erant.

390. 1. This legion will defend itself with great courage. 2. The boy wounded himself with the sword. 3. The man who is lazy injures himself. 4. Why do you not remain with me in the city? 5. The veteran soldiers had been stationed half way up the hill (on the middle of the hill). 6. When everything (all things) had been prepared (abs. abl.), I ordered the soldiers to make an attack.

SUGGESTED DRILL

(1) Explain the case of the reflexive pronouns in sentences 4, 5, and 7, 389. (2) Point out the reflexive pronouns in sentences 1 and 2, 389. (3) Explain the case of equitātū and of mīlitibus in sentence 3, 389. (4) Decline the phrase legiō veterāna. (5) Give the third person plural of possum in the present, past, imperfect, and future.

LESSON LXIV

PRESENT, PAST, AND FUTURE INFINITIVES OF REGULAR VERBS

THE INFINITIVES OF THE FOUR CONJUGATIONS

391. The Latin infinitive has three tenses, the present, the past, and the future. The infinitives of the four conjugations are formed as follows:

ACTIVE	PASSIVE
I.	
PRES. portāre, *to carry*	portārī, *to be carried*
PAST portāvisse, *to have carried*	portātus esse, *to have been carried*
FUT. portātūrus esse, *to be about to carry*	portātum īrī, *to be about to be carried*
II.	
PRES. monēre	monērī
PAST monuisse	monitus esse
FUT. monitūrus esse	monitum īrī
III.	
PRES. dūcere	dūcī
PAST dūxisse	ductus esse
FUT. ductūrus esse	ductum īrī
PRES. capere	capī
PAST cēpisse	captus esse
FUT. captūrus esse	captum īrī
IV.	
PRES. audīre	audīrī
PAST audīvisse	audītus esse
FUT. audītūrus esse	audītum īrī

FORMATION OF THE INFINITIVES

392. (1) In the first, second, and fourth conjugations the present passive infinitive is formed by changing the final **e** of the present active infinitive to **ī**. In the third conjugation the termination **-ere** is replaced by **ī**.

(2) The past active infinitive is formed with the termination **-isse,** which is added to the perfect stem.

(3) The past passive participle, which is used in forming the past passive infinitive, and the future active participle, which is used in forming the future active infinitive, agree in gender, number, and case with the subject.

(4) The ending **-um** is always retained with the future passive infinitive. The form used in this infinitive is not a participle.[1] The future passive infinitive is not much used.

EXERCISES

393. 1. Comparārī; comparāvisse; comparātus esse. 2. Audītūrus esse; audīvisse; audīrī. 3. Iēcisse; dēfendisse; mūnīvisse. 4. Mittī; mīsisse; missus esse. 5. Terrērī; territūrus esse; terruisse. 6. Trādūcī; trādūxisse; trāductūrus esse. 7. Vāstārī; timērī; petī; interficī; mūnīrī. 8. Iūvisse; relīquisse; fūgisse. 9. Ductūrus esse; ductum īrī; ductus esse. 10. Vincī; victus esse; victum īrī.

394. 1. To defend; to be defended; to have defended. 2. To hinder; to be hindered; to have been hindered. 3. To have begun; to have fortified; to have left. 4. To be sent; to have been sent; to be about to send. 5. To be conquered; to have conquered; to have been conquered. 6. To be increased; to have increased; to have persuaded.

SUGGESTED DRILL

(1) Indicate the stems of the infinitives in **393**. (2) Point out the difference between the future active infinitive and the past passive infinitive. (3) Decline the personal pronouns of the first and second persons. (4) Decline the reflexive pronoun of the third person.

---

[1] It is called the supine. The forms of the supine will be given later (**547**).

the present infinitive denotes
the same time as the verb;
ELEMENTARY LATIN 167
The future — time will but then
after the
main verb

LESSON LXV

INFINITIVE WITH SUBJECT ACCUSATIVE: INFINITIVES OF *SUM* AND *EŌ*

THE INFINITIVE WITH SUBJECT ACCUSATIVE

395. Verbs of *knowing, thinking, saying, hearing,* and *observing* may take a dependent infinitive with its subject in the accusative case. The infinitive when thus used is regularly translated by an English indicative introduced by *that.*

   a. The infinitive in this use will be present, past, or future according as the time to which it refers is present, past, or future, from the point of view of the verb on which it depends.

Hostēs fugere videō, *I see that the enemy are fleeing.*
Hostēs fugere vidēbam, *I saw that the enemy were fleeing.*
Hostēs fūgisse videō, *I see that the enemy have fled.*
Hostēs fūgisse vidēbam, *I saw that the enemy had fled.*
Puer dīcit frātrem ventūrum esse, *the boy says that his brother will come.*
Puer dīxit frātrem ventūrum esse, *the boy said that his brother would come.*

396.   THE INFINITIVES OF *SUM* AND *EŌ*

PRES.	esse	īre
PAST	fuisse	īsse (iisse)
FUT.	futūrus esse *or* fore	itūrus esse

   a. The predicate noun or adjective with the infinitive of **sum** is in the accusative if the subject is in the accusative.

Tē fortem esse videō, *I see that you are brave.*

Review verbs back to 154.

397. VOCABULARY

cēdō, -ere, cessī, cessum, yield, retreat

circiter, *adv.*, about

committō, -ere, commīsī, commissum, unite; do; proelium committere, begin battle

deinde, *adv.*, thereupon, then

perturbō, -āre, -āvī, -ātum, throw into disorder

pīlum, -ī, N., javelin

succēdō, -ere, successī, successum, advance, come up to

EXERCISES

398. 1. Puerum labōrāre vīdī. 2. Cognōvī iter longum esse. 3. Explōrātōrēs renūntiāvērunt montem ā Labiēnō tenērī. 4. Dōnum missum esse repperistī. 5. Legiōnēs proelium commīsisse lēgātus vidēbat. 6. Caesar dīxit Helvētiōs fortēs esse. 7. Hī hominēs dīcunt sē in Ītaliā duōs annōs fuisse.

The Helvetians Repulsed

Helvētiī sub collem successērunt atque proelium est commissum. Mīlitēs Rōmānī pīlīs celeriter hostēs perturbāvērunt, deinde gladiīs impetum in eōs fēcērunt. Multīs vulnerātīs (370), Helvētiōs reppulērunt, quī ad montem sē recēpērunt (*withdrew*). Is mōns circiter mīlle passūs aberat.

399. 1. We see that the boys are walking. 2. The soldier knows that the danger is great. 3. The leader hears that the enemy are fleeing. 4. You found out that the book had been sent. 5. The scout reported that the town had been captured. 6. The man said that the island was large. 7. Caesar heard that the Germans had crossed the river.

SUGGESTED DRILL

(1) Give all the infinitives of committō and perturbō. (2) Explain the case of longum in sentence 2, 398. (3) Give a synopsis of cēdō in the third person plural, active voice, indicative mood. (4) Give the principal parts of repellō and recipiō. (5) Give the present participles of the verbs in this lesson.

THE ROMAN FORUM (RESTORATION)

THIRTEENTH REVIEW LESSON

400. (1) Personal pronouns.

      (2) Reflexive pronouns.

      (3) The conjugation of **possum.**

      (4) The present participle.

      (5) The infinitives of the four conjugations.

      (6) The formation of adverbs.

      (7) The comparison of adverbs.

      (8) The genitive of description.

      (9) The objective genitive.

    (10) The ablative of description.

    (11) The ablative absolute.

    (12) The ablative of respect.

    (13) The infinitive with subject accusative.

401. Give Latin words with which the following English words are connected in derivation:

avert	commit	interim
cede	convert	medium
collocation	egotism	proximity
commission	instruction	veteran

LESSON LXVI

THE IMPERATIVE MOOD

402. The imperative mood in Latin, as in English, is used to express commands. It has the present and future tenses. The forms of the future, except in the case of a few words, are rarely used.

    a. The present has only the second person. In the singular number of the active voice it is the same as the present stem and may be found by dropping the **-re**

of the present active infinitive. In the singular number of
the passive it is the same as the present active infinitive.

PRESENT

ACTIVE	PASSIVE

I.

| amā, *love* (*thou*) | amāre, *be* (*thou*) *loved* |
| amāte, *love* (*ye*) | amāminī, *be* (*ye*) *loved* |

II.

| monē | monēre |
| monēte | monēminī |

III.

mitte	mittere
mittite	mittiminī
cape	capere
capite	capiminī

IV.

| audī | audīre |
| audīte | audīminī |

b. The verbs **dīcō**, **dūcō**, and **faciō** have the irregular
forms **dīc**, **dūc**, and **fac** in the singular of the present
active imperative. Their other imperative forms are
regular.

403. VOCABULARY

adveniō, -īre, advēnī, adven-
    tum, arrive
Bōiī, -ōrum, M. *pl.*, the Boii
brevis, breve, short
intellegō, -ere, intellēxī, in-
    tellēctum, know

latus, lateris, N., side, flank
    (*of an army*)
redintegrō, -āre, -āvī, -ātum,
    renew
Tulingī, -ōrum, M. *pl.*, the
    Tulingi

EXERCISES

404. 1. Amīcōs tuōs amā.   2. Illōs hominēs statim monē.
3. Breve tempus in eō vīcō manē.   4. Librum, puer, mihi dā.
5. Prōcēdite, mīlitēs, et proelium committite.   6. Castra,
mīlitēs, mūnīte.   7. Vīta eius hominis brevis fuit.   8. Gallī
intellēxērunt potentiam populī Rōmānī magnam esse.

An Unsuccessful Rally

Intereā Bōiī et Tulingī, sociī Helvētiōrum quī advēnerant,
impetum in Rōmānōs ā lateribus fēcērunt.   Hōc cognitō
Helvētiī signa convertērunt et proelium redintegrāvērunt.
Gallī ācriter pugnāvērunt sed dēnique repulsī ad montem
et in castra sua sē recēpērunt.   In eō locō ad multam noctem
sē dēfendērunt.   Multīs interfectīs Rōmānī castra et impedīmenta cēpērunt.

405. 1. Soldiers, fight bravely.   2. Boy, warn your brother.
3. Hear me, friends.   4. We know that the army is large.
5. The boy says that no one came.   6. That war was short,
but many were killed.   7. I know that the river is wide and
deep.

NINTH SUPPLEMENTARY REVIEW

VOCABULARY REVIEW

1. abdūcō, -dūcere, -dūxī, -ductum
2. aciēs, -ēī, F.
3. adhibeō, -ēre, -uī, -itum
4. aetās, -tātis, F.
5. antecēdō, -cēdere, -cessī
6. ascendō, -scendere, -scendī, -scēnsum
7. cēdō, -ere, cessī, cessum
8. cognōscō, -nōscere, -nōvī, -nitum
9. committō, -mittere, -mīsī, -missum
10. comparō, -āre, -āvī, -ātum
11. dēscendō, -scendere, -scendī, -scēnsum
12. ego, gen. meī
13. equitātus, -ūs, M.
14. ēvocō, -āre, -āvī, -ātum
15. graviter, adv.
16. interim, adv.
17. īnstruō, -struere, -strūxī, -strūctum
18. lūx, lūcis, F.
19. medius, -a, -um
20. noceō, -ēre, -uī, -itum
21. obiciō, -icere, -iēcī, -iectum
22. obtineō, -tinēre, -tinuī, -tentum
23. possum, posse, potuī
24. praedīcō, -dīcere, -dīxī, -dictum
25. praemittō, -mittere, -mīsī, -missum
26. praesidium, -ī, N.
27. prō, prep. with abl.
28. prōiciō, -icere, -iēcī, -iectum
29. reddō, -dere, -didī, -ditum
30. reiciō, -icere, -iēcī, -iectum
31. rīdeō, -ēre, rīsī, rīsum
32. succēdō, -cēdere, -cessī, -cessum
33. suī
34. teneō, -ēre, -uī
35. trāiciō, -icere, -iēcī, -iectum
36. tū, gen. tuī

---

1. lead away
2. line of battle
3. apply, employ
4. age
5. go before, precede
6. climb, ascend, mount
7. go, yield
8. learn, ascertain
9. commit, entrust (with proelium, begin)
10. get together, provide
11. descend
12. I
13. cavalry

14. call out
15. heavily, weightily, seriously
16. meanwhile
17. arrange
18. light
19. middle, middle of
20. injure
21. throw against, oppose
22. obtain, hold, have
23. be able
24. foretell
25. send ahead

26. garrison, guard
27. in front of, on behalf of
28. throw forward
29. give back
30. throw back
31. laugh
32. come up, succeed
33. (of) himself, herself, themselves
34. hold, keep
35. throw across, pierce
36. you

WORD STUDY

1. Two prefixes of importance in addition to those which have been given are the prepositions **prae**, meaning *before*, or *extremely*, and **sub**, meaning *under*. As we have seen in **aequus**, the diphthong **ae** becomes *e* in English derivatives, and therefore **prae** appears as *pre-* in many English words, such as *predict, prefer, precede*.

By assimilation **sub** becomes **suc-, suf-, sup-, sus-**.

2. Find two English derivatives from each of the following verbs:

ascendō   obiciō
committō   praedīcō

3. Explain the meaning of *interim* as an English word.

4. What is the meaning of *egotistical?*

5. What is the *antecedent* of a pronoun? Why is it so called?

6. With what Latin words are the following connected in derivation?

evoke   medium   project   ridicule
instruct   obtain   reject   success

LESSON LXVII

THE CONJUGATION OF *FERŌ*

406. The verb **ferō**, *bear, carry*, is irregular. Its principal parts are **ferō, ferre, tulī, lātum.**

PRESENT

ACTIVE		PASSIVE	
SINGULAR	PLURAL	SINGULAR	PLURAL
ferō	ferimus	feror	ferimur
fers	fertis	ferris	feriminī
fert	ferunt	fertur	feruntur

a. The imperfect and future are like those of **dūcō.**

IMPERFECT		FUTURE	
ACTIVE	PASSIVE	ACTIVE	PASSIVE
ferēbam	ferēbar	feram	ferar
ferēbās,	ferēbāris, -re,	ferēs,	ferēris, -re
etc.	*etc.*	*etc.*	*etc.*

b. The perfect system is formed regularly with the stem **tul-** in the active, and with the participle **lātus** in the passive.

Infinitives

	ACTIVE	PASSIVE
PRES.	ferre	ferrī
PAST	tulisse	lātus esse
FUT.	lātūrus esse	lātum īrī

Imperatives

ACTIVE		PASSIVE	
SINGULAR	PLURAL	SINGULAR	PLURAL
fer	ferte	ferre	feriminī

407. VOCABULARY

cīvis, cīvis, -ium, m., f., citizen

cōnferō, cōnferre, contulī, conlātum, collect, bring together

ferō, ferre, tulī, lātum, bear, carry, bring

īnferō, īnferre, intulī, inlātum, bring upon, cause

opus, operis, n., work, labor

pereō, -īre, -iī, -itum, perish

restituō, -ere, restituī, restitūtum, restore

EXERCISES

408. 1. Fert; ferēbat; feret. 2. Cōnfert; cōnfers; cōnferēbam. 3. Rōmānī bellum Gallīs[1] īnferunt. 4. Mīlitēs in ūnum locum impedīmenta cōnferēbant. 5. Bellum multa perīcula fert. 6. Eō tempore multī cīvēs periērunt et multī aliī ex urbe fūgērunt. 7. Opus quod facis magnum est.

THE TERMS OF PEACE

Hōc proeliō factō, Gallī lēgātōs (*envoys*) mīsērunt et pācem petiērunt. Caesar arma et obsidēs poposcit. Hīs trāditīs, Helvētiī domum redīre atque oppida et vīcōs restituere iussī sunt. Bōiī autem in fīnibus Haeduōrum mānsērunt quod Haeduī eīs amīcī erant.

409. 1. The Helvetians are collecting the arms. 2. This nation will make war on the Germans. 3. They could not bring aid. 4. Caesar says that the Gauls surrendered their arms. 5. Restore your towns and villages. 6. Caesar praised the work of the soldiers. 7. A great many (**complūrēs**) citizens assembled because they wished to see the leader of the army.

SUGGESTED DRILL

(1) Conjugate **cōnferō** and **īnferō** in the present indicative active, and the future indicative active. (2) Decline **cīvis** and **opus**, and state what is the class of stems to which each belongs. (3) Give the present imperatives of **restituō**, active and passive. (4) Give the past infinitives, active and passive, of **restituō**. (5) Conjugate **pereō** in the imperfect and the future of the indicative. (6) Give all the infinitives of **īnferō**.

---

[1] The phrase **bellum īnferre**, *make war on*, takes a dative (324).

LESSON LXVIII

SYNOPSIS OF *POSSUM* AND *FERŌ*

410. The synopsis of **possum** and of **ferō** (active) in the first person of the indicative is as follows:

PRES.	possum	ferō
IMPF.	poteram	ferēbam
FUT.	poterō	feram
PERF.	potuī	tulī
P. PERF.	potueram	tuleram
F. PERF.	potuerō	tulerō

The infinitives of **possum** are:

PRES. **posse**, *to be able*   PAST **potuisse**, *to have been able*

a. This verb has no future infinitive.

b. In irregular verbs, as in all others, the past infinitive is formed by adding **-isse** to the perfect stem.

c. The participles of **ferō** are as follows:

PRES.	ferēns
PAST	lātus
FUT. ACT.	lātūrus

ROMAN COIN

Possum has no participles.

411. VOCABULARY

Ariovistus, -ī, M., Ariovistus, *a German king*

Arvernī, -ōrum, M. *pl.*, the Arverni, *a Gallic tribe*

cliēns, clientis, clientium, M., dependent

contrā, *prep. w. acc.*, against, opposite

factiō, factiōnis, F., faction, party

ingēns, *gen.*, **ingentis,** huge, very large, very great

prīncipātus, -ūs, M., leadership

tegō, -ere, tēxī, tēctum, cover, protect

EXERCISES

412. 1. Gallī auxilium tulērunt. 2. Dīxit Gallōs auxilium tulisse. 3. Id facere potuit. 4. Intellegimus eum id facere potuisse. 5. Bellum celeriter cōnfectum est. 6. Populus Rōmānus hunc rēgem quī ē patriā suā fūgerat tēxit. 7. Dīviciācus multōs clientēs et amīcōs habēbat. 8. In eō flūmine est ingēns īnsula.

A Request for Help

Bellō Helvētiōrum cōnfectō, multī prīncipēs cīvitātum Galliae ad Caesarem vēnērunt, inter hōs Dīviciācus Haeduus. Auxilium ā Caesare contrā Ariovistum rēgem Germānōrum petēbant. Ōlim erant duae factiōnēs tōtīus Galliae. Alterīus Arvernī et Sēquanī prīncipātum tenēbant, alterīus Haeduī. Arvernī et Sēquanī auxilium ā Germānīs petiērunt, quōrum prīmō circiter quīndecim mīlia Rhēnum trānsiērunt.

413. 1. The Gauls could not defend the camp. 2. He says that the Gauls could not defend the camp. 3. The soldiers are collecting (**cōnferō**) grain. 4. We have heard that the soldiers are collecting grain. 5. Soldiers, bring aid. 6. The citizens feared the dependents of Orgetorix because they had weapons. 7. A very great number of Helvetians had been killed and others had been wounded.

SUGGESTED DRILL

(1) Give a synopsis of **possum** in the third person, singular and plural. (2) Give a synopsis of **ferō** in the third person singular of the passive and the third person plural of the active. (3) Give the participles of **īnferō** and **cōnferō**. (4) Decline the present participle of **tegō**. (5) Explain the case of **quī** in sentence 6, **412**. (6) Decline the adjective **ingēns**.

Formely

LESSON LXIX

DEPONENT VERBS

414. A deponent verb is one which is passive in form but active in meaning. Its principal parts are passive forms. Deponents have only two stems, the present and the participial.

a. The endings of the present infinitives which are used to indicate the conjugations are therefore as follows:

I.	II.	III.	IV.
-ārī	-ērī	-ī	-īrī

b. Deponents of the first and second conjugations are conjugated as follows:

> **cōnor, cōnārī, cōnātus sum,** *try.*
> **polliceor, pollicērī, pollicitus sum,** *promise.*

PRESENT

SINGULAR	PLURAL	SINGULAR	PLURAL
cōnor	cōnāmur	polliceor	pollicēmur
cōnāris, -re	cōnāminī	pollicēris, -re	pollicēminī
cōnātur	cōnantur	pollicētur	pollicentur

IMPERFECT

cōnābar	cōnābāmur	pollicēbar	pollicēbāmur
cōnābāris, -re	cōnābāminī	pollicēbāris, -re	pollicēbāminī
cōnābātur	cōnābantur	pollicēbātur	pollicēbantur

FUTURE

cōnābor	cōnābimur	pollicēbor	pollicēbimur
cōnāberis, -re	cōnābiminī	pollicēberis, -re	pollicēbiminī
cōnābitur	cōnābuntur	pollicēbitur	pollicēbuntur

Perfect

cōnātus sum   pollicitus sum

Past Perfect

cōnātus eram   pollicitus eram

Future Perfect

cōnātus erō   pollicitus erō

Imperatives

Sing. cōnāre   pollicēre
Plur. cōnāminī   pollicēminī

Infinitives

Pres. cōnārī   pollicērī
Past cōnātus esse   pollicitus esse
Fut. cōnātūrus esse   pollicitūrus esse

Participles

Pres. cōnāns   pollicēns
Past cōnātus, -a, -um   pollicitus, -a, -um
Fut. cōnātūrus, -a, -um   pollicitūrus, -a, -um

c. Deponents have the following active forms: the present and future participles, and the future infinitive. They have also the future passive participle, used with passive meaning. The past participle is usually active in meaning, like the other forms: **cōnātus**, *having tried*. Occasionally, however, it is used with passive meaning.

415.   **VOCABULARY**

cōnor, -ārī, -ātus sum, try
multitūdō, multitūdinis, f., multitude, great number
polliceor, -ērī, pollicitus sum, promise

posteā, *adv.*, afterwards
senātus, -ūs, m., senate
supplicium, -ī, n., punishment
vereor, -ērī, veritus sum, fear, be afraid of

EXERCISES

416. 1. Hī hominēs auxilium pollicentur. 2. Dīviciācus frūmentum cōnferre cōnātur. 3. Exīre cōnātī sunt quod fīnēs angustōs habēbant. 4. Gallī magnum numerum equitum pollicitī erant. 5. Urbem dēfendere cōnābuntur sed nōn poterunt. 6. Perīculum magnopere verēmur.

THE GERMANS AND THE HAEDUANS

Posteā plūrēs trāductī erant et eō tempore magna multitūdō eōrum in Galliā erat. Cum hīs Haeduī saepe armīs contenderant sed victī erant et obsidēs dederant. Auxilium anteā nōn petierant quod supplicia ab Ariovistō verēbantur. Dīviciācus quī sōlus obsidēs nōn dederat Rōmam vēnerat et auxilium ā senātū Rōmānō petīverat. Rōmānī autem auxilium nōn tulērunt.

417. 1. The man does not try to defend himself. 2. No one promised you a reward. 3. We cannot promise aid. 4. The soldier protected his brother with his shield. 5. The Sequani feared punishment from Ariovistus. 6. Why do you fear danger? 7. Fearing; promising; having feared; to have feared; to have promised.

SUGGESTED DRILL

(1) Conjugate **vereor** in the present indicative and the perfect indicative. (2) Give a synopsis of **cōnor** and of **polliceor** in the third person singular, giving English meanings. (3) Analyze **verēbantur**, indicating stem, tense sign, and personal endings. (4) Give a synopsis of **ferō** in the second person singular, active and passive. (5) Give the infinitives of **vereor**.

LESSON LXX

DEPONENT VERBS (Continued): ABLATIVE WITH ŪTOR, ETC.

DEPONENT VERBS (Continued)

418. Deponent verbs of the third conjugation ending in -or and those of the fourth conjugation are conjugated as follows:

> **sequor, sequī, secūtus sum,** *follow*
> **potior, potīrī, potītus sum,** *get possession of*

PRESENT

SINGULAR	PLURAL	SINGULAR	PLURAL
sequor	sequimur	potior	potīmur
sequeris, -re	sequiminī	potīris, -re	potīminī
sequitur	sequuntur	potītur	potiuntur

IMPERFECT

sequēbar	sequēbāmur	potiēbar	potiēbāmur
sequēbāris, -re	sequēbāminī	potiēbāris, -re	potiēbāminī
sequēbātur	sequēbantur	potiēbātur	potiēbantur

FUTURE

sequar	sequēmur	potiar	potiēmur
sequēris, -re	sequēminī	potiēris	potiēminī
sequētur	sequentur	potiētur	potientur

PERFECT

secūtus sum   potītus sum

PAST PERFECT

secūtus eram   potītus eram

Future Perfect

secūtus erō   potītus erō

Imperatives

Sing. sequere   potīre
Plur. sequiminī   potīminī

Infinitives

Pres. sequī   potīrī
Past   secūtus esse   potītus esse
Fut.   secūtūrus esse   potītūrus esse

Participles

Pres. sequēns   potiēns
Past   secūtus   potītus
Fut.   secūtūrus   potītūrus

THE ABLATIVE WITH *ŪTOR, FRUOR,* ETC.

419.   The deponents **ūtor, fruor, fungor, potior,** and **vēscor** take their objects in the ablative case.

Gladiō ūtitur, *he uses a sword.*
Oppidō potītī sunt, *they have gained possession of the town.*

420.   **VOCABULARY**

dēcēdō, -ere, dēcessī, dēces-   sequor, sequī, secūtus sum,
   sum, withdraw   follow
etiam, *adv.*, also, even   sōlum, *adv.*, only
exīstimō, -āre, -āvī, -ātum,   sustineō, -ēre, sustinuī, sus-
   think   tentum, endure, hold out
potior, -īrī, potītus sum, get   ūtor, ūtī, ūsus sum, use
   possession of   verbum, -ī, n., word

EXERCISES

421. 1. Hostēs exercitum nostrum sequēbantur. 2. Diūtius sequī nōn potest. 3. Cōnsidius explōrātōribus nōn ūsus
est. 4. Nostrī castrīs et impedīmentīs hostium potītī sunt.
5. Explōrātōrēs secūtus ad ingentem montem pervēnit. 6.
Ūsus; secūtus; ūtī; potīrī; sequī. 7. Verbīs fortibus ūteris.

THE CONDITION OF THE SEQUANI

Nōn sōlum Haeduī sed etiam Sēquanī auxilium ā Caesare
implōrābant. Ariovistus, quī maiōrem numerum Germānōrum trādūcere cupiēbat, Sēquanōs dē magnā parte agrī
ipsōrum dēcēdere iusserat. Itaque eī quī anteā sociī Ario-
vistī fuerant tum potentiam eius maximē verēbantur. Omnēs
Gallī dīxērunt sē nōn posse diūtius imperium eius sustinēre.
Exīstimābant Caesarem auxilium ferre posse.

422. 1. On that day our army followed the enemy. 2.
Why did they use boats? 3. At that time they could not
gain possession of the bridge. 4. They all tried to follow,
but they could not cross the river. 5. Having promised aid,
the leader withdrew.

SUGGESTED DRILL

(1) Conjugate **ūtor** in the present and future of the indicative.
(2) Give all the infinitives and participles of **ūtor**. (3) Give a synopsis of **sequor** and of **potior** in the third person singular. (4) Explain
the case of **explōrātōribus** in sentence 3, and of **castrīs** in sentence 4,
421. (5) Explain the case of **sē**, line 11, **421.** (6) Explain the use
of the infinitive **ferre** in line 12, **421.**

FOURTEENTH REVIEW LESSON

423. VOCABULARY REVIEW

aciēs, -ēī, F.

cīvis, cīvis, M. *and* F.

cliēns, clientis, M.

collis, collis, M.

equitātus, -ūs, M.

latus, lateris, N.

metus, -ūs, M.

multitūdō, -inis, F.

opus, operis, N.

prīncipātus, -ūs, M.

senātus, -ūs, M.

supplicium, -ī, N.

ego, meī

tū, tuī

brevis, -e

ingēns, *gen.* ingentis

medius, -a, -um

posterus, -a, -um

veterānus, -a, -um

circiter

deinde

dēnique

etiam

posteā

proximē

sōlum

adveniō, -venīre, -vēnī, -ventum

āvertō, -ere, āvertī, āversum

cēdō, -ere, cessī, cessum

committō, -mittere, -mīsī, -missum

cōnferō, -ferre, -tulī, -lātum

cōnor, -ārī, cōnātus sum

cōnspiciō, -spicere, -spexī, -spectum

convertō, -vertere, -vertī, -versum

dēcēdō, -cēdere, -cessī, -cessum

ferō, ferre, tulī, lātum

īnferō, -ferre, -tulī, -lātum

īnstruō, -ere, īnstrūxī, īnstrūctum

intellegō, -legere, -lēxī, -lēctum

lacessō, -ere, -īvī, -ītum

pereō, -īre, -iī *or* -īvī, -itum

polliceor, -ērī, pollicitus sum

possum, posse, potuī

potior, potīrī, potītus sum

redeō, -īre, -iī *or* -īvī, -itum

renūntiō, -āre, -āvī, -ātum

restituō, -ere, -uī, -ūtum

sequor, sequī, secūtus sum

sustineō, -ēre, -uī, sustentum

tegō, -ere, tēxī, tēctum

ūtor, ūtī, ūsus sum

vereor, verērī, veritus sum

424. RELATED ENGLISH WORDS

advent	confer	intelligent	senate
brevity	contradict	lateral	sequence
civic	infer	multitude	sustain
client	intellect	operation	use

LESSON LXXI

DEPONENT VERBS (Continued): PREDICATE NOMINATIVE WITH PASSIVE VERBS

DEPONENT VERBS (Continued)

425. Deponent verbs of the third conjugation ending in **-ior** are conjugated as follows:

ingredior, ingredī, ingressus sum, *enter*

PRESENT

SINGULAR
ingredior
ingrederis *or* ingredere
ingreditur

PLURAL
ingredimur
ingrediminī
ingrediuntur

IMPERFECT
ingrediēbar
ingrediēbāris *or* ingrediēbāre,
etc.

FUTURE
ingrediar
ingrediēris *or* ingrediēre,
etc.

PERFECT
ingressus sum,
etc.

PAST PERFECT
ingressus eram,
etc.

FUTURE PERFECT
ingressus erō,
etc.

Infinitives	*Participles*	*Imperative*
PRES. ingredī	PRES. ingrediēns	SING. ingredere
PAST ingressus esse	PAST ingressus	PLUR. ingrediminī
FUT. ingressūrus esse	FUT. ingressūrus	

THE PREDICATE NOMINATIVE WITH CERTAIN PASSIVE VERBS

426. Verbs meaning to *call, name, appoint, make,* and the like, when used in the passive, may be followed by a predicate nominative.

Ariovistus rēx appellātus est, *Ariovistus was called king.*

a. A predicate noun used with an infinitive which has its subject in the accusative is also in the accusative.

THE DEFECTIVE VERB *COEPĪ*

427. The verb **coepī,** *I began,* is used only in the perfect, past perfect, and future perfect. The other tenses are replaced by forms of **incipiō.**

428.   **VOCABULARY**

appellō, -āre, -āvī, -ātum, call, name

C., *abbreviation for* **Gaius,** *a Roman name*

coepī, coepisse, coeptum, began

ingredior, ingredī, ingressus sum, enter, invade (*sometimes followed by* **intrā** *and accusative*)

intrā, *prep. w. acc.,* within, into

Marius, -ī, M., Marius, *a Roman name;* Gaius Marius, *a famous Roman general*

memoria, -ae, F., memory

Vesontiō, Vesontiōnis, M., Vesontio, *a town of Gaul, now Besançon*

EXERCISES

429. 1. Celtae Gallī appellantur. 2. Tum frūmentum Vesontiōnem cōnferre coepērunt. 3. Hoc flūmen quod Helvētiī trānsībant Arar appellātur. 4. Caesar intrā fīnēs Gallōrum ingressus est et multa oppida eōrum cēpit. 5. Gallī magnīs scūtīs ūsī sunt. 6. Dīcis hoc oppidum appellārī Genavam. 7. Impigrē labōrāre coeperās quod patrī tuō placēre cupiēbās.

CAESAR PROMISES HELP

Caesar Haeduōs dēfendere cōnstituit quod hī ā senātū frātrēs appellātī erant. Itaque auxilium suum pollicitus est. Ōlim Germānī intrā prōvinciam ingressī erant atque magnam calamitātem intulerant. Dēnique ā C. Mariō superātī sunt, sed memoria eius bellī apud Rōmānōs manēbat.

STREET OF POMPEII

430. 1. The Haeduans were called friends by the Romans. 2. The Gauls began to set fire to their villages. 3. Orgetorix was called the leader of the Helvetians. 4. We shall gain possession of the weapons of the enemy. 5. The soldiers did not use javelins. 6. Those who had begun to cross the river were repulsed. 7. This town of the Gauls is called Vesontio. 8. The cavalry could not follow through the mountains.

SUGGESTED DRILL

(1) Conjugate **coepī** in the perfect and the past perfect of the indicative. (2) Give a synopsis of **ingredior** in the second person singular and the third person plural. (3) Name the verbs which take their objects in the ablative. (4) Explain the case of **Arar** in sentence 3, **429**. (5) Explain the case of **Genavam** in sentence 6, **429**.

LESSON LXXII

INTERROGATIVE PRONOUN: INTERROGATIVE PARTICLES

THE INTERROGATIVE PRONOUN

431. The interrogative pronoun **quis? quid?** *who? what?* is declined as follows in the singular:

Masc. and Fem.	*Neut.*
Nom. quis	quid
Gen. cuius	cuius
Dat. cui	cui
Acc. quem	quid
Abl. quō	quō

The plural forms are the same as those of the relative pronoun.

a. The interrogative adjective **quī, quae, quod,** is declined like the relative, except that the masculine nominative singular may be either **quī** or **quis.**

Quis hoc fēcit? *Who did this?* (pronoun)
Quod templum incēnsum est? *What temple was burned?* (adjective)

INTERROGATIVE PARTICLES

432. (1) Questions which merely ask for information and have no interrogative pronoun or adverb, usually have the enclitic **-ne** added to the first word.

Vēnitne legiō? *Has the legion come?*

(2) Questions which imply that the answer "yes" is expected are regularly introduced by **nōnne.**

Nōnne Caesar fortis erat? *Was not Caesar brave?*

433.   VOCABULARY

colloquium, -ī, N., conference, interview

cōnsulātus, -ūs, M., consulship

eō, *adv.,* to that place, there, thither

gravor, -ārī, gravātus sum, be unwilling

īnsolenter, *adv.,* insolently

queror, querī, questus sum, complain

quis, quid, who? what? (*for adj. forms, see* **431,** *a*)

respondeō, -ēre, respondī, respōnsum, answer, reply

EXERCISES

434. 1. Quis colloquium postulāvit? 2. Nōnne Caesar id postulāvit? 3. Nōnne Ariovistus ad colloquium vēnit? 4. Respōnditne īnsolenter lēgātīs quī ad eum vēnerant? 5. Quid Ariovistus timēbat? 6. Lēgātus cum ducibus eō pervēnit. 7. Cuius gladium hic puer fert? 8. Helvētiī in hōc itinere magnō numerō carrōrum ūsī sunt.

CAESAR REQUESTS A CONFERENCE

Caesar ad Ariovistum lēgātōs (*envoys*) mīsit et colloquium postulāvit. In cōnsulātū Caesaris Ariovistus ā senātū amīcus appellātus erat. Sed tamen ad colloquium venīre gravābātur et īnsolenter respondit. Caesar iterum lēgātōs mīsit et dē iniūriīs Haeduōrum questus est. Eadem respōnsa ab Ariovistō data sunt quae anteā (data erant).

435. 1. Who complained regarding the wrongs of the Haeduans? 2. Did not Caesar make war on the Helvetians? 3. Were the Romans defeated? 4. What did the man who ascended the mountain see? 5. Is this river wide? 6. What legion will be sent there?

SUGGESTED DRILL

(1) Explain the derivation and the meaning of the English words *colloquy* and *querulous*. (2) Explain the derivation of the Latin noun **respōnsum.** (3) Compare the adverb **īnsolenter** (from the adjective **īnsolēns**). (4) Decline **cōnsulātus** in the singular. (5) Decline the relative pronoun.

LESSON LXXIII

QUĪDAM, QUISQUE: IMPERSONAL VERBS

DECLENSION OF *QUĪDAM* AND *QUISQUE*

436. The indefinite pronoun or adjective **quīdam,** *a certain, a certain one,* is declined as follows:

SINGULAR

	Masc.	*Fem.*	*Neut.*
NOM.	quīdam	quaedam	quoddam *or* quiddam
GEN.	cuiusdam	cuiusdam	cuiusdam
DAT.	cuidam	cuidam	cuidam
ACC.	quendam	quandam	quoddam *or* quiddam
ABL.	quōdam	quādam	quōdam

PLURAL

NOM.	quīdam	quaedam	quaedam
GEN.	quōrundam	quārundam	quōrundam
DAT.	quibusdam	quibusdam	quibusdam
ACC.	quōsdam	quāsdam	quaedam
ABL.	quibusdam	quibusdam	quibusdam

a. The form **quiddam** is used as a pronoun, **quoddam** as an adjective.

b. **Quīdam** may sometimes be translated by the indefinite article *a* or *an.*

437. **Quisque,** *each,* when used as a pronoun is declined as follows in the singular:

	Masc. and Fem.	*Neut.*
NOM.	quisque	quidque
GEN.	cuiusque	cuiusque
DAT.	cuique	cuique
ACC.	quemque	quidque
ABL.	quōque	quōque

a. As an adjective the nominative is **quisque, quaeque, quodque,** and the other case forms are the same as those of the relative, with the suffix **-que.** The plural is rare.

IMPERSONAL VERBS

438. Impersonal verbs have only the third person singular, the infinitives, and occasionally the participles. They are sometimes translated by English impersonal verbs with *it* as subject, but the English equivalent is often a verb with a personal subject. Many of these may take a clause or an infinitive with or without the accusative as subject. Among the most important are **oportet** and **licet.**

Eum venīre oportet, *he ought to come* (*it is necessary for him to come*).

a. Many intransitive verbs also are used impersonally in the passive.

Pugnātur, *it is being fought* (*a fight is going on*).
Perventum est, *it was arrived* (*they arrived*).

439.   **VOCABULARY**

Cimberius, -ī, M., Cimberius, *a German chief*

licet, -ēre, licuit, it is permitted

Nasua, -ae, M., Nasua, *a German chief*

oportet, -ēre, oportuit, it is necessary, it is proper, one ought

quīdam, quaedam, quoddam *or* **quiddam,** a certain, a certain man, etc.

quisque, quidque, *pron.*, each one, each; *as adj.*, **quisque, quaeque, quodque,** each

Rhēnus, -ī, M., the Rhine

rīpa, -ae, F., bank (*of a stream*)

Suebī, -ōrum, M. *pl.*, the Suebi

EXERCISES

440. 1. Statim prōcēdere licet. 2. Amīcum manēre oportet. 3. Quisque sēcum frūmentum tulit. 4. Quendam mīlitem ad castra hostium mīsit. 5. Fortiter pugnātum est. 6. Diū ab Helvētiīs pugnātum erat. 7. Quīdam Gallus cum epistulā ad urbem missus est. 8. Quemque frūmentum domō portāre iussērunt.

THE SUEBI AT THE RHINE

Intereā nova manus Germānōrum ad rīpās Rhēnī vēnerat et trānsīre cōnābātur. Hī erant Suēbī, quae gēns est magnae virtūtis inter Germānōs.

Duo frātrēs, Nasua et Cimberius, eīs praeerant. Lēgātī Haeduōrum et Trēverōrum eam rem Caesarī ēnūntiāvērunt. Hīs rēbus audītīs, Caesar frūmentum comparāvit et ad Ariovistum contendit.

441. 1. We gave a reward to each. 2. A certain man demanded aid. 3. The soldier ought to fight bravely. 4. They ordered

ROMAN MOSAIC

each one to carry a weapon. 5. No one ought to fear. 6. The Germans did not attack Vesontio, because they could not cross the river.

––––––

SUGGESTED DRILL

(1) Decline together **quīdam cīvis**. (2) Give all the forms of **oportet** in the indicative. (3) Give the perfect infinitives of **licet** and **oportet**. (4) Explain the case of **amīcum** in sentence 2, and of **domō** in sentence 8, 440. (5) Give the Latin noun with which the English word *riparian* is connected in derivation, and explain its meaning in the phrase *riparian rights*.

LESSON LXXIV

SEMI-DEPONENTS: THE ENCLITIC *-QUE*

SEMI-DEPONENTS

442. There are four verbs which are deponent in the perfect system but which have active forms in the present system. Their principal parts are as follows:

> **audeō, -ēre, ausus sum,** *dare*
> **gaudeō, gaudēre, gāvīsus sum,** *rejoice*
> **soleō, solēre, solitus sum,** *be accustomed*
> **fīdō, fīdere, fīsus sum,** *trust*

a. The compounds of **fīdō,** also, are semi-deponents.

b. The synopsis of **audeō** in the first person singular of the indicative is as follows:

Pres.	audeō	Perf.	ausus sum
Impf.	audēbam	P. Perf.	ausus eram
Fut.	audēbō	F. Perf.	ausus erō

THE ENCLITIC *-QUE*

443. The enclitic conjunction **-que,** *and,* connects more closely than **et.** It is translated before the word to which it is joined.

Legiō equitātusque, *the legion and the cavalry.*

444.   **VOCABULARY**

audeō, audēre, ausus sum, dare

cingō, -ere, cīnxī, cīnctum, surround

facultās, -tātis, f., opportunity, supply

paene, *adv.,* almost

prior, prius, *comparative adjective,* former, first, previous

-que, and

soleō, solēre, solitus sum, be accustomed

ūsus, -ūs, m., use, advantage

EXERCISES

445. 1. Paene omnēs equitēs in eō proeliō interfectī sunt.
2. Quod ea legiō nōn prior trānsīre audēbat, proelium nōn
commissum est. 3. Mīlitēs veterānī nōn fugere solent, sed
eō diē perterritī sunt. 4. Nēmō dīcere ausus est. 5. Obsidēs
accipere solitī erant. 6. Dux mīlitēsque interfectī sunt. 7.
Caesarem eōs prohibēre oportet. 8. Quandam urbem incendērunt. 9. Mēcum īre licet.

THE RACE FOR VESONTIO

Ariovistus Vesontiōnem occupāre cōnātus est. Id erat
maximum oppidum Sēquanōrum et magnam facultātem habēbat eārum rērum quae ad bellum ūsuī (**196**) erant. Flūmen
paene tōtam urbem cingēbat atque ūnā ex parte erat mōns
magnā altitūdine. Quod hoc oppidum facile dēfendī poterat
Caesar quoque id occupāre cupiēbat. Itaque magnīs itineri-
bus eō contendit et prior advēnit.

446. 1. The soldiers did not dare complain. 2. They had
always been accustomed to do this. 3. The town and the
camp will be set on fire. 4. We ought to go at once. 5.
Caesar said that (**395**) the town was easily defended. 6. He
will hasten to that place with the cavalry. 7. Slave, do you
dare kill Gaius Marius?

SUGGESTED DRILL

(1) Give a synopsis of **soleō** in the third person singular and plural
in the indicative. (2) Give a synopsis of **fīdō** in the first person
singular and the third person singular in the indicative. (3) Decline
prior. (4) Give the accusative singular and plural of **quīdam.** (5)
Conjugate **cingō** in the perfect active and the past perfect passive of
the indicative.

LESSON LXXV

ALIQUIS, QUISQUAM: ABLATIVE OF CAUSE

THE INDEFINITES *ALIQUIS* AND *QUISQUAM*

447. The indefinite pronoun **aliquis**, *someone, anyone,* is declined as follows:

SINGULAR

	Masc.	Fem.	Neut.
Nom.	aliquis *or* aliquī	aliqua	aliquid *or* aliquod
Gen.	alicuius	alicuius	alicuius
Dat.	alicui	alicui	alicui
Acc.	aliquem	aliquam	aliquid *or* aliquod
Abl.	aliquō	aliquā	aliquō

PLURAL

Nom.	aliquī	aliquae	aliqua
Gen.	aliquōrum	aliquārum	aliquōrum
Dat.	aliquibus	aliquibus	aliquibus
Acc.	aliquōs	aliquās	aliqua
Abl.	aliquibus	aliquibus	aliquibus

a. The forms **aliquis** and **aliquid** in the singular are used as pronouns; the forms **aliquī, aliqua,** and **aliquod** are adjectives, with the meaning *some.*

448. The indefinite pronoun **quisquam**, *any one at all,* is declined as follows:

	Masc. and Fem.	Neut.
Nom.	quisquam	quicquam
Gen.	cuiusquam	cuiusquam
Dat.	cuiquam	cuiquam
Acc.	quemquam	quicquam
Abl.	quōquam	quōquam

a. **Quisquam** is used chiefly in sentences containing a negative or a comparative, or in conditions. It has no plural. The plural forms of **ūllus** are used when a plural is needed.

THE ABLATIVE OF CAUSE

449. The ablative with or without a preposition (**ab, dē, ex**) is used to express cause.

> **Multīs dē causīs,** *for many reasons (because of many reasons).*
>
> **Numerō suō glōriātī sunt,** *they boasted of their numbers (because of their numbers).*

450. VOCABULARY

aliquis, aliquid, *pron.,* some one; **aliquī, aliqua, aliquod,** *adj.,* some

fleō, flēre, flēvī, flētum, weep, lament

glōrior, -ārī, glōriātus sum, boast

magnitūdō, magnitūdinis, F., size, magnitude

quisquam, ⸤uicquam, any one at all

tabernāculum, -ī, N., tent

testāmentum, -ī, N., will

timor, timōris, M., fear

EXERCISES

451. 1. Lēgātus aliquem cum epistulā mīsit. 2. Nūllus sonus in eō locō audītus est neque quisquam vīsus est. 3. Caesar virtūte ūnīus legiōnis glōriātus est. 4. Intellegimus eum glōriātum esse. 5. Exīstimāvit eam legiōnem fortissimam esse.

PANIC IN THE ROMAN ARMY

In eō oppidō exercitus paucōs diēs mānsit. Hīs diēbus mīlitēs perterritī sunt quod Gallī dīxērunt Germānōs magnā virtūte et ingentī magnitūdine corporum esse. Is timor tōtum exercitum occupāvit. Multī flentēs ad tabernācula sua iērunt et testāmenta fēcērunt. Magnae silvae inter Ariovistum et exercitum Rōmānum erant, et iter erat perīculōsum.

452. 1. Some one saw the boy in the forest. 2. You often boast of the friendship of the Romans. 3. For (from) these reasons the town will be easily defended. 4. Roman soldiers were not always brave, but they defeated many enemies. 5. Diviciacus, weeping, implored aid from Caesar. 6. I have never given praise to anyone who did not work.

SUGGESTED DRILL

(1) Give a synopsis of **glōrior** in the third person singular in the indicative. (2) Explain what is meant by an *impersonal verb*. (3) Give all the forms of **licet** in the indicative. (4) Decline the interrogative pronoun. (5) Explain the case of **virtūte** in sentence 3, 451.

FIFTEENTH REVIEW LESSON

453.
(1) Interrogative pronouns.
(2) The declension of **quīdam** and **quisque**.
(3) The declension of **aliquis** and **quisquam**.
(4) Deponent verbs.
(5) The conjugation of **ferō**.
(6) Semi-deponent verbs.
(7) The imperative mood.
(8) The predicate nominative with passive verbs.
(9) The ablative of cause.
(10) The ablative with **ūtor**, etc.

454. Give Latin words with which the following English words are connected in derivation:

appeal	license	respond
audacious	magnitude	tabernacle
colloquy	memory	testament
faculty	priority	timorous
ingredient	querulous	

TENTH SUPPLEMENTARY REVIEW

VOCABULARY REVIEW

1. appellō, -āre, -āvī, -ātum
2. audeō, -ēre, ausus sum
3. cīvis, cīvis, M.
4. coepī, coepisse, coeptum
5. dormiō, -īre, -īvī, -ītum
6. etiam, *adv.*
7. exīstimō, -āre, -āvī, -ātum
8. expellō, -pellere, -pulī, -pulsum
9. exstruō, -struere, -strūxī, -strūctum
10. impellō, -pellere, -pulī, -pulsum
11. iūs, iūris, N.
12. legō, -ere, lēgī, lēctum
13. levis, -e
14. licet, -ēre, licuit
15. locō, -āre, -āvī, -ātum
16. magnitūdō, -dinis, F.
17. memoria, -ae, F.
18. multitūdō, -dinis, F.
19. -ne (*enclitic*)
20. obsideō, -sidēre, -sēdī, -sessum
21. oportet, -ēre, oportuit
22. perītus, -a, -um
23. posteā, *adv.*
24. potestās, -tātis, F.
25. -que, *conj.* (*enclitic*)
26. quis, quid
27. respondeō, -spondēre, -spondī, -spōnsum
28. sedeō, -ēre, sēdī, sessum
29. senātus, -ūs, M.
30. sentiō, -īre, sēnsī, sēnsum
31. sūmō, -ere, sūmpsī, sūmptum
32. supplicium, -ī, N.
33. sustineō, -tinēre, -tinuī, -tentum
34. timor, -ōris, M.

---

1. name, call
2. dare, venture
3. citizen
4. began
5. sleep
6. even, also
7. think, consider
8. drive out
9. pile up, erect
10. drive on, excite
11. justice, right
12. pick, gather, read
13. light (*in weight*)
14. it is lawful, permitted
15. place, put, set
16. size, importance
17. memory
18. multitude

19. (*sign of a question*)
20. besiege
21. it is fitting
22. skilled, experienced
23. afterwards
24. power, authority, chance
25. and
26. who (*interrogative*)
27. answer
28. sit
29. senate
30. feel, realize
31. take, assume
32. punishment
33. hold up, sustain
34. fear

WORD STUDY: LATIN SUFFIXES

1. It is usually difficult to give exact meanings to Latin suffixes. Often we can only say that they are used in forming certain classes of words. They differ from prefixes in that they are not usually added to whole words to form new ones. Instead, words with which suffixes are employed are usually altered by the loss or change of one or more letters when a suffix is added. Thus, **cīvitās** is derived from **cīvis**, but the ending -**tās** instead of being added to **cīvis** is used with **cīvi-**.

2. There are numerous English adjectives and nouns which end in -*ant* or -*ent*, such as *independent, patient, tenant, apparent, constant*. Most of these words came from Latin present participles, which have stems ending in -**ant**, -**ent**, or -**ient**. These different endings all became -*ant* in French, and hence we have some words, as for example *tenant*, with the ending -*ant*, although the form of the Latin word from which it comes would lead us to expect the ending -*ent*. In many cases, however, we have the ending which we should expect from the spelling of the original Latin word.

RELATED ENGLISH WORDS

3. Explain the meaning of the following words and give Latin words with which they are connected in derivation.

audacious	expulsion	license
civic	locate	memorial
dormitory	jury	

LESSON LXXVI

**THE SUBJUNCTIVE: PRESENT SUBJUNCTIVE OF FIRST AND
SECOND CONJUGATIONS**

THE SUBJUNCTIVE MOOD

455.   The subjunctive mood has four tenses, the present,
the imperfect, the perfect, and the past perfect.

The present subjunctive of the first and second conjugations is as follows:

ACTIVE

SINGULAR	PLURAL	SINGULAR	PLURAL
portem	portēmus	moneam	moneāmus
portēs	portētis	moneās	moneātis
portet	portent	moneat	moneant

PASSIVE

SINGULAR	PLURAL	SINGULAR	PLURAL
porter	portēmur	monear	moneāmur
portēris, -re	portēminī	moneāris, -re	moneāminī
portētur	portentur	moneātur	moneantur

a. The sign of the present subjunctive in the first
conjugation is **ē**, which replaces the characteristic **ā** of
the conjugation.   In the second conjugation the sign
is **ā**, which is added to the present stem.

THE SUBJUNCTIVE IN EXPRESSIONS OF DESIRE

456.   The subjunctive expresses a variety of ideas, among
the most important of which is *desire* (*will* or *wish*).

a. The expression of desire may consist in urging
someone to act with the speaker.

Eum iuvēmus, *let us help him.*

b. The act desired may be expressed in the form of an order to be carried out by someone else than the person addressed.

Exercitum statim parēmus, *let us prepare an army at once.*

c. The negative used with the subjunctive of desire is **nē.**

Nē eum moneāmus, *let us not warn him.*

457. VOCABULARY

centuriō, centuriōnis, M., centurion, *an officer in the
Roman army*
cupiditās, -tātis, F., eagerness,
desire
decimus, -a, -um, tenth
doceō, -ēre, docuī, doctum,
teach, tell

incūsō, -āre, -āvī, -ātum, reprimand
mēns, mentis, F., mind, disposition, attitude
nē, *adv.,* not (*with subj. in
expressions of desire,* etc.)
praecipuē, *adv.,* especially
vehementer, *adv.,* severely

EXERCISES

458. 1. Hōs mīlitēs moneāmus. 2. Servī gladiōs et scūta portent. 3. Centuriō in eō locō maneat. 4. Nē eum vehe-menter incūsēmus. 5. Impigrē hodiē labōrēmus quod hoc opus cōnficere dēbēmus.

ORDER AND COURAGE RESTORED

Convocātō conciliō Caesar mīlitēs et centuriōnēs vehemen-ter incūsāvit. Eōs docuit (*told*) nūllam causam esse timōris. Decimam legiōnem quae nōn timuerat praecipuē laudāvit. Verbīs eius mentēs eōrum conversae sunt et cupiditās bellī inlāta est. Tum castra mōvit et septem diēs iter fēcit ad ea loca in quibus Ariovistum esse audierat.

459. 1. Let us move camp at once. 2. Let the legion remain in camp. 3. Let us praise the centurions of this legion. 4. Let them not fear this enemy whom they have often conquered. 5. The mountain which overhung was of great height. 6. The legions have not dared to follow the Germans through the forests.

(1) Conjugate **doceō** and **incūsō** in the present subjunctive, active and passive. (2) Conjugate **cōnor** and **polliceor** in the present subjunctive. (3) Name the tense and the mood of each verb in the sentences of **458**. (4) Decline **quisque**. (5) Name the semi-deponent verbs.

LESSON LXXVII

CLAUSES OF PURPOSE: PRESENT SUBJUNCTIVE OF THIRD AND FOURTH CONJUGATIONS

CLAUSES OF PURPOSE

460. The subjunctive is used in subordinate clauses introduced by **ut**, *that,* or **nē**, *that not,* to express the purpose of the main act.

Fugit ut perīculum vītet, *he flees that he may avoid danger (in order to avoid danger).*

Auxilium mittit nē hostēs oppidum capiant, *he sends aid that the enemy may not capture the town.*

a. The act which is expressed by a clause of this form is one which is desired (or one the prevention of which is desired). Hence the force of the mood is the same as in the independent clauses of the preceding lesson, that is, it expresses *desire* or, more exactly, *will.*

b. In English, purpose is commonly expressed by the infinitive or by phrases introduced by *in order to,* or by clauses introduced by *that* or *in order that.*

He came to see his friend; he came in order to see his friend; he came in order that he might see his friend.

Such phrases or clauses cannot be translated into Latin by the infinitive, but are rendered by **ut** (or **nē**) and the subjunctive. If the purpose clause is negative, **nē** is used.

do not use the infinitive in Latin

THE PRESENT SUBJUNCTIVE OF THE THIRD AND FOURTH CONJUGATIONS

461.

ACTIVE

SINGULAR

dūcam	capiam	audiam
dūcās	capiās	audiās
dūcat	capiat	audiat

PLURAL

dūcāmus	capiāmus	audiāmus
dūcātis	capiātis	audiātis
dūcant	capiant	audiant

PASSIVE

SINGULAR

dūcar	capiar	audiar
dūcāris, -re	capiāris, -re	audiāris, -re
dūcātur	capiātur	audiātur

PLURAL

dūcāmur	capiāmur	audiāmur
dūcāminī	capiāminī	audiāminī
dūcantur	capiantur	audiantur

462. ## VOCABULARY

adventus, -ūs, M., arrival, approach

gaudeō, gaudēre, gāvīsus sum, rejoice

īnsidiae, -ārum, F. *pl.*, treachery, ambush

nē, *conj.*, that not (*in clauses of purpose*)

pedes, peditis, M., foot soldier; *pl.*, infantrymen, infantry

proficīscor, proficīscī, profectus sum, set out

quīntus, -a, -um, fifth

ut, *conj.*, that

uterque, utraque, utrumque, each of two, each

EXERCISES

463. 1. Uterque proficīscitur ut urbem capiat. 2. Ūnam legiōnem relinquit ut locus mūniātur. 3. Iter āvertunt ut cōpiās Rōmānās sequantur. 4. Aciem īnstruit ut proelium committat. 5. Auxilium implōrant nē urbēs incendantur. 6. Cum omnibus cōpiīs proficīscāmur. 7. Caesar gāvīsus est quod Ariovistus colloquium postulāverat.

A Conference Is Arranged

Cognitō Caesaris adventū, Ariovistus lēgātōs ad eum mīsit et colloquium postulāvit. Diēs colloquiō cōnstitūtus est ex eō diē quīntus. Uterque ad colloquium cum equitātū et sine peditibus vēnit quod Ariovistus dīxit sē verērī īnsidiās. Sed Caesar decimam legiōnem prō equitātū dūxit quod equitātuī fidem nōn habēbat.

464. 1. He sends envoys in order to demand (that he may demand) a conference. 2. He remains in the city to see his friend. 3. He sends the soldiers that the town may be defended. 4. He brings (leads) the legion that he may not be surrounded (**circumvenīre**) through treachery. 5. Let us bring the cavalry and one legion with us (**387**).

SUGGESTED DRILL

(1) Conjugate **mittō** and **veniō** in the present active subjunctive. (2) Conjugate **proficīscor** and **potior** in the present subjunctive. (3) Give the third person plural of the present active subjunctive of **laudō, moveō, dēfendō,** and **mūniō.** (4) Conjugate **proficīscor** in the future tense. (5) Indicate the tense sign and personal ending of **moveat.**

ROMAN SEAL RINGS

LESSON LXXVIII

RELATIVE CLAUSES OF PURPOSE: PRESENT SUBJUNCTIVE OF *SUM* AND *POSSUM*

RELATIVE CLAUSES OF PURPOSE

465. Sometimes a relative pronoun is used to introduce a purpose clause.

Lēgātum mittit quī colloquium postulet, *he sends an envoy who shall demand (to demand) an interview.*

a. The relative clause of purpose is frequently employed in dependence upon a main clause which has a form of **mittō** or some one of its compounds as its verb.

466. The present subjunctive of **sum** and **possum** is as follows:

Singular	Plural	Singular	Plural
sim	sīmus	possim	possīmus
sīs	sītis	possīs	possītis
sit	sint	possit	possint

467. VOCABULARY

arroganter, *adv.*, insolently
ita, *adv.*, so, thus
loquor, loquī, locūtus sum, speak

parātus, -a, -um, prepared
postulātum, -ī, N., demand, request
priusquam, *conj.*, before

EXERCISES

468. 1. Homō mittitur quī sit dux exercitūs. 2. Exercitum dīvidit ut hostēs circumvenīre possit. 3. Legiōnem in castrīs relinquit quae hostēs repellat. 4. Lēgātōs mittet quī eadem postulent. 5. Sint omnēs fortēs.

Ariovistus Is Defiant

In eō colloquiō Caesar iterum questus est dē iniūriīs quās Ariovistus fēcerat, et quaedam (*certain things*) postulāvit. Hīs postulātīs Ariovistus arroganter respondit, atque ita locūtus est: Ego in Galliam vēnī priusquam populus Rōmānus. Nōn ego bellum Gallīs intulī sed Gallī mihi bellum intulērunt. Omnēs cōpiās eōrum proeliō superāvī. Parātus sum iterum dēcertāre. Sī tū in Galliā manēbis hostis tuus erō. Sī dēcēdēs amīcus erō.

469. 1. He demands help, that the city may not be captured. 2. I am leaving ten men to fortify this place (who shall fortify). 3. They are collecting forces that they may be able to lay waste the fields. 4. Caesar enrolls two new legions in order to defend the province. 5. Let us be brave in danger.

SUGGESTED DRILL

(1) Conjugate **loquor** in the present subjunctive and the future indicative. (2) Explain the mood of **sit** in sentence 1, and of **sint** in sentence 5, **468**. (3) Give the principal parts of **questus, respondit, intulī**, and **vēnī**. (4) Decline **quīdam**. (5) Conjugate **dēcēdō** in the present indicative and subjunctive, active voice.

ROMAN HELMETS

LESSON LXXIX

SUBSTANTIVE CLAUSES WITH VERBS OF DESIRE: IMPERFECT SUBJUNCTIVE

THE SUBJUNCTIVE IN SUBSTANTIVE CLAUSES DEPENDING ON WORDS OF DESIRE

470. Many verbs expressing or implying an idea of desire, such as those meaning *to persuade, command, urge, determine, wish,* and the like, may take as object a clause with its verb in the subjunctive. The conjunction is **ut**, negative **nē**. A clause of this kind is usually translated into English by an infinitive phrase.

Hīs persuāsit ut <u>exīrent</u>, *he persuaded them to go forth.*

THE IMPERFECT SUBJUNCTIVE

471. The imperfect subjunctive of all regular verbs has the tense sign **rē**[1] before the personal endings. Its forms are made on the present stem.

ACTIVE

SINGULAR

I.	II.	III.		IV.
portārem	monērem	dūcerem	caperem	audīrem
portārēs	monērēs	dūcerēs	caperēs	audīrēs
portāret	monēret	dūceret	caperet	audīret

PLURAL

portārēmus	monērēmus	dūcerēmus	caperēmus	audīrēmus
portārētis	monērētis	dūcerētis	caperētis	audīrētis
portārent	monērent	dūcerent	caperent	audīrent

---

[1]As has been previously stated, a long vowel in a tense sign or stem ending becomes short before the personal endings -m, -t, -nt, -r, and -ntur.

PASSIVE

SINGULAR

portārer	monērer	dūcerei	caperer	audīrer
portārēris	monērēris	dūcerēris	caperēris	audīrēris
or	*or*	*or*	*or*	*or*
portārēre	monērēre	dūcerēre	caperēre	audīrēre
portārētur	monērētur	dūcerētur	caperētur	audīrētur

PLURAL

portārēmur	monērēmur	dūcerēmur	caperēmur	audīrēmur
portārēminī	monērēminī	dūcerēminī	caperēminī	audīrēminī
portārentur	monērentur	dūcerentur	caperentur	audīrentur

a. The imperfect subjunctive may be formed by adding the personal endings to the present active infinitive, with the necessary changes in quantity. This statement applies to all irregular verbs as well as regular verbs.

472.   **VOCABULARY**

colloquor, colloquī, collocūtus sum, confer, converse

comprehendō, -hendere, -hendī, -hēnsum, seize

discēdō, -cēdere, -cessī, -cessum, withdraw

hortor, -ārī, -ātus sum, urge

imperō, -āre, -āvī, -ātum, command (*with dative*)

lapis, lapidis, M., stone

patior, patī, passus sum, permit, allow

redūcō, -ere, redūxī, reductum, lead back

EXERCISES

473.   1. Eī persuādet ut dēcēdat.   2. Eī persuāsit ut dēcēderet.   3. Eōs hortātur ut impetum sustineant.   4. Caesar legiōnem hortātus est ut impetum hostium fortiter sustinēret.   5. Mīlitem ad amīcum mīsit quī eum hortārētur ut venīret.

A Treacherous Attack

Intereā equitēs Germānōrum appropinquāvērunt et tēla lapidēsque in Rōmānōs iacere coepērunt. Caesar ex colloquiō discessit et suōs (201) ad castra redūxit. Eīs imperāvit nē tēla in Germānōs iacerent. Posteā Ariovistus lēgātōs mīsit et aliud colloquium postulāvit. Caesar duōs lēgātōs mīsit quī cum eō colloquerentur. Sed Ariovistus eōs comprehendit neque dīcere passus est.

CAESAR'S TRIUMPH

474. 1. I persuaded the boy to remain. 2. The man persuaded his brother to withdraw. 3. The soldiers urged the centurions to lead them to the camp. 4. No one commanded (**imperāre**) you to do this. 5. The king persuaded the Germans to cross the river.

SUGGESTED DRILL

(1) Conjugate **hortor** and **colloquor** in the imperfect subjunctive. (2) Decline together **īdem lapsis.** (3) Give a synopsis of **potior** in the third person singular, in the indicative and in the present and the imperfect subjunctive. (4) Explain the mood of **hortārētur** and of **venīret in** sentence 5, 473. (5) Analyze the forms **sustinērent** and **hortārētur.**

LESSON LXXX

SUBJUNCTIVE OF *FERŌ* AND *EŌ*: ANTICIPATORY SUBJUNCTIVE

THE PRESENT AND IMPERFECT SUBJUNCTIVE OF *FERŌ* AND *EŌ*

475.   PRESENT

ACTIVE		PASSIVE	
SINGULAR	PLURAL	SINGULAR	PLURAL
feram	ferāmus	ferar	ferāmur
ferās	ferātis	ferāris *or* ferāre	ferāminī
ferat	ferant	ferātur	ferantur

IMPERFECT

ACTIVE		PASSIVE	
SINGULAR	PLURAL	SINGULAR	PLURAL
ferrem	ferrēmus	ferrer	**ferrēmur**
ferrēs	ferrētis	ferrēris *or* ferrēre	ferrēminī
ferret	ferrent	ferrētur	ferrentur

PRESENT		IMPERFECT	
SINGULAR	PLURAL	SINGULAR	PLURAL
eam	eāmus	īrem	īrēmus
eās	eātis	īrēs	īrētis
eat	eant	īret	īrent

THE ANTICIPATORY SUBJUNCTIVE

476. The subjunctive may be used in subordinate clauses to refer to an act as expected or anticipated.

Exspectāvit dum frāter redīret, *he waited until his brother should return.*

a. The Anticipatory Subjunctive is most frequently used after conjunctions meaning *until* or *before*.

477.   **VOCABULARY**

commeātus, -ūs, M., supplies

cōnsīdō, -sīdere, -sēdī, -sessum, encamp

contineō, -ēre, continuī, contentum, restrain

dum, *conj.*, until

interclūdō, -ere, interclūsī, interclūsum, cut off

postrīdiē, *adv.*, the next day

ultrā, *prep. w. acc.*, beyond

EXERCISES

478. 1. Auxilium mīsit priusquam urbs caperētur. 2. In castrīs exspectābant dum auxilium ferrētur. 3. Ad oppidum pervēnit priusquam hostēs fūgerent. 4. Ex urbe exeāmus ut proelium committāmus. 5. Domī puer manēbat dum frāter redīret. 6. Auxilium ferāmus et amīcōs iuvēmus.

CAESAR OFFERS BATTLE

Eōdem diē Ariovistus castra mōvit et sex mīlibus passuum ā Caesaris castrīs cōnsēdit. Postrīdiē castra ultrā Caesarem fēcit ut eum commeātū interclūderet. Caesar aciem īnstrūxit sed Ariovistus suōs castrīs (*in camp*) continuit, neque proelium commīsit. Equitēs autem Germānōrum cum equitātū Rōmānōrum proeliō contendēbant.

479. 1. The Germans waited until Caesar should move camp. 2. We seized the camp before the enemy fled. 3. The soldiers will set out to bring aid. 4. The centurion urged the legion to go by this road (that it should go, etc.). 5. Ariovistus restrained his men until the Romans should move their camp.

SUGGESTED DRILL

(1) Conjugate **cōnferō** in the present subjunctive passive and the imperfect subjunctive active. (2) Conjugate **trānseō** in the present and imperfect subjunctive. (3) Give a synopsis of **exeō** in the third person plural of the indicative and in the present and imperfect subjunctive. (4) Explain the mood of **fūgerent** in sentence 3, **478.**

SIXTEENTH REVIEW LESSON

480. VOCABULARY REVIEW

adventus, -ūs, M.

commeātus, -ūs, M.

cōnsulātus, -ūs, M.

cupiditās, -tātis, F.

facultās, -tātis, F.

īnsidiae, -ārum, F. *pl.*

lapis, lapidis, M.

mēns, mentis, F.

pedes, peditis, M.

postulātum, -ī, N.

rīpa, -ae, F.

tabernāculum, -ī, N.

testāmentum, -ī, N.

timor, timōris, M.

ūsus, -ūs, M.

parātus, -a, -um

prior, prius

arroganter

eō

īnsolenter

ita

paene

postrīdiē

praecipuē

vehementer

aliquis, aliquid

quīdam, quaedam, quoddam

quis? quid?

quisquam, quicquam

quisque, quidque

uterque, utraque, utrumque

appellō, -āre, -āvī, -ātum

audeō, -ēre, ausus sum

cingō, -ere, cīnxī, cīnctum

coepī, coepisse, coeptum

colloquor, colloquī, collocūtus sum

contineō, -ēre, continuī, contentum

doceō, -ēre, docuī, doctum

gaudeō, -ēre, gāvīsus sum

glōrior, -ārī, glōriātus sum

hortor, -ārī, hortātus sum

imperō, -āre, -āvī, -ātum

ingredior, ingredī, ingressus sum

licet, licēre, licuit

loquor, loquī, locūtus sum

oportet, -ēre, oportuit

patior, patī, passus sum

queror, querī, questus sum

redūcō, -ere, redūxī, reductum

soleō, -ēre, solitus sum

481. RELATED ENGLISH WORDS

arrogantly	docile	loquacious
comprehend	exhort	mental
contain	imperative	reduce
cupidity	insidious	vehemently

LESSON LXXXI

IMPERFECT SUBJUNCTIVE OF *SUM* AND *POSSUM:* RESULT CLAUSES

THE IMPERFECT SUBJUNCTIVE OF *SUM* AND *POSSUM*

482. The irregular verb **sum** and its compound, **possum**, are conjugated in the imperfect subjunctive as follows:

SINGULAR	PLURAL	SINGULAR	PLURAL
essem	essēmus	possem	possēmus
essēs	essētis	possēs	possētis
esset	essent	posset	possent

a. These forms may be found by adding the personal endings to the present infinitives (**471,** *a*).

THE SUBJUNCTIVE IN CLAUSES OF RESULT

483. Subordinate clauses expressing result are introduced by **ut** (occasionally by a relative pronoun) and have their verbs in the subjunctive.

ita arroganter respondit ut omnēs īrātī essent, *he answered so arrogantly that all were angry.*

a. The negative used in clauses of result is **nōn.**

b. The subjunctive in these clauses usually states a fact and is translated by the English indicative, as in the example above.

484. ### VOCABULARY

dēligō, -ere, dēlēgī, dēlēctum, choose, select

dīligenter, *adv.,* diligently

idōneus, -a, -um, suitable, appropriate

perficiō, -ere, perfēcī, perfectum, complete

tam, *adv.,* so (*with adjectives or adverbs*)

undique, *adv.,* on all sides

EXERCISES

485. 1. Tam celeriter mīlitēs castra undique circumvēnē-
runt ut nēmō fugere posset. 2. Puerī tam dīligenter labōrāvērunt ut multī eōs laudārent. 3. Illīs hominibus persuā-
simus ut nōbīs amīcī essent. 4. Legiō pervenīre contendēbat
priusquam oppidum expugnārētur. 5. Mīlitēs ita ācriter
pugnāvērunt ut omnēs hostēs fugerent.

THE ROMANS FORTIFY ANOTHER CAMP

Ubi *(when)* Caesar vīdit Germānōs castrīs sē continēre,
aliud cōnsilium cēpit *(formed)*. Locum idōneum dēlēgit et
castra parva mūnīre coepit. Ariovistus equitēs ad eum
locum mīsit quī Rōmānōs terrērent. Hī autem repulsī sunt
atque opus perfectum est.

486. 1. The Gauls fought so fiercely that we could not
drive them back. 2. The horsemen were so brave that they
dared to make an attack on the legion. 3. We could not
persuade the soldiers to choose (that they choose) a suitable
place. 4. The Romans tried to complete the work before
the Helvetians should cross the river.

SUGGESTED DRILL

(1) Give a synopsis of **sum** in the third person singular of the indicative and of the present and the imperfect subjunctive. (2) Give a
synopsis of **possum** in the third person plural of the indicative and of
the present and the imperfect subjunctive. (3) Explain the subjunctive **expugnārētur** in sentence 4, 485. (4) Compare the adverb **dīligenter** (from the adjective **dīligens**). (5) Conjugate **perficiō** in the
present and the imperfect subjunctive, active voice.

LESSON LXXXII

PERFECT SUBJUNCTIVE: INDIRECT QUESTIONS

THE PERFECT SUBJUNCTIVE, ACTIVE VOICE

487. The perfect active subjunctive is formed on the perfect stem, with the tense sign **erī**.

SINGULAR

I.	II.	III.	IV.
portāverim	monuerim	dūxerim	audīverim
portāverīs	monuerīs	dūxerīs	audīverīs
portāverit	monuerit	dūxerit	audīverit

PLURAL

portāverīmus	monuerīmus	dūxerīmus	audīverīmus
portāverītis	monuerītis	dūxerītis	audīverītis
portāverint	monuerint	dūxerint	audīverint

THE PERFECT SUBJUNCTIVE, PASSIVE VOICE

488. The perfect passive subjunctive is made up of the past participle and the present subjunctive of **sum**.

portātus sim	monitus sim	ductus sim	audītus sim
portātus sīs,	monitus sīs,	ductus sīs,	audītus sīs,
etc.	*etc.*	*etc.*	*etc.*

INDIRECT QUESTIONS

489. An indirect question is a question which is quoted with changed form. Indirect questions depend on words of *asking, knowing, perceiving,* and the like:

> *He asked who the man was.* (Direct, *Who is the man?*)

In Latin, an indirect question has its verb in the subjunctive.

> **Sciō cūr timeās,** *I know why you fear.* (Direct, **Cūr timēs?** *Why do you fear?*)

490. **VOCABULARY**

arbitror, -ārī, arbitrātus sum, think

cōnfīdō, -ere, cōnfīsus sum (442), trust (*usually takes dative*)

dēmum, *adv.*, at last

ēdūcō, -ere, ēdūxī, ēductum, lead out

quaerō, -ere, quaesīvī, quae- sītum, ask

sciō, scīre, scīvī, scītum, know

vesper, vesperī, м., evening

EXERCISES

491. 1. Quaerō quis hic homō sit. 2. Nēmō intellegit quis hoc dōnum mīserit. 3. Scīmus cūr omnēs hunc puerum monuerint. 4. Nōn reperīre possum in quō locō amīcī nostrī habitāverint. 5. Pater tuus huic hominī nōn cōnfīdit quod eum honestum esse nōn arbitrātur. 6. Tam diū in silvā mānsit ut ante noctem domum pervenīre nōn posset.

The Battle Begins

Caesar duās legiōnēs in castrīs minōribus relīquit nē commeātū prohibērētur. Reliquōs in castra maiōra redūxit. Ariovistus statim partem cōpiārum mīsit quae impetum in eās legiōnēs faceret. Ācriter ad vesperum pugnātum est (438, *a*), sed Germānī repulsī sunt. Tum dēmum Ariovistus omnēs cōpiās ēdūxit ut proeliō dēcertāret.

492. 1. We know who has heard this. 2. The man asks who has promised a reward. 3. No one thinks that the enemy are brave. 4. The leader knows who has captured the town. 5. We shall find out where you have been. 6. The camp was so placed that the soldiers could see the bank of the river.

SUGGESTED DRILL

(1) Conjugate **possum** in the perfect indicative and the perfect subjunctive. (2) Conjugate **ferō** in the perfect subjunctive, active and passive. (3) Give a synopsis of **cōnfīdō** in the third person singular of the indicative. (4) Explain the mood of **mīserit** in sentence 2, and of **posset** in sentence 6, 491. (5) Explain the mood of **faceret**, line 10, 491, and of **dēcertāret**, line 12, 491.

LESSON LXXXIII

PAST PERFECT SUBJUNCTIVE

THE PAST PERFECT SUBJUNCTIVE, ACTIVE VOICE

493. The past perfect subjunctive in the active voice is formed on the perfect stem with the tense sign **issē**.

SINGULAR

I.	II.	III.	IV.
portāvissem	monuissem	dūxissem	audīvissem
portāvissēs	monuissēs	dūxissēs	audīvissēs
portāvisset	monuisset	dūxisset	audīvisset

PLURAL

portāvissēmus	monuissēmus	dūxissēmus	audīvissēmus
portāvissētis	monuissētis	dūxissētis	audīvissētis
portāvissent	monuissent	dūxissent	audīvissent

THE PAST PERFECT SUBJUNCTIVE, PASSIVE VOICE

494. The past perfect subjunctive in the passive voice is made up of the past participle and the imperfect subjunctive of sum.

I.	II.	III.	IV.
portātus essem	monitus essem	ductus essem	audītus essem
portātus essēs,	monitus essēs,	ductus essēs,	audītus essēs,
etc.	*etc.*	*etc.*	*etc.*

495. **VOCABULARY**

comminus, *adv.*, hand to hand
dexter, dextra, dextrum,
  right hand, right
firmus, -a, -um, firm, strong
minimē, *adv.*, least
premō, -ere, pressī, pressum,
  press hard, press

prōcurrō, -ere, prōcurrī, prō-cursum, run forward
sinister, sinistra, sinistrum,
  left hand, left
videor, vidērī, vīsus sum
  (*passive of* **videō** *as deponent*), seem

EXERCISES

496. 1. Puer quaesīvit cūr amīcus suus auxilium postulā-
visset. 2. Lēgātus repperit cūr mīlitēs urbem nōn dēfendis-
sent. 3. Crassus auxilium tulit nē ea pars repellerētur. 4.
Tam celeriter prōcurrērunt ut statim comminus pugnārētur.
5. Centuriō locum castrīs (*for a camp*) dēlēgit quī idōneus
vidēbātur.

A HARD-FOUGHT BATTLE

Caesar a dextrō cornū proelium commīsit quod ea pars
hostium minimē firma erat. Mīlitēs Rōmānī ācriter impetum
fēcērunt et Germānī celeriter prōcurrērunt. Comminus pugnātum est. Germānī ā sinistrā parte repulsī sunt sed ā
dextrā parte vehementer Rōmānōs premēbant. Ad eam
partem P. Crassus quī equitātuī praeerat auxilium tulit.

497. 1. No one knew why the soldiers had come. 2. We
asked why the soldiers had not been sent. 3. We know
who is defending the town. 4. The centurion persuaded
the scouts to set out. 5. Caesar made an attack before the
enemy fortified their camp.

SUGGESTED DRILL

(1) Give a synopsis of **pugnō** and of **portō** in the third person singular, active voice, in the indicative and the subjunctive. (2) Give
the tense signs of the past perfect indicative, the perfect subjunctive,
and the past perfect subjunctive in the active voice. (3) Explain the
mood of **repellerētur** in sentence 3, **496.** (4) Decline in the singular
the words **cornū dextrum.**

LESSON LXXXIV

INDIRECT DISCOURSE

498. A direct quotation is one which repeats the exact words of the original speaker.

He said, "I will come."

An indirect quotation is one which repeats the thought, but not the exact words of the original speaker.

He said that he would come.

In English, an indirect quotation is commonly introduced by the conjunction *that;* sometimes no conjunction is used.

499. In Latin, indirect quotations are expressed as follows:

(1) A main clause containing a statement has its verb in the infinitive with the subject in the accusative.

(2) A main clause containing a command has its verb in the subjunctive.

(3) All subordinate clauses have their verbs in the subjunctive.

Lēgātus dīxit locum quem centuriōnēs dēlēgissent nōn idōneum esse, *the lieutenant said that the place which the centurions had chosen was not suitable.*

a. The constructions of indirect discourse are used after words of *saying, thinking, knowing, perceiving,* and the like. For this use in simple sentences see **395.**

500.   **VOCABULARY**

incolumis, -e, safe
nam, *conj.*, for
regiō, regiōnis, F., region
remaneō, -manēre, -mānsī, -mānsum, remain

salūs, salūtis, F., safety
tergum, -ī, N., back
uxor, uxōris, F., wife
vertō, -ere, vertī, versum, turn; terga vertere, flee

EXERCISES

501. 1. Nūntius dīcit hostēs oppidum mūnīre quod impetum timeant. 2. Labiēnus cognōverat eās legiōnēs quae trāns flūmen essent in perīculō magnō esse. 3. Cōnsidius renūntiāvit Gallōs eum montem tenēre ad quem Labiēnus profectus esset. 4. Ariovistus dīxit sē bellum gerere quod Gallī sē oppugnāvissent. 5. In eā regiōne diū remānsī.

ROUT OF THE GERMANS

Dēnique Germānī repulsī sunt et terga vertērunt. Ad flūmen Rhēnum contendērunt quī ex eō locō circiter quīnque mīlia passuum aberat. Ibi paucī trānsiērunt et sibi salūtem reppererunt. In hīs fuit Ariovistus, sed fīlia eius atque duae uxōrēs interfectae sunt. Nam Ariovistus duās uxōrēs habēbat. Eī lēgātī quōs Caesar mīserat repertī sunt et incolumēs reductī sunt.

502. 1. The centurion said that the place which had been chosen for a camp was not suitable. 2. We think the boy is working because he fears his father. 3. The scouts reported to Caesar that the army which was approaching was large. 4. The enemy crossed the river so quickly that we were not able to fortify our camp. 5. The soldiers saw that Caesar was in danger.

SUGGESTED DRILL

(1) Indicate the base of the nouns **regiō** and **salūs**. (2) Give the three stems of the verb **vertō**. (3) Give the principal parts of **proficīscor** and of **reperiō**. (4) Conjugate **absum** in the imperfect indicative and imperfect subjunctive. (5) Give all the infinitives of **premō**, active and passive.

ROMAN CHARIOT RACE

ELEVENTH SUPPLEMENTARY REVIEW

VOCABULARY REVIEW

1. adventus, -ūs, M.
2. celer, celeris, celere
3. cōnfīdō, -fīdere, -fīsus sum
4. cōnsuētūdō, -dinis, F.
5. contineō, -tinēre, -tinuī, -tentum
6. cupiditās, -tātis, F.
7. dēligō, -ligere, -lēgī, -lēctum
8. dēpōnō, -pōnere, -posuī, -positum
9. dexter, -tra, -trum
10. dīligenter, *adv.*
11. discēdō, -cēdere, -cessī, -cessum
12. doceō, -ēre, -uī, -tum
13. dolor, -ōris, M.
14. ēdūcō, -dūcere, -dūxī, -ductum
15. expōnō, -pōnere, -posuī, -positum
16. idōneus, -a, -um
17. imperātor, -ōris, M.
18. imperō, -āre, -āvī, -ātum
19. incolumis, -e
20. interclūdō, -clūdere, -clūsī, -clūsum
21. mēns, mentis, F.
22. mors, mortis, F.
23. nam, *conj.*
24. necessārius, -a, -um
25. ōdī, ōdisse
26. officium, -ī, N.
27. oppōnō, -pōnere, -posuī, -positum
28. ostendō, -tendere, -tendī, -tentum
29. perficiō, -ficere, -fēcī, -fectum
30. premō, -ere, pressī, pressum
31. quaerō, -ere, quaesīvī, quaesītum
32. redūcō, -dūcere, -dūxī, -ductum
33. remaneō, -manēre, -mānsī, -mānsum
34. salūs, -ūtis, F.
35. sciō, scīre, scīvī, scītum
36. serviō, -īre, -īvī, -ītum
37. sinister, -tra, -trum
38. vulnus, -neris, N.

---

1. a coming (to), arrival
2. swift
3. trust
4. custom, habit
5. hold together, contain, confine

6. desire, greed
7. select, choose
8. put down, put aside
9. right (hand), *as adj.*
10. with care
11. go away, depart
12. teach, show
13. grief
14. lead out
15. set forth, explain
16. fit, suitable
17. commander, general
18. command, order
19. unharmed, safe
20. shut off, cut off, stop
21. mind
22. death

23. for
24. necessary, urgent
25. hate
26. duty, service, courtesy
27. put against, oppose
28. show
29. accomplish
30. press, oppress
31. seek, inquire
32. lead back
33. stay behind, remain
34. safety
35. know
36. serve
37. left (hand), *as adj.*
38. wound

WORD STUDY

1. Among the suffixes which are used in forming nouns are -ia, -tia, -ium, (-t)iō, -dō, -tās, -tūs, -tus (-sus)

Examples of their use in forming nouns from other nouns, from adjectives, and from verbs are the following:

From nouns:	From adjectives:	From verbs:
altitūdō (altus)	cīvitās (cīvis)	adventus (adveniō)
amīcitia (amīcus)	servitūs (servus)	cupiditās (cupiō)
celeritās (celer)	virtūs (vir)	oppugnātiō (oppugnō)

2. Some of these suffixes are represented in English derivatives from Latin as follows:

-ia appears as *-y*
  memoria, *memory*

-tia appears as *-ce* (or *-cy*)
  dīligentia, *diligence*

-ium appears as *-y* (or *-e*)
  subsidium, *subsidy*

(-t)iō appears as *(-t)ion*
  nātiō, *nation*

-tās appears as *-ty*
  nobilitās, *nobility*

-tus often drops **t**
  adventus, *advent*

LESSON LXXXV

INDIRECT DISCOURSE (Continued): *EŌ* (Completed)

INDIRECT DISCOURSE (Continued)

503. The infinitive in indirect discourse is present, past, or future, according as the verb in the direct discourse expressed present, past, or future time.

The subjunctive is regularly present or perfect if the verb on which the indirect discourse depends is present or future. It is regularly past or past perfect if the verb on which the indirect discourse depends is in any tense of past time.

THE CONJUGATION OF *EŌ* (Completed)

504. The imperatives, participles, and infinitives of **eō** are as follows:

Imperatives	*Participles*	*Infinitives*
SING. ī	PRES. iēns (*gen.* euntis)	PRES. īre
PLUR. īte	PAST itum	PAST īsse (iisse)
	FUT. itūrus	FUT. itūrus esse

505.   **VOCABULARY**

citerior, -ius, *comparative adj.*, nearer, hither

crēdō, -dere, -didī, -ditum, believe

pecūnia, -ae, F., money

praeficiō, -ficere, -fēcī, -fectum, put in command of

redigō, -ere, redēgī, redāctum, reduce

servitūs, servitūtis, F., slavery, servitude

Ubiī, -ōrum, M. *pl.*, the Ubii, *a German tribe*

EXERCISES

506. 1. Centuriō oppidō[1] praefectus est. 2. Labiēnus centuriōnem oppidō praefēcit. 3. Caesar vīdit Belgās exercitum condūxisse. 4. Omnēs existimābant hostēs impetum

---

[1] See 324.

factūrōs esse. 5. Lēgātus dīcit Germānōs discēdere quod pugnāre nōn cupiant. 6. Belgae crēdidērunt Rōmānōs in Galliā remanēre ut eam regiōnem in servitūtem redigerent. 7. Gallī auxilium petīvērunt et pecūniam pollicitī sunt.

THE END OF THE CAMPAIGN

Hōc proeliō cognitō trāns Rhēnum, Suēbī quī ad rīpās Rhēnī vēnerant domum redīre coepērunt. Ubiī quī eās regiōnēs incolēbant impetum in eōs in itinere fēcērunt atque magnum numerum interfēcērunt. Itaque duo bella ūnā aestāte cōnfecta sunt. (Haec erant bellum Helvētiōrum et bellum Germānōrum.) Caesar Labiēnum castrīs praefēcit; ipse in Galliam citeriōrem profectus est.

507. 1. The Ubii said that their fathers had inhabited that region. 2. The Romans found out that the Germans were brave. 3. Labienus knew that the scouts would set out. 4. The Ubii had not been reduced to (**in**) slavery. 5. We did not promise money to the slave.

SUGGESTED DRILL

(1) Decline together **meus liber.** (2) Explain the case of **oppidō** in sentence 2, 506. (3) Explain the case of **hostēs** in sentence 4, 506. (4) Give the accusative singular and the genitive plural of **citerior.** (5) Explain the mood of **redigerent** in sentence 6, 506.

SEVENTEENTH REVIEW LESSON

508. (1) The imperative, infinitives, and participles of **eō.**

(2) The present subjunctive of regular verbs.

(3) The present subjunctive of **sum** and **possum.**

(4) The subjunctive of regular verbs.

(5) The subjunctive of **sum** and **possum.**

(6) The perfect and past perfect subjunctive.

(7) The use of the subjunctive in main clauses.

(8) Clauses of purpose.

(9) Substantive clauses of desire.

(10) The anticipatory subjunctive.

(11) Indirect questions.

(12) Indirect discourse.

509. Give Latin words with which the following English words are connected in derivation:

arbitration	pecuniary	salutary
confide	perfect	servitude
credit	pressure	sinister
dexterity	remain	version
firm	requisition	vespers

LESSON LXXXVI

TENSES OF SUBJUNCTIVE IN SUBORDINATE CLAUSES: DESCRIPTIVE CLAUSES OF SITUATION

TENSES IN SUBORDINATE CLAUSES

510. The relation between the tense of a subjunctive[1] in a subordinate clause and the tense of the verb of the main clause on which it depends is usually as follows:

(1) If the tense of the main verb denotes present or future time, the dependent subjunctive is present or perfect.

(2) If the tense of the main verb denotes past time, the tense of the dependent subjunctive is imperfect or past perfect.

(3) The present and imperfect tenses of the subjunctive in subordinate clauses denote acts incomplete at the time of the

---

[1] The relation between the tense of a dependent indicative and that of the main verb is sufficiently evident from the English to cause the pupil no difficulty.

main verb. The perfect and past perfect denote acts complete at the time of the main verb.

    a. If the main verb is a perfect which is equivalent to an English present perfect, the dependent subjunctive is sometimes present or perfect.

    b. A result clause occasionally has its verb in the perfect after a main tense of past time.

DESCRIPTIVE CLAUSES OF SITUATION

511. A clause introduced by **cum** meaning *when,* with its verb in the imperfect or past perfect subjunctive, is used to describe the situation in which the act of the main clause took place.

    Cum pōns factus esset, exercitus flūmen trānsiit, *when the bridge had been made, the army crossed the river.*

512.   **VOCABULARY**

coniūrō, -āre, -āvī, -ātum, league together, plot

cum, *conj.,* when, since, although

lībertās, -tātis, F., liberty

mereor, merērī, meritus sum, deserve

ob, *prep. with accusative,* on account of

occīdō, -ere, occīdī, occīsum, kill

tantus, -a, -um, so great

inter sē, among themselves, to one another, one another

EXERCISES

513. 1. Mīlitēs eō diē magnam laudem meritī sunt. 2. Cum Belgae inter sē coniūrāvissent, bellum parāre coepērunt. 3. Ob eam rem Caesar statim profectus est. 4. Timor tantus erat ut multī flērent. 5. Cum nūntius hoc dīxisset, discessit. 6. Cum multī occīsī essent, reliquī fūgērunt.

PLOTS AMONG THE BELGIANS

Cum Caesar in citeriōre Galliā esset, Belgae contrā populum Rōmānum coniūrāre coepērunt. Eae gentēs quae proximae

erant ā Rōmānīs superātae erant. Exercitus Rōmānus in
Galliā hiemābat, quod numquam anteā factum erat. Itaque
Belgae potentiam populī Rōmānī timēbant et lībertātem suam
dēfendere cōnstituērunt. Cōpiās in ūnum locum condūxērunt
et bellum parāvērunt.

INTERIOR OF A HOUSE AT POMPEII (RESTORATION)

514. 1. When the lieutenant had drawn up the line of
battle, the enemy advanced. 2. The danger was so great
that all remained in the city. 3. On account of this fact
(*thing*) a legion was sent. 4. When the Belgians had seen
this, they began to league together. 5. We cannot remain
longer in this region.

———

SUGGESTED DRILL

(1) Conjugate **sum** and **possum** in the past perfect indicative and
the past perfect subjunctive. (2) Give a synopsis of **possum** in the
third person, singular and plural, of the indicative and subjunctive.
(3) Give the infinitives of **exeō** and **trānseō**. (4) Explain the mood
of **coniūrāvissent** in sentence 4, and of **flērent** in sentence 6, **513**.
(5) Conjugate **occīdō** in the perfect subjunctive, active voice.

LESSON LXXXVII

CONJUGATION OF *FIŌ*: SUBSTANTIVE CLAUSES OF FACT

THE CONJUGATION OF *FIŌ*

515. The verb **fīō**, *become* or *be made*, is used as the passive of **faciō** in the present system. The perfect system of **faciō** in the passive is regularly formed with the past participle and the forms of **sum**. The endings of **fīō** are those of the active voice. Its forms will be found in the Appendix, section 35.

> *a.* In this verb the vowel **i** is long before another vowel except in the imperfect subjunctive and the present infinitive.
>
> *b.* The third person singular, when followed by **ut** and the subjunctive, is commonly translated *it happens, it results, the result is.*

SUBSTANTIVE CLAUSES OF FACT [1] INTRODUCED BY *UT*

516. Some verbs and phrases which express the bringing about of an act or situation may take as object (or as subject in the passive) a dependent clause introduced by **ut**, with its verb in the subjunctive.

The words with which this type of clause is most frequently used are **faciō** and its compounds, and words meaning *to happen.*

> **Fīēbat ut omnēs timērent**, *it resulted (the result was) that all feared.*
>
> **Ea rēs effēcit ut castra tūta essent**, *this fact brought it about that the camp was safe (made the camp safe).*

---

[1] With the compounds of **faciō** a substantive clause of desire is sometimes used (470).

517. VOCABULARY

certus, -a, -um, certain

fīō, fierī, factus sum, become, be made

frūmentārius, -a, -um, of grain; **rēs frūmentāria,** grain supply

pābulum, -ī, N., forage

Pedius, -ī, M., Pedius, *a Roman name*

Q., *abbreviation for* **Quīntus,** *a Roman name*

Rēmī, -ōrum, M. *pl.*, the Remi, *a tribe of Gaul*

ulterior, ulterius, farther

certiōrem (certiōrēs) facere, to inform (*lit.* to make more certain); **certior (certiōrēs) fierī,** to be informed

a. The phrases **certiōrem (-ēs) facere, certior (-ēs) fierī,** may be followed by an infinitive with subject accusative.

Caesarem certiōrem fēcērunt hostēs fūgisse, *they informed Caesar that the enemy had fled.*

EXERCISES

518. 1. Fīēbat ut nōn facile domō exīre possent. 2. Dumnorīx fit dux equitātūs. 3. Hic vir certior factus est moram esse perīculōsam. 4. Dē hīs rēbus omnēs certiōrēs fīunt. 5. Rēmī Caesarem certiōrem faciunt.

Caesar Organizes a Larger Army

Caesar ā Labiēnō dē eā rē certior factus est. Itaque duās novās legiōnēs in Galliā citeriōre cōnscrīpsit. Q. Pedium lēgātum mīsit quī eās in Galliam ulteriōrem dūceret. Ipse, cum cōpia pābulī esset, ad exercitum vēnit. Rē frūmentāriā comparātā castra mōvit et quīndecim diēbus ad fīnēs Belgārum pervēnit. Cum eō (*there*) vēnisset, Rēmī quī proximī Galliae ex Belgīs sunt lēgātōs mīsērunt et pācem petiērunt.

519. 1. All things (**omnia**) which you command are being done. 2. The lieutenant is being informed concerning the danger. 3. The centurion was informed that the enemy were approaching. 4. We have informed the man that this

place is dangerous.   5. When the camp had been moved, the
Remi sent envoys.

(1) Decline the phrase **rēs frūmentāria** (used only in the singular).
(2) Give the Latin noun from which the adjective **frūmentārius** is
derived.   (3) Conjugate the verb **petō** in the perfect and the past perfect subjunctive passive.   (4) Explain the case of **dux** in sentence 2,
518.   (5) Explain the mood of **dūceret**, line 7, 518.

LESSON LXXXVIII

CUM CAUSAL CLAUSES: GENITIVE OF MATERIAL

CUM CAUSAL CLAUSES

520. A subordinate clause introduced by **cum** meaning
since, has its verb in the subjunctive.

> **Cum sē dēfendere nōn possent, auxilium ā Caesare
> petēbant,** *since they could not defend themselves, they
> requested aid from Caesar.*

THE GENITIVE OF MATERIAL

521. The genitive may be used to denote the material of
which something is composed or the persons making up a
collective noun.

> **Multitūdō Belgārum convēnit,** *a multitude of Belgians
> assembled.*

a. This use is found chiefly with collective nouns.

522.   VOCABULARY

adsum, adesse, adfuī, adfutū-   līberāliter, *adv.*, generously
  rus, be present, be at hand   onus, oneris, N., burden,
fluō, -ere, flūxī, flow   weight
gravis, -e, heavy, hard to bear,   ōrdō, ōrdinis, M., rank, order
  serious   vallēs, vallis, -ium, F., valley

EXERCISES

523. 1. Cum magnus numerus mīlitum in oppidō esset, hostēs impetum nōn fēcērunt. 2. Ariovistus magnam multitūdinem Germānōrum trādūxerat. 3. Cum iniūriae hostium gravēs sint, auxilium tuum petimus. 4. Quod onus armōrum magnum erat, nostrī vix flūmen trānsiērunt. 5. Huic puerō persuādēre potes ut domī maneat. 6. Eō diē omnēs ōrdinēs aderant. 7. Hoc flūmen per magnam vallem fluit, et multīs locīs trānsītur.

Submission of the Remi

Dīxērunt sē parātōs esse obsidēs dare et Rōmānōs frūmentō iuvāre. Dē hīs rēbus quae apud Belgās fīēbant, et dē numerō quem quaeque cīvitās ad hoc bellum pollicita erat Caesarem certiōrem fēcērunt. Caesar eīs līberāliter respondit et obsidēs eōrum accēpit. Dīviciācum Haeduum hortātus est ut cōpiae Haeduōrum in fīnēs Belgārum dūcerentur.

524. 1. Since Ariovistus remained in camp, Caesar led back his forces to the town. 2. Since the scouts are not present, we shall send three soldiers. 3. A multitude of Gauls and Germans were killed in flight. 4. The road was so narrow that a few could defend it. 5. When the first ranks had crossed, the rest followed at once.

SUGGESTED DRILL

(1) Explain the case of **Germānōrum** in sentence 2, and of **puerō** in sentence 5, 523. (2) Explain the case of **diē** in sentence 6, 523. (3) Explain the mood of **esset** in sentence 1, 523. (4) Give a synopsis of **adsum** in the third person plural of the indicative and the subjunctive. (5) Give the genitive plural of **ōrdō** and **vallēs**.

LESSON LXXXIX

CONJUGATION OF *VOLŌ: CUM* ADVERSATIVE CLAUSES

THE IRREGULAR VERB *VOLŌ*

525. The verb **volō**, *wish, be willing*, is irregular. Its principal parts are **volō, velle, voluī.**

PRESENT

Indicative		*Subjunctive*	
SINGULAR	PLURAL	SINGULAR	PLURAL
volō	volumus	velim	velīmus
vīs	vultis	velīs	velītis
vult	volunt	velit	velint

IMPERFECT

volēbam	volēbāmus	veliem	vellēmus
volēbās	volebātis	vellēs	vellētīs
volēbat	volēbant	vellet	vellent

FUTURE

volam	volēmus
volēs	volētis
volet	volent

PERFECT

voluī	voluimus	voluerim	voluerīmus

PAST PERFECT

volueram	voluerāmus	voluissem	voluissēmus

FUTURE PERFECT

voluerō	voluerimus

Participle	*Infinitives*	
volēns	PRES. velle	PAST voluisse

a. This verb has no imperatives.

CUM ADVERSATIVE CLAUSES

526. A subordinate clause introduced by **cum**, meaning *although*, has its verb in the subjunctive.

Cum perīculum magnum sit, tamen impetum faciēmus, *although the danger is great, still we shall make an attack.*

a. The adverb **tamen** usually stands in the main clause with which an adversative clause is connected.

527. **VOCABULARY**

Axona, -ae, F., the Aisne, *a river of France*
bene, *adv.,* well
Bibrax, Bibractis, F., Bibrax, *a town of Gaul*
difficultās, -tātis, F., difficulty

extrēmus, -a, -um, last, farthest, farthest part of
prōpōnō, -ere, prōposuī, prōpositum, point out, explain
tardē, *adv.,* slowly
volō, velle, voluī, wish, will

EXERCISES

528. 1. Cum paucī in oppidō essent, tamen hostēs id expugnāre nōn poterant. 2. Caesar proelium committere volēbat. 3. Cum nōn bene meritī sītis, tamen vōs iuvābimus. 4. Tardius appropinquāvērunt quod magna onera portābant. 5. Fīēbat ut nēmō huic hominī cōnfīderet. 6. Magnae difficultātēs itineris prōpōnēbantur, sed tamen omnēs proficīscī volēbant. 7. Vult, volet, vīs, volent.

LOCATION OF THE ROMAN CAMP

Ipse exercitum trāns flūmen Axonam, quod est in extrēmīs fīnibus Rēmōrum, dūxit et ibi castra posuit. Rīpae eius flūminis latus castrōrum mūniēbant. Itaque factum est ut commeātūs ad eum sine perīculō portārī possent. Nam fīnēs Rēmōrum post eum erant. Ab hīs castrīs oppidum Rēmōrum nōmine (**366**) Bibrax aberat mīlia passuum octō. Id Belgae magnō impetū oppugnāre coepērunt.

529. 1. Although the town is large, still a few soldiers can defend it. 2. This man wishes to live in the city. 3. Although the river was not deep, the legion advanced slowly. 4. The centurions could not persuade the soldiers to cross (**470**) the ditch. 5. The Germans wish to cross the Rhine.

SUGGESTED DRILL

(1) Give the derivation of the English words *extreme, tardy,* and *proposition.* (2) Give the Latin adjective from which the noun **difficultās** is derived. (3) Explain the case of **hominī** in sentence 5, 528. (4) Give the principal parts of **volēbant** and **cōnfīdāmus.** (5) Explain the mood of **cōnfīderet** in sentence 5, 528.

LESSON XC

CONJUGATION OF *NŌLŌ*: CLAUSES OF FEAR

CONJUGATION OF *NŌLŌ*

530. The verb **nōlō** is a compound of **volō** and **nōn.** Its forms will be found in the Appendix, section 36.

CONSTRUCTIONS WITH EXPRESSIONS OF FEAR

531. Verbs and other expressions of fear may take a dependent clause with the subjunctive, introduced by **nē,** meaning *that,* or **ut,** meaning *that not.*

Verēbantur nē exercitus noster in Galliā manēret, *they feared that our army would remain in Gaul.*

Timeō ut sē fortiter dēfendant, *I fear that they will not defend themselves bravely.*

a. The English future tense depending on a word or phrase of fear in the present tense is translated by the present subjunctive.

532.   VOCABULARY

aedificium, -ī, N., building, house

dēdō, -ere, dēdidī, dēditum, give up, yield, surrender

dēpopulor, -ārī, dēpopulātus sum, lay waste

Iccius, -ī, M., Iccius, *a chief of the Remi*

nōlō, nōlle, nōluī, not wish, be unwilling

paulisper, *adv.,* a little while

propinquus, -a, -um, near

EXERCISES

533. 1. Labiēnus veritus est nē hostēs flūmen trānsīrent. 2. Belgae, quī obsidēs mittere nōlēbant, paulisper restitērunt. 3. Verēmur nē aedificia incendantur. 4. Gallī timēbant ut sē dēfendere possent. 5. Cum aedificia vīcōsque trāns Rhēnum habērent, eō redīre volēbant. 6. Iccius sē hostibus dēdere nōluit.

THE DEFENSE OF BIBRAX

Oppidānī vix sē dēfendēbant. Iccius quī oppidō praefuit nūntiōs ad Caesarem mīsit quī auxilium peterent. Dīxit sē nōn posse diūtius sustinēre. Cum Caesar haec cognōvisset, auxilium statim mīsit. Hostēs ab oppidō discessērunt sed agrōs Rēmōrum dēpopulātī sunt et multa aedificia vīcōsque incendērunt. Ad castra Caesaris contendērunt et sua castra in locō propinquō posuērunt.

534. 1. We fear that the town may be captured. 2. The army was unwilling to advance. 3. The Romans feared that the enemy would lay waste the province. 4. The Haeduans were unwilling to furnish the grain which they had promised. 5. We feared that the messenger would not come.

SUGGESTED DRILL

(1) State the difference between the use of conjunctions in purpose clauses and in clauses of fear. (2) Point out the difference between the forms of negative clauses of purpose and of negative clauses of result. (3) Name the three kinds of **cum** clauses, giving the meaning of **cum** with each. (4) State what tenses of the subjunctive are used with **cum** meaning *when*.

EIGHTEENTH REVIEW LESSON

535.

VOCABULARY REVIEW

aedificium, -ī, N.

difficultās, -tātis, F.

lībertās, -tātis, F.

onus, oneris, N.

ōrdō, ōrdinis, M.

pābulum, -ī, N.

pecūnia, -ae, F.

regiō, -ōnis, F.

salūs, salūtis, F.

servitūs, -tūtis, F.

tergum, -ī, N.

uxor, uxōris, F.

vallēs, vallis, F.

vesper, vesperī, M.

citerior, citerius

dexter, -tra, -trum

extrēmus, -a, -um

firmus, -a, -um

frūmentārius, -a, -um

gravis, grave

idōneus, -a, -um

incolumis, incolume

propinquus, -a, -um

sinister, -tra, -trum

tantus, -a, -um

ulterior, ulterius

adsum, -esse, -fuī, -futūrus

arbitror, -ārī, arbitrātus sum

cōnfīdō, -ere, cōnfīsus sum

coniūrō, -āre, -āvī, -ātum

dēdō, -ere, dēdidī, dēditum

dēligō, -ere, dēlēgī, dēlēctum

dēpopulor, -ārī, -ātus sum

fīō, fierī, factus sum

mereor, -ērī, meritus sum

nōlō, nōlle, nōluī

occīdō, -ere, occīdī, occīsum

perficiō, -ere, perfēcī, perfectum

praeficiō, -ere, praefēcī, praefectum

premō, -ere, pressī, pressum

prōpōnō, -ere, prōposuī, prōpositum

quaerō, -ere, quaesīvī, quaesītum

redigō, -ere, redēgī, redāctum

sciō, scīre, scīvī, scītum

vertō, vertere, vertī, versum

volō, velle, voluī

bene

comminus

dēmum

līberāliter

minimē

paulisper

tam

tardē

undique

cum

nam

ubi

ob

536.

RELATED ENGLISH WORDS

certain

difficulty

extreme

grave

merit

ordinal

propinquity

propose

tardy

ulterior

valley

volition

LESSON XCI

FUTURE PASSIVE PARTICIPLE: DATIVE OF AGENT

THE FUTURE PASSIVE PARTICIPLE

537. The Latin verb has a future passive participle, formed on the present stem, with the endings **-ndus, -nda,** and **-ndum.**

I.	II.	III.	IV.
amandus, -a, -um	monendus	dūcendus	audiendus
		capiendus	

a. This participle refers to something that is to be done or ought to be done.

Homō monendus est, *the man is to be (must be) warned.*

THE DATIVE OF AGENT

538. With the future passive participle, the person by whom the act must be done or ought to be done is regularly indicated by the dative.

Homō frātrī monendus est, *the man must be warned by his brother.*

a. In translating expressions of obligation or necessity into Latin with this construction it is often necessary to change the verb from the active to the passive.

We must send help (help must be sent by us), **auxilium nōbīs mittendum est.**

539.   **VOCABULARY**

cotīdiē, *adv.*, daily, every day
fortūna, -ae, F., fortune
opīniō, opīniōnis, F., belief, expectation
rēgīna, -ae, F., queen

sōl, sōlis, M., the sun
supersedeō, -sedēre, -sēdī, -sessum, refrain from
umquam, *adv.*, ever (*used with negatives*)

EXERCISES

540. 1. Caesarī aciēs īnstruenda est.   2. Castra mīlitibus dēfendenda sunt.   3. Ōlim fortūna eius cīvitātis melior erat quod cīvēs meliōrēs habēbat.   4. Rēmī verēbantur nē oppidum caperētur.   5. Domum redīre nōn vult.   6. Auxilium nōbīs statim ferendum est.   7. Eō diē iter nostrum per silvam magnam fuit neque sōlem vīdimus.   8. Rēx et rēgīna fūgērunt neque umquam ad urbem rediērunt.

BATTLE AT THE AISNE

Prīmō Caesar propter multitūdinem hostium et propter opīniōnem virtūtis proeliō supersedēbat.   Equitēs eius autem cum equitibus Belgārum cotīdiē proeliō contendēbant.   Cum ipse vīdisset Rōmānōs nōn minus fortēs esse, (in) locō idōneō aciem īnstrūxit.   Hostēs item cōpiās suās īnstrūxērunt.   Sed eō diē proelium nōn commissum est.   Posterō diē Belgae ad flūmen Axonam contendērunt et trānsīre cōnātī sunt.   Sed multīs interfectīs repulsī sunt.

541. 1. The army ought to cross the river (the river ought to be crossed, *etc.*).   2. The centurion ought to lead back the soldiers to camp.   3. No one ought to be sent into danger by the leader.   4. The enemy led out their army every day, but they did not begin battle.   5. The towns of our allies ought not to be burned by the legion.

SUGGESTED DRILL

(1) Explain the case of **mīlitibus** in sentence 2, and of **nōbīs** in sentence 6, 540.   (2) Give the future active and the future passive participles of **postulō, habeō, dīcō,** and **mūniō.**   (3) Give a synopsis of **volō** in the third person singular of the indicative and the subjunctive. (4) Give a synopsis of **nōlō** in the second person plural of the indicative and the subjunctive.   (5) Explain the mood of **caperētur** in sentence 4, 540.

LESSON XCII

CONJUGATION OF *MĀLŌ*   GENITIVE OF OBJECT

THE CONJUGATION OF *MĀLŌ*

542. The verb **mālō**, *prefer*, is a compound of **magis** and **volō**. Its forms will be found in the Appendix, section 36.

Mālō has no imperatives or participles.

THE GENITIVE WITH CERTAIN VERBS

543. The verbs **meminī** and **reminīscor**, *remember*, and **oblīvīscor**, *forget*, frequently take a noun in the genitive as object. But if the object is a neuter pronoun, or a neuter adjective used as a noun, it is always in the accusative.

544.   **VOCABULARY**

ēgredior, ēgredī, ēgressus sum, set out, depart from

mālō, mālle, māluī, prefer

meminī, meminisse, *defective verb*, remember (*the perfect is translated as present, the past perfect as past, and the future perfect as future*)

oblīvīscor, oblīvīscī, oblītus sum, forget

prīstinus, -a, -um, former, old-time

reminīscor, reminīscī, remember, recall

secundus, -a, -um, second

vigilia, -ae, F., watch (*one fourth of the night*)

EXERCISES

545. 1. Caesar veterum iniūriārum Helvētiōrum reminīscēbātur. 2. Prīstinae virtūtis eōrum nōn oblītus est. 3. Hās condiciōnēs pācis nōn accēpērunt quod in lībertāte manēre mālēbant. 4. Domō exīre māvult quod numquam domī contentus fuit. 5. Semper perīculōrum eius bellī meminerō. 6. Cōpiae īnstruendae sunt et proelium committendum est.

The Belgians Disperse

Cum Belgae magnam cōpiam reī frūmentāriae nōn habērent, in eō locō nōn diū remanēre poterant. Itaque conciliō
convocātō, domum redīre cōnstituērunt. Secundā vigiliā
castrīs ēgressī sunt. Cum quisque prīmum locum itineris
peteret, fēcērunt ut Rōmānī eōs fugere exīstimārent.

546. 1. The Romans remembered the victory of the Helvetians. 2. On that day Caesar preferred to refrain from
battle. 3. Labienus did not forget the flight of the cavalry
of the Gauls. 4. The Belgians remembered the liberty in
which their fathers had lived (remained). 5. The soldiers
seemed to fear the Germans.

SUGGESTED DRILL

(1) Conjugate **volō, nōlō,** and **mālō,** in the present indicative and
the present subjunctive. (2) Give the future passive participles of
ēgredior and **convocō.** (3) Explain the case of **virtūtis** in sentence 2,
and of **domō** in sentence 4, 545. (4) Conjugate **ēgredior** and **oblīvīscor**
in the present indicative. (5) Conjugate **meminī** in the perfect
subjunctive.

LESSON XCIII

THE SUPINE: PLACE CONSTRUCTIONS

THE SUPINE

547. The Supine is a verbal noun with only two case forms, the accusative and the ablative of the singular number. The accusative ends in **-um** and the ablative in **-ū**.

I.	II.	III.		IV.
portātum	monitum	ductum	captum	audītum
portātū	monitū	ductū	captū	audītū

a. The accusative of the supine may be used to express purpose in a clause in which the finite verb expresses motion.

Lēgātōs pācem petītum mīsērunt, *they sent envoys to ask peace.*

b. The ablative of the supine is used with a few adjectives as an ablative of respect. It is usually translated by the English present infinitive.

Optimum factū, *best to do (the best thing to do).*

REVIEW OF PLACE CONSTRUCTIONS

548. *a.* Place to Which is regularly expressed by the accusative with **ad** or **in**.

b. Place Where is regularly expressed by the ablative with **in**.

c. Place from Which is regularly expressed by the ablative with **ab**, **dē**, or **ex**.

d. With names of towns or small islands, and with **domus**, Place to Which is expressed by the accusative without a preposition, and Place from Which by the ablative without a preposition.

e. With names of towns and small islands, and with
domus, Place Where is expressed by the locative, which
in the singular of the first and second declensions is
identical with the genitive; with other words it is identical with the ablative.

f. The locative of **domus** is **domī.** A few words,
among which are **locus** and **pars,** may omit the preposition in expressing Place Where, especially if modified
by an adjective.

549. <center>**VOCABULARY**</center>

agmen, agminis, N., line,
column (*of an army*)

cōnservō, -āre, -āvī, -ātum,
spare, protect

incrēdibilis, -e, incredible, ex-
traordinary

moror, -ārī, morātus sum,
delay

Noviodūnum, -ī, N., Noviodunum, *a town of Gaul*

novissimus, -a, -um (*superlative of* **novus**), last; rear

**subsequor, -sequī, -secūtus
sum,** follow, follow closely

Suessiōnēs, -um, M. *pl.*, the
Suessiones, *a tribe of Gaul*

EXERCISES

550. 1. Haeduī ad Caesarem auxilium rogātum vēnērunt.
2. Id facillimum est factū. 3. Omnēs quī arma trādidērunt
ab eō cōnservātī sunt. 4. Proximā nocte domum vēnērunt
et paulisper domī mānsērunt. 5. Domō proficīscī volēbant
quod numquam contentī fuerant. 6. Caesar Noviodūnī nōn
diū morātus est. 7. In eā īnsulā magnus numerus equōrum
erat. 8. Incrēdibilī celeritāte flūmen trānsiērunt.

THE ROMANS PURSUE

Prīmā lūce Caesar omnem equitātum mīsit quī novissimum
agmen morārētur. Labiēnum cum tribus legiōnibus subsequī
iussit. Hae magnam multitūdinem hostium fugientium con-
cīdērunt. Caesar exercitum in fīnēs Suessiōnum dūxit quī
Rēmīs proximī sunt. Suessiōnēs in oppidum Noviodūnum

convēnērunt sed cum Caesar omnia comparāvisset lēgātōs
pācem petītum mīsērunt.

551. 1. Those who have returned home ought to be protected. 2. The Belgians set out for home in the second
watch. 3. Iccius sent men to ask aid. 4. Some will remain
at home, others will set out for the city. 5. This is the best
thing to do (is best to do). 6. The courage of these men is
incredible.

<hr>

SUGGESTED DRILL

(1) Decline **domus.** (2) Give a synopsis of **moror** in the third
person singular of the indicative and the subjunctive. (3) Give a
synopsis of **subsequor** in the third person plural of the indicative and
the subjunctive. (4) Give all the infinitives and all the participles of
cōnservō. (5) Give the supines of **videō** and **dīcō.**

CIRCUS MAXIMUS

LESSON XCIV

THE GERUND

552. The Gerund is a verbal noun of the second declension. It is in the neuter gender, and its only forms are the genitive, dative, accusative, and ablative cases of the singular number. Its nominative is supplied by the infinitive. Its declension is as follows:

	I.	II.	III.	IV.
Gen.	portandī	monendī	dūcendī	audiendī
Dat.	portandō	monendō	dūcendō	audiendō
Acc.	portandum	monendum	dūcendum	audiendum
Abl.	portandō	monendō	dūcendō	audiendō

a. The gerund of **capiō** is declined like the gerund of **audiō**.

553. (1) The genitive of the gerund is used chiefly as an objective genitive with an adjective or a noun. With the ablative **causā** it expresses purpose.

> **Cupidus bellandī,** *desirous of engaging in war.*
> **Resistendī causā,** *for the sake (purpose) of resisting.*

(2) The dative of the gerund is little used.

(3) The accusative of the gerund is frequently used as the object of the preposition **ad** to express purpose.

> **Ad oppugnandum,** *for attacking, to attack.*

(4) The ablative may be used to express means or cause, or as the object of the prepositions **ab, dē, ex,** or **in.**

> **pugnandō,** *by fighting.*
> **in quaerendō,** *on inquiring.*

a. The gerund when used as the object of a preposition cannot have an object. For expressions of this kind the Latin employs a different construction.

VIEW OF MODERN ROME FROM THE CAPITOLINE HILL

554. **VOCABULARY**

accēdō, -ere, accessī, accessum, approach (*usually with* **ad** *and the accusative*)

Ambiānī, -ōrum, M. *pl.,* the Ambiani, *a tribe of Gaul*

bellō, -āre, -āvī, -ātum, engage in war, carry on war

Bellovacī, -ōrum, M. *pl.,* the Bellovaci, *a tribe of Gaul*

cohors, cohortis, F., cohort, *one of the ten divisions of the legion*

cupidus, -a, -um, desirous, fond of

pandō, -ere, pandī, passum, hold out

parcō, -ere, pepercī, parsum, spare (*with dative*)

EXERCISES

555. 1. Ariovistus cupidus bellandī erat. 2. Spem amīcōs videndī nōn habēbam. 3. Pācem petendī causā vēnērunt. 4. Ad hoc oppidum cum cohortibus accēdet. 5. Omnia ad proficīscendum parāvērunt. 6. In quaerendō Caesar repperit arma trādita esse.

SURRENDER OF THE BELLOVACI

Obsidibus acceptīs Caesar eīs pepercit et in fīnēs Bellovacōrum profectus est. Cum ad oppidum eōrum accessisset, puerī fēminaeque ex mūrō manūs pandērunt, et pācem implōrāvērunt. Prō hīs Dīviciācus Haeduus locūtus est. Caesar eīs quoque pepercit sed magnum numerum obsidum poposcit. Hīs datīs et armīs trāditīs ab eō locō in fīnēs Ambiānōrum pervēnit quī sē sine morā dēdidērunt.

556. 1. They have hope of capturing the city. 2. The enemy prepared everything for making an attack (for attacking). 3. I have this army for the purpose of carrying on war. 4. The Belgians preferred to return home. 5. You cannot help your friend by pleading (**implōrāre**). 6. Caesar protected the Bellovaci because he thought this was best (to do).

SUGGESTED DRILL

(1) Point out the gerunds in sentences 1-6, 555. (2) Give the gerunds of **habeō** and **moror**. (3) Give the past infinitives, active and passive, of **dēdō**. (4) Explain the case of **obsidibus**, line 1, and of **eīs**, line 5, 555. (5) Give the principal parts of **patior** and of **pandō**.

LESSON XCV

THE GERUNDIVE: ORDINAL NUMERALS

557. The future passive participle of a transitive verb is often used in agreement with a noun or pronoun in phrases which are equivalent in meaning to a gerund with an object.[1]

Spēs urbis capiendae. The meaning is the same as **Spēs urbem capiendī,** *hope of capturing the city.*

The future passive participle when thus used is called the Gerundive. The gerundive may be used in either number and in any case to agree with the noun or pronoun to which it belongs.

    a. Since the gerund cannot stand as the object of a preposition and at the same time govern an object, gerundive phrases are frequently used with the forms of transitive verbs. The English translation of such phrases is the same as if the gerundive were a gerund having as its object the word with which the gerundive agrees.

    b. The case uses of the gerundive construction are in general the same as those of the gerund.

Cupidus oppidī expugnandī, *desirous of storming the town.*

Auxilī ferendī causā, *for the purpose (sake) of bringing aid.*

Ad eās rēs cōnficiendās, *for accomplishing these things.*

Dē auxiliō mittendō, *about (concerning) sending aid.*

Lapidibus portandīs, *by carrying stones.*

---

[1] The gerundive construction was not a substitute for the gerund in the thought of the Romans, but was probably the usage from which the gerund was derived.

558. The following distinctions between the gerund and gerundive are to be observed:

GERUND	GERUNDIVE
A noun	A participle
Active in meaning	Passive
Neuter gender	All genders
Used only in the singular	Both numbers

ORDINAL NUMERALS

559. The first twenty ordinals are as follows:

prīmus,	*first*	ūndecimus,	*eleventh*
secundus,	*second*	duodecimus,	*twelfth*
tertius,	*third*	tertius decimus,	*thirteenth*
quārtus,	*fourth*	quārtus decimus,	*fourteenth*
quīntus,	*fifth*	quīntus decimus,	*fifteenth*
sextus,	*sixth*	sextus decimus,	*sixteenth*
septimus,	*seventh*	septimus decimus,	*seventeenth*
octāvus,	*eighth*	duodēvīcēsimus,	*eighteenth*
nōnus,	*ninth*	ūndēvīcēsimus,	*nineteenth*
decimus,	*tenth*	vīcēsimus,	*twentieth*

a. The ordinals are declined as adjectives of the first and second declensions. Compound ordinals, such as **tertius decimus,** have both parts declined.

560. VOCABULARY

accidō, -ere, accidī, happen

experior, -īrī, expertus sum, try

Nervii, -ōrum, M. *pl.,* the Nervii, *a tribe of Belgians*

plēnus, -a, -um, full

Sabis, Sabis, M., the Sambre, *a river of Gaul*

tempestās, -tātis, F., storm, tempest

ūnā, *adv.,* together, at the same time

EXERCISES

561. 1. Hostēs quī trāns flūmen cōnsēdērunt spem oppidī capiendī habent. 2. Ad eās rēs cōnficiendās Orgetorīx dēlēctus est. 3. Lapidibus iaciendīs multōs vulnerāvērunt. 4. Pācis petendae causā lēgātōs mīsī. 5. Accidit ut lūna plēna esset. 6. Tempestātēs tantae erant ut proficīscī nōn possēmus.

THE NERVII PREPARE FOR WAR

Proximī hīs erant Nerviī quī maximē ferī inter eōs exīstimābantur. Hī trāns Sabim cōnsēderant ibique adventum Rōmānōrum exspectābant. Ūnā cum hīs erant duae gentēs fīnitimae quae eandem fortūnam bellī experīrī volēbant. Hīs rēbus cognitīs Caesar centuriōnēs explōrātōrēsque praemīsit quī locum castrīs (**196**) dēligerent.

562. 1. The cohort was left in the town for the purpose of defending the townspeople. 2. We shall send a legion to capture the town (**ad** *with gerundive phrase*). 3. By throwing stones we drove back the enemy who were crossing the river. 4. Orgetorix will be chosen to accomplish these things. 5. The Nervii set out that they might try the fortune of war.

SUGGESTED DRILL

(1) Point out the gerundives in **561**. (2) Give the gerunds of **capiō**. (3) State whether **capiendī** in sentence 1, **561**, is a gerund or a gerundive, and give proof. (4) Give a synopsis of **iaciō** in the third person plural. (5) Conjugate **possum** in the imperfect indicative and the imperfect subjunctive.

NINETEENTH REVIEW LESSON

563.　(1) The conjugation of **fīō**.
(2) The conjugation of **volō, nōlō, mālō**.
(3) Future passive participles.
(4) The supine.
(5) The gerund.
(6) The gerundive.
(7) The genitive of material.
(8) The genitive with verbs of remembering and forgetting.
(9) The dative of agent.
(10) **cum** descriptive clauses.
(11) **cum** causal clauses.
(12) **cum** adversative clauses.
(13) Clauses of fear.

564.　Give Latin words with which the following English words are connected in derivation:

accession	fortune	reminiscence
accident	incredible	second
conservation	moratorium	solar
cupidity	oblivion	subsequent
egress	opinion	tempest
experiment	pristine	vigil

ROMAN KITCHEN RANGE

LESSON XCVI

REVIEW OF PARTICIPLES: NEGATIVE COMMANDS

REVIEW OF PARTICIPLES

565. The Latin verb has four participles, the present active, the past passive, and the future, active and passive.

PRESENT		PAST		FUTURE	
ACTIVE	PASSIVE	ACTIVE	PASSIVE	ACTIVE	PASSIVE
portāns	—	—	portātus	portātūrus	portandus
monēns	—	—	monitus	monitūrus	monendus
dūcēns	—	—	ductus	ductūrus	dūcendus
capiēns	—	—	captus	captūrus	capiendus
audiēns	—	—	audītus	audītūrus	audiendus

a. In English there is a present passive participle, *being carried,* etc., and a past active participle, *having carried,* etc. These two participles are lacking in the Latin verb.

b. Deponent verbs have the same number of participles as other verbs: **cōnāns, cōnātus, cōnātūrus, cōnandus,** etc. The past participle of a deponent verb is usually active in meaning, but sometimes it is passive. The sense of the sentence in which the participle stands will make it possible to decide in which voice it is used.

c. The present participle is declined as an adjective of the third declension: **portāns, portantis,** etc. The other participles are declined as adjectives of the first and second declensions: **portātus, -a, -um,** *etc.*

NEGATIVE COMMANDS

566. Negative commands (prohibitions) in the second person are frequently expressed by the imperative of **nōlō** (**nōlī, nōlīte**), followed by the infinitive of the verb expressing the act forbidden: **Nōlī eum iuvāre,** *do not help him.*

567. VOCABULARY

efficiō, -ere, effēcī, effectum, bring about

fugō, -āre, -āvī, -ātum, put to flight, rout

expedītus, -a, -um, unimpeded, ready for action

lateō, -ēre, -uī, lurk, remain concealed

nesciō, -īre, -īvī, not know

silvestris, -tre, wooded, forest covered

vergō, -ere, slope

EXERCISES

568. 1. Belgae crēdidērunt Rōmānōs in Galliā remanēre quod eam regiōnem in servitūtem redigere vellent. 2. Nōlī huic puerō pecūniam dare. 3. Nesciō ubi castra posita sint. 4. Hostēs, flūmen trānsīre cōnātī, fugātī sunt. 5. Nōlī exercitum in perīculum dūcere. 6. Haec rēs effēcit ut Germānī discēdere nōllent. 7. Nōlīte hostium impetum timēre.

POSITION OF THE ARMIES

Locum castrīs dēlēgērunt in colle quī ad flūmen Sabim vergēbat. Trāns id flūmen alter collis erat cuius pars magna erat silvestris. In hīs silvīs hostēs latēbant. Altitūdō flūminis nōn magna erat. Caesar equitātū praemissō subsequitur omnibus cōpiīs. Quod hostibus appropinquābat duās legiōnēs expedītās dūcēbat.

569. 1. We shall find out who is in the town. 2. The boy said that his brother who had been in the war had been wounded. 3. The Romans did not know in what place the Nervii were lurking. 4. Having promised aid, we returned to Gaul. 5. Do not receive money from this man.

———

SUGGESTED DRILL

(1) Name a Latin noun with which **servitūs** is connected in derivation. (2) Give the noun from which **silvestris** is derived. (3) Give an English word which is connected in derivation with **pecūnia**. (4) Explain the mood of **vellent** in sentence 1, 568. (5) Explain the mood of **sint** in sentence 3, 568. (6) Give the principal parts of **dō**, **crēdō**, **dēdō**, and **trādō**.

LESSON XCVII

CONDITIONS AND CONCLUSIONS: NON-COMMITTAL CONDITIONAL SENTENCES

CONDITIONAL SENTENCES

570. A conditional sentence is a complex sentence, the subordinate clause of which is introduced by *if*. The subordinate clause is called the Condition, the main clause is called the Conclusion.

NON-COMMITTAL CONDITIONAL SENTENCES [1]

571. In Latin, a conditional sentence which does not imply that the condition is either true or false regularly has both verbs in the indicative.

> **Sī puer domī est, māter laeta est,** *if the boy is at home, his mother is glad.*
>
> **Sī hostēs flūmen trānsiērunt, nostrī pontem nōn dēfendērunt,** *if the enemy have crossed the river, our men did not defend the bridge.*

a. Sometimes an imperative or a subjunctive of desire is used in the conclusion of a conditional sentence of this kind instead of an indicative.

> **Sī pācem cupitis, arma trādite,** *if you desire peace, surrender your arms.*

b. A non-committal conditional sentence referring to future time is commonly called a Future More Vivid conditional sentence. The verb of its conditional clause is usually translated by an English present tense, but the Latin sentence has the verb of the condition as well as of the conclusion in the future or future perfect.

---

[1] Conditional sentences of this type are sometimes called *neutral* conditional sentences.

572. **VOCABULARY**

claudō, -ere, clausī, clausum,
close

nisi, *conj.*, if not, unless

pellō, -ere, pepulī, pulsum,
rout, put to flight

prōvolō, -āre, -āvī, rush forth,
fly forth

subitō, *adv.*, suddenly

trānsgredior, -gredī, -gressus
sum, cross

EXERCISES

573. 1. Sī hostēs in silvā latent, perīculum est. 2. Sī Gallī flūmen trānsgrediuntur, perīculum nostrum magnum est. 3. Peditēs ad proelium committendum prōcessērunt. 4. Equitātus proelī committendī causā praemissus est. 5. Sī omnēs legiōnēs in castrīs sunt, portās claudite. 6. Nisi peditēs pervenient, hostēs flūmen trānsgredientur.

BEGINNING OF THE BATTLE

Equitēs Rōmānī flūmen trānsgressī cum equitātū hostium proelium commīsērunt. Hostēs ad silvās sē recēpērunt ac rūrsus ex silvīs in nostrōs impetum fēcērunt. Interim sex legiōnēs quae vēnerant castra mūnīre coepērunt. Tum hostēs quī in silvīs latēbant subitō prōvolāvērunt impetumque in nostrōs equitēs fēcērunt. Hīs pulsīs flūmen trānsiērunt et incrēdibilī celeritāte ad castra contendērunt.

574. 1. If the cavalry are crossing the river, the enemy do not see them. 2. The legion set out for the purpose of burning the town. 3. Caesar did not think the enemy would cross the river. 4. If the enemy are collecting an army, they wish to wage war. 5. We do not know in what place the Belgians are lurking.

SUGGESTED DRILL

(1) Explain the meaning and the derivation of the English words *latent* and *transgress*. (2) Give the rules for the use of moods and tenses in indirect discourse. (3) State what the difference is between the English and the Latin usage in regard to conjunctions introducing indirect discourse. (4) Give the method of expressing negative commands. (5) Give the past and future infinitives of **trānsgredior**.

LESSON XCVIII

CONDITIONAL SENTENCES CONTRARY TO FACT: REVIEW OF CASES WITH PREPOSITIONS

CONDITIONAL SENTENCES, CONTRARY TO FACT

575. A conditional sentence which implies by its form that the condition is not true and that the actual situation is not that which is referred to in the conclusion is called a conditional sentence Contrary to Fact.

If he had seen the danger, he would have avoided it (implying that he did not see the danger and that he did not avoid it).

576. In Latin, a conditional sentence contrary to fact has its verbs in the imperfect or the past perfect subjunctive; the imperfect to express present time, and the past perfect to express past time.

Sī fortēs mīlitēs habērēmus, in perīculō nōn essēmus,
if we had brave soldiers, we should not be in danger.

Sī fortēs mīlitēs habuissēmus, in perīculō nōn fuissēmus,
if we had had brave soldiers, we should not have been in danger.

REVIEW OF CASES WITH PREPOSITIONS

577. The following prepositions used in this book always have their objects in the ablative case: **ā (ab), dē, ē (ex), cum, prō, sine.**

In phrases denoting the place toward which motion is directed, **in** and **sub** have their objects in the accusative case; in phrases denoting the place in which something exists or some act is done, they have their objects in the ablative case.

All other prepositions used in this book have their objects in the accusative case.

578.　　　　　　　**VOCABULARY**

agō, -ere, ēgī, āctum, drive, do, carry on

exercitātus, -a, -um, trained

incursus, -ūs, M., attack

mīlitāris, -e, military; rēs mīlitāris, military science, warfare

necessitās, -tātis, F., necessity, urgency

ratiō, ratiōnis, F., theory, reason

superior, superius, *compar. adj.*, higher, preceding, previous

VIEW ON THE APPIAN WAY

EXERCISES

579.　1. Sī hostēs in silvā latērent, perīculum esset.　**2.** Sī peditēs sē recēpissent, castra capta essent.　3. Sī omnēs legiōnēs in castrīs essent, nōn timērēmus.　4. Sī lēgātī Caesaris imperia exspectāvissent, exercitus repulsus esset.　5. Hic locus mīlitibus dēfendendus est.

Roman Discipline

Caesarī omnia ūnō tempore agenda erant. Incursus hos-
tium magnam partem eārum rērum impediēbat quās ratiō
reī mīlitāris postulābat. Mīlitēs autem superiōribus proeliīs
exercitātī fuerant, et lēgātī quī legiōnibus praeerant imperium Caesaris nōn exspectāvērunt. Itaque exercitus īnstrūc-
tus est magis ut (*as*) necessitās temporis (postulābat) quam
ut ratiō reī mīlitāris postulābat.

580. 1. If the soldiers had fortified the camp, the enemy
would not have made an attack. 2. If the soldier had set
out from the camp, he would have been captured. 3. If the
enemy were not laying waste our fields, we should not be
asking aid of (from) the Romans. 4. If you are brave soldiers, defend the camp. 5. If the man were not lazy, he
would be working today.

---

suggested drill

(1) Name the class of conditional sentences to which sentences 1, 2,
and 3, 579, belong. (2) Point out the verb of the conclusion in each
of these three sentences. (3) Explain the use of the tenses of the
verbs in sentence 3, 579. (4) Explain the case of **mīlitibus** in sentence 5 and of **Caesarī**, line 6, 579.

LESSON XCIX

FUTURE LESS VIVID CONDITIONAL SENTENCES: *ISTE*

future less vivid conditional sentences

581. A conditional sentence which implies doubt on the
part of the speaker or writer as to the fulfillment of the
condition, and which has as its conclusion a verb denoting
an act as conceivable or imaginable, is called a Future Less
Vivid conditional sentence. Its verbs stand in the present
(or perfect) subjunctive.

> **Sī hostem videat, fugiat,** *if he should see the enemy, he*
> *would flee.*

a. The perfect is used in the place of the present when the completion of the act is prominent in thought.

b. The verbs of a future more vivid conditional sentence are translated with the auxiliaries *shall* and *will*, or (in the condition) by the present tense. The verbs of a future less vivid conditional sentence are translated with *should* and *would*.

THE DEMONSTRATIVE *ISTE*

582. Besides **hic, ille,** and **is,** there is another demonstrative, **iste,** translated *that of yours,* or simply *that.* It is less frequently used than the others and commonly refers to something associated with the person addressed. It is declined like **ille.**

Masc.	*Fem.*	*Neut.*
iste	ista	istud
istīus	istīus	istīus, *etc.*

a. **Iste** is sometimes used to express contempt.

583.   **VOCABULARY**

cōgō, -ere, coēgī, coāctum, collect, compel

duodecimus, -a, -um, twelfth

nūdō, -āre, -āvī, -ātum, strip, leave unprotected

revertor, revertī, revertī, reversum, return (*deponent in present system*)

septimus, -a, -um, seventh

spērō, -āre, -āvī, -ātum, hope

EXERCISES

584. 1. Istud dōnum parvum esse vidētur. 2. Sī amīcus meus essēs, nōn haec dīcerēs. 3. Tantus erat numerus Germānōrum ut Gallī quī eam regiōnem incolēbant eīs resistere nōn possent. 4. Sī discessissent, Caesar eōs secūtus esset. 5. Magnae cōpiae coactae sunt quod hostēs appropinquābant. 6. Mīlitēs spērant lēgātum auxilium missūrum esse.[1]

---

[1] **Spērō** is followed by indirect discourse.

The Nervii in the Roman Camp

Pars hostium ab Rōmānīs repulsa statim fūgit. Sed cum castra Rōmāna nūdāta essent, magnus numerus Nerviōrum ad eum locum contendit. Eō tempore equitēs Rōmānī in castra sē recipiēbant, sed, hostibus vīsīs in castrīs, aliam in partem fugam petiērunt. Interim duodecima legiō et septima ab hostibus premēbantur.

585. 1. They fled so swiftly that the legion which had crossed the river did not make an attack. 2. Since the scouts who had been sent ahead had not seen the enemy, the soldiers did not fear danger. 3. If the town had been captured, many would have been killed. 4. If the legion should cross the river, the cavalry would flee.

SUGGESTED DRILL

(1) Explain the mood of **possent** in sentence 3, 584. (2) State what form of conditional sentences is illustrated by 2 and 4, 584. (3) Conjugate **revertor** in the present indicative and the perfect indicative.

LESSON C

FUTURE IMPERATIVE: SUBJUNCTIVE BY ATTRACTION

THE FUTURE IMPERATIVE

586. The forms of the future imperative are found in the second and third persons. They are as follows:

ACTIVE

SINGULAR

2.	portātō	monētō	mittitō	capitō	audītō
3.	portātō	monētō	mittitō	capitō	audītō

PLURAL

2.	portātōte	monētōte	mittitōte	capitōte	audītōte
3.	portantō	monentō	mittuntō	capiuntō	audiuntō

PASSIVE

SINGULAR

2.	portātor	monētor	mittitor	capitor	audītor
3.	portātor	monētor	mittitor	capitor	audītor

PLURAL

2.	[Lacking]	——	——	——	——
3.	portantor	monentor	mittuntor	capiuntor	audiuntor

a. The future imperative is used when there is a clear reference to future time indicated by an adverb or other expression of time. It is translated *thou shalt carry, he shall carry,* or *let him carry,* etc.

b. The verbs **meminī** and **sciō** regularly (and **habeō** occasionally) use the future imperative instead of the present.

THE SUBJUNCTIVE BY ATTRACTION

587. Sometimes a subordinate clause which would otherwise have its verb in the indicative takes the subjunctive because it is closely dependent on a subjunctive or an infinitive.

Ita ācriter pugnāvērunt ut omnēs quī in proeliō essent vulnerārentur, *they fought so fiercely that all who were in the battle were wounded.*

588.   **VOCABULARY**

Atuatucī, -ōrum, M. *pl.,* the Atuatuci *a Belgian tribe*

cohortor, -ārī, -ātus sum, urge, encourage

dīmittō, -ere, dīmīsī, dīmissum, send away, dismiss

paulum, *adv.,* a little

hīberna, -ōrum, N. *pl.,* winter quarters, winter camp

rōbur, -ōris, M., oak, strength

supersum, -esse, -fuī, -futūrus, be left, survive

tardō, -āre, -āvī, -ātum, hinder, check

EXERCISES

589. 1. Mementōte hanc patriam meam esse. 2. Scītō
mē amīcum eius hominis semper fuisse. 3. Gallī tempestātēs nōn timēbant quod nāvēs eōrum ex rōbore factae sunt.
4. Equitēs dīmissī sunt sed legiōnēs in hībernīs manent. 5.
Signum datum est ut eī quī profectī essent reverterentur.

END OF THE BATTLE

Tum Caesar scūtum cēpit et ipse in prīmam aciem prōcessit. Centuriōnēs mīlitēsque cohortātus est. Eius adventus
spem mīlitibus intulit et impetus hostium paulum tardātus
est. Eōdem tempore Labiēnus, quī advēnerat, auxilium mīsit
et omnēs hostēs fugātī sunt. Posteā eī quī supererant sē
dēdidērunt. Eō bellō cōnfectō Atuatucī quī sociī Nerviōrum
fuerant Caesarī resistere cōnātī sunt. Sed oppidum eōrum
captum est et paene omnēs servī factī sunt. Tum Caesar
legiōnēs in hībernīs relīquit atque in Ītaliam profectus est.

590. 1. They came to the camp because they wished to
beg for peace. 2. We sent them away because we did not
trust them (*dative*). 3. Remember that your fathers were
brave men. 4. Be assured (know) that the danger is not
great.

SUGGESTED DRILL

(1) Conjugate **supersum** in the present and the imperfect subjunctive. (2) Mention two other compounds of **sum**. (3) Give the rule for
the use of tenses of the subjunctive in subordinate clauses. (4) Give
the future imperatives of **probō**, **videō**, and **mūniō**. (5) Give all the
imperatives, present and future, of **laudō**.

TWENTIETH REVIEW LESSON

591. Vocabulary Review

agmen, agminis, N.
cohors, cohortis, F.
incursus, -ūs, M.
necessitās, -tātis, F.
opīniō, -ōnis, F.
ratiō, -ōnis, F.
rōbur, rōboris, N.
sōl, sōlis, M.
tempestās, -tātis, F.
vigilia, -ae, F.
cupidus, -a, -um
exercitātus, -a, -um
incrēdibilis, -e
mīlitāris, -e
plēnus, -a, -um
prīstinus, -a, -um
secundus, -a, -um
silvestris, -e
superior, superius
cotīdiē
paulum
subitō
umquam
ūnā
nisi

accēdō, -ere, accessī, accessum
accidō, -ere, accidī
agō, -ere, ēgī, āctum
attribuō, -ere, attribuī, attribūtum
claudō, -ere, clausī, clausum
cōgō, -ere, coēgī, coāctum
cohortor, -ārī, cohortātus sum
cōnsīdō, -ere, cōnsēdī, cōnsessum
efficiō, -ficere, -fēcī, -fectum
ēgredior, ēgredī, ēgressus sum
lateō, -ēre, -uī
mālō, mālle, māluī
meminī, meminisse
moror, -ārī, morātus sum
nesciō, -scīre, -scīvī
oblīvīscor, oblīvīscī, oblītus sum
parcō, -ere, pepercī, parsum
pandō, -ere, pandī, passum
pellō, -ere, pepulī, pulsum
reminīscor, reminīscī
spērō, -āre, -āvī, -ātum
supersedeō, -sedēre, -sēdī, -sessum
supersum, -esse, -fuī, -futūrus
trānsgredior, -gredī, -gressus sum
vergō, vergere

592. Related English Words

act	expedite	retard
agent	latent	revert
close	necessity	superior
cogent	nude	transgress
efficient	rational	verge

TWELFTH SUPPLEMENTARY REVIEW

VOCABULARY REVIEW

1. adsum, adesse, adfuī
2. agō, -ere, ēgī, āctum
3. amplē, *adv.*
4. amplus, -a, -um
5. bene, *adv.*
6. certus, -a, -um
7. claudō, -ere, clausī, clausum
8. cōgō, -ere, coēgī, coāctum
9. cohors, cohortis, F
10. cōnservō, -āre, -āvī, -ātum
11. cōnsistō, -sistere, -stitī
12. crēber, -bra, -brum
13. cupidus, -a, -um
14. dēficiō, -ficere, -fēcī, -fectum
15. dēsistō, -sistere, -stitī, -stitum
16. dēspērō, -āre, -āvī, -ātum
17. difficultās, -tātis, F.
18. dignitās, -tātis, F.
19. dīmittō, -mittere, -mīsī, -missum
20. enim, *conj.* (*postpositive*)
21. ēripiō, -ripere, -ripuī, -reptum
22. exitus, -ūs, M.
23. fortūna, -ae, F.
24. factum, -ī, N.
25. frūmentārius, -a, -um
26. gravis, -e
27. iam, *adv.*
28. intermittō, -mittere, -mīsī, -missum
29. lībertās, -tātis, F.
30. mīlitāris, -e
31. nōtus, -a, -um
32. ob, *prep. with acc.*
33. ōrdō, -dinis, M.
34. pecūnia, -ae, F.
35. pellō, -ere, pepulī, pulsum
36. plēnus, -a, -um
37. praecipiō, -cipere, -cēpī, -ceptum
38. praeficiō, -ficere, -fēcī, -fectum
39. prīmus . . . decimus
40. propinquus, -a, -um
41. prōpōnō, -pōnere, -posuī, -positum
42. ratiō, -ōnis, F.
43. redigō, -igere, -ēgī, -āctum
44. reficiō, -ficere, -fēcī, -fectum
45. rēgīna, -ae, F.
46. rēs frūmentāria
47. rēs mīlitāris
48. servitūs, -tūtis, F.
49. spērō, -āre, -āvī, -ātum
50. tālis, -e

1. be near, be present
2. drive, do
3. fully
4. large, distinguished
5. well
6. fixed, certain
7. close, confine
8. drive together, collect, compel
9. cohort
10. save fully, preserve
11. take one's place, stop
12. frequent, thick
13. desirous, eager
14. fail, revolt, rebel
15. desist from, cease
16. lose hope, despair
17. difficulty
18. worth, position
19. send away
20. for
21. snatch away
22. a going forth, outcome, departure
23. fortune, wealth
24. thing done, act, deed
25. pertaining to grain
26. heavy, serious
27. by this time, already
28. interrupt, discontinue
29. freedom
30. military
31. known
32. on account of
33. rank, class
34. money
35. drive, defeat
36. full
37. order, instruct, advise
38. put in charge of
39. first . . . tenth
40. near; *as noun*, a relative
41. put before, propose
42. account, theory, manner
43. drive back, reduce, render
44. repair
45. queen
46. grain supplies
47. military affairs, art of war
48. slavery
49. hope
50. such

WORD STUDY

1. In the following phrases explain the meaning and origin of the italicized words:

A *cogent* reason

Conservation of national resources

A narrow *exit*

The *gravity* of the situation

A brief *intermission*

A *notorious* fact

The *expulsion* of the king

On account of *propinquity*

Ordinal numerals

A wise *precept*

EUTROPIUS' HISTORY OF ROME
(SELECTIONS)

BOOK ONE

Romulus and the Founding of Rome

Rōmānum imperium ā Rōmulō exōrdium habet, quī
Rheae Silviae, Vestālis virginis, fīlius et, quantum putātus
est, Mārtis erat. Is decem et octō annōs nātus urbem
exiguam in Palātīnō monte cōnstituit, post Trōiae excidium annō trecentēsimō nōnāgēsimō quārtō.   5

Conditā cīvitāte, quam ex nōmine suō Rōmam vocāvit,
haec ferē ēgit. Multitūdinem fīnitimōrum in cīvitātem
recēpit, centum ex seniōribus lēgit, quōrum cōnsiliō omnia
ageret, quōs senātōrēs nōmināvit propter senectūtem. Tum,
cum uxōrēs ipse et populus suus nōn habērent, invītāvit 10
ad spectāculum lūdōrum vīcīnās urbī Rōmae nātiōnēs
atque eārum virginēs rapuit. Commōtīs bellīs propter
raptārum iniūriam Caenīnēnsēs vīcit, Antemnātēs, Crus-
tumīnōs, Sabīnōs, Fīdēnātēs, Vēientēs. Haec omnia oppida
urbem cingunt. Et cum ortā subitō tempestāte nōn com- 15
pāruisset, annō rēgnī trīcēsimō septimō ad deōs trānsīsse
crēditus est et cōnsecrātus. Deinde Rōmae per quīnōs diēs
senātōrēs imperāvērunt et hīs rēgnantibus annus ūnus
complētus est.

Numa, the Peaceful King

Posteā Numa Pompilius rēx creātus est, quī bellum 20
quidem nūllum gessit, sed nōn minus cīvitātī quam
Rōmulus prōfuit. Nam et lēgēs Rōmānīs mōrēsque
cōnstituit, quī cōnsuētūdine proeliōrum iam latrōnēs ac

sēmibarbarī putābantur, et annum dēscrīpsit in decem
mēnsēs prius sine aliquā supputātiōne cōnfūsum, et īnfīnīta
Rōmae sacra ac templa cōnstituit. Morbō dēcessit quad-
rāgēsimō et tertiō imperiī annō.

Tullus Hostilius, the Warrior

5　Huic successit Tullus Hostīlius. Hic bella reparāvit,
Albānōs vīcit, quī ab urbe Rōmā duodecimō mīliāriō sunt,
Vēientēs et Fīdēnātēs, quōrum aliī sextō mīliāriō absunt
ab urbe Rōmā, aliī octāvō decimō, bellō superāvit, urbem
ampliāvit adiectō Caeliō monte. Cum trīgintā et duōs
10　annōs rēgnāsset, fulmine ictus cum domō suā ārsit.

Ancus Marcius. Expansion of Roman Power

Post hunc Ancus Mārcius, Numae ex fīliā nepōs, suscēpit imperium. Contrā Latīnōs dīmicāvit, Aventīnum
montem cīvitātī adiēcit et Iāniculum, apud ōstium Tiberis
cīvitātem suprā mare sextō decimō mīliāriō ab urbe Rōmā
15　condidit. Vīcēsimō et quārtō annō imperiī morbō periit.

Tarquin the Elder. Development of the City

Deinde rēgnum Prīscus Tarquinius accēpit. Hic numerum senātōrum duplicāvit, circum Rōmae aedificāvit,
lūdōs Rōmānōs īnstituit, quī ad nostram memoriam per-
manent. Vīcit īdem etiam Sabīnōs et nōn parum agrōrum
20　sublātum īsdem urbis Rōmae territōriō iūnxit, prīmusque
triumphāns urbem intrāvit. Mūrōs fēcit et cloācās,
Capitōlium inchoāvit. Trīcēsimō octāvō imperiī annō per
Ancī fīliōs occīsus est, rēgis eius, cui ipse successerat.

Servius Tullius. Further Expansion

Post hunc Servius Tullius suscēpit imperium, genitus ex
25　nōbilī fēminā, captīvā tamen et ancillā. Hic quoque
Sabīnōs subēgit, montēs trēs, Quirīnālem, Vīminālem,

Ēsquilīnum, urbī adiūnxit, fossās circum mūrum dūxit.
Prīmus omnium cēnsum ōrdināvit, quī adhūc per orbem
terrārum incognitus erat. Sub eō Rōma omnibus in
cēnsum dēlātīs habuit capita LXXXIII mīlia cīvium Rōmānōrum cum hīs, quī in agrīs erant. Occīsus est scelere 5
generī suī Tarquinī Superbī, fīliī eius rēgis, cui ipse successerat, et fīliae, quam Tarquinius habēbat uxōrem.

Tarquin the Proud. End of the Kings

L. Tarquinius Superbus, septimus atque ultimus rēgum,
Volscōs, quae gēns ad Campāniam euntibus nōn longē ab
urbe est, vīcit, Gabiōs cīvitātem et Suessam Pōmētiam 10
subēgit, cum Tuscīs pācem fēcit et templum Iovī in Capitōliō aedificāvit. Posteā Ardeam oppugnāns, in octāvō
decimō mīliāriō ab urbe Rōmā positam cīvitātem, imperium
perdidit. Cumque imperāsset annōs quattuor et vīgintī
cum uxōre et līberīs suīs fūgit. Ita Rōmae rēgnātum est 15
per septem rēgēs annīs ducentīs quadrāgintā tribus, cum
adhūc Rōma, ubi plūrimum, vix usque ad quīntum deci-
mum mīliārium possidēret.

Beginning of the Republic

Hinc cōnsulēs coepēre, prō ūnō rēge duo, hāc causā
creātī, ut, sī ūnus malus esse voluisset, alter eum habēns 20
potestātem similem coercēret. Et placuit nē imperium
longius quam annuum habērent, nē per diūturnitātem potes-
tātis īnsolentiōrēs redderentur, sed cīvīlēs semper essent,
quī sē post annum scīrent futūrōs esse prīvātōs. Fuērunt
igitur annō prīmō ab expulsīs rēgibus cōnsulēs L. Iūnius 25
Brūtus, quī maximē ēgerat ut Tarquinius pellerētur, et
Tarquinius Collātīnus, marītus Lucrētiae. Sed Tarquiniō
Collātīnō statim sublāta est dignitās. Placuerat enim, nē
quisquam in urbe manēret, quī Tarquinius vocārētur. Ergō
acceptō omnī patrimōniō suō ex urbe migrāvit et locō 30
ipsīus factus est L. Valerius Pūblicola cōnsul.

Wars of the Early Republic

Commōvit tamen bellum urbī Rōmae rēx Tarquinius,
quī fuerat expulsus, et collēctīs multīs gentibus, ut in
rēgnum posset restituī, dīmicāvit. In prīmā pugnā Brūtus
cōnsul et Arrūns, Tarquinī fīlius in vicem sē occīdērunt,
5 Rōmānī tamen ex eā pugnā victōrēs recessērunt. Brūtum
mātrōnae Rōmānae, dēfēnsōrem pudīcitiae suae, quasi
commūnem patrem per annum lūxērunt. Valerius Pūblicola Sp. Lucrētium Tricipitīnum collēgam sibi fēcit,
Lucrētiae patrem, quō morbō mortuō iterum Horātium
10 Pulvillum collēgam sibi sūmpsit. Ita prīmus annus quīnque cōnsulēs habuit, cum Tarquinius Collātīnus propter
nōmen urbe cessisset, Brūtus in proeliō perīsset, Sp.
Lucrētius morbō mortuus esset.

Secundō quoque annō iterum Tarquinius ut reciperētur
15 in rēgnum bellum Rōmānīs intulit, auxilium eī ferente
Porsennā, Tusciae rēge, et Rōmam paene cēpit. Vērum
tum quoque victus est.

Tertiō annō post rēgēs exāctōs Tarquinius cum suscipī
nōn posset in rēgnum neque eī Porsenna, quī pācem cum
20 Rōmānīs fēcerat, praestāret auxilium, Tusculum sē contulit, quae cīvitās nōn longē ab urbe est, atque ibi per
quattuordecim annōs prīvātus cum uxōre cōnsenuit.

Quārtō annō post rēgēs exāctōs cum Sabīnī Rōmānīs
bellum intulissent, victī sunt, et dē hīs triumphātum est.

Death of Brutus. The Dictatorship

25 Quīntō annō L. Valerius ille, Brūtī collēga et quater
cōnsul, fātāliter mortuus est, adeō pauper, ut collātīs ā
populō nummīs sūmptum habuerit sepultūrae. Quem
mātrōnae sīcutī Brūtum annum lūxērunt.

Nōnō annō post rēgēs exāctōs cum gener Tarquinī ad
30 iniūriam socerī vindicandam ingentem collēgisset exercitum, nova Rōmae dignitās est creāta, quae dictātūra
appellātur, maior quam cōnsulātus. Eōdem annō etiam

magister equitum factus est, quī dictātōrī obsequerētur.
Dictātor autem Rōmae prīmus fuit T. Larcius, magister
equitum prīmus Sp. Cassius.

The Establishment of the Tribunate

Sextō decimō annō post rēgēs exāctōs sēditiōnem populus
Rōmae fēcit, tamquam ā senātū atque cōnsulibus pre- 5
merētur. Tum et ipse sibi tribūnōs plēbis quasi propriōs
iūdicēs et dēfēnsōrēs creāvit, per quōs contrā senātum et
cōnsulēs tūtus esse posset.

War with the Volscians

Sequentī annō Volscī contrā Rōmānōs bellum reparā-
vērunt, et victī aciē etiam Coriolōs cīvitātem, quam habē- 10
bant optimam, perdidērunt.

Octāvō decimō annō postquam rēgēs ēiectī erant, expulsus ex urbe Q. Mārcius, dux Rōmānus, quī Coriolōs
cēperat, Volscōrum cīvitātem, ad ipsōs Volscōs contendit
īrātus et auxilia contrā Rōmānōs accēpit. Rōmānōs saepe 15
vīcit, usque ad quīntum mīliārium urbis accessit, oppugnātūrus etiam patriam suam, lēgātīs, quī pācem petēbant,
repudiātīs, nisi ad eum māter Veturia et uxor Volumnia
ex urbe vēnissent, quārum flētū et dēprecātiōne superātus
remōvit exercitum. Atque hic secundus post Tarquinium 20
fuit, quī dux contrā patriam suam esset.

The Fabii and the War with Veii

C. Fabiō et L. Virgīniō cōnsulibus trecentī nōbilēs
hominēs, quī ex Fabiā familiā erant, contrā Vēientēs
bellum sōlī suscēpērunt, prōmittentēs senātuī et populō per
sē omne certāmen implendum. Itaque profectī, omnēs 25
nōbilēs et quī singulī magnōrum exercituum ducēs esse
dēbērent, in proeliō concidērunt. Ūnus omnīnō super-
fuit ex tantā familiā, quī propter aetātem puerīlem
dūcī nōn potuerat ad pugnam. Post haec cēnsus in urbe

habitus est et inventa sunt cīvium capita CXVII mīlia
CCCXIX.

Cincinnatus Made Dictator

Sequentī tamen annō cum in Algidō monte ab urbe duodecimō fermē mīliāriō Rōmānus obsidērētur exercitus, L.
5 Quīntius Cincinnātus dictātor est factus, quī agrum quattuor iugerum possidēns manibus suīs colēbat. Is cum in
opere et arāns esset inventus, sūdōre dētersō togam praetextam accēpit et caesīs hostibus līberāvit exercitum.

Wars with Fidenae and Veii

Annō trecentēsimō et quīntō decimō ab urbe conditā
10 Fīdēnātēs contrā Rōmānōs rebellāvērunt. Auxilium hīs
praestābant Vēientēs et rēx Vēientium Tolumnius. Quae
ambae cīvitātēs tam vīcīnae urbī sunt, ut Fīdēnae sextō,
Vēī octāvō decimō mīliāriō absint. Coniūnxērunt sē hīs et
Volscī. Sed Mam. Aemiliō dictātōre et L. Quīntiō Cin-
15 cinnātō magistrō equitum victī etiam rēgem perdidērunt.
Fīdēnae captae et excīsae.

Post vīgintī deinde annōs Vēientānī rebellāvērunt. Dictātor contrā ipsōs missus est Fūrius Camillus, quī prīmum
eōs vīcit aciē, mox etiam cīvitātem diū obsidēns cēpit,
20 antīquissimam Ītaliae atque dītissimam. Post eam cēpit et
Faliscōs, nōn minus nōbilem cīvitātem. Sed commōta est
eī invidia, quasi praedam male dīvīsisset, damnātusque ob
eam causam et expulsus cīvitāte.

Capture of Rome by the Gauls

Statim Gallī Senonēs ad urbem vēnērunt et victōs Rōmā-
25 nōs ūndecimō mīliāriō ā Rōmā apud flūmen Alliam secūtī
etiam urbem occupāvērunt. Neque dēfendī quicquam nisi
Capitōlium potuit; quod cum diū obsēdissent et iam Rōmānī famē labōrārent, acceptō aurō, nē Capitōlium obsi-
dērent, recessērunt. Sed ā Camillō, quī in vīcīnā cīvitāte

exulābat, Gallīs superventum est gravissimēque victī sunt.
Posteā tamen etiam secūtus eōs Camillus ita cecīdit, ut et
aurum, quod hīs datum fuerat, et omnia, quae cēperant,
mīlitāria signa revocāret. Ita tertiō triumphāns urbem
ingressus est et appellātus secundus Rōmulus, quasi et ipse ᵴ
patriae conditor.

BOOK SIX

(Chapters 17-25)

Caesar's Wars in Gaul

Annō urbis conditae sexcentēsimō nōnāgēsimō tertiō
C. Iūlius Caesar, quī posteā imperāvit, cum L. Bibulō cōnsul est factus. Dēcrēta est eī Gallia et Īllyricum cum
legiōnibus decem. Is prīmus vīcit Helvētiōs, quī nunc 10
Sēquanī appellantur, deinde vincendō per bella gravissima
usque ad Ōceanum Britannicum prōcessit. Domuit autem
annīs novem ferē omnem Galliam, quae inter Alpēs, flūmen
Rhodanum, Rhēnum et Ōceanum est et circuitū patet ad
bis et trīciēs centēna mīlia passuum. Britannīs mox bellum 15
intulit, quibus ante eum nē nōmen quidem Rōmānōrum cognitum erat, eōsque victōs obsidibus acceptīs stīpendiāriōs
fēcit. Galliae autem tribūtī nōmine annuum imperāvit
stīpendium quadringentiēs, Germānōsque trāns Rhēnum
adgressus inmānissimīs proeliīs vīcit. Inter tot successūs 20
ter male pugnāvit, apud Arvernōs semel praesēns et absēns
in Germāniā bis. Nam lēgātī eius duo, Titūrius et Aurunculēius, per īnsidiās caesī sunt.

Defeat of Crassus by the Parthians

Circā eadem tempora, annō urbis conditae sexcentēsimō
nōnāgēsimō septimō, M. Licinius Crassus, collēga Cn. Pom- 25
pēī Magnī in cōnsulātū secundō, contrā Parthōs missus est
et cum circā Carrās contrā ōmen et auspicia dīmicāsset, ā

Surēnā, Orōdis rēgis duce, victus ad postrēmum interfectus
est cum fīliō, clārissimō et praestantissimō iuvene. Reliquiae exercitūs per C. Cassium quaestōrem servātae sunt,
quī singulārī animō perditās rēs tantā virtūte restituit, ut
5 Persās rediēns trāns Euphrāten crēbrīs proeliīs vinceret.

Beginning of the Civil War

Hinc iam bellum cīvīle successit exsecrandum et lacri-
mābile, quō praeter calamitātēs, quae in proeliīs accidērunt,
etiam populī Rōmānī fortūna mūtāta est. Caesar enim
rediēns ex Galliā victor coepit poscere alterum cōnsulātum
10 atque ita, ut sine dubietāte aliquā eī dēferrētur. Contrādictum est ā Mārcellō cōnsule, ā Bibulō, ā Pompēiō, ā
Catōne, iussusque dīmissīs exercitibus ad urbem redīre.
Propter quam iniūriam ab Arīminō, ubi mīlitēs congregātōs habēbat, adversum patriam cum exercitū vēnit. Cōn-
15 sulēs cum Pompēiō senātusque omnis atque ūniversa nōbilitās ex urbe fūgit et in Graeciam trānsiit. Apud Ēpīrum,
Macedoniam, Achāiam Pompēiō duce senātus contrā Caesarem bellum parāvit.

The War in Spain and Greece

Caesar vacuam urbem ingressus dictātōrem sē fēcit. Inde
20 Hispāniās petiit. Ibi Pompēī exercitūs validissimōs et
fortissimōs cum tribus ducibus, L. Āfrāniō, M. Petrēiō,
M. Varrōne, superāvit. Inde regressus in Graeciam trānsiit, adversum Pompēium dīmicāvit. Prīmō proeliō victus
est et fugātus, ēvāsit tamen, quia nocte interveniente Pom-
25 pēius sequī nōluit, dīxitque Caesar nec Pompēium scīre
vincere et illō tantum diē sē potuisse superārī. Deinde in
Thessaliā apud Palaeopharsālum prōductīs utrimque in-
gentibus cōpiīs dīmicāvērunt. Pompēī aciēs habuit XL
mīlia peditum, equitēs in sinistrō cornū sexcentōs, in dextrō
30 quīngentōs, praetereā tōtīus Orientis auxilia, tōtam nōbili-
tātem, innumerōs senātōrēs, praetōriōs, cōnsulārēs et quī

magnōrum iam bellōrum victōrēs fuissent. Caesar in aciē
suā habuit peditum nōn integra xxx mīlia, equitēs mīlle.

Pompey's Defeat and Death

Numquam adhūc Rōmānae cōpiae in ūnum neque
maiōrēs neque meliōribus ducibus convēnerant, tōtum
terrārum orbem facile subāctūrae, sī contrā barbarōs dūce- 5
rentur. Pugnātum tum est ingentī contentiōne, victusque
ad postrēmum Pompēius et castra eius dīrepta sunt. Ipse
fugātus Alexandrīam petiit, ut ā rēge Aegyptī, cui tūtor ā
senātū datus fuerat propter iuvenīlem eius aetātem, acci-
peret auxilia. Quī fortūnam magis quam amīcitiam secūtus 10
occīdit Pompēium, caput eius et ānulum Caesarī mīsit. Quō
cōnspectō Caesar etiam lacrimās fūdisse dīcitur, tantī virī
intuēns caput et generī quondam suī.

Caesar in Egypt and Asia Minor

Mox Caesar Alexandrīam vēnit. Ipsī quoque Ptolemaeus parāre voluit īnsidiās, quā causā bellum rēgī inlātum 15
est. Victus in Nīlō periit inventumque est eius corpus cum
lōrīcā aureā. Caesar Alexandrīā potītus rēgnum Cleopatrae
dedit, Ptolemaeī sorōrī. Rediēns inde Caesar Pharnacēn,
Mithridātis Magnī fīlium, quī Pompēiō in auxilium apud
Thessaliam fuerat, rebellantem in Pontō et multās populī 20
Rōmānī prōvinciās occupantem vīcit aciē, posteā ad mortem
coēgit.

Renewal of the War in Africa

Inde Rōmam regressus tertiō sē cōnsulem fēcit cum M.
Aemiliō Lepidō, quī eī magister equitum dictātōrī ante
annum fuerat. Inde in Āfricam profectus est, ubi īnfīnīta 25
nōbilitās cum Iubā, Mauritāniae rēge, bellum reparāverat.
Ducēs autem Rōmānī erant P. Cornēlius Scīpiō ex genere
antīquissimō Scīpiōnis Āfricānī (hic etiam socer Pompēī
Magnī fuerat), M. Petrēius, Q. Vārus, M. Porcius Catō,

L. Cornēlius Faustus, Sullae dictātōris fīlius. Contrā hōs
commissō proeliō post multās dīmicātiōnēs victor fuit
Caesar. Catō, Scīpiō, Petrēius, Iuba ipsī sē occīdērunt.
Faustus, Sullae quondam dictātōris fīlius, Pompēī gener, ā
5 Caesare interfectus est.

End of the Civil War

Post annum Caesar Rōmam regressus quārtō sē cōnsulem fēcit et statim ad Hispāniās est profectus, ubi Pompēī fīliī, Cn. Pompēius et Sex. Pompēius, ingēns bellum
praeparāverant. Multa proelia fuērunt, ultimum apud
10 Mundam cīvitātem, in quō adeō Caesar paene victus est,
ut fugientibus suīs sē voluerit occīdere, nē post tantam
reī mīlitāris glōriam in potestātem adulēscentium nātus
annōs sex et quīnquāgintā venīret. Dēnique revocātīs suīs
vīcit. Ex Pompēī fīliīs maior occīsus est, minor fūgit.

Caesar the Ruler of Rome. His Death

15 Inde Caesar bellīs cīvīlibus tōtō orbe compositīs Rōmam
rediit. Agere īnsolentius coepit et contrā cōnsuētūdinem
Rōmānae lībertātis. Cum ergō et honōrēs ex suā voluntāte
praestāret, quī ā populō anteā dēferēbantur, nec senātuī ad
sē venientī adsurgeret aliaque rēgia ac paene tyrannica
20 faceret, coniūrātum est in eum ā sexāgintā vel amplius
senātōribus equitibusque Rōmānīs. Praecipuī fuērunt
inter coniūrātōs duo Brūtī ex eō genere Brūtī, quī prīmus
Rōmae cōnsul fuerat et rēgēs expulerat, et C. Cassius et
Servīlius Casca. Ergō Caesar, cum senātūs diē inter
25 cēterōs vēnisset ad cūriam, tribus et vīgintī vulneribus
cōnfossus est.

NOTES

Eutropius was a Roman historian who wrote in the latter part of the fourth century A. D. His book, which was called *Breviarium ab Urbe Condita*, was a brief history of Rome from the founding of the city to the year 364 A. D.

Page 259, l. 1. imperium, *state* (literally *authority*).

quī Rhēae Silviae, etc., order for translation, **quī erat fīlius Rhēae Silviae, Vestālis virginis, et (quantum putātus est) Mārtis.**

2. quantum putātus est, *as it was believed* (literally, *as he was thought*).

3. decem et octō annōs nātus, *at the age of eighteen years* (literally, *having been born eighteen years*); **annōs** is accusative of duration of time.

4. Palātīnō monte, *the Palatine Hill,* one of the seven hills of Rome.

5. annō trecentēsimō, etc., according to the common legend Rome was founded in the year 753 B. C. Some authorities give 754.

6. Conditā cīvitāte, *after he had founded the city, when the city was founded* (literally *with the city founded,* ablative absolute).

7. haec ferē ēgit, *his further achievements were about as follows* (*he did about these things*).

8. quōrum . . . ageret, *by whose advice he should act in all matters* (*should do everything*); a relative clause of purpose.

10. cum, *since.*

uxōrēs, object of **habērent.**

12. Commōtīs bellīs, *when war broke out,* ablative absolute.

propter raptārum iniūriam, a genitive modifying the object of a preposition often stands between the preposition and the object.

14. Sabīnōs, in apposition with the three proper names preceding. The towns whose inhabitants are referred to were Sabine towns. The other two towns (Fidenae and Veii) were Etruscan towns.

15. nōn compāruisset, *had disappeared.*

17. cōnsecrātus (est), *was deified.*

Rōmae, locative case.

per quīnōs diēs, *for five days each.*

18. **hīs rēgnantibus,** *under their rule.*

21. **cīvitātī,** dative with **prōfuit.** Most compounds of **sum** take the dative.

22. **et,** correlative with **et** in line 1, p. 260, *both . . . and.* The first **et** may be omitted in translation.

Rōmānīs, *for the Romans,* a dative of reference.

23. **cōnsuētūdine proeliōrum,** *from their continual battles (from their custom of battles).*

Page 260, l. 1. **in decem mēnsēs,** others say that Numa divided the year into twelve months.

2. **cōnfūsum,** agrees with **annum.**

3. **Morbō dēcessit,** *died a natural death (died from illness)* ; **morbō** is ablative of cause.

5. **Huic,** dative with a compound of **sub** (**successit**).

6. **duodecimō mīliāriō,** *twelve miles (at the twelfth milestone).* The form of expression in Caesar, Cicero, or any other writer of the best period would have been **duodecim mīlia** (or **mīlibus**) **passuum.**

7. **quōrum aliī . . . aliī,** translate as if **quōrum** referred to the names of the towns instead of to their inhabitants: *one of which . . . the other.* A Latin writer of the best period would use **alterī . . . alterī.**

9. **adiectō Caeliō monte,** *by adding the Caelian Hill.*

10. **rēgnāsset,** contracted form of **rēgnāvisset.**

ārsit, *was consumed;* from **ārdeō,** *to burn,* in intransitive sense.

11. **Numae ex fīliā nepōs,** *a grandson of Numa, the son of his daughter.*

suscēpit imperium, *succeeded to the throne.*

13. **Iāniculum,** part of the object of **adiēcit.** The Janiculum is on the opposite side of the Tiber from the other hills and is not usually reckoned as one of the seven hills.

apud ōstium, the conjunction **et** is understood before **apud,** and also before **Aventīnum** in line 12. Conjunctions are omitted more freely in Latin than in English.

14. **cīvitātem,** the name of the city was Ostia. It was the seaport of Rome.

suprā mare, *on the sea.*

17. **circum** (noun), the Circus Maximus, an enclosure between the Palatine and the Aventine hills, for races and other sports.

18. **lūdōs Rōmānōs,** this was a particular celebration occurring in September of each year.

19. **īdem,** translate simply *he* (subject of **vīcit**). It is sometimes difficult to indicate in English the exact emphasis given by this word.

nōn parum agrōrum, *a large area of their country (not a little of their land)*; the phrase is object of **iūnxit.** The word **parum,** which is sometimes an adverb, is here a noun.

20. **sublātum īsdem . . . iūnxit,** *he took from them* (**īsdem**) *a large area of their country and annexed it to;* **īsdem** is a dative of reference used with a word of taking away.

sublātum, perfect participle of **tollō,** in agreement with **parum.** The participle is occasionally translated as here by a verb coordinate with the main verb of its sentence.

21. **triumphāns,** *with a triumphal procession.*

Mūrōs fēcit, this wall was known as the Servian Wall, and was commonly believed to have been built by the king who followed Tarquinius Priscus.

22. **per fīliōs.** The accusative with **per** is here equivalent to the ablative of agent, **ā fīliīs.**

23. **rēgis eius,** in apposition with **Ancī.**

24. **genitus ex,** *a son of.*

Page 261, l. 1. dūxit, *extended.*

3. **omnibus in cēnsum dēlātīs,** *when all had been enumerated.*

4. **capita lxxxiii mīlia cīvium Rōmānōrum,** *a population of eighty-three thousand Roman citizens.* **mīlia** is a noun in apposition with **capita,** which means *heads,* as in the phrase ''so many head of cattle.''

7. **fīliae,** genitive, depending on **scelere,** connected by **et** with **generī. uxōrem,** *as his wife.*

9. **quae gēns,** *a nation which.*

ad Campāniam euntibus, *in the direction of Campania (for those going toward),* a special use of the dative of reference. The participle is used as a substantive.

10. **Gabiōs cīvitātem,** *the city of Gabii.* When the name of a city is given with the word **urbs** (or **cīvitās**) it usually stands in apposition. The English equivalent is *of* and the proper name.

11. **Capitōliō** here means the Capitoline Hill; in line 22, p. 260, **Capitōlium** means the Capitoline temple.

12. **in octāvō decimō mīliāriō,** the preposition might have been omitted without affecting the meaning, as in line 7, p. 260.

13. **positam,** *situated.*

14. **perdidit,** he was compelled to flee because of the indignation aroused by a crime committed by one of his sons.

cumque imperāsset, etc., *and after a reign of twenty-four years.* **-que** is always translated before the word to which it is added.

imperāsset, contracted form of **imperāvisset.**

15. **Rōmae,** the same case as **Rōmae** in line 17, p. 259.

rēgnātum est per septem rēgēs, *the reigns of seven kings lasted.* The verb is impersonal. The use of **per septem rēgēs** is like that of **per fīliōs,** line 22, p. 260.

16. **annīs,** the use of the ablative instead of the accusative to express duration is irregular.

cum, *although.*

17. **ubi plūrimum,** *at its greatest extent (where most).*

18. **possidēret,** *exercised authority.*

19. **Hinc cōnsulēs coepēre,** *after this the consulship was established.*

coepēre, the ending **-ērunt** is more frequently used than **-ēre** in the third person plural of the perfect, but some writers use both.

duo, in apposition with **cōnsulēs.**

20. **malus,** may here be translated *troublesome to the state.*

voluisset, subjunctive by attraction.

eum, object of **coercēret.**

21. **placuit nē habērent,** *it was thought best that they should not hold (it was pleasing that,* etc.)

22. **nē redderentur,** *that they might not become (be rendered).*

23. **cīvīlēs,** *of the character of citizens.*

24. **quī scīrent,** *since they knew.*

sē futūrōs esse prīvātōs, indirect discourse.

25. **ab expulsīs rēgibus,** *after the expulsion of the kings.*

26. **maximē ēgerat ut Tarquinius pellerētur,** *had been especially active in bringing about the expulsion of Tarquinius.*

27. **Lucrētiae,** she was the victim of the crime which had been the cause of the uprising against Tarquinius.

Tarquiniō Collātīnō, *from Tarquinius Collatinus.* The case is the same as that of **īsdem,** line 20, p. 260.

28. **nē quisquam,** *that no one.*

30. **locō ipsīus,** *in his place.*

31. **cōnsul,** predicate nominative with **factus est.**

Page 262, l. 1. urbī, dative of reference with the phrase **bellum commōvit.**

Rōmae, dative, in apposition with **urbī.**

3. **restituī,** present passive infinitive.

4. **in vicem sē occīdērunt,** *killed each other.*

7. **lūxērunt,** from **lūgeō.**

9. **patrem,** in apposition with **Sp. Lucrētium Tricipitīnum.**

quō . . . mortuō, *and when he (Tricipitinus) fell ill and died,* ablative absolute.

10. **collēgam sibi,** *as his colleague.* **sibi** in line 10, and also in line 8, is dative of reference.

12. urbe, *from the city.*

perīsset, from **pereō.**

15. Rōmānīs, dative with a form of **īnferre,** a compound of **in** which does not express motion.

ferente Porsennā, ablative absolute; **auxilium** is object of **ferente.**

18. post rēgēs exāctōs means the same as **ab expulsīs rēgibus,** line 25, p. 261.

20. Tusculum, *to Tusculum.*

21. quae cīvitās, the order of translation is the same as that of **quae gēns,** line 9, p. 261.

22. prīvātus, *in private life.*

cōnsenuit, from **cōnsenēscō.**

24. dē hīs triumphātum est, *a triumph was celebrated for the victory over them.* The verb is impersonal like **rēgnātum est,** line 15, p. 261.

25. ille, following the noun with which it agrees, means *the celebrated.*

26. fātāliter mortuus est, translate like **morbō dēcessit,** line 3, p. 260 (**fātāliter,** *by fate*).

27. sūmptum habuerit sepultūrae, *the expense of his funeral was paid* (*he had the expense of his funeral*).

29. ad iniūriam socerī vindicandam, *to avenge the overthrow of his father-in-law.*

30. ingentem, modifies **exercitum.**

Page 263, l. 1. dictātōrī, dative with a compound of **ob.**

obsequerētur, subjunctive in a relative clause of purpose.

5. tamquam premerētur, *on the ground that they were oppressed.*

6. Tum et ipse, *then, also, they;* **ipse** is singular to agree with **populus,** but the English idiom requires a plural.

16. urbis, we should say ''from the city.''

oppugnātūrus patriam suam, *intending to attack his native city.*

20. secundus post Tarquinium, *the first after Tarquinius.* The Latin counts the starting point of a series in reckoning the position of any member of the series.

25. omne certāmen implendum, *that the whole undertaking* (*struggle*) *would be carried out.* This construction is not according to the usage of Latin of the best period.

omnēs nōbilēs et quī . . . dēbērent, *all of them* (*being*) *men of high rank and each one capable of commanding a great army.*

Page 264, l. 7. togam praetextam, the toga praetexta, which had a purple border, was worn by the more important officials of the government and also by young boys. The toga worn by the adult private citizen was white.

12. **sextō mīliāriō absint,** *is (only) six miles distant.*

20. **dītissimam,** superlative of **dīves.**

22. **quasi,** *on the ground that.*

24. **Statim,** *just at this time.*

victōs, translate by a relative clause, *whom they had defeated.*

25. **secūtī,** *pursuing.*

28. **labōrārent,** *were suffering.*

Page 265, l. 1. Gallīs superventum est, *the Gauls were surprised.* Impersonal construction.

gravissimē, *overwhelmingly.*

2. **eōs ita cecīdit,** *so thoroughly crushed them.*

5. **quasi,** *as if he were.*

11. **Sēquanī,** the Sequani and Helvetians were originally different tribes, but either they had been united at the time of Eutropius, or else Eutropius confused their identity.

vincendō per bella gravissima, *conquering in hard-fought wars.* **vincendō** is a gerund used somewhat freely as an ablative of manner.

12. **Ōceanum Britannicum,** *the English Channel.*

14. **circuitū,** *in circumference.*

ad bis et trīciēs centēna mīlia passuum, *about 3,200 miles.*

16. **nē . . . quidem,** the emphatic word stands between **nē** and **quidem.**

17. **eōs victōs,** *when he had conquered them.*

18. **Galliae imperāvit,** *he levied upon Gaul.*

annuum, modifies **stīpendium.**

19. **quadringentiēs** (supply **centēna mīlia sēstertium**), *forty million sesterces,* a little over $1,600,000.

21. **male pugnāvit,** *met with defeat.*

27. **circā,** *near,* an unusual meaning of the word.

Page 266, l. 4. quī . . . restituit, *who was a man of unusual courage, and remedied the disaster.*

5. **Persās,** object of **vinceret.**

6. **exsecrandum,** *deplorable.*

7. **quō,** *by which.*

10. **Contrādictum est,** *he was opposed;* the verb is impersonal.

13. **iniūriam,** *affront.*

congregātōs habēbat, translate like the past perfect of **congregō.**

15. **nōbilitās,** *nobles.*

16. **fūgit,** singular, to agree with the nearest part of the compound subject.

17. **Pompēiō duce,** *under the leadership of Pompey.*

20. **petiit,** *went to (sought).*

24. **nocte interveniente,** *as night had come on.*

25. nec Pompēium scīre vincere, *that Pompey did not know how to conquer.*

27. Palaeopharsālum, the town is usually called Pharsalus.

Page 267, l. 1. fuissent, subjunctive in a relative descriptive clause.

2. nōn integra, *not quite (not entire).*

3. Numquam ... subāctūrae, *never before had larger or more skilfully commanded Roman forces met, forces which might easily have subdued the whole world.* The employment of the future active participle here is not according to the best Latin usage. The negatives neque ... neque do not destroy the effect of the preceding negative, numquam.

5. dūcerentur, a somewhat irregular use of a condition. It is in sense contrary to fact in past time (had been led), but the form suggests merely anticipation from a past point of view.

6. Pugnātum est ingentī contentiōne, *the battle was fought with great stubbornness.*

victus, supply est.

10. Quī, *he.*

fortūnam magis quam amīcitiam secūtus, *having regard for his own fortunes rather than for friendship.*

11. Quō cōnspectō, *at the sight.*

13. generī, Pompey had married Caesar's daughter, but she had died before the beginning of the civil war.

14. Ipsī parāre voluit īnsidiās, *wished to deal treacherously with him.* Ipsī is a dative of reference.

16. Victus periit, *he was defeated and lost his life.*

17. Alexandrīā, ablative with potior.

18. Pharnacēn, object of vīcit; rebellantem and occupantem agree with Pharnacēn. It was after this battle that Caesar sent the famous message vēnī, vīdī, vīcī.

21. ad mortem coēgit, Eutropius implies that Caesar compelled Pharnaces to commit suicide. But other historians say that he was killed by one of his generals.

24. eī dictātōrī, *when he (Caesar) was dictator;* eī is a dative of reference and dictātōrī is in apposition with it.

ante annum, *a year before.*

25. īnfīnīta nōbilitās, *a great many of the nobles* (who had fled from Rome).

Page 268, l. 6. Post annum, *a year later.*

9. ultimum, supply proelium.

10. adeō paene, *so nearly.*

11. fugientibus suīs, *when his men began to flee,* ablative absolute.

12. **nātus annōs sex et quīnquāgintā,** *at the age of fifty-six.*

14. **maior,** *the older;* **minor,** *the younger.* The word **nātū** is understood.

15. **bellīs cīvīlibus compositīs,** *when the civil wars had been ended.*

16. **Agere īnsolentius,** *to conduct himself somewhat arrogantly.*

17. **et,** coordinate with **nec** and **-que.** Omit in translation.
honōrēs, *offices.*

19. **rēgia,** *king-like.*

20. **coniūrātum est in eum,** *a conspiracy was formed against him,* impersonal.

24. **senātūs diē,** *on the day of the meeting of the senate.*

APPENDIX

SUMMARY OF DECLENSIONS AND CONJUGATIONS
NOUNS

1. FIRST DECLENSION, ā-stems

	SINGULAR	PLURAL
Nom.	rosa	rosae
Gen.	rosae	rosārum
Dat.	rosae	rosīs
Acc.	rosam	rosās
Abl.	rosā	rosīs

2. SECOND DECLENSION, o-stems

SINGULAR

N.	amīcus	puer	ager	vir	templum
G.	amīcī	puerī	agrī	virī	templī
D.	amīcō	puerō	agrō	virō	templō
Ac.	amīcum	puerum	agrum	virum	templum
Ab.	amīcō	puerō	agrō	virō	templō

PLURAL

N.	amīcī	puerī	agrī	**virī**	templa
G.	amīcōrum	puerōrum	agrōrum	virōrum	templōrum
D.	amīcīs	puerīs	agrīs	virīs	templīs
Ac.	amīcōs	puerōs	agrōs	virōs	templa
Ab.	amīcīs	puerīs	agrīs	virīs	templīs

NOTE. The vocative singular of -**us** nouns ends in -**e**: **amīce**. The genitive singular and the vocative singular of **fīlius** and of proper nouns in -**ius** end in -**ī**: **fīlī**.

3. THIRD DECLENSION

A. CONSONANT STEMS

SINGULAR

N.	lēx	mīles	frāter	homō
G.	lēgis	mīlitis	frātris	hominis
D.	lēgī	mīlitī	frātrī	hominī
Ac.	lēgem	mīlitem	frātrem	hominem
Ab.	lēge	mīlite	frātre	homine

PLURAL

N.	lēgēs	mīlitēs	frātrēs	hominēs
G.	lēgum	mīlitum	frātrum	hominum
D.	lēgibus	mīlitibus	frātribus	hominibus
Ac.	lēgēs	mīlitēs	frātrēs	hominēs
Ab.	lēgibus	mīlitibus	frātribus	hominibus

SINGULAR

N.	flūmen	caput	corpus	iter
G.	flūminis	capitis	corporis	itineris
D.	flūminī	capitī	corporī	itinerī
Ac.	flūmen	caput	corpus	iter
Ab.	flūmine	capite	corpore	itinere

PLURAL

N.	flūmina	capita	corpora	itinera
G.	flūminum	capitum	corporum	itinerum
D.	flūminibus	capitibus	corporibus	itineribus
Ac.	flūmina	capita	corpora	itinera
Ab.	flūminibus	capitibus	corporibus	itineribus

B. i-stems

SINGULAR

N.	hostis	caedēs	ignis	turris
G.	hostis	caedis	ignis	turris
D.	hostī	caedī	ignī	turrī
Ac.	hostem	caedem	ignem	turrim or -em
Ab.	hoste	caede	ignī or -e	turrī or -e

PLURAL

N.	hostēs	caedēs	ignēs	turrēs
G.	hostium	caedium	ignium	turrium
D.	hostibus	caedibus	ignibus	turribus
Ac.	hostīs or -ēs	caedīs or -ēs	ignīs or -ēs	turrīs or -ēs
Ab.	hostibus	caedibus	ignibus	turribus

SINGULAR

N.	īnsigne	calcar	animal
G.	īnsignis	calcāris	animālis
D.	īnsignī	calcarī	animālī
Ac.	īnsigne	calcar	animal
Ab.	īnsignī	calcārī	animālī

PLURAL

N.	īnsignia	calcāria	animālia
G.	īnsignium	calcārium	animālium
D.	īnsignibus	calcāribus	animālibus
Ac.	īnsignia	calcāria	animālia
Ab.	īnsignibus	calcāribus	animālibus

C. Mixed Stems

	SINGULAR	PLURAL	SINGULAR	PLURAL
N.	urbs	urbēs	gēns	gentēs
G.	urbis	urbium	gentis	gentium
D.	urbī	urbibus	gentī	gentibus
Ac.	urbem	urbēs or -īs	gentem	gentēs or -īs
Ab.	urbe	urbibus	gente	gentibus

D. Irregular Nouns

	SINGULAR	PLURAL	SINGULAR	PLURAL
N.	vīs	vīrēs	bōs	bovēs
G.	—	vīrium	bovis	boum
D.	—	vīribus	bovī	būbus or bōbus
Ac.	vim	vīrīs or -ēs	bovem	bovēs
Ab.	vī	vīribus	bove	būbus or bōbus

4.   FOURTH DECLENSION, u-stems

	SINGULAR	PLURAL	SINGULAR	PLURAL
N.	exercitus	exercitūs	cornū	cornua
G.	exercitūs	exercituum	cornūs	cornuum
D.	exercituī or -ū	exercitibus	cornū	cornibus
Ac.	exercitum	exercitūs	cornū	cornua
Ab.	exercitū	exercitibus	cornū	cornibus

	SINGULAR	PLURAL
N.	domus	domūs
G.	domūs	domuum or domōrum
D.	domuī or domō	domibus
Ac.	domum	domūs or domōs
Ab.	domū or domō	domibus
Loc.	domī	

5.   FIFTH DECLENSION, ē-stems

	SINGULAR	PLURAL	SINGULAR	PLURAL
N.	diēs	diēs	rēs	rēs
G.	diēī	diērum	reī	rērum
D.	diēī	diēbus	reī	rēbus
Ac.	diem	diēs	rem	rēs
Ab.	diē	diēbus	rē	rēbus

ADJECTIVES

6.   FIRST AND SECOND DECLENSIONS

bonus, *good*

	SINGULAR			PLURAL		
	Masc.	*Fem.*	*Neut.*	*Masc.*	*Fem.*	*Neut.*
N.	bonus	bona	bonum	bonī	bonae	bona
G.	bonī	bonae	bonī	bonōrum	bonārum	bonōrum
D.	bonō	bonae	bonō	bonīs	bonīs	bonīs
Ac.	bonum	bonam	bonum	bonōs	bonās	bona
Ab.	bonō	bonā	bonō	bonīs	bonīs	bonīs

miser, *unhappy*

	SINGULAR			PLURAL		
N.	miser	misera	miserum	miserī	miserae	misera
G.	miserī	miserae	miserī	miserōrum	miserārum	miserōrum
D.	miserō	miserae	miserō	miserīs	miserīs	miserīs
Ac.	miserum	miseram	miserum	miserōs	miserās	misera
Ab.	miserō	miserā	miserō	miserīs	miserīs	miserīs

pulcher, *beautiful*

	SINGULAR			PLURAL		
N.	pulcher	pulchra	pulchrum	pulchrī	pulchrae	pulchra
G.	pulchrī	pulchrae	pulchrī	pulchrōrum	pulchrārum	pulchrōrum
D.	pulchrō	pulchrae	pulchrō	pulchrīs	pulchrīs	pulchrīs
Ac.	pulchrum	pulchram	pulchrum	pulchrōs	pulchrās	pulchra
Ab.	pulchrō	pulchrā	pulchrō	pulchrīs	pulchrīs	pulchrīs

7. ## THIRD DECLENSION

A. THREE TERMINATIONS—(i-stems)

ācer, *sharp*

	SINGULAR			PLURAL		
	Masc.	*Fem.*	*Neut.*	*Masc.*	*Fem.*	*Neut.*
N	ācer	ācris	ācre	ācrēs	ācrēs	ācria
G.	ācris	ācris	ācris	ācrium	ācrium	ācrium
D.	ācrī	ācrī	ācrī	ācribus	ācribus	ācribus
Ac.	ācrem	ācrem	ācre	ācrēs *or* -īs	ācrēs *or* -īs	ācria
Ab.	ācrī	ācrī	ācrī	ācribus	ācribus	ācribus

B. TWO TERMINATIONS—(i-stems)

omnis, *all*

	SINGULAR		PLURAL	
	Masc. and Fem.	*Neut.*	*Masc. and Fem.*	*Neut.*
N.	omnis	omne	omnēs	omnia
G.	omnis	omnis	omnium	omnium
D.	omnī	omnī	omnibus	omnibus
Ac.	omnem	omne	omnēs *or* -īs	omnia
Ab.	omnī	omnī	omnibus	omnibus

C. ONE TERMINATION

i-stems

fēlīx, *fortunate*   **potēns,** *powerful*   **vetus,** *old*
(*a consonant stem*)

		SINGULAR			
M. and F.	*N.*	*M. and F.*	*N.*	*M. and F.*	*N.*
N. fēlīx	fēlīx	potēns	potēns	vetus	vetus
G. fēlīcis	fēlīcis	potentis	potentis	veteris	veteris
D. fēlīcī	fēlīcī	potentī	potentī	veterī	veterī
Ac. fēlīcem	fēlīx	potentem	potēns	veterem	vetus
Ab. fēlīcī	fēlīcī	potentī, -e	potentī, -e	vetere	vetere

		PLURAL			
N. fēlīcēs	fēlīcia	potentēs	potentia	veterēs	vetera
G. fēlīcium	fēlīcium	potentium	potentium	veterum	veterum
D. fēlīcibus	fēlīcibus	potentibus	potentibus	veteribus	veteribus
Ac. fēlīcēs, -īs	fēlīcia	potentēs, -īs	potentia	veterēs	vetera
Ab. fēlīcibus	fēlīcibus	potentibus	potentibus	veteribus	veteribus

8.   PRESENT PARTICIPLES

	SINGULAR			PLURAL	
Masc. and Fem.	*Neut.*		*Masc. and Fem.*	*Neut.*
N.	portāns	portāns		portantēs	portantia
G.	portantis	portantis		portantium	portantium
D.	portantī	portantī		portantibus	portantibus
Ac.	portantem	portāns		portantēs (-īs)	portantia
Ab.	portante (-ī)	portante (-ī)		portantibus	portantibus

9.   IRREGULAR ADJECTIVES

N.	sōlus	sōla	sōlum	alter	altera	alterum
G.	sōlīus	sōlīus	sōlīus	alterīus	alterīus	alterīus
D.	sōlī	sōlī	sōlī	alterī	alterī	alterī
Ac.	sōlum	sōlam	sōlum	alterum	alteram	alterum
Ab.	sōlō	sōlā	sōlō	alterō	alterā	alterō

(*The plurals are like those of* **bonus** *and* **miser.**)

10   REGULAR COMPARISON OF ADJECTIVES

Positive	*Comparative*	*Superlative*
lātus	lātior, lātius	lātissimus, -a, -um
fortis	fortior, fortius	fortissimus, -a, -um
fēlīx	fēlīcior, fēlīcius	fēlīcissimus, -a, -um
miser	miserior, miserius	miserrimus, -a, -um
facilis	facilior, facilius	facillimus, -a, -um

11.   IRREGULAR COMPARISON OF ADJECTIVES

Positive	*Comparative*	*Superlative*
bonus	melior, melius	optimus, -a, -um
malus	peior, peius	pessimus, -a, -um
magnus	maior, maius	maximus, -a, -um
parvus	minor, minus	minimus, -a, -um
multus	—, plūs	plūrimus, -a, -um

12. DECLENSION OF COMPARATIVES

lātior, *broader*

SINGULAR		PLURAL	
Masc. and Fem.	*Neut.*	*Masc. and Fem.*	*Neut.*
N. lātior	lātius	lātiōrēs	lātiōra
G. lātiōris	lātiōris	lātiōrum	lātiōrum
D. lātiōrī	· lātiōrī	lātiōribus	lātiōribus
Ac. lātiōrem	lātius	lātiōrēs	lātiōra
Ab. lātiōre	lātiōre	lātiōribus	lātiōribus

plūs, *more*

SINGULAR		PLURAL	
Masc. and Fem.	*Neut.*	*Masc. and Fem.*	*Neut.*
N. ———	plūs	plūrēs	plūra
G. ———	plūris	plūrium	plūrium
D. ———	———	plūribus	plūribus
Ac. ———	plūs	plūrēs *or* -īs	plūra
Ab. ———	———	plūribus	plūribus

13. REGULAR COMPARISON OF ADVERBS

Positive	*Comparative*	*Superlative*
lātē	lātius	lātissimē
fortiter	fortius	fortissimē
ācriter	ācrius	ācerrimē
facile	facilius	facillimē

IRREGULAR COMPARISON OF ADVERBS

bene	melius	optimē
male	peius	pessimē
magnopere	magis	maximē
multum	magis	maximē
multum	plūs	plūrimum
parum	minus	minimē
prope	propius	proximē
saepe	saepius	saepissimē
diū	diūtius	diūtissimē

14.   NUMERALS

Numeral adjectives are of three classes: *cardinals*, answering the question *how many?* as *one*, *two*, etc.; *ordinals*, answering the question *which in order?* as *first*, *second*, etc.; and *distributives*, answering the question *how many each?* as *one each*, *two each*, etc.

Roman Numerals	*Cardinal*	*Ordinal*	*Distributive*
I.	ūnus, -a, -um	prīmus, -a, -um	singulī, -ae, -a
II.	duo, -ae, -o	secundus *or* alter	bīnī
III.	trēs, tria	tertius	ternī *or* trīnī
IV.	quattuor	quārtus	quaternī
V.	quīnque	quīntus	quīnī
VI.	sex	sextus	sēnī
VII.	septem	septimus	septēnī
VIII.	octō	octāvus	octōnī
IX.	novem	nōnus	novēnī
X.	decem	decimus	dēnī
XI.	ūndecim	ūndecimus	ūndēnī
XII.	duodecim	duodecimus	duodēnī
XIII.	tredecim	tertius decimus	ternī dēnī
XIV.	quattuordecim	quārtus decimus	quaternī dēnī
XV.	quīndecim	quīntus decimus	quīnī dēnī
XVI.	sēdecim	sextus decimus	sēnī dēnī
XVII.	septendecim	septimus decimus	septēnī dēnī
XVIII.	duodēvīgintī	duodēvīcēsimus	duodēvīcēnī
XIX.	ūndēvīgintī	ūndēvīcēsimus	ūndēvīcēnī
XX.	vīgintī	vīcēsimus	vīcēnī
XXI.	ūnus et vīgintī (vīgintī ūnus)	vīcēsimus prīmus	vīcēnī singulī
XXVIII.	duodētrīgintā	duodētrīcēsimus	duodētrīcēnī
XXIX.	ūndētrīgintā	ūndētrīcēsimus	ūndētrīcēnī
XXX.	trīgintā	trīcēsimus	trīcēnī
XL.	quadrāgintā	quadrāgēsimus	quadrāgēnī
L.	quīnquāgintā	quīnquāgēsimus	quīnquāgēnī
LX.	sexāgintā	sexāgēsimus	sexāgēnī
LXX.	septuāgintā	septuāgēsimus	septuāgēnī
LXXX.	octōgintā	octōgēsimus	octōgēnī
XC.	nōnāgintā	nōnāgēsimus	nōnāgēnī
C.	centum	centēsimus	centēnī

CI.	centum (et) ūnus	centēsimus (et) prīmus	centēnī (et) singulī
CC.	ducentī, -ae, -a	ducentēsimus	ducēnī
CCC.	trecentī	trecentēsimus	trecēnī
CCCC.	quadringentī	quadringentēsimus	quadringēnī
D.	quīngentī	quīngentēsimus	quīngēnī
DC.	sescentī	sescentēsimus	sescēnī
DCC.	septingentī	septingentēsimus	septingēnī
DCCC.	octingentī	octingentēsimus	octingēnī
DCCCC.	nōngentī	nōngentēsimus	nōngēnī
M.	mīlle	mīllēsimus	singula mīlia
MM.	duo mīlia	bis mīllēsimus	bīna mīlia

15.

DECLENSION OF duo AND trēs

	duo, *two*			trēs, *three*	
	Masc.	*Fem.*	*Neut.*	*Masc. and Fem.*	*Neut.*
N.	duo	duae	duo	trēs	tria
G.	duōrum	duārum	duōrum	trium	trium
D.	duōbus	duābus	duōbus	tribus	tribus
Ac.	duōs, duo	duās	duo	trēs, trīs	tria
Ab.	duōbus	duābus	duōbus	tribus	tribus

PRONOUNS

16.

PERSONAL PRONOUNS

First person, **ego**, *I*		Second person, **tū**, *you* (*thou*)	
SINGULAR	PLURAL	SINGULAR	PLURAL
N. ego	nōs	tū	vōs
G. meī	⎰ nostrum ⎱ nostrī	tuī	⎰ vestrum ⎱ vestrī
D. mihi	nōbīs	tibi	vōbīs
Ac. mē	nōs	tē	vōs
Ab. mē	nōbīs	tē	vōbīs

a. There is no personal pronoun of the third person. Its place is taken either by a demonstrative pronoun (usually **is**, *he*, **ea**, *she*, **id**, *it*), or, if the antecedent is the subject of the sentence or clause, by the reflexive pronouns.

17.   REFLEXIVE PRONOUNS

	First person, **meī,** *of myself*		Second person, **tuī,** *of yourself*		Third person, **suī,** *of himself, etc.*	
	SING.	PLUR.	SING.	PLUR.	SING.	PLUR.
G.	meī	nostrī	tuī	vestrī	suī	suī
D.	mihi	nōbīs	tibi	vōbīs	sibi	sibi
Ac.	mē	nōs	tē	vōs	sē	sē
Ab.	mē	nōbīs	tē	vōbīs	sē	sē

18.   POSSESSIVE PRONOUNS

1st pers. meus, -a, -um, *my*

2d pers. tuus, -a, -um, *your* (of one)

3d pers. suus, -a, -um, *his, her, its* (when referring to the subject)

eius (gen. sing. of **is**) *his, her, its* (when not referring to the subject)

noster, -tra, -trum, *our*

vester, -tra, -trum, *your* (of more than one)

suus, -a, -um, *their* (when referring to the subject)

eōrum, eārum, eōrum (gen. plur. of **is**) *their* (when not referring to the subject)

19.   DEMONSTRATIVE PRONOUNS

hic, *this*

	SINGULAR			PLURAL		
	Masc.	*Fem.*	*Neut.*	*Masc.*	*Fem.*	*Neut.*
N.	hic	haec	hoc	hī	hae	haec
G.	huius	huius	huius	hōrum	hārum	hōrum
D.	huic	huic	huic	hīs	hīs	hīs
Ac.	hunc	hanc	hoc	hōs	hās	haec
Ab.	hōc	hāc	hōc	hīs	hīs	hīs

ille, *that*

	SINGULAR			PLURAL		
	Masc.	*Fem.*	*Neut.*	*Masc.*	*Fem.*	*Neut.*
N.	ille	illa	illud	illī	illae	illa
G.	illīus	illīus	illīus	illōrum	illārum	illōrum
D.	illī	illī	illī	illīs	illīs	illīs
Ac.	illum	illam	illud	illōs	illās	illa
Ab.	illō	illā	illō	illīs	illīs	illīs

a. **iste** is declined like **ille**

is, *this, that, he, she, it*

| | SINGULAR | | | PLURAL | | |
	Masc.	Fem.	Neut.	Masc.	Fem.	Neut.
N.	is	ea	id	iī, eī	eae	ea
G.	eius	eius	eius	eōrum	eārum	eōrum
D.	eī	eī	eī	iīs, eīs	iīs, eīs	iīs, eīs
Ac.	eum	eam	id	eōs	eās	ea
Ab.	eō	eā	eō	iīs, eīs	iīs, eīs	iīs, eīs

20. THE IDENTIFYING PRONOUN

īdem, *the same*

| | SINGULAR | | | | PLURAL | | |
	Masc.	Fem.	Neut.		Masc.	Fem.	Neut.
N.	īdem	eadem	idem	N.	īdem or eīdem	eaedem	eadem
G.	eiusdem	eiusdem	eiusdem	G.	eōrundem	eārundem	eōrundem
D.	eīdem	eīdem	eīdem	D.	īsdem or eīsdem	īsdem or eīsdem	īsdem or eīsdem
Ac.	eundem	eandem	idem	Ac.	eōsdem	eāsdem	eadem
Ab.	eōdem	eādem	eōdem	Ab.	īsdem or eīsdem	īsdem or eīsdem	īsdem or eīsdem

21. THE INTENSIVE PRONOUN

ipse, *self*

| | SINGULAR | | | PLURAL | | |
	Masc.	Fem.	Neut.	Masc.	Fem.	Neut.
N.	ipse	ipsa	ipsum	ipsī	ipsae	ipsa
G.	ipsīus	ipsīus	ipsīus	ipsōrum	ipsārum	ipsōrum
D.	ipsī	ipsī	ipsī	ipsīs	ipsīs	ipsīs
Ac.	ipsum	ipsam	ipsum	ipsōs	ipsās	ipsa
Ab.	ipsō	ipsā	ipsō	ipsīs	ipsīs	ipsīs

22. THE RELATIVE PRONOUN

quī, *who*

| | SINGULAR | | | PLURAL | | |
	Masc.	Fem.	Neut.	Masc.	Fem.	Neut.
N.	quī	quae	quod	quī	quae	quae
G.	cuius	cuius	cuius	quōrum	quārum	quōrum
D.	cui	cui	cui	quibus	quibus	quibus
Ac.	quem	quam	quod	quōs	quās	quae
Ab.	quō	quā	quō	quibus	quibus	quibus

23. INTERROGATIVE PRONOUN AND ADJECTIVE

	SINGULAR			PLURAL		
	Masc.	Fem.	Neut.	Masc.	Fem.	Neut.
N.	quis	quae	quid	quī	quae	quae
G.	cuius	cuius	cuius	quōrum	quārum	quōrum
D.	cui	cui	cui	quibus	quibus	quibus
Ac.	quem	quam	quid	quōs	quās	quae
Ab.	quō	quā	quō	quibus	quibus	quibus

a. In the nominative singular masculine the adjective form is sometimes quī. In the nominative and accusative singular neuter it is always quod.

24. INDEFINITE PRONOUNS

quisque, *each*   **quisquam,** *anyone*

	SINGULAR				
	Masc.	Fem.	Neut.	Masc. and Fem.	Neut.
N.	quisque	quaeque	quidque, quodque	quisquam	quicquam (quidquam)
G.	cuiusque	cuiusque	cuiusque	cuiusquam	cuiusquam
D.	cuique	cuique	cuique	cuiquam	cuiquam
Ac.	quemque	quamque	quidque, quodque	quemquam	quicquam (quidquam)
Ab.	quōque	quāque	quōque	quōquam	quōquam
	Plural rare			*Plural missing*	

quīdam, *a certain*

	SINGULAR		
	Masc.	Fem.	Neut.
N.	quīdam	quaedam	quiddam (quoddam)
G.	cuiusdam	cuiusdam	cuiusdam
D.	cuidam	cuidam	cuidam
Ac.	quendam	quandam	quiddam (quoddam)
Ab.	quōdam	quādam	quōdam

	PLURAL		
N.	quīdam	quaedam	quaedam
G.	quōrundam	quārundam	quōrundam
D.	quibusdam	quibusdam	quibusdam
Ac.	quōsdam	quāsdam	quaedam
Ab.	quibusdam	quibusdam	quibusdam

aliquis, *some*

SINGULAR

	Masc.	Fem.	Neut.
N.	aliquis (aliquī)	aliqua	aliquid (aliquod)
G.	alicuius	alicuius	alicuius
D.	alicui	alicui	alicui
Ac.	aliquem	aliquam	aliquid (aliquod)
Ab.	aliquō	aliquā	aliquō

PLURAL

N.	aliquī	aliquae	aliqua
G.	aliquōrum	aliquārum	aliquōrum
D.	aliquibus	aliquibus	aliquibus
Ac.	aliquōs	aliquās	aliqua
Ab.	aliquibus	aliquibus	aliquibus

REGULAR VERBS

25.

FIRST CONJUGATION

ACTIVE VOICE

Principal parts: **portō, portāre, portāvī, portātum**

Present

INDICATIVE	SUBJUNCTIVE

SINGULAR

portō, *I carry*	portem
portās, *you carry*	portēs
portat, *he carries*	portet

PLURAL

portāmus, *we carry*	portēmus
portātis, *you carry*	portētis
portant, *they carry*	portent

Imperfect

SINGULAR

portābam, *I was carrying*	portārem
portābās, *you were carrying*	portārēs
portābat, *he was carrying*	portāret

PLURAL

portābāmus, *we were carrying*	portārēmus
portābātis, *you were carrying*	portārētis
portābant, *they were carrying*	portārent

INDICATIVE	SUBJUNCTIVE

Future

SINGULAR

portābō, *I shall carry*
portābis, *you will carry*
portābit, *he will carry*

PLURAL

portābimus, *we shall carry*
portābitis, *you will carry*
portābunt, *they will carry*

Perfect

SINGULAR

portāvī, *I have carried, I carried*   portāverim
portāvistī, *you have carried, etc.*   portāverīs
portāvit, *he has carried, etc.*   portāverit

PLURAL

portāvimus, *we have carried, etc.*   portāverīmus
portāvistis, *you have carried, etc.*   portāverītis
portāvērunt, -ēre, *they have carried, etc.*   portāverint

Past Perfect

SINGULAR

portāveram, *I had carried*   portāvissem
portāverās, *you had carried*   portāvissēs
portāverat, *he had carried*   portāvisset

PLURAL

portāverāmus, *we had carried*   portāvissēmus
portāverātis, *you had carried*   portāvissētis
portāverant, *they had carried*   portāvissent

Future Perfect

SINGULAR

portāverō, *I shall have carried*
portāveris, *you will have carried*
portāverit, *he will have carried*

PLURAL

portāverimus, *we shall have carried*
portāveritis, *you will have carried*
portāverint, *they will have carried*

IMPERATIVE

Present		*Future*	
Sing. 2.	portā, *carry* (thou)	Sing. 2.	portātō, *thou shalt carry*
Plur. 2.	portāte, *carry* (ye)	3.	portātō, *he shall carry*
		Plur. 2.	portātōte, *ye shall carry*
		3.	portantō, *they shall carry*

INFINITIVES

Pres. portāre, *to carry*
Past portāvisse, *to have carried*
Fut. portātūrus esse, *to be about to carry*

PARTICIPLES

Pres. portāns, *carrying*
Fut. portātūrus, *about to carry*

GERUND

G. portandī, *of carrying*
D. portandō, *to (for) carrying*
Ac. portandum, *carrying*
Ab. portandō, *from, by carrying*

SUPINE

Ac. portātum, *to carry*
Ab. portātū, *to carry*

26.   PASSIVE VOICE

Present

INDICATIVE	SUBJUNCTIVE
SINGULAR	SINGULAR
portor, *I am carried*	porter
portāris, -re, *you are carried*	portēris, -re
portātur, *he is carried*	portētur
PLURAL	PLURAL
portāmur, *we are carried*	portēmur
portāminī, *you are carried*	portēminī
portantur, *they are carried*	portentur

Imperfect

SINGULAR	SINGULAR
portābar, *I was (being) carried*	portārer
portābāris, -re, *you were carried*	portārēris, -re
portābātur, *he was carried*	portārētur
PLURAL	PLURAL
portābāmur, *we were (being) carried*	portārēmur
portābāminī, *you were (being) carried*	portārēminī
portābantur, *they were (being) carried*	portārentur

INDICATIVE   **SUBJUNCTIVE**

Future

SINGULAR

portābor, *I shall be carried*
portāberis, -re, *you will be carried*
portābitur, *he will be carried*

PLURAL

portābimur, *we shall be carried*
portābiminī, *you will be carried*
portābuntur, *they will be carried*

Perfect

SINGULAR   SINGULAR

portātus sum, *I have been carried*   portātus sim
portātus es, *you have been carried*   portātus sīs
portātus est, *he has been carried*   portātus sit

PLURAL   PLURAL

portātī sumus, *we have been carried*   portātī sīmus
portātī estis, *you have been carried*   portātī sītis
portātī sunt, *they have been carried*   portātī sint

Past Perfect

SINGULAR   SINGULAR

portātus eram, *I had been carried*   portātus essem
portātus erās, *you had been carried*   portātus essēs
portātus erat, *he had been carried*   portātus esset

PLURAL   PLURAL

portātī erāmus, *we had been carried*   portātī essēmus
portātī erātis, *you had been carried*   portātī essētis
portātī erant, *they had been carried*   portātī essent

Future Perfect

SINGULAR

portātus erō, *I shall have been carried*
portātus eris, *you will have been carried*
portātus erit, *he will have been carried*

PLURAL

portātī erimus, *we shall have been carried*
portātī eritis, *you will have been carried*
portātī erunt, *they will have been carried*

IMPERATIVE

Present	Future
Sing. 2. portāre, *be (thou) carried*	*Sing. 2.* portātor, *thou shalt be carried*
Plur. 2. portāminī, *be (ye) carried*	*3.* portātor, *he shall be carried*
	Plur. 2. ———
	3. portantor, *they shall be carried*

INFINITIVES	PARTICIPLES
Pres. amārī, *to be loved*	*Past* portātus, *having been carried*
Past amātus esse, *to have been loved*	*Fut.* portandus, *to be carried*
Fut. amātum īrī, *to be about to be loved*	

27.   SECOND, THIRD, AND FOURTH CONJUGATIONS

moneō, monēre, monuī, monitum   capiō, capere, cēpī, captum
dūcō, dūcere, dūxī, ductum   audiō, audīre, audīvī, audītum

ACTIVE VOICE

INDICATIVE

Present	moneō	dūcō	capiō	audiō
	monēs	dūcis	capis	audīs
	monet	dūcit	capit	audit
	monēmus	dūcimus	capimus	audīmus
	monētis	dūcitis	capitis	audītis
	monent	dūcunt	capiunt	audiunt
Imperfect	monēbam	dūcēbam	capiēbam	audiēbam
	monēbās	dūcēbās	capiēbās	audiēbās
	monēbat	dūcēbat	capiēbat	audiēbat
	monēbāmus	dūcēbāmus	capiēbāmus	audiēbāmus
	monēbātis	dūcēbātis	capiēbātis	audiēbātis
	monēbant	dūcēbant	capiēbant	audiēbant
Future	monēbō	dūcam	capiam	audiam
	monēbis	dūcēs	capiēs	audiēs
	monēbit	dūcet	capiet	audiet
	monēbimus	dūcēmus	capiēmus	audiēmus
	monēbitis	dūcētis	capiētis	audiētis
	monēbunt	dūcent	capient	audient
Perfect	monuī	dūxī	cēpī	audīvī
Past Perf.	monueram	dūxeram	cēperam	audīveram
Fut. Perf.	monuerō	dūxerō	cēperō	audīverō

SUBJUNCTIVE

Present	moneam	dūcam	capiam	audiam
	moneās	dūcās	capiās	audiās
	moneat	dūcat	capiat	audiat
	moneāmus	dūcāmus	capiāmus	audiāmus
	moneātis	dūcātis	capiātis	audiātis
	moneant	dūcant	capiant	audiant
Imperfect	monērem	dūcerem	caperem	audīrem
	monērēs	dūcerēs	caperēs	audīrēs
	monēret	dūceret	caperet	audīret
	monērēmus	dūcerēmus	caperēmus	audīrēmus
	monērētis	dūcerētis	caperētis	audīrētis
	monērent	dūcerent	caperent	audīrent
Perfect	monuerim	dūxerim	cēperim	audīverim
Past Perf.	monuissem	dūxissem	cēpissem	audīvissem

IMPERATIVE

Present	monē	dūc	cape	audī
	monēte	dūcite	capite	audīte
Future	2 monētō	dūcitō	capitō	audītō
	3 monētō	dūcitō	capitō	audītō
	2 monētōte	dūcitōte	capitōte	audītōte
	3 monentō	dūcuntō	capiunto	audiuntō

PARTICIPLES

Present	monēns	dūcēns	capiēns	audiēns
Future	monitūrus	ductūrus	captūrus	audītūrus

INFINITIVE

Present	monēre	dūcere	capere	audīre
Past	monuisse	dūxisse	cēpisse	audīvisse
Future	monitūrus esse	ductūrus esse	captūrus esse	audītūrus esse

GERUND

	monendī	dūcendī	capiendī	audiendī
	monendō	dūcendō	capiendō	audiendō
	etc.	etc.	etc.	etc.

SUPINE

	monitum	ductum	captum	audītum
	monitū	ductū	captū	audītū

28.

INDICATIVE

Present			
Present	moneor	dūcor	capior	audior
	monēris, -re	dūceris, -re	caperis, -re	audīris, -re
	monētur	dūcitur	capitur	audītur
	monēmur	dūcimur	capimur	audīmur
	monēminī	dūciminī	capiminī	audīminī
	monentur	dūcuntur	capiuntur	audiuntur
Imperfect	monēbar	dūcēbar	capiēbar	audiēbar
	monēbāris, -re	dūcēbāris, -re	capiēbāris, -re	audiēbāris, -re
	monēbātur	dūcēbātur	capiēbātur	audiēbātur
	monēbāmur	dūcēbāmur	capiēbāmur	audiēbāmur
	monēbāminī	dūcēbāminī	capiēbāminī	audiēbāminī
	monēbantur	dūcēbantur	capiēbantur	audiēbantur
Future	monēbor	dūcar	capiar	audiar
	monēberis, -re	dūcēris, -re	capiēris, -re	audiēris, -re
	monēbitur	dūcētur	capiētur	audiētur
	monēbimur	dūcēmur	capiēmur	audiēmur
	monēbiminī	dūcēminī	capiēminī	audiēminī
	monēbuntur	dūcentur	capientur	audientur
Perfect	monitus sum	ductus sum	captus sum	audītus sum
Past Perf.	monitus eram	ductus eram	captus eram	audītus eram
Fut. Perf.	monitus erō	ductus erō	captus erō	audītus erō

SUBJUNCTIVE

Present	monear	dūcar	capiar	audiar
	moneāris, -re	dūcāris, -re	capiāris, -re	audiāris, -re
	moneātur	dūcātur	capiātur	audiātur
	moneāmur	dūcāmur	capiāmur	audiāmur
	moneāminī	dūcāminī	capiāminī	audiāminī
	moneantur	dūcantur	capiantur	audiantur
Imperfect	monērer	dūcerer	caperer	audīrer
	monērēris, -re	dūcerēris, -re	caperēris, -re	audīrēris, -re
	monērētur	dūcerētur	caperētur	audīrētur
	monērēmur	dūcerēmur	caperēmur	audīrēmur
	monērēminī	dūcerēminī	caperēminī	audīrēminī
	monērentur	dūcerentur	caperentur	audīrentur

| *Perfect* | monitus sim | ductus sim | captus sim | audītus sim |
| *Past Perf.* | monitus essem | ductus essem | captus essem | audītus essem |

IMPERATIVE

Present	monēre	dūcere	capere	audīre
	monēminī	dūciminī	capiminī	audīminī
Future	2 ———	———	———	———
	3 monentor	dūcuntor	capiuntor	audiuntor

PARTICIPLES

| *Past* | monitus | ductus | captus | audītus |
| *Future* | monendus | dūcendus | capiendus | audiendus |

INFINITIVE

Present	monērī	dūcī	capī	audīrī
Perfect	monitus esse	ductus esse	captus esse	audītus esse
Future	monitum īrī	ductum īrī	captum īrī	audītum īrī

29. DEPONENT VERBS

I. cōnor, cōnārī, cōnātus sum
II. polliceor, pollicērī, pollicitus sum
III. sequor, sequī, secūtus sum
IV. potior, potīrī, potītus sum

INDICATIVE

	I.	II.	III.	IV.
Pres.	cōnor	polliceor	sequor	potior
	cōnāris, -re	pollicēris, -re	sequeris, -re	potīris, -re
	cōnātur	pollicētur	sequitur	potītur
	cōnāmur	pollicēmur	sequimur	potīmur
	cōnāminī	pollicēminī	sequiminī	potīminī
	cōnāntur	pollicentur	sequuntur	potiuntur
Impf.	cōnābar	pollicēbar	sequēbar	potiēbar
Fut.	cōnābor	pollicēbor	sequar	potiar
Perf.	cōnātus sum	pollicitus sum	secūtus sum	potītus sum
P. Pf.	cōnātus eram	pollicitus eram	secūtus eram	potītus eram
F. Pf.	cōnātus erō	pollicitus erō	secūtus erō	potītus erō

SUBJUNCTIVE

Pres.	cōner	pollicear	sequar	potiar
Impf.	cōnārer	pollicērer	sequerer	potīrer
Perf.	cōnātus sim	pollicitus sim	secūtus sim	potītus sim
P. Pf.	cōnātus essem	pollicitus essem	secūtus essem	potītus essem

IMPERATIVE

| Pres. | cōnāre | pollicēre | sequere | potīre |
| Fut. | cōnātor | pollicētor | sequitor | potītor |

INFINITIVE

Pres.	cōnārī	pollicērī	sequī	potīrī
Past	cōnātus esse	pollicitus esse	secūtus esse	potītus esse
Fut.	cōnātūrus esse	pollicitūrus esse	secūtūrus esse	potītūrus esse

PARTICIPLE

Pres.	cōnāns	pollicēns	sequēns	potiēns
Past	cōnātus	pollicitus	secūtus	potītus
F. Act.	cōnātūrus	pollicitūrus	secūtūrus	potītūrus
F. Pass.	cōnandus	pollicendus	sequendus	potiendus

GERUND

cōnandī, etc.   pollicendī, etc.   sequendī, etc.   potiendī, etc.

SUPINE

| cōnātum | pollicitum | secūtum | potītum |
| cōnātū | pollicitū | secūtū | potītū |

IRREGULAR VERBS

30. Conjugation of **sum**.

Principal parts: **sum, esse, fuī, futūrus**

INDICATIVE

Present

SINGULAR	PLURAL
sum, *I am*	sumus, *we are*
es, *you are*	estis, *you are*
est, *he, she, it is*	sunt, *they are*

Imperfect

eram, *I was*	erāmus, *we were*
erās, *you were*	erātis, *you were*
erat, *he, she, it was*	erant, *they were*

Future

erō, *I shall be*	erimus, *we shall be*
eris, *you will be*	eritis, *you will be*
erit, *he, she, it will be*	erunt, *they will be*

Perfect

fuī, *I have been, I was*	fuimus, *we have been, we were*
fuistī, *you have been, you were*	fuistis, *you have been, you were*
fuit, *he, she, it has been, was*	fuērunt *or* -ēre, *they have been, etc.*

Past Perfect

fueram, *I had been*	fuerāmus, *we had been*
fuerās, *you had been*	fuerātis, *you had been*
fuerat, *he, she, it had been*	fuerant, *they had been*

Future Perfect

fuerō, *I shall have been*	fuerimus, *we shall have been*
fueris, *you will have been*	fueritis, *you will have been*
fuerit, *he, she, it will have been*	fuerint, *they will have been*

SUBJUNCTIVE

Present		Imperfect	
SINGULAR	PLURAL	SINGULAR	PLURAL
sim	sīmus	essem	essēmus
sīs	sītis	essēs	essētis
sit	sint	esset	essent

Perfect		Past Perfect	
fuerim	fuerīmus	fuissem	fuissēmus
fuerīs	fuerītis	fuissēs	fuissētis
fuerit	fuerint	fuisset	fuissent

IMPERATIVE

Present

2d pers. es, *be (thou)*	este, *be (ye)*

Future

2d pers.	estō, *be, thou shalt be*	estōte, *be, ye shall be*	
3d pers.	estō, *let him be, he shall be*	suntō, *let them be, they shall be*	

PARTICIPLE

Fut.   futūrus, *about to be*

INFINITIVE

Pres.	esse, *to be*
Perf.	fuisse, *to have been*
Fut.	futūrus esse *or* fore, *to be about to be*

31. CONJUGATION OF **possum.**

Principal parts: **possum, posse, potuī**

INDICATIVE		SUBJUNCTIVE	

Present

SINGULAR	PLURAL	SINGULAR	PLURAL
possum	possumus	possim	possīmus
potes	potestis	possīs	possītis
potest	possunt	possit	possint

Imperfect

poteram	poterāmus	possem	possēmus
poterās	poterātis	possēs	possētis
poterat	poterant	posset	possent

Future

poterō	poterimus

Perfect

potuī	potuimus	potuerim	potuerīmus

Past Perfect

potueram	potuerāmus	potuissem	potuissēmus

Future Perfect

potuerō	potuerimus

INFINITIVE

Pres.	posse	*Past*	potuisse

32. CONJUGATION OF **prōsum**.

Principal parts:　**prōsum, prōdesse, prōfuī**

INDICATIVE		SUBJUNCTIVE	
	Present		
prōsum	prōsumus	prōsim	prōsīmus
prōdes	prōdestis	prōsīs	prōsītis
prōdest	prōsunt	prōsit	prōsint

The remaining forms of the present system are conjugated like **sum**, with the prefix **prōd-**. The perfect system is regularly formed with the stem **prōfu-**.

33. CONJUGATION OF **ferō**.

Principal parts:　**ferō, ferre, tulī, lātum**

INDICATIVE

Present

Active		Passive	
ferō	ferimus	feror	ferimur
fers	fertis	ferris, -re	feriminī
fert	ferunt	fertur	feruntur

Imperfect

ferēbam	ferēbāmus	ferēbar	ferēbāmur

Future

feram	ferēmus	ferar	ferēmur

Perfect

tulī	tulīmus	lātus sum	lātī sumus

Past Perfect

tuleram	tulerāmus	lātus eram	lātī erāmus

Future Perfect

tulerō	tulerimus	lātus erō	lātī erimus

SUBJUNCTIVE

Present

feram	ferāmus	ferar	ferāmur

Imperfect

ferrem	ferrēmus	ferrer	ferrēmur

Perfect

| tulerim | tulerīmus | | lātus sım | lātī sīmus |

Past Perfect

| tulissem | tulissēmus | | lātus essem | lātī essēmus |

IMPERATIVE
Present

| *2* fer | ferte | | ferre | feriminī |

Future

| *2* fertō | fertōte | | fertor | ——— |
| *3* fertō | feruntō | | fertor | feruntor |

| INFINITIVE | | | PARTICIPLES | |

Active		*Passive*	*Active*		*Passive*
Pres.	ferre	ferrī	*Pres.*	ferēns	*Past*	lātus
Past	tulisse	lātus esse	*Fut.*	lātūrus	*Fut.*	ferendus
Fut.	lātūrus esse	lātum īrī				

| GERUND | | SUPINE | |
| ferendī, etc. | | *Acc.* lātum | *Abl.* lātū |

34. CONJUGATION OF **eō**.

Principal parts: **eō, īre, iī** *or* **īvī, itum**

Present

INDICATIVE		SUBJUNCTIVE	
eō	īmus	eam	eāmus
īs	ītis	eās	eātis
it	eunt	eat	eant

Imperfect

| ībam | ībāmus | īrem | īrēmus |

Future

| ībō | ībimus | | |

Perfect

| iī *or* īvī | iimus *or* īvimus | ierim *or* īverim | ierīmus *or* īverīmus |

Past Perfect

ieram (īveram) ierāmus (īverāmus) īssem (īvissem) īssēmus (īvissēmus)

Future Perfect

ierō *or* īverō   ierimus *or* īverimus

IMPERATIVE		INFINITIVE		PARTICIPLE	
Pres.	ī, īte	*Pres.*	īre	*Pres.*	iēns (*Gen.* euntis)
Fut.	ītō, ītōte	*Perf.*	iisse *or* īsse	*Fut.*	itūrus
	īto, euntō	*Fut.*	itūrus esse		

GERUND	SUPINE
eundī, etc.	itum, itū

35. Conjugation of fīō.

Principal parts: **fīō, fierī, factus sum**

Present

INDICATIVE		SUBJUNCTIVE	
fīō	—	fīam	fīāmus
fīs	—	fīās	fīātis
fit	fīunt	fīat	fīant

Imperfect

fīēbam	fīēbāmus	fierem	fierēmus

Future

fīam	fīēmus

Perfect

factus sum	factus sim

Past Perfect

factus eram	factus essem

Future Perfect

factus erō

IMPERATIVE	INFINITIVE		PARTICIPLE	
Pres. fī, fīte	*Pres.*	fierī	*Perf.*	factus
	Perf.	factus esse	*Fut.*	faciendus
	Fut.	factum īrī		

36. Conjugation of **volō**, and its compounds.

volō, velle, voluī, *be willing.*
nōlō, nōlle, nōluī, *be unwilling.*
mālō, mālle, māluī, *prefer.*

INDICATIVE

Pres.	volō	nōlō	mālō
	vīs	nōn vīs	māvīs
	vult	nōn vult	māvult
	volumus	nōlumus	mālumus
	vultis	nōn vultis	māvultis
	volunt	nōlunt	mālunt
Imperfect	volēbam	nōlēbam	mālēbam
Fut.	volam	nōlam	mālam
Perf.	voluī	nōluī	māluī
Past Perf.	volueram	nōlueram	mālueram
Fut. Perf.	voluerō	nōluerō	māluerō

SUBJUNCTIVE

Pres.	velim	nōlim	mālim
Imperfect	vellem	nōllem	māllem
Perf.	voluerim	nōluerim	māluerim
Past Perf.	voluissem	nōluissem	māluissem

IMPERATIVE

Pres.	nōlī	nōlīte
Fut.	nōlītō	nōlītōte
	nōlītō	nōluntō

INFINITIVE

Pres.	velle	nōlle	mālle
Perf.	voluisse	nōluisse	māluisse

PARTICIPLE

Pres.	volēns	nōlēns	

REVIEW OF SYNTAX
AGREEMENT

37. 1. Adjectives and participles agree in gender, number, and case with the nouns to which they belong (55).

2. A relative pronoun agrees with its antecedent in gender and number, but its case depends on its use in its own clause (288).

3. A noun in apposition agrees in case with the noun which it explains (62).

4. A verb agrees with its subject in person and number (44).

CASES
THE NOMINATIVE

38. 1. The subject of a finite verb is in the nominative case (11).

2. A predicate noun used with a finite form of **sum** is in the nominative case (50, 2).

THE GENITIVE

39. 1. The genitive is used to denote a person or thing referred to as possessing something (11).

2. The genitive is used to refer to the whole of something, of which a part is denoted by the word on which the genitive depends (265).

3. The genitive, modified by an adjective, may be used to describe a person or thing (352).

4. Nouns and adjectives which denote actions sometimes take a dependent genitive in a relation similar to that of a direct object to the verb on which it depends (381).

5. The genitive may be used to denote the material of which something is composed, or the persons or objects making up a collective noun (521).

6. The verbs **meminī** and **reminīscor**, *remember,* and **oblīvīscor,** *forget,* frequently take a genitive as object. But if the object is a neuter pronoun or adjective it always stands in the accusative (543).

THE DATIVE

40. 1. The indirect object is in the dative (26).

2. The dative is used in dependence on adjectives of *attitude, quality,* or *relation* to indicate the person or thing toward which the attitude is directed or in reference to which the quality or relation is said to exist (27).

3. Verbs meaning to *favor, please, trust, obey, serve, resist, envy, threaten, pardon, spare,* and *persuade,* take their (apparent) objects in the dative (125).

4. The possessor of something may be denoted by the dative with the thing possessed in the nominative as the subject of a form of the verb meaning *to be* (325).

5. The purpose or end which something serves or is intended to serve is often expressed by the dative (196).

6. With many verbs compounded with **ante, ob, prae,** or **sub,** a noun or pronoun connected in sense with the preposition is put in the dative. The dative is also thus used with compounds of **ad** and **in** when motion is not expressed, and occasionally with the compounds of a few other prepositions (324).

7. The dative is often used to indicate a person who is likely to be affected favorably or unfavorably by an act or situation, or with reference to whom an act is said to be done or a situation to exist. Occasionally this use of the dative is found with words referring to things (245).

8. With the future passive participle the dative is used to indicate the person by whom the act must be done or ought to be done (538).

THE ACCUSATIVE

41. 1. The direct object of a verb is in the accusative (11).

2. A noun used to tell how long an act or situation continues is put in the accusative (177).

3. A noun used to express extent in space is put in the accusative (312).

4. With the names of towns and small islands, also with **domus,** the accusative without a preposition is used to name the place to which motion is directed. With other words in this construction a preposition, **ad** or **in,** is used (313).

THE ABLATIVE

42. 1. The ablative represents a combination of ideas, the original force of which is expressed by English phrases with the prepositions *from, in,* or *with* (33).

2. Verbs meaning to *separate, remove, deprive of, lack, be absent,* and the like, take the ablative of separation, often with **ab** or **ex** (329).

3. With names of towns and small islands, also with **domus,** the ablative without a preposition is used to express the idea of place from which. With other words in this construction, a preposition, **ab, dē,** or **ex,** is used (330).

4. With passive verbs, the noun or pronoun which indicates the person by whom the act is done is put in the ablative with **ā** or **ab** (98).

5. With the comparative form of an adjective (occasionally of an

adverb), if **quam** is omitted, the noun or pronoun indicating the person or thing with which comparison is made is put in the ablative without a preposition (340).

6. The ablative with **in** is used to indicate the place where something is or where some act occurs (110).

7. The ablative without a preposition is used to indicate the time at which or within which an act occurs or a situation exists (211).

8. The ablative with the preposition **cum** is used to indicate the person with whom one is associated in doing an act (104).

9. The manner is which an act is done may be expressed by the ablative with **cum**. But **cum** may be omitted if the noun is modified by an adjective (277).

10. The means or instrument with which an act is done is expressed by the ablative without a preposition (130).

11. The way or route by which one goes may be expressed by the ablative without a preposition (318).

12. The ablative without a preposition is used to express the degree or measure of difference between two things (346).

13. A noun or pronoun in the ablative, together with an adjective, a participle, or another noun in agreement, may be used to indicate some circumstance or event loosely connected with the rest of the sentence (370).

14. The ablative without a preposition may be used to indicate in what respect a statement is true (366).

15. The ablative modified by an adjective may be used to describe a person or thing (353).

16. The ablative with or without a preposition may be used to express cause (449).

17. The deponents **ūtor, fruor, fungor, potior,** and **vēscor** take their objects in the ablative (419).

THE VOCATIVE

43. The vocative is used to denote the person addressed (34).

THE LOCATIVE

44. With the names of towns and small islands, also with **domus,** the place where some act occurs or something exists is denoted by the locative (299).

    a. The locative has the same form as the genitive in the singular of nouns of the first and second declension; elsewhere it has the same form as the ablative. The locative of **domus** is **domī.**

MOODS

THE INDICATIVE

45. The indicative is used in statements of fact and in questions which imply that the answer expected is a statement of fact.

THE SUBJUNCTIVE

46. 1. The most important use of the subjunctive is to refer to an act as desired (456).

2. In a main clause the expression of desire may consist: (1) in urging someone to act with the speaker (456, *a*), (2) in giving an order to be carried out by someone else than the person addressed (456, *b*).

3. A subordinate clause expressing the purpose of the main act has its verb in the subjunctive. Purpose clauses are introduced by **ut** or **nē**, or a relative pronoun (460).

4. A substantive clause depending on a verb which expresses or implies desire has its verb in the subjunctive (470).

5. Verbs and other expressions of fear may take a dependent clause with the subjunctive introduced by **nē**, *that*, or **ut**, *that not* (531).

6. The subjunctive may be used in a subordinate clause to refer to an act as anticipated or expected (476).

7. The subjunctive is used in subordinate clauses expressing result (483).

8. A substantive clause depending on a verb or phrase which expresses the bringing about of an act or of a situation has its verb in the subjunctive (516).

9. A clause introduced by **cum** meaning *when*, if used to describe the situation in which the main act took place, has its verb in the imperfect or past perfect subjunctive **(511).**

10. A **cum** clause introduced by **cum** meaning *since* has its verb in the subjunctive (520).

11. A clause introduced by **cum** meaning *although* has its verb in the subjunctive (526).

12. An indirect question has its verb in the subjunctive (489).

13. Sometimes a subordinate clause which would otherwise have its verb in the indicative takes the subjunctive because it is closely dependent on a subjunctive or an infinitive (587).

CONDITIONAL SENTENCES

47. 1. Non-committal conditional sentences have their verbs in the indicative (571).

2. Future less vivid conditional sentences have their verbs in the present or perfect subjunctive (581).

3. Conditional sentences contrary to fact have their verbs in the imperfect subjunctive to refer to present time, and the past perfect to refer to past time (576).

THE IMPERATIVE

48. The imperative is used to express affirmative commands. The forms of the present tense are usually employed except in the case of the verbs meminī and sciō, of which the future is used with present meaning (402, 586).

THE INFINITIVE

49. 1. The infinitive is sometimes used to complete the meaning of the finite verb of the clause in which it stands (272).

2. Words of *knowing, thinking, saying, hearing,* and *observing* may take as object an infinitive with its subject in the accusative (395).

INDIRECT DISCOURSE

50. In Latin, indirect quotations are expressed as follows: (*a*) A main clause containing a statement of fact has its verb in the infinitive with the subject in the accusative.

(*b*) A main clause expressing a command has its verb in the subjunctive.

(*c*) All subordinate clauses have their verbs in the subjunctive (499).

THE SUPINE

51. 1. The accusative of the supine is used to express purpose in clauses in which the finite verb expresses motion (547, *a*).

2. The ablative of the supine is used as an ablative of respect with a few adjectives (547, *b*).

THE GERUND

52. The gerund is a verbal noun, used only in four cases and in the singular number (552).

THE GERUNDIVE

53. The gerundive is a participle and is used in agreement with a noun or pronoun (557).

RELATION OF TENSES

54. The tense of a subjunctive in a dependent clause usually bears a certain relation to the tense of the verb in the main clause.

(*a*) If the main verb denotes present or future time, the dependent subjunctive is regularly present or perfect.

(*b*) If the main verb denotes past time the dependent subjunctive is regularly imperfect or past perfect (510).

FAMILIAR LATIN PHRASES

Ad astra per aspera, To the stars through difficulties (motto of Kansas).

Ad utrumque parātus, Prepared for either result.

Alter ego est amicus, A friend is one's second self.

Aurī sacra famēs, Accursed greed for gold.

E plūribus ūnum, One (formed) from many (motto of the United States).

Ex animō, Sincerely.

Esse quam vidērī, To be rather than to seem.

Fāta viam invenient, The fates will find a way.

Ferē libenter hominēs id quod volunt crēdunt, Men usually believe willingly that which they wish.

Fīat lūx, Let there be light.

Fīat iūstitia, Let justice be done.

Fortēs fortūna iuvat, Fortune favors the brave.

Homō sum, hūmānī nihil ā mē aliēnum putō, I am a man, and I regard nothing as foreign to me which has to do with humanity.

Horribile dictū, Horrible to relate.

In hōc signō vincēs, In this sign you shall conquer.

Labōrāre est ōrāre, To labor is to pray.

Labor omnia vincit, Toil conquers all things.

Mēns sāna in corpore sānō, A sound mind in a sound body.

Mēns sibi cōnscia rēctī, A mind conscious in itself (to itself) of right.

Mīrābile dictū, Wonderful to say.

Montānī semper līberī, Mountaineers are always freemen (motto of West Virginia).

Nōn prōgredī est regredī, Not to go forward is to go backward.

Nōn sibi sed omnibus, Not for one's self but for all.

Pāce tuā, With your permission.

Possunt quia posse videntur, They can because they think they can.

Quod erat dēmōnstrandum (abbr. *Q.E.D.*), Which was to be proved.

Semper parātus, Always ready.

Sīc ītur ad astra, Thus one rises to fame (to the stars).

Sīc semper tyrannīs, Ever thus to tyrants (motto of Virginia).

Sīc trānsit glōria mundī, Thus passes away the glory of the world.

Sine diē, Without a day (said of an assembly which adjourns without a date fixed for meeting again).

Tempora mūtantur et nōs mūtāmur in illīs, The times change and we change with them (in them).

Vincit quī patitur, He conquers who endures.

Vincit quī sē vincit, He conquers who conquers himself.

LATIN WORD FORMATION

1. PREFIXES

We sometimes attach one or more syllables to the beginning of a word and thus form a new word of somewhat different meaning. By placing the syllable *un-* at the beginning of *prepared* we form the word *unprepared*. In Latin the word **addūcō** is formed in like manner by placing **ad** before **dūcō**. A syllable or group of syllables which is thus used in the formation of words is called a Prefix.

2. SUFFIXES

A word is sometimes formed by adding one or more syllables to the end of another word. Thus by adding *-ly* to the adjective *rapid* we get the adverb *rapidly*. A syllable or group of syllables thus used is called a Suffix.

3. CHANGES IN SPELLING

Often the form of a Latin prefix was changed because of the letter which immediately followed it. This change came about for the reason that the Romans found it difficult to pronounce certain groups of consonants, and therefore they changed these groups, perhaps through careless and inaccurate pronunciation at first, into forms which were less difficult. The spelling was finally changed to correspond with the pronunciation. Thus when **ad** was used as a prefix with **cēdō**, the new word came to be **accēdō** instead of **adcēdō**. This change by which a letter is made the same as that which follows it is called Assimilation.

In addition to this change in the spelling of prefixes, a vowel in the middle of a word was often changed when a prefix was joined to the original word. Thus from **re-** and **teneō** we have **retineō**.

4. LATIN PREFIXES

Most Latin prefixes are prepositions. The prepositions **ad** and **dē**. for example, are among the most frequently used prefixes. There are, however, a few prefixes which are never found as separate words. The syllable **re-** of **redūcō** is of this kind. Such a prefix is called an Inseparable Prefix.

The most important prefixes for the work of the first year are as follows:

(1) **ā, ab, abs,** *from, away.*

> **abdūcō** (=ab+dūcō), *lead away.*

NOTE. Before vowels the form **ab** is always used. Thus **abeō** (=ab+eō), *go away.* Before consonants both **ā** and **ab** are used. The

310

form **abs** is found before **c** and **t**: **abscīdō** (=abs+caedō), *cut away*, **abstrahō** (=abs+trahō), *drag away, draw away*.

(2) **ad**, *to, toward*.

      addūcō (=ad+dūcō), *lead to*.

NOTE. Other meanings than those given above are sometimes found. Among them are *at, by, up, upon*. Sometimes **ad** is used merely to emphasize the meaning of the word to which it is added. By assimilation it becomes **ac-, ag-, al-, an-, ap-, ar-, as-, at-**. Some of these changes did not take place until later than the time when the most important Latin literature was written, but they are seen in English derivatives, such as *aggressive, alleviate, annex, approve, arrive, assume, attract*.

(3) **com- (con-)**, *together, entirely, completely*.

      condūcō (=com-+dūcō), *lead together, bring together*.

NOTE. **com-**, used as an inseparable prefix, is an old form of the preposition **cum**, *with*. By assimilation it becomes **col-, con-, cor-**. Sometimes it is found as **co-**.

(4) **dē**, *from, away*.

      dēdūcō (=dē+dūcō), *lead away, withdraw*.

NOTE. Other meanings of **dē** sometimes found in compounds are *not* and *thoroughly*.

(5) **ē, ex**, *out, out from, thoroughly*.

      ēdūcō (=ē+dūcō), *lead out*.

NOTE 1. The prefix appears as **ex** before vowels and *h*, and before certain consonants; elsewhere it appears as **ē**.

NOTE 2. The three prepositions **ā (ab)**, **dē**, and **ē (ex)** are closely related in meaning. The general meaning of **ā, ab** is *away from*, of **dē**, *down from*, of **ē, ex**, *out from*. In compounds these meanings are not always distinguished.

(6) **in**, *in, into*.

      indūcō (=in+dūcō), *lead in, lead into*.

NOTE. By assimilation **in** becomes **il-, im-, ir-**.

(7) **in-**, *not*.

      incrēdibilis (=in+crēdibilis, *credible*), *not credible*.

NOTE. This is an inseparable prefix and has no connection with the preceding word. It is often represented in English by *un-* or *in-*. The English prefix *un-* is not derived from **in-**, but both go back to a common source.

(8) **inter,** *between.*

> interpōnō (=inter+pōnō), *place between.*

(9) **per,** *through, thoroughly.*

> perdūcō (=per+dūcō), *lead through.*

NOTE. With adjectives and adverbs **per** sometimes means *very.* Thus, **persaepe,** *very often.*

(10) **prae,** *before, in advance.*

> praemittō (=prae+mittō), *send in advance.*

NOTE. In English derivatives **prae** becomes *pre-.* Examples are *prefer, precede, pretend.*

(11) **prō,** *before, forward.*

> prōdūcō (=prō+dūcō), *lead forward.*

(12) **sub,** *under, up to, to the aid of.*

> submittō (=sub+mittō), *send to the aid of.*

NOTE. By assimilation **sub** becomes **suc-, suf-, sug-, sup-,** and sometimes **sum-** and **sur-.** Examples in English derivatives are *succeed, suffer, suggest, support, summon.*

5. LATIN SUFFIXES

It is usually difficult to give exact meanings to Latin suffixes. Often we can only say that they are used in forming certain classes of words. They differ from prefixes in that they are not usually added to whole words to form new ones, but are instead employed with a form which is formed by dropping or changing one or more letters of the original word. Thus cīvitās is said to be derived from cīvis, but the ending –tās instead of being added to cīvis is used with cīvi–.

Some suffixes which are often used in nouns are **-ia, -tia, -ium, -iō, (-tiō), -dō, -tās, -tūs, -tus (-sus).**

Examples are as follows:

(1) From nouns:

> cīvitās (cīvis)
> pecūnia (pecus)
> servitūs (servus)
> virtūs (vir)

(2) From adjectives:

> altitūdō (altus)
> amīcitia (amīcus)
> celeritās (celer)
> dignitās (dignus)
> dīligentia (dīligēns)

(3) From verbs:

> adventus (adveniō)
> cupiditās (cupiō, cupidus)
> iūdicium (iūdicō)
> oppugnātiō (oppugnō)
> potestās (possum, potēns)
> praesidium (praesideō)

NOTE. In some of the examples given above the word in parentheses does not show the exact order of derivation, but it serves to indicate a common relation. Thus, iūdicium is derived from iūdex.

6. ENGLISH DERIVATIVES

We have seen that prefixes are very often changed by assimilation, and that the diphthong ae becomes e in English derivatives. Suffixes also are frequently changed. Some of these changes are as follows:

The suffix -ia regularly appears in English as y.

> memoria, *memory.*

-tia as -ce (or cy).

> dīligentia, *diligence.*

-ium as -y (or e).

> subsidium, *subsidy.*

-(t)iō as (-t)ion.

> nātiō, *nation.*

-tūdō as -tude.

> magnitūdō, *magnitude.*

-tās as -ty.

> nōbilitās, *nobility.*

-tus often drops -s.

> adventus, *advent.*

Some Latin suffixes do not often appear in any form in English words. Thus, -tūs may be seen as -tue in virtue, but it is rarely found in other words. *Servitude* does not come from servitūs.

7. Find the more important English derivatives from the following:

FIRST HALF YEAR

Required		Optional	
capiō	moveō	agō	pācō
dīcō	putō	cognōscō	parō
dūcō	servō	habeō	pugnō
locō	videō	iūdicō	spectō
mittō	vocō	moveō	teneō

SECOND HALF YEAR

Required		Optional	
audiō	scrībō	audeō	pellō
doceō	sedeō	cōnsulō	pōnō
faciō	sūmō	dō	terreō
iaciō	timeō	fīdō	trahō
nāvigō	vincō	mūniō	veniō

NOTE. It will be observed that a great many derivatives come from the past passive participle.

8. The following forms of arrangement for note-books for this work are suggested.

TYPE 1 (Without Definitions)

locō, locāre, locāvī, locātum—*place*.   locate, local, locality, location, locus, collocate, collocation, dislocate, localization, localize, locally, locative, locomotive, locomotor.

TYPE 2 (With Definitions)

vocō, vocāre, vocāvī, vocātum—*call*.

vocation—a *calling,* occupation.

vocational—pertaining to a vocation or *calling*.

vocal—pertaining to voice.

evoke—*call* out.

convoke—*call* together.

vocative—case of *calling,* case of address.

revoke—*call* back, remand.

invoke—*call* upon, ask for.

vociferous—with large *calling* power, with loud tones.

invocation—a *calling* upon, a prayer.

TYPE 3 (With Examples of Use in English)

mittō, mittere, mīsī, missum—*send*.

mission—He was sent on a mission to Europe.

missionary—He was sent as a missionary to China.

missive—The letter was a formidable missive.

missile—Stones were the missiles of early warfare.

transmit—They will transmit the message to us.

remission—He preached the remission of sins.

commit—She was committed to his care.

submit—They submitted to the inevitable.

submissive—The slave was not submissive.

omit—Omit the non-essential.

LATIN-ENGLISH VOCABULARY

A

ā, ab, *prep. with abl.*, from, by

absēns, absentis, absent

absum, abesse, āfuī, āfutūrus, be absent, be distant, be away

ac, *see* atque

accēdō, -ere, accessī, accessum, approach

accidō, -ere, accidī, happen

accipiō, -ere, accēpī, acceptum, receive, accept

accūsō, -āre, -āvī, -ātum, accuse, censure

ācer, ācris, ācre, spirited, fierce, bold, sharp, keen

Achāia, -ae, F., Achaia, *a district of Greece*

aciēs, -ēī, F., edge; line of battle, battle

ācriter, *adv.*, fiercely, eagerly, spiritedly

ad, *prep. with acc.*, to, toward; near

adeō, *adv.*, to such an extent, so, so very

adgredior, adgredī, adgressus sum, approach; attack

adhibeō, -ēre, -uī, -itum, summon

adhūc, *adv.*, as yet, to this time, before this time

adiciō, -ere, adiēcī, adiectum, add; throw to

adiungō, -iungere, -iūnxī, -iūnctum, join to, annex

adsum, -esse, -fuī, -futūrus, be present, be at hand

adsurgō, -surgere, -surrēxī, -surrēctum, rise

adulēscēns, -centis, M., young man

advenïō, -venīre, -vēnī, -ventum, arrive, come up

adventus, -ūs, M., coming, arrival, approach

adversum, *prep. with acc.*, against

adversus, -a, -um, opposed, unsuccessful, unfavorable

aedificium, -ī, N., building

aedificō, -āre, -āvī, -ātum, build

Aegyptus, -ī, F., Egypt

Aemilius, -ī, M., Aemilius, *a Roman name*

aestās, -tātis, F., summer

aetās, -tātis, F., age

Āfrānius, -ī, M., Afranius, *a Roman name*

Āfrica, -ae, F., Africa

Āfricānus, -ī, M., Africanus, *a name given to two of the Scipios because of their victories over the Carthaginians, a nation of northern Africa*

ager, agrī, M., field, land

agmen, agminis, N., column, army; novissimum agmen, the rear line

agō, -ere, ēgī, āctum, do, drive

agricola, -ae, M., farmer

Albānī, -ōrum, M. *pl.*, the inhabitants of Alba

albus, -a, -um, white

Alexandrīa, -ae, F., Alexandria

Algidus, -ī, M., Algidus, *a mountain southeast of Rome*

aliquis, aliquid, *and* aliquī, aliqua, aliquod, some one, some thing, some

alius, alia, aliud, another

Allia, -ae, F., the Allia, *a small river north of Rome*

1

Alpēs, -ium, F. *pl.*, the Alps

alter, altera, alterum, the other; second

altitūdō, -dinis, F., height; depth

altus, -a, -um, high, tall, deep

ambō, ambae, ambō, both

ambulō, -āre, -āvī, -ātum, walk

amīcitia, -ae, F., friendship

amīcus, -ī, M., friend

āmittō, -ere, āmīsī, āmissum, lose

amō, -āre, -āvī, -ātum, love

ampliō, -āre, -āvī, -ātum, increase, extend

amplius, *comparative adv.*, more

ancilla, -ae, F., maid servant, servant

Ancus, -ī, M., *see* **Mārcius**

angustus, -a, -um, narrow

animal, animālis, N., animal

animus, -ī, M., mind, courage, spirit

annus, -ī, M., year

annuus, -a, -um, lasting a year, for a year, yearly

ante, *prep. with acc.*, before, in front of; *adv.*, before, previously

anteā, *adv.*, formerly, before

Antemnātēs, -ium, M. *pl.*, the inhabitants of Antemnae

antīquus, -a, -um, old, ancient

ānulus, -ī, M., ring

Ap., *abbreviation for* **Appius**, *a Roman first name*

appellō, -āre, -āvī, -ātum, call, name

appropinquō, -āre, -āvī, -ātum, approach

apud, *prep. with acc.*, among, in the presence of; near; in, with

aqua, -ae, F., water

Aquītānī, -ōrum, M. *pl.*, the Aquitanians, *a people of Gaul*

Arar, **Araris**, M., the Saône, *a river of Gaul*

arbitror, arbitrārī, arbitrātus sum, think

Ardea, -ae, F., Ardea, *a city of Latium*

ārdeō, -ēre, ārsī, ārsūrus, take fire, burn

Arīminum, -ī, N., Ariminum, *a city in northeastern Italy*

Ariovistus, -ī, M., Ariovistus, *a German king*

arma, -ōrum, N. *pl.*, arms, weapons

armātus, -a, -um, armed

armō, -āre, -āvī, -ātum, arm

arō, arāre, arāvī, arātum, plow

arroganter, *adv.*, insolently

Arrūns, **Arruntis**, M., Arruns, *a son of Tarquinius Superbus*

Arvernī, -ōrum, M. *pl.*, the Arverni, *a Gallic tribe*

ascendō, -ere, ascendī, ascēnsum, ascend

atque (*before vowels or consonants*) *or* **ac** (*before consonants only*), *conj.*, and

attribuō, -tribuere, -tribuī, -tribūtum, assign

Atuātucī, -ōrum, M. *pl.*, the Atuatuci, *a Belgian tribe*

auctōritās, -tātis, F., authority, influence

audeō, -ēre, ausus sum, *semi-deponent*, dare

audiō, -īre, -īvī, -ītum, hear

augeō, -ēre, auxī, auctum, increase, add to

aureus, -a, -um, golden, of gold

aurum, -ī, N., gold

Aurunculēius, -ī, M., Aurunculeius, *a Roman name;* Lucius Aurunculeius Cotta, *one of Caesar's officers*

auspicium, -ī, N., auspices, sign

autem, *conj.,* but, however; moreover

auxilium, -ī, N., aid, help; *pl.,* auxiliaries

Aventīnus, -a, -um, Aventine; **Aventīnus Mōns,** the Aventine Hill, *one of the seven hills of Rome*

āvertō, -ere, āvertī, āversum, turn away

Axona, -ae, F., the Aisne, *a river of France*

B

barbarus, -ī, M., barbarian, foreigner *(not Greek or Roman)*

Belgae, -ārum, M. *pl.,* the Belgians

bellō, -āre, -āvī, -ātum, engage in war, carry on war

Bellovacī, -ōrum, the Bellovaci, *a tribe of Gaul*

bellum, -ī, N., war

bene, *adv.,* well

beneficium, -ī, N., favor, kindness

benignus, -a, -um, kind

Bibracte, Bibractis, N., Bibracte, *a town of the Haeduans*

Bibrax, Bibractis, F., Bibrax, *a town of the Remi*

Bibulus, -ī, M., Bibulus, *a Roman name*

bis, *adv.,* twice

Bōiī, -ōrum, M. *pl.,* the Boii, *a Gallic tribe*

bonus, -a, -um, good

bōs, bovis, M., F., ox, cow; *pl.,* cattle

brevis, breve, short

Britannia, -ae, F., Britain, Great Britain

Britannī, -ōrum, M. *pl.,* the Britons

Britannicus, -a, -um, British

Brūtus, -ī, M., Brutus, *a Roman name;* Lucius Junius Brutus, *one of the first two consuls at Rome*

C

C., *abbreviation for* **Gāius,** *a Roman first name*

caedēs, caedis, F., slaughter, massacre

caedō, -ere, cecīdī, caesum, cut down; kill, vanquish

Caelius, -a, -um, Caelian; **Caelius Mōns,** the Caelian Hill, *one of the seven hills of Rome*

Caenīnēnsēs, -ium, M. *pl.,* the inhabitants of Caenina

Caesar, Caesaris, M., Caesar, *a Roman name;* Gaius Julius Caesar, *a famous Roman soldier and statesman*

calamitās, -tātis, F., calamity, disaster

calcar, calcāris, N., spur

Camillus, -ī, M., Camillus, *a Roman name;* Furius Camillus, *the conqueror of Veii*

Campānia, -ae, F., Campania, *a district lying southeast of Latium*

capiō, -ere, cēpī, captum, take, capture; **cōnsilium capere,** form a plan

Capitōlium, -ī, N., (1) the Capitol, *the temple of Jupiter at Rome on the Capitoline Hill;* (2) the Capitoline Hill

captīvus, -ī, M., (**captīva, -ae,** F.), captive, prisoner

caput, capitis, N., head

Carrae, -ārum, F. *pl.*, Carrhae, *a city of Asia*

carrus, -ī, M., cart

cārus, -a, -um, dear

Casca, -ae, M., Casca, *a Roman name*

Cassius, -ī, M., Cassius, *a Roman name;* Lucius Cassius, *a Roman consul who was killed in battle with the Helvetians*

castellum, -ī, N., fort, redoubt

castra, -ōrum, N. *pl.*, camp

Catō, -ōnis, M., Cato, *a Roman name*

causa, -ae, F., cause, reason; *abl.,* for the sake of, for the purpose of

eēdō, -ere, cessī, cessum, yield, retreat, withdraw

celeritās, -tātis, F., speed

celeriter, *adv.,* swiftly, rapidly, quickly

cēlō, -āre, -āvī, -ātum, conceal

Celtae, -ārum, M. *pl.*, the Celts

cēnsus, -ūs, M., census, enumeration

centēnī, -ae, -a, *distributive num.,* a hundred each, a hundred

centum, *indecl. num.,* one hundred

centuriō, -ōnis, M., centurion, *an officer in the Roman army*

certāmen, certāminis, N., struggle

certē, *adv.,* certainly, at any rate, at least

certus, -a, -um, certain

cessō, -āre, -āvī, -ātum, cease, be unused, fall into disuse

cēterī, -ōrum, M. *pl.*, the rest, the others

Cimberius, -ī, M., Cimberius, *a German chief*

Cincinnātus, -ī, M., *a Roman name;* Lucius Quinctius Cincinnatus, *the famous dictator*

cingō, -ere, cīnxī, cīnctum, surround

circā, *prep. with acc.,* near, about

circiter, *adv.,* and *prep. with acc.,* about

circuitus, -ūs, M., circuit, circumference

circum, *prep. with acc.,* around

circumdō, -dare, -dedī, -datum, surround

circumveniō, -venīre, -vēnī, -ventum, surround

circus, -ī, M., circle, enclosure for sports, race course

citerior, citerius, *comparative adj.,* nearer, hither

citrā, *prep. with acc.,* on this side of

cīvīlis, -e, belonging to citizens, civil; courteous

cīvis, cīvis, M., F., citizen

cīvitās, -tātis, F., state, city

clārus, -a, -um, famous, distinguished

Claudius, -ī, M., Claudius, *a Roman name*

claudō, -ere, clausī, clausum, close

Cleopatra, -ae, F., Cleopatra, *queen of Egypt*

cliēns, clientis, M., dependent

cloāca, -ae, F., sewer

Cn., *abbreviation for* **Gnaeus,** *a Roman first name*

coepī, coepisse, coeptum, *defective verb,* began

coerceō, -ēre, -uī, -itum, restrain

cognōscō, -ere, cognōvī, cognitum, find out; *perf.,* know cōgō, -ere, coēgī, coāctum, collect, compel

cohors, cohortis, F., cohort, *a division of the legion*

cohortor, -ārī, -ātus sum, urge, encourage

Collātīnus, -ī, M., *a Roman name;* Tarquinius Collatinus, *one of the first two consuls at Rome*

collēga, -ae, M., colleague

colligō, -ere, collēgī, collēctum, collect

collis, -is, M., hill

collocō, -āre, -āvī, -ātum, place, station

colloquium, -ī, N., conference, interview

colloquor, colloquī, collocūtus sum, confer, converse

colō, -ere, coluī, cultum, till, cultivate

commeātus, -ūs, M., supplies

commemorō, -āre, -āvī, -ātum, call to mind, mention

comminus, *adv.*, hand to hand

committō, -mittere, -mīsī, -missum, unite, do; proelium committere, begin battle

commoveō, -movēre, -mōvī, -mōtum, stir up, arouse

commūnis, -e, common

compāreō, -ēre, -uī, appear, be seen

comparō, -āre, -āvī, -ātum, prepare, get ready

compleō, -ēre, -ēvī, -ētum, fill, fill up, complete

complūrēs, -a (-ia), several, some

compōnō, -pōnere, -posuī, -positum, arrange, settle

comprehendō, -hendere, -hendī, -hēnsum, seize

concidō, -ere, concidī, fall, be slain

concīdō, -cīdere, -cīdī, -cīsum, cut to pieces, kill

concilium, -ī, N., council

conditor, -tōris, M., founder

condiciō, -ōnis, F., condition, terms

condō, -ere, condidī, conditum, found, build; put away

condōnō, -āre, -āvī, -ātum, pardon

condūcō, -dūcere, -dūxī, -ductum, bring together, collect

cōnferō, -ferre, -tulī, -lātum, collect; sē cōnferre, to withdraw

cōnficiō, -ere, cōnfēcī, cōnfectum, finish, complete

cōnfīdō, -fīdere, -fīsus sum, *semideponent*, trust

cōnfodiō, -fodere, -fōdī, -fossum, stab

cōnfūsus, -a, -um, confused, lacking order

congregō, -āre, -āvī, -ātum, collect

coniciō, -ere, coniēcī, coniectum, throw

coniungō, -iungere, -iūnxī, -iūnctum, unite

coniūrātus, -ī, M., a conspirator

coniūrō, -āre, -āvī, -ātum, league together, conspire, plot

cōnor, -ārī, cōnātus sum, try, attempt

cōnscrībō, -ere, cōnscrīpsī, cōnscrīptum, enroll

consecrō, -āre, -āvī, -ātum, dedicate, deify

cōnsenēscō, -ere, cōnsenuī, grow old

cōnservō, -āre, -āvī, -ātum, protect, spare

Cōnsidius, -ī, M., Considius, *an officer in Caesar's army*

cōnsīdō, -ere, cōnsēdī, cōnsessum, encamp

cōnsilium, -ī, N., plan, counsel, judgment, advice

cōnspiciō, -spicere, -spexī, -spectum, perceive, see, catch sight of

cōnstituō, -ere, cōnstituī, cōnstitūtum, decide, determine; establish, appoint; construct; station, draw up

cōnsuētūdō, -dinis, F., habit, practice, usage

cōnsul, cōnsulis, M., consul, *one of the two chief magistrates of Rome, elected annually*

cōnsulāris, -e, consular, of the consul; *masculine as noun*, ex-consul

cōnsulātus, -ūs, M., consulship

contendō, -ere, contendī, contentum, fight, contend; hasten, go to

contentiō, -ōnis, F., struggle

contentus, -a, -um, contented, satisfied

contineō, -tinēre, -tinuī, -tentum, restrain

contrā, *prep. with acc.*, against

contrādīcō, -dīcere, -dīxī, -dictum, oppose

conveniō, -venīre, -vēnī, -ventum, come together, assemble

convertō, -ere, convertī, conversum, turn, change; signa convertere, wheel about

convocō, -āre, -āvī, -ātum, call together, summon

cōpia, -ae, F., plenty, supply; *pl.*, forces, troops

Coriolī, -ōrum, M. *pl.*, Corioli, *a town in Latium*

Cornēlia, -ae, F., Cornelia, *name of a girl or woman*

Cornēlius, -ī, M., Cornelius, *a Roman name*

cornū, cornūs, N., horn; wing (*of an army*)

corpus, corporis, N., body

corrumpō, -ere, corrūpī, corruptum, destroy, corrupt, seduce

cotīdiē, *adv.*, daily, every day

Crassus, -ī, M., Crassus, *a Roman name;* Marcus Licinius Crassus, *one of the members of the First Triumvirate*

crēber, crēbra, crēbrum, numerous

crēdō, -ere, crēdidī, crēditum, believe

creō, -āre, -āvī, -ātum, create; elect, appoint

Crustumīnī, -ōrum, M. *pl.*, the inhabitants of Crustumerium

cum, *prep. with abl.*, with

cum, *conj.*, when, since, although

cupiditās, -tātis, F., desire

cupidus, -a, -um, desirous, fond

cupiō, -ere, cupīvī, cupītum, wish, desire

cūr, *adv.*, why?

cūria, -ae, F., the senate house

D

damnō, -āre, -āvī, -ātum, condemn

dē, *prep. with abl.*, from, about, concerning (*original meaning, down from*)

dēbeō, -ēre, -uī, -itum, owe, ought

dēcēdō, -cēdere, -cessī, -cessum, withdraw; die

decem, *indecl. num.*, ten

decemvir, -ī, M., decemvir, *a mem-*

ber of a body of officials consisting of ten men

dēcernō, -cernere, -crēvī, -crētum, decide; decree, vote

dēcertō, -āre, -āvī, -ātum, fight to a finish; **proeliō dēcertāre,** fight a (decisive) battle

decimus, -a, -um, tenth

dēdō, -ere, dēdidī, dēditum, yield, surrender, give up

dēfendō, -ere, dēfendī, dēfēnsum, defend

dēfēnsor, -sōris, M., defender

dēferō, -ferre, -tulī, -lātum, report; confer, bestow

dēfessus, -a, -um, tired out, exhausted

dēiciō, -ere, dēiēcī, dēiectum, cast down, dislodge; disappoint

deinde, *adv.*, next, thereupon, then

dēleō, -ēre, -ēvī, -ētum, destroy, blot out

dēligō, -ligere, -lēgī, -lēctum, select, choose

dēmōnstrō, -āre, -āvī, -ātum, show, point out

dēmum, *adv.*, at last

dēnique, *adv.*, finally

dēpopulor, -ārī, -ātus sum, lay waste

dēprecātiō, -ōnis, F., warding off by prayer, pleading

dēscrībō, -scrībere, -scrīpsī, -scrīptum, mark off, divide

dēserō, -ere, dēseruī, dēsertum, desert, abandon

dētergeō, -tergēre, -tersī, -tersum, wipe away

dēterreō, -ēre, -uī, -itum, prevent, deter, hinder

deus, -ī, M., a god

dexter, -tra, -trum, right, right hand

dīcō, -ere, dīxī, dictum, say

dictātor, -tōris, M., dictator

dictātūra, -ae, F., dictatorship

diēs, -ēī, M. *and* F., day

difficilis, -e, difficult

difficultās, -tātis, F., difficulty

dignitās, -tātis, F., dignity, authority, official position, rank

dīligenter, *adv.*, diligently

dīmicātiō, -ōnis, F., struggle

dīmicō, -āre, -āvī, -ātum, fight, struggle

dīmittō, -ere, dīmīsī, dīmissum, send away, dismiss

dīripiō, -ere, dīripuī, dīreptum, tear apart; plunder

discēdō, -cedere, -cessī, -cessum, withdraw

dītissimus, -a, -um, *superlative adj.*, richest

diū, *adv.*, long, for a long time

diūturnitās, -tātis, F., long duration

dīves, *gen.* **dīvitis,** wealthy, rich

Dīviciācus, -ī, M., Diviciacus, *a Haeduan chief*

dīvidō, -ere, dīvīsī, dīvīsum, divide, separate

dīvīsus, -a, -um, *p. part. as adj.*, divided

dō, dare, dedī, datum, give

doceō, -ēre, docuī, doctum, teach, tell

domicilium, -ī, N., home, dwelling place, residence

dominus, -ī, M., master

domō, -āre, -uī, -itum, subdue

domus, -ūs, F., house, home

dōnum, -ī, N., gift, present

dubietās, -tātis, F., doubt

ducentī, -ae, -a, *numeral adj.*, two hundred

dūcō, -ere, dūxī, ductum, lead; construct; consider, think

dum, *conj.*, until; while

Dumnorīx, -īgis, M., Dumnorix, *a Haeduan chief*

duo, duae, duo, *numeral adj.*, two

duodecim, *numeral adj.*, twelve

duodēvīgintī, *numeral adj.*, eighteen

duodecimus, -a, -um, twelfth

duplicō, -āre, -āvī, -ātum, double

dux, ducis, M., leader, guide; general

E

ē, ex, *prep. with abl.*, from

ēdūcō, -dūcere, -dūxī, -ductum, lead out

efficiō, -ere, effēcī, effectum, bring about, cause

ego, meī, *personal pronoun*, I (*pl.*, nōs)

ēgredior, ēgredī, ēgressus sum, go out from, set out, depart

ēiciō, -ere, ēiēcī, ēiectum, drive out

emō, emere, ēmī, ēmptum, buy

enim, *conj.* (*post positive*), for

ēnūntiō, -āre, -āvī, -ātum, make known, report, disclose

eō, īre, īvī *or* iī, itum, go

eō, *adv.*, to that place, there (*with expressions of motion*)

Ēpīrus, -ī, F., Epirus, *a district of Greece*

epistula, -ae, F., letter

eques, equitis, M., cavalryman, horseman; *pl.*, cavalry

equitātus, -ūs, M., cavalry

equus, -ī, M., horse

ergō, *adv.*, therefore

errō, -āre, -āvī, -ātum, wander

Ēsquilīnus, -ī, M., the Esquiline, *one of the seven hills of Rome*

et, *conj.*, and

etiam, *adv.*, even, also

Euphrātēs, -is, M., the Euphrates

ēvādō, -ere, ēvāsī, ēvāsum, escape

excēdō, -ere, excessī, excessum, withdraw, go out

excidium, -ī, N., downfall, destruction

excīdō, -ere, excīdī, excīsum, demolish

exeō, -īre, -iī *or* -īvī, -itum, go forth, go out of, go from

exercitātus, -a, -um, trained

exercitus, -ūs, M., army

exigō, -ere, exēgī, exāctum, drive out

exiguus, -a, -um, small

exīstimō, -āre, -āvī, -ātum, think

exōrdium, -ī, M., beginning, origin

expellō, -ere, expulī, expulsum, drive out

experior, -īrī, expertus sum, try

explōrātor, -tōris, M., scout

explōrō, -āre, -āvī, -ātum, explore

expugnō, -āre, -āvī, -ātum, take by storm, capture

exsecrandus, -a, -um, detestable

exspectō, -āre, -āvī, -ātum, wait for, expect

exulō, -āre, -āvī, -ātum, be in exile

extrēmus, -a, -um, farthest, farthest part of, last

F

Fabius, -ī, M., Fabius, *a Roman name*

Fabius, -a, -um, of the Fabii, Fabian

facile, *adv.,* easily

facilis, -e, easy

faciō, -ere, fēcī, factum, make, do

factiō, factiōnis, F., faction, party

facultās, -tātis, F., opportunity, supply

Faliscī, -ōrum, M. *pl.,* Falerii, *a city of Etruria*

famēs, famis, F., hunger

familia, -ae, F., household, family

fātāliter, *adv.,* according to fate, by the decree of fate

Faustus, -ī, M., Faustus, *a Roman name*

faveō, -ēre, fāvī, fautūrus, favor

fēlīx, fēlīcis, happy, fortunate

fēmina, -ae, F., woman

ferē, *adv.,* nearly, about

fermē, *adv.,* about

ferō, ferre, tulī, lātum, bear, carry, bring

ferus, -a, -um, fierce

Fīdēnae, -ārum, F. *pl.,* Fidenae, *an ancient town near Rome*

Fīdēnātēs, -ium, M. *pl.,* the inhabitants of Fidenae

fidēs, -eī, F., faith, confidence

fīlia, -ae, F., daughter

fīlius, -ī, M., son

fīnis, -is, M., limit, end; *pl.,* territories, boundaries

fīnitimus, -a, -um, neighboring; **fīnitimī, -ōrum,** M. *pl.,* neighbors

fīō, fierī, factus sum, *used as passive of* **facio,** be made, be done; happen, become

firmus, -a, -um, firm

fleō, flēre, flēvī, flētum, weep

flētus, -ūs, M., weeping

flūctus, -ūs, M., wave

flūmen, flūminis, N., river

fluō, -ere, flūxī, flūxum, flow

fortis, -e, brave

fortiter, *adv.,* bravely

fortūna, -ae, F., fortune

fossa, -ae, F., ditch

frāter, frātris, M., brother

frūmentārius, -a, -um, of grain; **rēs frūmentāria,** grain supply, provisions

frūmentum, -ī, M., grain

fuga, -ae, F., flight

fugiō, -ere, fūgī, fugitūrus, flee

fugō, -āre, -āvī, -ātum, put to flight, rout

fulmen, fulminis, N., thunderbolt

fundō, -ere, fūdī, fūsum, pour out, shed

Fūrius, -ī, M., Furius, *a Roman name*

G

Gabiī, -ōrum, M. *pl.,* Gabii, *an old city of Latium*

Gallia, -ae, F., Gaul

Gallus, -ī, M., a Gaul

gaudeō, -ēre, gāvīsus sum, rejoice, be glad

Genava, -ae, F., Geneva

gener, generī, M., son-in-law

genitus, -a, -um, sprung from, descended from

gēns, gentis, F., tribe, nation, race

genus, generis, N., birth; family

Germānia, -ae, F., Germany

Germānī, -ōrum, M. *pl.,* the Germans

gerō, -ere, gessī, gestum, carry; **bellum gerere,** wage war

gladius, -ī, M., sword

glōria, -ae, F., glory

glōrior, -ārī, glōriātus sum, boast

Graecia, -ae, F., Greece

Reverio

grātia, -ae, F., favor, good will, gratitude

grātus, -a, -um, pleasing

gravis, -e, heavy, serious, hard to bear

graviter, *adv.,* heavily, severely

gravor, -ārī, gravātus sum, be unwilling

H

habeō, -ēre, -uī, -itum, have, hold

habitō, -āre, -āvī, -ātum, live, dwell

Haeduus, -ī, M., a Haeduan; *pl.,* the Haeduans, *a tribe of Gaul*

Helvētiī, -ōrum, M. *pl.,* the Helvetians

Hibernia, -ae, F., Ireland

hic, haec, hoc, this; *pl.,* these

hiemō, -āre, -āvī, -ātum, winter, spend the winter

hinc, *adv.,* from here, from this point, after this

Hispānia, -ae, F., Spain

hodiē, *adv.,* today

homō, hominis, M., man, human being

honestus, -a, -um, honorable

honor, -ōris, M., honor, office

hōra, -ae, F., hour

Horātius, -ī, M., Horatius, *a Roman name;* Horatius Pulvillus, *successor to Lucretius Tricipitinus in the consulship*

hortor, -ārī, -ātus sum, urge, encourage

hortus, -ī, M., garden

Hostīlius, -ī, M., Hostilius, *a Roman name*

hostis, -is, M. *and* F., enemy, public enemy; *pl.,* the enemy

I

iaciō, -ere, iēcī, iactus, throw

iam, *adv.,* now, already

Iāniculum, -ī, N., the Janiculum, *a hill west of the Tiber*

ibi, *adv.,* there, in that place

Iccius, -ī, M., Iccius, *a chief of the Remi*

(īcō), īcere, īcī, ictum, strike

īdem, eadem, idem, same, the same

idōneus, -a, -um, suitable, appropriate

igitur, *adv.,* therefore

ignis, -is, M., fire

ille, illa, illud, that; *pl.,* those

Īllyricum, -ī, N., Illyria, *a region bordering on the eastern coast of the Adriatic Sea*

immānis, -e, enormous, very great; fierce

impedīmentum, -ī, N., hindrance; *pl.,* baggage

impediō, -īre, -īvī, -ītum, hinder

impedītus, -a, -um, impeded, hindered, at a disadvantage

impendeō, -ēre, overhang, impend

imperium, -ī, N., power, authority, command, supreme power; reign

imperō, -āre, -āvī, -ātum, command, order; govern, rule

impetus, -ūs, M., attack, impetuosity, violence

impiger, -gra, -grum, energetic, industrious

impigrē, *adv.,* industriously, energetically

impleō, -plēre, -plēvī, -plētum, complete, finish

implōrō, -āre, -āvī, -ātum, entreat, ask for, ask, implore improvīsō, *adv.*, unexpectedly

in, *prep. with acc.*, into

in, *prep. with abl.*, in, on

incendō, -ere, incendī, incēnsum, set on fire, burn

inchoō, -āre, -āvī, -ātum, begin

incipiō, -ere, incēpī, inceptum, begin

incognitus, -a, -um, unknown

incolō, -ere, incoluī, inhabit

incolumis, -e, safe

incrēdibilis, -e, incredible

incursus, -ūs, M., attack

incūsō, -āre, -āvī, -ātum, reprimand

inde, *adv.*, from that place, from there; next

indicium, -ī, M., disclosure, information; per indicium, through informers

īnferō, -ferre, -tulī, -lātum, bring upon, cause, arouse; bellum īnferre, make war on

īnfīnītus, -a, -um, countless

ingēns, *gen.* ingentis, hūge, very great

ingredior, ingredī, ingressus sum, go into, enter, invade; *sometimes followed by* intrā *and accusative*

inimīcus, -a, -um, unfriendly, hostile

inimīcus, -ī, M., enemy

inīquus, -a, -um, unfavorable, unjust

iniūria, -ae, F., injury, injustice, wrong, affront

innumerus, -a, -um, countless, innumerable

īnsidiae, -ārum, F. *pl.*, treachery; plot, ambush

īnsigne, īnsignis, N., badge, decoration

īnsolēns, *gen.*, īnsolentis, arrogant

īnsolenter, *adv.*, insolently

īnstituō, -ere, īnstituī, īnstitūtum, set up, establish

īnstruō, -struere, -strūxī, -strūctum, draw up, arrange

īnsula, -ae, F., island

integer, -gra, -grum, whole, entire

intellegō, -ere, intellēxī, intellēctum, know

inter, *prep. with acc.*, between, among

interclūdō, -clūdere, -clūsī, -clūsum, cut off

intereā, *adv.*, meanwhile

interficiō, -ficere, -fēcī, -fectum, kill

interim, *adv.*, meanwhile

interveniō, -venīre, -vēnī, -ventum, come between, intervene

intrā, *prep. with acc.*, within, into

intrō, -āre, -āvī, -ātum, enter

intueor, -ērī, intuitus sum, look at, look upon

inveniō, -venīre, -vēnī, -ventum, find

invicem *or* in vicem, *adv.*, in turn, in succession

invidia, -ae, F., envy, hatred, unpopularity

invītō, -āre, -āvī, -ātum, invite

invītus, -a, -um, unwilling

ipse, ipsa, ipsum, himself, herself, itself

īrātus, -a, -um, angry, angry at

is, ea, id, this, that; he, she, it

iste, ista, istud, that of yours, that

ita, *adv.*, so, thus, in such a way

Italia, -ae, F., Italy

itaque, *adv.*, and so, accordingly

item, *adv.*, also

īter, itineris, N., journey, march, road, route

iterum, adv., again

Iuba, -ae, M., Juba, an African king

iubeō, -ēre, iussī, iussum, order, command

iūdex, iūdicis, M., judge

iūgerum, -ī (gen. pl., iūgerum), N., juger, acre (a little less than two-thirds of an English acre)

iūgum, -ī, N., yoke; ridge (of hills or mountains)

Iūlius, -ī, M., Julius, a Roman name

iungō, -ere, iūnxī, iūnctum, join, annex

Iūnius, -ī, M., Junius, a Roman name

Iuppiter, Iovis, M., Jupiter

iūstitia, -ae, F., justice

iuvenīlis, -e, youthful

iuvenis, -is, M., young man

iuvō, -āre, iūvī, iūtum, help, assist

L

L., abbreviation for Lūcius, a Roman first name.

Labiēnus, -ī, M., Labienus, an officer in Caesar's army

labōrō, -āre, -āvī, -ātum, labor, work, suffer

lacessō, -ere, lacessīvī, lacessītum, harass, attack

lacrima, -ae, F., tear

lacrimābilis, -e, lamentable

lapis, lapidis, M., stone

Larcius, -ī, M., Larcius, a Roman name

lātē, adv., widely, extensively

lateō, -ēre, -uī, lurk, remain concealed

Latīnī, -ōrum, M. pl., the Latins, the inhabitants of Latium

lātitūdō, -inis, F., width

latrō, latrōnis, M., brigand, robber

latus, lateris, N., side, flank

lātus, -a, -um, wide

laudō, -āre, -āvī, -ātum, praise

laus, laudis, F., praise

lēgātus, -ī, M., lieutenant, envoy

legiō, legiōnis, F., legion

legō, -ere, lēgī, lēctum, choose; read

lēx, lēgis, F., law

Lepidus, -ī, M., Lepidus, a Roman name

liber, librī, M., book

līber, lībera, līberum, free

līberāliter, adv., generously, graciously

līberī, -ōrum, M. pl., children (the free members of the household)

līberō, -āre, -āvī, -ātum, free, release, extricate

lībertās, -tātis, F., liberty

licet, licēre, licuit, impersonal verb, it is permitted

Licinius, -ī, M., Licinius, a Roman name

locus, -ī, M. (usually neuter in pl.), place

longē, adv., far, at a distance, by far

longitūdō, -inis, F., length

longus, -a, -um, long

loquor, loquī, locūtus sum, speak

lōrīca, -ae, F., coat of mail

Lucrētia, -ae, F., Lucretia, a Roman matron whose suicide, because of having suffered outrage from the son of Tarquinius Superbus, caused the expulsion of the kings from Rome

Lucrētius, -ī, M., Lucretius, *a Roman name;* Spurius Lucretius Tricipitinus, *one of the early consuls at Rome*

lūdus, -ī, M., game, sport

lūgeō, -ēre, lūxī, lūctum, mourn, mourn for

lūna, -ae, F., .moon

lūx, lūcis, F., light

M

M., *abbreviation for* **Mārcus,** *a Roman first name*

Macedonia, -ae, F.. Macedonia

magis, *adv.* (*comparative of* **magnopere**), more

magister -trī, M. master; **magister equitum,** master of the horse

magnitūdō, -inis, F.. size, greatness, magnitude

magnopere, *adv.,* greatly

magnus, -a, -um, large; **Pompēius Magnus,** Pompey the Great

male, *adv.,* badly

mālō, mālle, māluī, prefer

malus, -a, -um, bad, wicked, injurious, harmful

Mām., *abbreviation for* **Māmercus,** *a Roman first name*

maneō, -ēre, mānsī, mānsūrus, remain

manus, -ūs, F.. hand, band, company

Mārcellus, -ī, M., Marcellus, *a Roman name*

Mārcius, -ī, M., *a Roman name;* Ancus Marcius, *the fourth king of Rome*

mare maris, N., sea

marītus, -ī, M., husband

Marius, ī, M., Marius, *a Roman name*

Mārs, Mārtis, M., Mars, *the Roman god of war*

māter, mātris, F., mother

mātrōna, -ae, F., matron, married woman

Maurītānia, -ae, F., Mauretania, *a country of Africa*

maximē, *adv.,* *superl. of* **magnopere**

medius, -a, -um, middle, the middle of; **in mediō colle,** half way up the hill

meminī, meminisse, *defective verb,* remember

memoria, -ae, F., memory

mens. mentis, F., mind, disposition, attitude

mēnsis, mēnsis, M., month

mereor, merērī, meritus sum, deserve

metus, -ūs, M., fear

meus, -a, -um, mine

migrō, -āre, -āvī, -ātum, depart

mīles, mīlitis, M., soldier

mīliārium, -ī. N., milestone

mīlitāris, -e, military; **rēs mīlitāris,** warfare, military science

mīlitō, -āre, -āvī, -ātum, serve as a soldier

mīlle, *indecl. num.,* a thousand

minimē, *adv.* (*superlative of* **parum**), least

minus, *adv.* (*comparative*), less

miser, misera, miserum, unhappy, unfortunate

Mithridātēs, -is, M., Mithridates

mittō, -ere, mīsī, missum, send

moneō, -ēre, -uī, -itum, warn. advise, remind

mōns, montis, M., mountain

mora, -ae, F., delay

morbus, -ī, M., disease

morior, morī, mortuus sum, die

moror, morārī, morātus sum, delay

mors, mortis, F., death

mōs, mōris, M., custom

moveō, -ēre, mōvī, mōtum, move, cause, stir up

mox, *adv.*, soon, afterwards

multitūdō, -inis, F., large number, multitude

multus, -a, -um, much; *pl.*, many

Munda, -ae, F., Munda, *a city of Spain*

mūniō, -īre, -īvī, -ītum, fortify

mūrus, -ī, M., wall

mūtō, -āre, -āvī, -ātum, change

N

nam, *conj.*, for

nāscor, nāscī, nātus sum, be born

Nasua, -ae, M., Nasua, *a German chief*

nātiō, -ōnis, F., nation, inhabitant of a state

nātūra, -ae, F., nature

nātus, -a, -um, *see* **nāscor**

nauta, -ae, M., sailor

nāvis, -is, F., ship, boat

nē, *adv.*, not; *conj.*, that . . . not

nec, *see* **neque**

necessitās, -tātis, F., necessity, urgency

necō, -āre, -āvī, -ātum, kill

nēmō, *dat.* **nēminī** (*no gen or abl.*), M., no one

nepōs, nepōtis, M., grandson

Nīlus, -ī, M., the Nile

neque *or* **nec**, *conj.*, nor, and . . . not; **neque . . . neque**, neither . . . nor

Nervii, -ōrum, M. *pl.*, the Nervii, *a tribe of Belgians*

nesciō, -īre, -īvī, not know

neuter, -tra, -trum, neither

nihil, N. *indecl.*, nothing

nisi, *conj.*, unless

nōbilis, -e, well known, of noble birth

nōbilitās, -tātis, F., nobility, the nobles, aristocracy.

noceō, -ēre, -uī, -itum (*with dative*), injure

nōlō, nōlle, nōluī, be unwilling, not wish

nōmen, nōminis, N., name

nōminō, -āre, -āvī, -ātum, name, call

nōn, *adv.*, not

nōnāgēsimus, -a, -um, ninetieth

nōndum, *adv.*, not yet

nōn numquam, *adv.*, sometimes

nōnus, -a, -um, ninth

noster, nostra, nostrum, our, ours

novem, *indecl. num.*, nine

Noviodūnum, -ī, N., Noviodunum, *a town of Gaul*

novissimus, -a, -um, *superlative of* **novus**, newest, last; **novissimum agmen**, rear line

novus, -a, -um, new

nox, noctis, F., night

nūdō, -āre, -āvī, -ātum, strip, leave unprotected

nūllus, -a, -um, no, none

Numa, -ae, M., Numa, *a Roman name;* Numa Pompilius, *the second king of Rome*

numerus, -ī, M., number

nummus, -ī, M., coin, money

numquam, *adv.*, never

nunc, *adv.*, now

nūntius, -ī, M., message, messenger

O

ob, *prep. with acc.,* on account of

oblīvīscor, oblīvīscī, oblītus sum, forget

obsequor, -sequī, -secūtus sum, yield to, submit to, be under the authority of

obses, obsidis, M., hostage

obsideō, -sidēre, -sēdī, -sessum, besiege, blockade

Ōceanus, -ī, M., the ocean

occīdō, -ere, occīdī, occīsum, kill

occupō, -āre, -āvī, -ātum, seize, take possession of

Ocelum, -ī, N., Ocelum, *a town of Gaul*

octāvus, -a, -um, eighth; **octāvus decimus,** eighteenth

octō, *indecl. num.,* eight

octōgintā, *indecl. num.,* eighty

oculus, -ī, M., eye

ōlim, *adv.,* formerly, once

ōmen, ōminis, N., omen

omnīnō, *adv.,* at all

omnis, -e, all, every

onus, oneris, N., burden, weight

opīniō, -ōnis, F., opinion, expectation, belief

oportet, oportēre, oportuit, *impersonal verb,* it is necessary (*translated as personal verb,* one ought)

oppidānus, -ī, M., a townsman, inhabitant of a town

oppidum, -ī, N., town

oppugnō, -āre, -āvī, -ātum, attack

opus, operis, N., work, labor, task

orbis, orbis, M., circle; **orbis terrārum,** the world

ōrdinō, -āre, -āvī, -ātum, arrange

ōrdō, ōrdinis, M., order, rank

Orgetorix, -īgis, M., Orgetorix, *a Helvetian chief*

Oriēns, Orientis, M., the East, the Orient

orior, -īrī, ortus sum, arise, spring up

Orōdēs, -is, M., Orodes, *a king of the Parthians*

ōstium, -ī, N., door, mouth

P

P., *abbreviation for* **Pūblius**

pābulum, -ī, N., forage, fodder

pācō, -āre, -āvī, -ātum, subdue, make peaceful

paene, *adv.,* almost

Palaeopharsālus, -ī, M., Old Pharsalus

Palātīnus, -a, -um, Palatine

pandō, -ere, pandī, passum, stretch out, hold out

parātus, -a, -um, prepared

parcō, -ere, pepercī, parsum, spare

parō, -āre, -āvī, -ātum, prepare

pars, partis, F., part

Parthī, -ōrum, M. *pl.,* the Parthians

parum, *adv.,* too little, not enough

parvus, -a, -um, small

passus, -ūs, M., pace (4 *ft.* 10½ *in.*); **mīlle passūs** *or* **passuum,** one mile

pateō, -ēre, -uī, extend, be open

pater, patris, M., father

patior, patī, passus sum, permit, allow

patria, -ae, F., native land, country

patrimōnium, -ī, N., inheritance

paucī, -ae, -a (*sing. rarely used*), few; M. *pl. as noun,* a few

paulisper, *adv.,* for a little while

paulum, *adv.*, a little, somewhat

pauper, *gen.*, pauperis, poor

pāx, pācis, F., peace

pecūnia, -ae, F., money

pedes, peditis, M., foot soldier; *pl.*, infantry

pedester, -tris, -tre, on foot, foot, infantry (*as adjective*)

Pedius, -ī, M., *a Roman name;* Q. Pedius, *one of Caesar's officers*

pellō, -ere, pepulī, pulsum, rout, put to flight, drive out

per, *prep. with acc.*, through, by means of

pereō, -īre, -iī, -itum, perish, die

perditus, -a, -um, desperate, ruined

perdō, -ere, perdidī, perditum, lose

perficiō, -ere, perfēcī, perfectum, complete

perīculōsus, -a, -um, dangerous

perīculum, -ī, N., danger

permaneō, -manēre, -mānsī, -mānsum, continue, remain

Persae, -ārum, M. *pl.*, Persians

persuādeō, -suādēre, -suāsī, -suāsum, persuade

perterreō, -ēre, -uī, -itum, frighten thoroughly

pertineō, -ēre, -uī, extend, pertain

perturbō, -āre, -āvī, -ātum, throw into confusion *or* disorder

perveniō, -īre, pervēnī, perventum, arrive

pēs, pedis, M., foot

petō, -ere, petīvī *or* petiī, petītum, seek, ask for, beg for, go to

Petrēius, -ī, M., Petreius, *a Roman name*

phalanx, phalangis, F., phalanx

Pharnacēs, -is, M., Pharnaces

piger, pigra, pigrum, lazy

pīlum, -ī, N., javelin

placeō, -ēre, -uī, -itum, please

plēbs, plēbis, F., the common people, plebeians

plēnus, -a, -um, full

plūrimus, -a, -um, *see* multus

poena, -ae, F., punishment, penalty

polliceor, -ērī, pollicitus sum, promise

Pōmētia, -ae, F., *see* Suessa

Pompēius, -ī, M., Pompey, *a famous Roman general*

Pompilius, -ī, M., *see* Numa

pōnō, -ere, posuī, positum, place, locate, pitch (a camp)

pōns, pontis, M., bridge

Pontus, -ī, M., Pontus, *a country of Asia Minor*

populus, -ī, M., people

Porcius, -ī, M., Porcius, *a Roman name*

Porsenna, -ae, M., Porsenna, *a king of Etruria*

porta, -ae, F., gate

portō, -āre, -āvī, -ātum, carry

poscō, -ere, poposcī, demand

possideō, -sidēre, -sēdī, -sessum, possess, hold

possum, posse, potuī, be able, can

post, *prep. with acc.*, behind, after; *as adv.*, afterwards

posteā, *adv.*, afterwards

posterus, -a, -um, the following

postquam, *conj.*, after

postrēmus, -a, -um, (*superl. of* posterus), last; ad postrēmum, at last

postrīdiē, *adv.*, the next day

postulātum, -ī, N., demand

postulō, -āre, -āvī, -ātum, demand, ask

potēns, *gen.*, potentis, powerful

potentia, -ae, F., power, influence

potestās, -tātis, F., power

potior, potīrī, potītus sum, gain possession of

praecēdō, -cēdere, -cessī, -cessum, surpass, excel

praecipuē, *adv.*, especially

praecipuus, -a, -um, distinguished, chief

praeda, -ae, F., booty, spoil

praedicō, -āre, -āvī, -ātum, boast, announce

praeficiō, -ficere, -fēcī, -fectum, put in command of

praemittō, -mittere, -mīsī, missum, send ahead

praemium, -ī, N., reward

praeparō, -āre, -āvī, -ātum, prepare, make preparations for

praesēns, *gen.*, praesentis, present, in person

praestāns, *gen.*, praestantis, distinguished, prominent

praestō, -stāre, -stitī, -stātum, *transitive*, furnish, bestow; *intrans.*, surpass

praesum, -esse, -fuī, -futūrus, be in charge *or* command of

praeter, *prep. with acc.*, beyond, more than

praetereā, *adv.*, besides

praetextus, -a, -um, bordered

praetōrius, -ī, M., ex-praetor

premō, -ere, pressī, pressum, press, press hard; oppress

prīmō, *adv.*, at first

prīmum, *adv.*, first

prīmus, -a, -um, first

prīnceps, prīncipis, M., leader, chief

prīncipātus, -ī, M., leadership

prior, prius, *comparative adjective,* former, first

Prīscus, -ī, *see* Tarquinius

prīstinus, -a, -um, former, old time

prius, *adv.*, previously

priusquam, *conj.*, before

prīvātus, -ī, M., a private citizen

prō, *prep. with abl.*, in front of; for, on behalf of, in place of

probō, -āre, -āvī, -ātum, approve, approve of

prōcēdō, -cēdere, -cessī, -cessum, advance

prōcurrō, -currere, -currī, -cursum, run forward

prōdūcō, -dūcere, -dūxī, -ductum, lead out

proelium, -ī, N., battle

profectiō, -ōnis, F., setting out, departure

proficīscor, proficīscī, profectus sum, set out

prohibeō, -ēre, -uī, -itum, keep back, prevent, restrain

prōmittō, -mittere, -mīsī, -missum, promise

prōmoveō, -movēre, -mōvī, -mōtum, move forward

properō, -āre, -āvī, -ātum, hasten

propinquus, -a, -um, neighboring, near

prōpōnō, -ere, prōposuī, prōpositum, point out, explain, offer

proprius, -a, -um, own, special

propter, *prep. with acc.*, on account of

prōsum, prōdesse, prōfuī, prōfutūrus, benefit

prōvincia, -ae, F., province; the Province, *the southeastern part of Gaul* prōvolō, -āre, -āvī, -ātum, rush forth

proximē, adv., last, most recently

proximus, -a, -um, nearest, next, very near

Ptolemaeus, -ī, M., Ptolemy

Pūblicola, -ae, M., Publicola, a Roman name; Lucius Valerius Publicola, one of the early consuls at Rome

pudīcitia, -ae, F., chastity, virtue, honor

puella, -ae, F., girl

puer, -ī, M., boy

puerīlis, -e, childish, youthful

pugna, -ae, F., fight, battle

pugnō, -āre, -āvī, -ātum, fight, engage in battle

pulcher, -chra, -chrum, beautiful

Pulvillus, -ī, M., see Horātius

putō, -āre, -āvī, -ātum, think, consider

Q

Q., abbreviation for Quīntus, a Roman first name

quadrāgēsimus, -a, -um, fortieth

quadrāgintā, indecl. num., forty

quadringentiēs, adv., four hundred times

quaerō, -ere, -quaesīvī, quaesītum, ask

quaestor, -tōris, M., quaestor, one of a group of Roman officials who had charge of the financial affairs of the state and of the army

quam, adv., than, how, as

quantum, adv., as much as, as far as

quārtō, adv., for the fourth time

quārtus, -a, -um, fourth

quasi, adv., as if, as

quater, adv., four times

quattuor, indecl. num., four

quattuordecim, indecl. num., fourteen

-que, enclitic conj., and

queror, querī, questus sum, complain

quī, quae, quod, relative pronoun, who, which, that

quia, conj., because

quīdam, quaedam, quoddam (quiddam), a certain, some, a certain man, etc.

quidem, adv., indeed; nē ... quidem, not even

quīngentī, -ae, -a, numeral adj., five hundred

quīnī, -ae, -a, distributive num., five each

quīnquāgintā, indecl. num., fifty

quīnque, indecl. num., five

Quīntius, -ī, M., a Roman name; see Cincinnātus

quīntus, -a, -um, fifth

Quirīnālis, -is, M., the Quirinal, one of the seven hills of Rome

quis, quid, interrogative pronoun, who? what?

quisquam, quicquam, any, any person, anything

quisque, quidque, pronoun; and quisque, quaeque, quodque, adj., each

quō, conj., that, in order that

quod, conj., because

quondam, adv., formerly, once

quoque, adv., also

R

rapiō, -ere, rapuī, raptum, carry off, seize

ratiō, ratiōnis, F., theory, reason

rebellō, -āre, -āvī, -ātum, renew a war, revolt

recēdō, -cēdere, -cessī, -cessum, withdraw

recipiō, -ere, recēpī, receptum, receive, take back; sē recipere, retreat, withdraw

reddō, -dere, -didī, -ditum, render

redeō, -īre, -iī, -itum, return

recipiō, -ere, recēpī, receptum, reduce

redintegrō, -āre, -āvī, -ātum, renew

redūcō, -dūcere, -dūxī, -ductum, lead back, bring back

rēgīna, -ae, F., queen

regiō, regiōnis, F., region

rēgius, -a, -um, royal, regal, like a king

rēgnō, -āre, -āvī, -ātum, reign

rēgnum, -ī, N., royal authority, kingdom, reign

regredior, regredī, regressus sum, return

relinquō, -ere, relīquī, relictum, leave

reliquiae, -ārum, F. pl., remnant

reliquus, -a, -um, remaining, rest of; reliquī, as noun, the rest

Rēmī, -ōrum, M. pl., the Remi, a Belgian tribe

reminīscor, reminīscī, remember, recall

removeō, -movēre, -mōvī, -mōtum, remove, withdraw

renovō, -āre, -āvī, -ātum, renew

renūntiō, -āre, -āvī, -ātum, bring back word, report

reparō, -āre, -āvī, -ātum, restore, renew

repellō, -ere, reppulī, repulsum, drive back, beat back, repulse

reperiō, -īre, repperī, repertum, find, find out

repudiō, -āre, -āvī, -ātum, reject, refuse

rēs, reī, F., thing, affair

resistō, resistere, restitī, resist (*takes dative*)

respondeō, -ēre, respondī, respōnsum, answer, reply

respōnsum, -ī, N., reply

restituō, -ere, restituī, restitūtum, restore

revertor, revertī, revertī, reversum (*deponent in present system*), return

revocō, -āre, -āvī, -ātum, recall, recover

rēx, rēgis, M., king

Rhēa, -ae, F., Rhea, *an old Italian name;* Rhea Silvia, *the mother of Romulus and Remus*

Rhēnus, -ī, M., the Rhine

Rhodanus, -ī, M., the Rhone

rīpa, -ae, F., bank (*of a river*)

rōbur, rōboris, N., oak; strength

rogō, -āre, -āvī, -ātum, ask

Rōma, -ae, F., Rome

Rōmānus, -a, -um, Roman

Rōmānus, -ī, M., a Roman

Rōmulus, -ī, M., Romulus, *the traditional founder of Rome*

rosa, -ae, F., rose

rūrsus, *adv.*, again

S

Sabīnī, -ōrum, M. *pl.*, the Sabines

Sabis, -is, M., the San.bre, *a river of France*

sacrum, -ī, N., sanctuary, sacred place *or* building

saepe, *adv.*, often

sagitta, -ae, F., arrow

salūs, salūtis, F., safety

satis, *adv.*, enough

saxum, -ī, N., rock, stone

scelus, sceleris, N., crime

schola, -ae, F., school

sciō, scīre, scīvī, scītum, know

Scīpiō, -ōnis, M., Scipio, *a Roman name*

scūtum, -ī, N., shield

secundus, -a, -um, second; favorable

sed, *conj.*, but

sēdecim, *numeral adj.*, sixteen

sēditiō, -ōnis, F., insurrection

semel, *adv.*, once

sēmibarbarus, -a, -um, half civilized

semper, *adv.*, always

senātor, -tōris, M., senator

senātus, -ūs, M., senate

senectūs, -tūtis, F., old age, age

senior, -ōris, *compar. of* senex, older; *as noun*, old man

Senonēs, -um, M. *pl.*, the Senones, *a tribe of the Gauls*

septem, *indecl. num.*, seven

septendecim, *indecl. num.*, seventeen

septimus, -a, -um, seventh

sepultūra, -ae, F., burial

Sēquanī, -ōrum, M. *pl.*, the Sequani

sequor, sequī, secūtus sum, follow

Servīlius, -ī, M., Servilius, *a Roman name*

servitūs, -tūtis, F., slavery

Servius, -ī, M., Servius, *a Roman name;* Servius Tullius, *the sixth king of Rome*

servō, -āre, -āvī, -ātum, save

servus, -ī, M., slave, servant

sex, *indecl. num.*, six

Sex., *abbreviation for* Sextus

sexāgintā, *indecl. num.*, sixty

sexcentēsimus, -a, -um, six-hundredth

sexcentī, -ae, -a, *num. adj.*, six hundred

sextus, -a, -um, sixth; sextus decimus, sixteenth

Sextus, -ī, M., Sextus, *a Roman first name*

sī, *conj.*, if

sīcutī, *adv.*, just as, as

signum, -ī, N., sign, signal, standard; signa convertere, wheel about

silva, -ae, F., forest

silvestris, -tre, wooded, forest covered

Silvia, -ae, F., *see* Rhēa

similis, -e, like, similar

sine, *prep. with abl.*, without.

singulāris, -e, remarkable, unusual

singulī, -ae, -a, one at a time, separate, individually

sinister, -tra, -trum, left, left hand

socer, socerī, M., father-in-law

socius, -ī, M., ally

sōl, sōlis, M., the sun

soleō, -ēre, solitus sum, *semi-deponent*, be accustomed

sōlum, *adv.*, only; nōn sōlum ... sed etiam, not only ... but also

sōlus, -a, -um, only, alone

sonus, -ī, M., sound

soror, sorōris, F., sister

Sp., *abbreviation for* Spurius, *a Roman first name*

spectāculum, -ī, N., show, a spectacle; spectāculum lūdōrum, an exhibition of games spērō, -āre, -āvī, -ātum, hope

spēs, speī, F., hope

statua, -ae, F., statue

statim, adv., at once

stīpendiārius, -a, -um, subject to tribute, tributary

stīpendium, -ī, N., tribute, tax; military service

stō, stāre, stetī, stātūrus, stand

studeō, -ēre, -uī, desire, be eager for

stuprum, -ī, N., defilement, dishonor

sub, prep. with acc. or abl., under, beneath; at the foot of

subdūcō, -dūcere, -dūxī, -ductum, withdraw

subigō, -ere, subēgī, subāctum, subdue, conquer

subitō, adv., suddenly

subsequor, subsequī, subsecūtus sum, follow up, follow closely

subsidium, -ī, N., reinforcements, reserves

succēdō, -cēdere, -cessī, -cessum, come up close to, advance; follow, succeed

successus, -ūs, M., success

sūdor, sūdōris, M., sweat, perspiration

Suēbī, -ōrum, M. pl., the Suebi, a German tribe

Suessa, -ae, F., a city of Latium, commonly called Suessa Pometia

Suessiōnēs, -um, M. pl., the Suessiones, a Belgian tribe

suī, reflexive pron., of himself, herself, itself, themselves

Sulla, -ae, M., Sulla, a Roman name

sum, esse, fuī, futūrus, be

summus, -a, -um, highest, supreme; highest part of

sūmō, -ere, sūmpsī, sūmptum, take

sūmptus, -ūs, M., expense

Superbus, -ī, M., see Tarquinius

superior, superius, compar. adj., higher; preceding, previous

superō, -āre, -āvī, -ātum, defeat, overcome, conquer

supersedeō, -sedēre, -sēdī, -sessum, refrain from

supersum, -esse, -fuī, -futūrus, survive, be left

superveniō, -venīre, -vēnī, -ventum, come upon, surprise

supplicium, -ī, N., punishment

supportō, -āre, -āvī, -ātum, bring up, furnish

supputātiō, -ōnis, F., reckoning, computation

suprā, prep. with acc., above

Surēna, -ae, M., Surena, a Parthian general

suscipiō, -cipere, -cēpī, -ceptum, undertake, assume, receive

sustineō, -ēre, sustinuī, sustentum, sustain, withstand, hold out

suus, -a, -um, his, her, its, their

T

T., abbreviation for Titus, a Roman first name

tabernāculum, -ī, N., tent

tam, adv., so

tamquam, adv., as if

tamen, adv., nevertheless, still

tantum, adv., so greatly; only, merely

tantus, -a, -um, so great

tardē, adv., slowly

tardō, -āre, -āvī, -ātum, hinder, check

Tarquinius, -ī, M., Tarquinius, *the name of two Roman kings; Tarquinius Priscus (Tarquin the Elder) was the fifth of the kings, and Tarquinius Superbus (Tarquin the Proud) was the seventh*

tegō, -ere, tēxī, tēctum, cover, protect

tēlum, -ī, N., weapon

tempestās, -tātis, F., storm

templum, -ī, N., temple

tempus, temporis, N., time

tendō, -ere, tetendī, tentum *or* **tēnsum,** hold out, extend

teneō, -ēre, -uī, hold

ter, *adv.,* three times

tergum, -ī, N., back

terra, -ae, F., land, earth

terreō, -ēre, -uī, -itum, frighten, terrify

territōrium, -ī, N., territory

tertiō, *adv.,* for the third time

tertius, -a, -um, third

testāmentum, -ī, N., will

Thessālia, -ae, F., Thessaly

Tiberis, -is, M., the Tiber

timeō, -ēre, -uī, fear

timor, timōris, M., fear

Titurius, -ī, M., *a Roman name;* Quintus Titurius Sabinus, *one of Caesar's officers*

toga, -ae, F., toga

tollō, -ere, sustulī, sublātum, lift; take away

Tolumnius, -ī, M., Tolumnius, *a king of Veii*

tot, *indecl. adj.,* so many

tōtus, -a, -um, all, entire

trādō, -ere, trādidī, trāditum, surrender, give up

trādūcō, -dūcere, -dūxī, -ductum, lead across

trāns, *prep. with acc.,* across, beyond

trānseō, -īre, -iī *or* **-īvī, -itum,** cross

trānsgredior, -gredī, -gressus sum, cross

trānsportō, -āre, -āvī, -ātum, convey across

trecentēsimus, -a, -um, three hundredth

trecentī, -ae, -a, *num. adj.,* three hundred

trēs, tria, *gen.* **trium.,** three

tribūnus, -ī, M., tribune

tribūtum, -ī, N., tribute

trīciēs, *adv.,* thirty times

Tricipitīnus, -ī, M., *see* **Lucrētius**

trīduum, -ī, N., three days

trīgintā, *indecl. num.,* thirty

triumphō, -āre, -āvī, -ātum, celebrate a triumph

trīcēsimus, -a, -um, thirtieth

Trōia, -ae, F., Troy

tū, tuī, *personal pronoun,* you; *pl.,* **vōs**

tuba, -ae, F., trumpet

Tulingī, -ōrum, M. *pl.,* the Tulingī, *a Gallic tribe*

Tullius, -ī, M., Tullius, *a Roman name*

Tullus, -ī, M., Tullus, *a Roman name;* Tullus Hostilius, *the third king of Rome*

tum, *adv.,* then

tumultus, -ūs, M., disturbance, insurrection, uprising

turris, -is, F., tower

Tuscia, -ae, F., Etruria

Tuscī, -ōrum, M. *pl.,* the Etruscans, *inhabitants of Etruria*

Tusculum, -ī, N., Tusculum, *an ancient town not far from Rome*

tūtor, tūtōris, M., guardian, protector

tūtus, -a, -um, safe

tuus, -a, -um, your, yours

tyrannicus, -a, -um, despotic, tyrannical

U

ubi, *adv.*, where, when

Ubiī, -ōrum, M. *pl.*, the Ubii, *a German tribe*

ūllus, -a, -um, any

ulterior, ulterius, *comparative adj.*, farther

ultimus, -a, -um, *superl.*, farthest, last

ultrā, *prep. with acc.*, beyond

umquam, *adv.*, ever

ūnā, *adv.*, together, at the same time

ūndecim, *numeral adj.*, eleven

ūndecimus, -a, -um, eleventh

ūndēvīgintī, *numeral adj.*, nineteen

undique, *adv.*, on all sides

ūniversus, -a, -um, all together, entire, all

ūnus, -a, -um, one

urbs, urbis, F., city

usque, *adv.*, as far as

ūsus, -ūs, M., use, experience, advantage

ut, *conj.*, that, in order that

ut, *adv.*, as

uter, -tra, -trum, which of two

uterque, utraque, utrumque, each of two, each

ūtilis, -e, useful

ūtor, ūtī, ūsus sum, use

utrimque, *adv.*, on both sides

uxor, uxōris, F., wife

V

vacuus, -a, -um, vacant

Valerius, -ī, Valerius, *a Roman name*

validus, -a, -um, strong, powerful

vallēs, vallis, F., valley

Varrō, Varrōnis, M., Varro, *a Roman name*

Vārus, -ī, M., Varus, *a Roman name*

vāstō, -āre, -āvī, -ātum, lay waste

vehementer, *adv.*, severely

Vēī, Vēiōrum, M. *pl.*, Veii, *an ancient town of Etruria*

Vēientānī, -ōrum, M. *pl.*, *same as* Vēientēs

Vēientēs, -ium, M. *pl.*, the inhabitants of Veii

vel, *conj.*, or

vēndō, -ere, vēndidī, vēnditum, sell

veniō, -īre, vēnī, ventum, come

ventus, -ī, M., wind

vereor, -ērī, veritus sum, fear

vergō, -ere, slope

vertō, -ere, vertī, versum, turn

vērum, *adv.*, but

Vesontiō, -ōnis, M., Vesontio, *a town of Gaul, now Besançon*

vesper, vesperī, M., evening

Vestālis, -e, Vestal, of Vesta

vester, -tra, -trum, your, yours

veterānus, -a, -um, veteran

Veturia, -ae, Veturia, *a woman's name*

vetus, veteris, old, former, of long standing

vexō, -āre, -āvī, -ātum, lay waste, overrun, harass, plunder

via, -ae, F., street, road, way

vīcēsimus, -a, -um, twentieth

vīcīnus, -a, -um, near, neighboring

vicem, *see* **invicem**

victor, -tōris, M., conqueror

victōria, -ae, F., victory

vīcus, -ī, M., village

videō, -ēre, vīdī, vīsum, see; *pass. as dep.,* seem

vigilia, -ae, F., watch

vīgintī, *indecl. num.,* twenty

Vīminālis, -is, M., the Viminal, *one of the seven hills of Rome*

vincō, -ere, vīcī, victum, conquer, defeat

vindicō, -āre, -āvī, -ātum, avenge

vir, virī, M., man

Virgīnius, -ī, M., Virginius, *a Roman name*

virgō, -inis, F., virgin, maiden, girl, young woman

virtūs, -tūtis, F., courage, manliness

vīs, F., force, violence; *pl.* strength

vīta, -ae, F., life

vītō, -āre, -āvī, -ātum, avoid

vix, *adv.,* scarcely, with difficulty

vocō, -āre, -āvī, -ātum, call

volō, velle, voluī, wish, be willing

Volscī, -ōrum, M. *pl.,* Volscians

Volumnia, -ae, F., Volumnia, *a woman's name*

voluntās, -tātis, F., wish, will

vōx, vōcis, F., voice, word, utterance

vulnerō, -āre, -āvī, -ātum, wound

vulnus, vulneris, N., a wound

ENGLISH-LATIN VOCABULARY

A

able, be able, possum, posse, potuī

absent, be absent, absum, abesse, āfuī, āfutūrus

account, on account of, propter, *prep. with acc.*

accustomed, be accustomed, soleō, -ēre, solitus sum

advance, prōcēdō, -cēdere, -cessī, -cessum

advice, cōnsilium, cōnsilī, N.

again, rūrsus, iterum, *advs.*

aid, auxilium, auxilī, N.

all, omnis, omne

ally, socius, -ī, M.

alone, sōlus, -a, -um

also, item, *adv.*

although, cum, *conj.*

always, semper, *adv.*

among, apud, *prep. with acc.*

and, et, atque, -que, *conjs.*

angry, īrātus, -a, -um

animal, animal, animālis, N.

another, alius, alia, aliud

answer, respōnsum, -ī, N.

any one (*in a negative sentence*), quisquam

approach, appropinquō, -āre, -āvī, -ātum

approve, approve of, probō, -āre, -āvī, -ātum

Aquitanians, Aquītānī, -ōrum, M. *pl.*

Ariovistus, Ariovistus, -ī, M.

arm, armō, -āre, -āvī, -ātum

arms, arma, armōrum, N. *pl.*

army, exercitus, -ūs, M.

arrive, perveniō, -venīre, -vēnī, -ventum

arrow, sagitta, -ae, F.

ascend, ascendō, -ere, ascendī, ascēnsum

ask, rogō, -āre, -āvī, -ātum; quaerō, -ere, quaesīvī, quaesītum; **ask for**, petō, -ere, petīvī, petītum

assemble (*intransitive*), conveniō, -venīre, -vēnī, -ventum

at once, statim, *adv.*

attack (*noun*), impetus, -ūs, M.

attack (*verb*), oppugnō, -āre, -āvī, ātum

avoid, vītō, -āre, -āvī, -ātum

await, exspectō, -āre, -āvī, -ātum

B

badge, īnsigne, īnsignis, N.

bank (*of a river*), rīpa, -ae, F.

battle, proelium, -ī, N.

be, sum, esse, fuī, futūrus

beautiful, pulcher, -chra, -chrum

because, quod, *conj.*

before, ante, *prep. with acc.*

before, priusquam, *conj.*

beg for, petō, -ere, petīvī, petītum

began, have begun, coepī, coepisse, coeptum (*perfect tenses only*)

begin, incipiō, -ere, incēpī, inceptum; **begin battle**, proelium committere

behind, post, *prep. with acc.*

Belgians, Belgae, -ārum, M. *pl.*

between, inter, *prep. with acc.*

beyond, trāns, *prep. with acc.*

boast, glōrior, -ārī, glōriātus sum

boat, nāvis, nāvis, F.

body, corpus, corporis, N.

book, liber, librī, M.

boy, puer, puerī, M.

brave, fortis, forte

bravely, fortiter, *adv.*

bridge, pōns, pontis, M.

bring, ferō, ferre, tulī, lātum

bring together, condūcō, -dūcere, -dūxī, -ductum

Britain, Great Britain, Britannia, -ae, F.

brother, frāter, frātris, M.

build, aedificō, -āre, -āvī, -ātum

burn, incendō, -ere, incendī, incēnsum

but, sed, *conj.*

buy, emō, -ere, ēmī, ēmptum

by, ā, ab, *prep. with abl.*

C

Caesar, Caesar, Caesaris, M.

call, vocō, -āre, -āvī, -ātum; (*name*), appellō, -āre, -āvī, -ātum

call together, convocō, -āre, -āvī, -ātum

camp, castra, -ōrum, N. *pl.*

can, am able, possum, posse, potuī

capture, expugnō, -āre, -āvī, -ātum; capiō, -ere, cēpī, captum

carry, portō, -āre, -āvī, -ātum

carry on, gerō, -ere, gessī, gestum

cart, carrus, -ī, M.

Cassius, Cassius, -ī, M.

cattle, bovēs (*sing.* bōs, bovis), M. *and* F.

cause, causa, -ae, F.

cavalry, equitātus, -ūs, M.

Celts, Celtae, -ārum, M. *pl.*

centurion, centuriō, -ōnis, M.

certain, quīdam, quaedam, quoddam *or* quiddam

certainly, certē, *adv.*

choose, dēligō, -ere, dēlēgī, dēlēctum

citizen, cīvis, cīvis, M., F.

city, urbs, urbis, F.

cohort, cohors, cohortis, F.

collect (*trans.*), condūcō, -dūcere, -dūxī, -ductum; cōnferō, -ferre, -tulī, -lātum

come, veniō, -īre, vēnī, ventum

command, imperō, -āre, -āvī, -ātum

command, be in command of, praesum, -esse, -fuī, -futūrus

complain, queror, querī, questus sum

complete, perficiō, -ficere, -fēcī, -fectum; cōnficiō, -ficere, -fēcī, -fectum

concerning, dē, *prep. with abl.*

conference, colloquium, -ī, N.

conquer, vincō, -ere, vīcī, victum

Considius, Cōnsidius, -ī, M.

Cornelia, Cornēlia, -ae, F.

council, concilium, -ī, N.

country, native country, patria, -ae, F.

courage, virtūs, virtūtis, F.

courage, animus, -ī, M.

cross, trānseō, -īre, -iī, -itum

D

danger, perīculum, -ī, N.

dangerous, perīculōsus, -a, -um

dare, audeō, -ere, ausus sum

daughter, fīlia, -ae, F.

day, diēs, diēī, M. *and* F.

daybreak, prīma lūx

deep, altus, -a, -um

defeat, superō, -āre, -āvī, -ātum

defend, dēfendō, -ere, dēfendī, dēfēnsum

delay, mora, -ae, F.

demand, postulō, -āre, -āvī, -ātum

dependent, cliēns, clientis, M.

desert, dēserō, -ere, -uī, -tum

deserve, mereor, -ērī, meritus sum

desire, studeō, -ēre, -uī (*takes dative*); cupiō, -ere, cupīvī, cupītum

destroy, dēleō, -ēre, -ēvī, -ētum

difficult, difficilis, -e

difficulty, with difficulty, vix, *adv.*

disclose, ēnūntiō, -āre, -āvī, -ātum

distant, be distant, absum, abesse, āfuī, āfutūrus

distinguished, clārus, -a, -um

ditch, fossa, -ae, F.

Diviciacus, Dīviciācus, -ī, M.

do, faciō, -ere, fēcī, factum; **be done,** fīō, fierī, factus sum

draw up, īnstruō, -struere, -strūxī, -strūctum

drive back, repellō, -ere, reppulī, repulsum

E

each, *as pron.,* quisque, quidque; *adj.,* quisque, quaeque, quodque

easily, facile, *adv.*

easy, facilis, -e

enemy (*a public enemy*), hostis, hostis, M.; (*a personal enemy*), inimīcus, -ī, M.

energetic, impiger, impigra, impigrum

energetically, impigrē, *adv.*

enough, satis, *adv. and indecl. noun*

enroll, cōnscrībō, -scrībere, -scrīpsī, -scrīptum

envoy, lēgātus, -ī, M.

every, omnis, -e; **everything,** omnia, -ium; **every day,** cotīdiē, *adv.*

extend, pateō, -ēre, -uī

expect, exspectō, -āre, -āvī, -ātum

explore, explōrō, -āre, -āvī, -ātum

F

fact (*thing*), rēs, reī, F.

famous, clārus, -a, -um

far, longē, *adv.*

farmer, agricola, -ae, M.

father, pater, patris, M.

favor, faveō, -ēre, fāvī, fautum

fear (*noun*), metus -ūs, M.

fear (*verb*), timeō, -ere, -uī; vereor, -ērī, veritus sum

few, paucī, -ae, -a, *as substantive,* paucī, -ōrum, M. *pl.*

field, ager, agrī, M.

fierce, ferus, -a, -um

fiercely, ācriter, *adv.*

fight (*verb*), pugnō, -āre, -āvī, -ātum

fill, fill up, compleō, -ēre, -ēvī, -ētum

find, find out, reperiō, -īre, repperī, repertum

fire, ignis, ignis, M.

first, prīmus, -a, -um

first, at first, prīmō, *adv.*

five, quīnque, *indecl. num.*

flee, fugiō, -ere, fūgī, fugitūrus

flight, fuga, -ae, F.

follow, sequor, sequī, secūtus sum

foot, pēs, pedis, M.

forces, cōpiae, -ārum, F. *pl.*

forest, silva, -ae, F.

forget, oblīvīscor, oblīvīscī, oblītus sum

former, prīstinus, -a, -um

formerly, ōlim, *adv.*

formerly, anteā, *adv.*

fort, castellum, -ī, N.

fortify, mūniō, -īre, -īvī, -ītum

fortune, fortūna, -ae, F.

four, quattuor, *indecl. num.*

friend, amīcus, -ī, M.

friendship, amīcitia, -ae, F.
frighten, terreō, -ēre, -uī, -itum
from, ē, ex; ā, ab; dē, *preps. with abl.*
furnish, supportō, -āre, -āvī, -ātum

G

gain possession of, potior, potīrī, potītus sum
Gaius, Gāius, -ī, M.
gate, porta, -ae, F.
Gaul (*a country*), Gallia, -ae, F.
Gaul, a Gaul (*an inhabitant of the country of Gaul*), Gallus, -ī, M.
Geneva, Genava, -ae, F.
German, a German, Germānus, -ī, M.
gift, dōnum, -ī, N.
girl, puella, -ae, F.
give, dō, dare, dedī, datum
go, eō, īre, īvī *or* iī, itum
go forth, exeō, -īre, -iī, -itum
good, bonus, -a, -um
grain, frūmentum, -ī, N.
Great Britain, Britannia, -ae, F.
greatly, magnopere, *adv.*

H

Haeduan, a Haeduan, Haeduus, -ī, M.
hand, manus, -ūs, F.
happen, accidō, -ere, accidī
happy, fēlīx, fēlīcis
hasten, contendō, -ere, contendī, contentum
hasten, properō, -āre, -āvī, -ātum
have, habeō, -ēre, -uī, -itum
he, is
head, caput, capitis, N.
hear, audiō, -īre, -īvī, -ītum
height, altitūdō, -dinis, F.
help (*noun*), auxilium, -ī, N.
help (*verb*), iuvō, -āre, iūvī, iūtum

Helvetians, the Helvetians, Helvētiī, -ōrum, M. *pl.*
her, *reflexive,* suus, -a, -um; *when not reflexive,* eius
herself, *see* **self**
high, altus, -a, -um
hill, collis, collis, M.
himself, *see* **self**
hinder, impediō, -īre, -īvī, -ītum; dēterreō, -ēre, -uī, -itum
his, *reflexive,* suus, -a, -um; *when not reflexive,* eius
hold out, tendō, -ere, tetendī, tentum *or* tēnsum
home, domus, -ūs, F.
honorable, honestus, -a, -um
hope, spēs, speī, F.
horse, equus, -ī, M.
horseman, eques, equitis, M.
hostage, obses, obsidis, M.
hour, hōra, -ae, F.
hundred, one hundred, centum, *indecl. num.*

I

I, ego, *gen.,* meī
Iccius, Iccius, -ī, M.
if, sī, *conj.;* **if not,** nisi
implore, implōrō, -āre, -āvī, -ātum
in, in, *prep. with abl.*
incredible, incrēdibilis, -e
industrious, impiger, -gra, -grum
industriously, impigrē, *adv.*
infantry, cōpiae pedestrēs, cōpiārum pedestrium, F.
inform, certiōrem (certiōrēs) facere
inhabit, incolō, -ere, -uī
inhabitant of a town, oppidānus, -ī, M.
injure, noceō, -ēre, -uī, -itum (*takes dative*)

injury, iniūria, -ae, F.

into, in, *prep. with acc.*

invite, invītō, -āre, -āvī, -ātum

Ireland, Hibernia, -ae, F.

island, īnsula, -ae, F.

it, id

Italy, Ītalia, -ae, F.

its, *reflexive,* suus, -a, -um; *when not reflexive,* eius

itself, *see* self

javelin, pīlum, -ī, N.

journey, iter, itineris, N.

K

kill, interficiō, -ficere, -fēcī, -fectum

kind, benignus, -a, -um

king, rēx, rēgis, M.

know, *perf. of* cognōscō, -ere, cognōvī, cognitum; sciō, scīre, scīvī, scītum; intellegō, -legere, -lēxī, -lēctum

L

Labienus, Labiēnus, -ī, M.

large, magnus, -a, -um

law, lēx, lēgis, F.

lay waste, vāstō, -āre, -āvī, -ātum; dēpopulor, -ārī, dēpopulātus sum

lazy, piger, pigra, pigrum

lead, dūcō, -ere, dūxī, ductum

lead back, redūcō, -dūcere, -dūxī, -ductum

lead out, ēdūcō, -ere, ēdūxī, ēductum

leader, dux, ducis, M.

league together, coniūrō, -āre, -āvī, -ātum

leave, relinquō, -ere, relīquī, relictum

legion, legiō, -ōnis, F.

letter, epistula, -ae, F.

liberty, lībertās, lībertātis, F.

lieutenant, lēgātus, -ī, M.

life, vīta, -ae, F.

line of battle, aciēs, -ēī, F.

live (*dwell*), habitō, -āre, -āvī, -ātum

long, longus, -a, -um

long, for a long time, diū, *adv.*

lose, āmittō, -mittere, -mīsī, -missum

love, amō, -āre, -āvī, -ātum

Lucius, Lūcius, -ī, M.

lurk, lateō, -ēre, -uī

M

make, faciō, -ere, fēcī, factum; **make war on,** bellum īnferō, īnferre, etc.

man, homō, hominis, M.; vir, virī, M.

many, multī, multae, multa; *pl. of* multus

march, iter, itineris, N.

Marius, Marius, -ī, M.

master, dominus, -ī, M.

meanwhile, intereā, *adv.*

messenger, nūntius, -ī, M.

middle, middle of, medius, -a, -um

mile, mīlle passūs *or* passuum; *pl.,* mīlia passuum.

money, pecūnia, -ae, F.

more, magis, *adv.*

mountain, mōns, montis, M.

move, moveō, -ēre, mōvī, mōtum

much, multus, -a, -um; *when used with comparative,* multō, *abl. of neuter*

multitude, multitūdō, -dinis, F.

my, mine, meus, -a, -um

N

name, nōmen, nōminis, N.

narrow, angustus, -a, -um

nation, gēns, gentis, F.

native country, patria, -ae, F.

nature, nātūra, -ae, F.

neighboring, fīnitimus, -a, -um

neither (conj.), neque; neither ...
nor, neque ... neque

neither (of two), neuter, -tra,
-trum

Nervii, Nerviī, -ōrum, M. pl.

never, numquam, adv.

nevertheless, tamen, adv.

new, novus, -a, -um

next to, proximus, -a, -um

night, nox, noctis, F.

no (adj.), nūllus, -a, -um

no one, nēmō; dat., nēminī (no
gen.)

not, nōn, adv.; with subjunctive of
desire, nē

not yet, nōndum, adv.

nothing, nihil, indeclinable, N.

now, nunc, adv.

number, numerus, -ī, M.

O

Ocelum, Ocelum, -ī, N.

often, saepe, adv.

old, vetus, gen., veteris

on, in, prep. with abl.

on account of, ob, prep. with acc.;
propter, prep. with acc.

on this side of, citrā, prep. with
acc.

one, ūnus, -a, -um; one . . . another, alius . . . alius; one . . .
the other, alter . . . alter

order, iubeō, -ēre, iussī, iussum

Orgetorix, Orgetorīx, Orgetorīgis, M.

other, the other (of two), alter,
altera, alterum; another, alius,
alia, aliud

ought, dēbeō, -ēre, -uī, -itum

our, ours, noster, -tra, -trum

ourselves, see self

overhang, impendeō, -ēre

overrun, vexō, -āre, -āvī, -ātum

P

part, pars, partis, F.

peace, pāx, pācis, F.

people, populus, -ī, M.

persuade, persuādeō, -suādēre,
-suāsī, -suāsum (takes dative)

place (noun), locus, -ī, M. (usually
neuter in plural)

place (verb), collocō, -āre, -āvī,
-ātum

plan, cōnsilium, -ī, N.

please, placeō, -ēre, -uī (takes
dative)

pleasing, grātus, -a, -um

point out, dēmōnstrō, -āre, -āvī,
-ātum

power, potentia, -ae, F.; imperium, -ī, N.

powerful, potēns, gen., potentis

praise, laus, laudis, F.

praise, laudō, -āre, -āvī, -ātum

prefer, mālō, mālle, māluī

prepare, comparō, -āre, -āvī, -ātum

present, be present, adsum, -esse,
-fuī, -futūrus

present, dōnum, -ī, N.

prisoner, captīvus, -ī, M.

promise, polliceor, -ērī, pollicitus
sum

protect, tegō, -ere, -tēxī, -tēctum;
cōnservō, -āre, -āvī, -ātum

province, prōvincia, -ae, F.

punishment, supplicium, -ī, N.

purpose, for the purpose, causā
with genitive

Q

quickly, celeriter, adv.

R

rank, ōrdō, ōrdinis, M.

reason, causa, -ae, F.

receive, accipiō, -cipere, -cēpī, -ceptum

reduce, redigō, -ere, redēgī, redāctum

refrain, supersedeō, -sedēre, -sēdī, -sessum

regarding, dē, *prep. with abl.*

region, regiō, regiōnis, F.

reject, repudiō, -āre, -āvī, -ātum

remain, maneō, -ēre, mānsī, mānsum

remember, meminī, meminisse; reminīscor, reminīscī

Remi, Rēmī, -ōrum, M. *pl.*

renew, renovō, -āre, -āvī, -ātum

report, ēnūntiō, -āre, -āvī, -ātum; renūntiō, -āre, -āvī, -ātum

repulse, repellō, -ere, reppulī, repulsum

residence, domicilium, -ī, N.

resist, resistō, -ere, restitī (*takes dative*)

rest, the rest, reliquī, -ōrum, M. *pl.*

restore, restituō, -ere, restituī, restitūtum

restrain, contineō, -tinēre, -tinuī, -tentum

return, redeō, -īre, -iī, -itum

reward, praemium, -ī, N.

Rhine, Rhēnus, -ī, M.

river, flūmen, flūminis, N.

road, iter, itineris, N.

road, via, -ae, F.

Roman (*adj.*), Rōmānus, -a, -um

Roman, a Roman, Rōmānus, -ī, M.

Rome, Rōma, -ae, F.

rose, rosa, -ae, F.

route, iter, itineris, N.

royal authority, royal power, rēgnum, -ī, N.

S

safe, tūtus, -a, -um

sailor, nauta, -ae, M.

same, īdem, eadem, idem

say, dīcō, -ere, dīxī, dictum

school, schola, -ae, F.

scout, explōrātor, -tōris, M.

second, secundus, -a, -um

see, videō, -ēre, vīdī, vīsum

seem, videor, vidērī, vīsus sum

seize, occupō, -āre, -āvī, -ātum

self, himself, herself, itself, ipse, ipsa, ipsum; *reflexive*, suī

send, mittō, -ere, mīsī, missum

send ahead, praemittō, -mittere, -mīsī, -missum

separate, dīvidō, -ere, dīvīsī, dīvīsum

Sequani, Sēquanī, -ōrum, M. *pl.*

set on fire, set fire to, incendō, -ere, incendī, incēnsum

set out, proficīscor, proficīscī, profectus sum

seven, septem, *indecl. num.*

several, complūrēs, -ium

Sextus, Sextus, -ī, M.

she, ea

shield, scūtum, -ī, N.

ship, nāvis, nāvis, F.

short, brevis, breve

signal, signum, -ī, N.

since, cum, *conj.*

slaughter, caedēs, caedis, F.

slave, servus, -ī, M.

slavery, servitūs, -tūtis, F.

slowly, tardē, *adv.*

small, parvus, -a, -um

so, tam, *adv.*

so great, tantus, -a, -um

soldier, mīles, mīlitis, M.

some . . . others, aliī . . . aliī

some one, aliquis

sometimes, nōn numquam

son, fīlius, fīlī, M.

sound, sonus, -ī, M.

speed, celeritās, -tātis, F.

spend the winter, hiemō, -āre, -āvī, -ātum

spirit, animus, -ī, M.

spur, calcar, calcāris, N.

stand, stō, stāre, stetī, stātūrus

state, cīvitās, -tātis, F.

station, collocō, -āre, -āvī, -ātum

statue, statua, -ae, F.

still, tamen, adv.

stone, saxum, -ī, N.

street, via, -ae, F.

strength, vīrēs, vīrium (pl. of vīs)

subdue, pācō, -āre, -āvī, -ātum

suitable, idōneus, -a, -um

summer, aestās, -tātis, F.

supreme, summus, -a, -um (superlative of superus)

surpass, praecēdō, -cēdere, -cessī, -cessum

surrender, trādō, -ere, trādidī, trāditum; dēdō, -ere, dēdidī, dēditum

surround, circumveniō, -venīre, -vēnī, -ventum

swiftly, celeriter, adv.

sword, gladius, -ī, M.

T

take, capiō, -ere, cēpī, captum

tall, altus, -a, -um

temple, templum, -ī, N.

ten, decem, indecl. num.

territories, fīnēs, -ium, M. (pl. of fīnis)

than, quam, conj.

that, conj., ut; that . . . not, nē

that, demonstrative, ille, illa, illud (unemphatic), is, ea, id

their, reflexive, suus, -a, -um; when not reflexive, eōrum, eārum

themselves, reflexive, suī

then, tum, adv.

there (in that place), ibi, adv.; (to that place), eō, adv.

thing, rēs, reī, F.

think, arbitror, -ārī, arbitrātus sum

third, tertius, -a, -um

this, hic, haec, hoc

three, trēs, tria

three days, trīduum, -ī, N.

through, per, prep. with acc.

time, tempus, temporis, N.

time, for a long time, diū, adv.

tired out, dēfessus, -a, -um

to, ad, prep. with acc.

today, hodiē, adv.

tower, turris, turris, F.

town, oppidum, -ī, N.

townspeople, oppidānī, -ōrum, M. pl.

treachery, īnsidiae, -ārum, F. pl.

trust, cōnfīdō, -ere, cōnfīsus sum

try, cōnor, -ārī, cōnātus sum; experior, -īrī, expertus sum

two, duo, duae, duo

two days, bīduum, -ī, N.

two hundred, ducentī, -ae, -a

U

Ubii, Ubiī, -ōrum, M. pl.

unexpectedly, imprōvīsō, adv.

unfavorable, inīquus, -a, -um

unhappy, miser, misera, miserum

unknown, incognitus, -a, -um

unless, nisi, conj.

until, dum, conj.

unwilling, be unwilling, nōlō,
nōlle, nōluī
unwilling, invītus, -a, -um
urge, hortor, -ārī, hortātus sum
use, ūtor, ūtī, ūsus sum
useful, ūtilis, -e

V

valley, vallēs, vallis, F.
Vesontio, Vesontiō, -ōnis, F.
veteran, veterānus, -a, -um
victory, victōria, -ae, F.
village, vīcus, -ī, M.
violence, vīs, F.
voice, vōx, vōcis, F.

W

wage, gerō, gerere, gessī, gestum
wait, wait for, exspectō, -āre, -āvī,
-ātum
walk, ambulō, -āre, -āvī, -ātum
wall, mūrus, -ī, M.
wander, errō, -āre, -āvī, -ātum
war, bellum, -ī, N.
warn, moneō, -ēre, -uī, -itum
watch, vigilia, -ae, F.
water, aqua, -ae, F.
wave, flūctus, -ūs, M.
weapon, tēlum, -ī, N.
weapons, arma, -ōrum
weep, fleō, flēre, flēvī, flētum
what, interrog., pron., quid; as
adj., quis (quī), quae, quod
where, ubi, adv.

white, albus, -a, -um
who, what, interrog., quis, quid
who, which, what, relative, quī,
quae, quod
whole, tōtus, -a, -um
why, cūr, adv.
when, cum
wide, lātus, -a, -um
widely, lātē, adv.
width, lātitūdō, -dinis, F.
wing (of an army), cornū, -ūs, N.
winter (verb), spend the winter,
hiemō, -āre, -āvī, -ātum
wish, cupiō, -ere, cupīvī, cupītum
wish, volō, velle, voluī
with, cum, prep. with abl.
withdraw, dēcēdō, -ere, dēcessī
dēcessum; excēdō, -cēdere,
-cessī, -cessum
woman, fēmina, -ae, F.
work (noun), opus, operis, N.
work (verb), labōrō, -āre, -āvī,
-ātum
wound (verb), vulnerō, -āre, -āvī,
-ātum
wrong, iniūria, -ae, F.

Y

year, annus, -ī, M.
you, tū, singular; vōs, plural.
your, yours, tuus, -a, -um, referring to one person; vester, vestra, vestrum, referring to more
than one person.

INDEX

(Numbers refer to sections.)

34

SUPPLEMENTARY READING

PERSEUS

Perseus and his mother were set adrift on the sea by Acrisius, king of Argos, the grandfather of Perseus, because an oracle had declared that Acrisius would some day perish at the hands of his grandson.

Jupiter, however, saved the mother and child, bringing them to the Island of Seriphus, where they were kindly received by Polydectes, the king.

When Perseus reached manhood he was ordered by Polydectes to bring him the head of Medusa, an undertaking which was likely to prove fatal. But Apollo and Minerva directed him on his journey and gave him a special equipment for his task. With the aid thus afforded, he accomplished the perilous exploit in safety and escaped from the companions of Medusa, who sought to kill him. On his way back he rescued Andromeda, daughter of Cepheus, the king of the Ethiopians, who was about to be devoured by a sea serpent. He married Andromeda, and soon after returned with her to the island from which he had been sent by the crafty Polydectes. Finding that his mother had taken refuge from the king, he turned the latter into stone through the magic power of the head of Medusa. Afterward, while taking part in athletic games he accidentally killed his grandfather, Acrisius, thus fulfilling the oracle which Acrisius had vainly sought to escape.

SUPPLEMENTARY READING
MATERIAL

THE STORY OF PERSEUS

1. Set Adrift

Haec nārrantur ā poētīs dē Perseō. Perseus fīlius erat
Iovis, maximī deōrum. Avus eius Ācrisius appellābātur.
Ācrisius volēbat Perseum, nepōtem suum, necāre; nam propter
ōrāculum puerum timēbat. Comprehendit igitur Perseum,
adhūc īnfantem, et cum mātre in arcā ligneā inclūsit. Tum
arcam ipsam in mare coniēcit. Danaē, Perseī māter, magnopere territa est; tempestās enim magna mare turbābat. Per- 5
seus autem in sinū mātris dormiēbat.

---

1. Haec, *these things, i.e.,* the following stories. This substantive use of
the neuter plural of *hic* is very common.

2. Ācrisius: predicate nominative after the passive of a verb of calling.

6. Danaē: a Greek name, with genitive ending in *-ēs,* acc. in *-ēn.*

7. enim: postpositive, *i.e.,* it stands after one or more words of its sentence; *nam* (see l. 3) regularly stands first in a sentence. Another postpositive word is *autem,* l. 8.

In section 1 point out two appositives; an ablative of agent.

---

2. avus, -ī, *m.,* grandfather.

3. nepōs, -ōtis, *m.,* grandson, neph-
ew.

4. ōrāculum, -ī, *n.* [ōrō], oracle.

**com-prehendō, -hendere, -hendī,
-hēnsum,** *tr.,* seize, arrest.

5. ad-hūc, *adv.,* until now, as yet.

in-fāns, *gen.* **-fantis,** *adj.,* infant;
subst., m. and f., infant, babe.

arca, -ae, *f.,* chest, box.

ligneus, -a, -um, *adj.,* [lignum], of
wood, wooden.

inclūdō, -clūdere, -clūsī, -clūsus, *tr.*
[in+claudō], shut up, enclose.

6. coniciō, -icere, -iēcī, -iectum,
tr. [com-+iaciō], throw together;
hurl, cast.

7. enim, *conj.* (*postpositive*), for.

turbō, -āre, -āvī, -ātum, *tr.* [turba],
disturb, throw into confusion.

8. autem, *conj.,* but, on the other
hand, however; furthermore.

sinus, -ūs, *m.,* a fold; bosom.

dormiō, -īre, -īvī, -ītum, *intr.,* sleep.

2. Cast on an Island

Iuppiter tamen haec omnia vīdit, et fīlium suum servāre
10 cōnstituit. Fēcit igitur mare tranquillum, et arcam ad īnsulam Serīphum perdūxit. Huius īnsulae Polydectēs tum rēx
erat. Postquam arca ad lītus appulsa est, Danaē in harēnā
quiētem capiēbat. Post breve tempus ā piscātōre quōdam
reperta est, et ad domum rēgis Polydectis adducta est. Ille
15 mātrem et puerum benignē excēpit, et sēdem tūtam in fīnibus
suīs dedit. Danaē hoc dōnum libenter accēpit, et prō tantō
beneficiō rēgī grātiās ēgit.

---

9. tamen: usually postpositive, but sometimes stands first in its clause;
the same is true of *igitur*, l. 4.

10. mare tranquillum: two accusatives after a verb of making. One
accusative may be an adjective, as here.

11. Serīphum: in apposition with *īnsulam*. We usually say in English
"the island of," "the city of."

12. Postquam: with *postquam* and *ubi* the perfect is the tense most frequently employed. In translation, with the English equivalents "after"
or "when," we sometimes employ the past perfect tense, sometimes the
past.

13. piscātōre quōdam: the forms of *quīdam* sometimes precede and
sometimes follow the word they modify.

16. dedit: *eīs*, dative of indirect object, is to be understood.

In section 2 point out a complementary infinitive; a dative of indirect
object.

---

10. tranquillus, -a, -um, *adj.*, calm,
still.

**11. per-dūcō, -dūcere, -dūxī, -duc-
tum,** *tr.*, lead through, lead, bring,
conduct.

12. appellō, -ere, -pulī, -pulsum, *tr.*
[ad+pellō], drive to, bring to; *with
or without* nāvem, land, put in.

harēna (*sometimes spelled* **arēna**),
-ae, *f.*, sand; shore, beach.

13. quiēs, -ētis, *f.*, rest; peace, quiet.

piscātor, -ōris, *m.* [piscor, to fish],
fisherman.

14. domus, -ūs, (-ī), *f.*, home, house.

ad-dūcō, -dūcere, -dūxī, -ductum,
tr., lead to, conduct, bring; incite,
induce.

15. benignē, *adv.* [benignus], kindly.

excipiō, -cipere, -cēpī, -ceptum, *tr.*
[ex+capiō], take out, take up,
catch; receive, entertain.

sēdēs, -is, *f.* [sedeō], seat, chair;
residence, abode.

17. grātia, -ae, *f.* [grātus], favor, influence; gratitude, thanks, re-
quital; **grātiās agere,** to express
thanks; **grātiam referre,** to make
requital, to requite; **grātiā** (*with
gen.*), for the sake of.

3. PERSEUS SENT ON HIS TRAVELS

Perseus igitur multōs annōs ibi habitāvit, et cum mātre suā vītam ēgit beātam. At Polydectēs Danaēn magnopere amābat atque eam in mātrimōnium dūcere volēbat. Hoc 20 tamen cōnsilium Perseō minimē grātum erat. Polydectēs igitur Perseum dīmittere cōnstituit. Tum iuvenem ad sē vocāvit et haec dīxit: "Turpe est vītam hanc ignāvam agere; iam dūdum tū adulēscēns es; quousque hīc manēbis? Tempus est arma capere et virtūtem praestāre. Hinc abī, et 25 caput Medūsae mihi refer."

---

18. annōs: accusative of duration of time.

21. Perseō: dependent on *grātum;* for the case see App. 40, 2.

23. haec: used as in l. 1; with *dīxit, spoke as follows.*

agere: subject of *est;* an infinitive used as a noun is in the neuter gender; hence the predicate adjective, *turpe,* is neuter.

24. iam dūdum es, *you have long been;* with *iam dūdum* a present tense is translated by an English present perfect, an imperfect by an English past perfect; *iam dūdum erās* would mean *you had long been.*

25. abī: imperative of *abeō.* What is the imperative of *eō?*

26. refer: the present imperative of *ferō* and its compounds is irregular. See App. 33.

---

19. beātus, -a, -um, *adj.,* happy, prosperous.

20. atque, *conj.,* and also, and.

mātrimōnium, -ī, *n.* [**māter**], marriage; **in mātrimōnium dare,** give in marriage, arrange a marriage for; **in mātrimōnium dūcere,** marry.

21. minimē, *superl. adv.* [**minimus**], least, very little; by no means, not at all.

23. vocō, -āre, -āvī, -ātum, *tr.* [**vōx**], call, summon.

turpis, -e, *adj.,* unseemly, shameful, disgraceful.

ignāvus, -a, -um, *adj.* [**in-+gnāvus,** busy], inactive, cowardly.

24. dūdum, *adv.,* before, formerly; **iam dūdum,** this long time, a long time ago.

adulēscēns, adulēscentis, -ium, *adj.* [*pr. part.* of **adolēscō**], youthful; *subst., m.,* a young man, a youth.

quo-usque, *adv.,* till when? how long?

25. prae-stō, -stāre, -stitī, -stitum, *intr. and tr.,* stand before; excel, be better; exhibit, show.

hinc, *adv.* [**hic**], from this place, hence.

ab-eō, -īre, -iī, -itum, *intr.,* go away, depart.

26. re-ferō, -ferre, -tulī, -lātum, *tr.,* bear back, bring back; **pedem referre,** withdraw, retire, retreat; **grātiam referre,** requite.

4. Perseus Gets His Outfit

Perseus, ubi haec audīvit, ex īnsulā discessit et, postquam ad continentem vēnit, Medūsam quaesīvit. Diū frūstrā quaerēbat; nam nātūram locī ignōrābat. Tandem Apollō et
30 Minerva viam dēmōnstrāvērunt. Prīmum ad Graeās, sorōrēs Medūsae, pervēnit. Ab hīs tālāria et galeam magicam accēpit. Apollō autem et Minerva falcem et speculum dēdērunt. Tum postquam tālāria pedibus induit, in āera ascendit. Diū per āera volābat; tandem tamen ad eum locum
35 vēnit ubi Medūsa cum cēterīs Gorgonibus habitābat. Gorgonēs autem mōnstra erant speciē horribilī; capita enim eārum serpentibus omnīnō contēcta erant; manūs etiam ex aere factae erant.

---

27. Perseus: in Latin, when the verbs of a principal and a subordinate clause express action by the same person or thing, the noun or pronoun used to denote the subject frequently stands before the subordinate clause.

haec, *this;* see note on *haec,* l. 23.

31. galeam magicam: this rendered the wearer invisible.

33. pedibus, *on his feet;* dative, used with the compound *induit.*

āera: a word of Greek origin, which retains its Greek accusative form.

36. speciē horribilī, *of horrible aspect,* ablative of description.

37. aere: from *aes.*

---

28. continēns, -entis, *f.* [contineō], continent, mainland.

frūstrā, *adv.,* in vain, to no purpose.

29. ignōrō, -āre, -āvī, -ātum, *tr.,* not know, be unaware of.

tandem, *adv.,* at length, finally.

30. prīmum, *adv.* [prīmus], in the first place, first of all; **cum prīmum,** as soon as; **quam prīmum,** as soon as possible.

31. tālāria, -ium, *n. pl.,* winged sandals.

galea, -ae, *f.,* helmet.

magicus, -a, -um, *adj.,* magical. magic.

32. falx, falcis, *f.,* sickle.

speculum, -ī, *n.* [speciō, look], mirror

33. induō, -duere, -duī, -dūtum, *tr.,* put on.

āēr, āeris, *m.,* the air.

35. cēterī, -ae, -a, *adj., pl.,* the other, the rest of.

36. mōnstrum, -ī, *n.,* [moneō], a divine omen, portent; monster.

speciēs, -ēī, *f.,* appearance, aspect.

horribilis, -e, *adj.* [horreō], terrible, fearful, dreadful.

omnīnō, *adv.* [omnis], altogether, entirely; at all; only.

con-tegō, -tegere, -tēxī, -tēctum, *tr.* cover.

aes, aeris, *n.,* copper, bronze.

5. The Gorgon's Head

Rēs erat difficillima abscīdere caput Gorgonis; eius enim
cōnspectū hominēs in saxum vertēbantur. Propter hanc cau- 40
sam Minerva illud speculum dederat. Perseus igitur tergum
vertit, et in speculum īnspiciēbat; hōc modō ad locum vēnit
ubi Medūsa dormiēbat. Tum falce suā caput eius ūnō ictū
abscīdit. Cēterae Gorgonēs statim ē somnō excitātae sunt
et, ubi rem vīdērunt, īrā commōtae sunt. Arma rapuērunt, 45
et Perseum occīdere volēbant; ille autem, dum fugit, galeam
magicam induit et, ubi hoc fēcit, statim ē cōnspectū eārum
ēvāsit.

40. vertēbantur: the Latin imperfect, like the English past, often expresses repeated or customary action.

42. speculum: ancient mirrors consisted of polished metal plates.

hōc modō: ablative of manner.

46. dum fugit, *while he fled, while fleeing;* when a *dum* clause denotes
situation, it takes the present indicative, regardless of the tense of the
principal verb.

In section 5 what is the subject of the first sentence? Account for the
case of *ictū*, 43; for the tense of *fēcit*, 47. What different forces have the
perfects *vertit, vēnit,* and the imperfects *īnspiciēbat, dormiēbat,* 42-43?

39. abscīdō, -cīdere, -cīdī, -cīsum,
tr. [abs+caedō], cut off.

40. cōnspectus, -ūs, *m.* [cōnspiciō],
sight, view.

vertō, -ere, vertī, versum, *tr.,* turn.

43. ictus, -ūs, *m.,* blow, stroke.

44. somnus, -ī, *m.,* sleep.

excitō, -āre, -āvī, -ātum, *tr.,* call
out, rouse.

45. īra, -ae, *f.,* anger, wrath, ire.

**com-moveō, -movēre, -mōvī, -mō-
tum,** *tr.,* move deeply, excite,
arouse, alarm.

rapiō, -ere, rapuī, raptum, *tr.,* seize,
carry off.

46. occīdō, -cīdere, -cīdī, -cīsum, *tr.*
[ob+caedō], cut down, kill.

dum, *conj.,* while; until.

48. ē-vādō, -vādere, -vāsī, -vāsum,
intr., come out, make one's way;
escape.

6. The Sea Serpent

Post haec Perseus in fīnēs Aethiopum vēnit. Ibi Cēpheus
quīdam illō tempore rēgnābat. Hic Neptūnum, maris deum, 50

49. Cēpheus quīdam, *a certain Cepheus,* or *a man named Cepheus.*

50. tempore: ablative of time.

Hic: a pronoun referring to Cepheus.

ōlim offenderat. Neptūnus autem mōnstrum saevissimum mīserat. Hoc cotīdiē ē marī veniēbat et hominēs dēvorābat. Ob hanc causam pavor animōs omnium occupāverat. Cēpheus igitur ōrāculum deī Hammōnis cōnsuluit, atque ā deō iussus

55 est fīliam mōnstrō trādere. Eius autem fīlia, nōmine Andromeda, virgō fōrmōsissima erat. Cēpheus, ubi haec audīvit, magnum dolōrem percēpit. Volēbat tamen cīvēs suōs ē tantō perīculō extrahere, atque ob eam causam cōnstituit imperāta Hammōnis facere.

---

52. marī: it should be remembered that neuter nouns with the genitive plural in *-ium* have the ending *-ī* in the ablative singular.

53. omnium, *of all* (*i.e., men*); a substantive use of an adjective; compare the neuter *haec*, l. 23.

54. ōrāculum: the word may mean the seat of an oracle, as here, or the reply given by an oracle. The consultation of oracles sprang from the belief that information and advice could be obtained from certain divinities. Oracles were usually given by oral utterances of a priest or priestess in a state of real or pretended frenzy, or by signs. The temple (with its oracle) of the Egyptian god Hammon stood in an oasis of the Libyan desert. His oracles were signs interpreted by a priest. The most famous oracle of antiquity was that of Apollo at Delphi, in Greece, where the oracular response was delivered by a priestess in a state of excitement resembling madness.

55. mōnstrō: *trādere* takes an indirect object.

nōmine: ablative of respect.

56. Cēpheus, ubi: the order for translation is explained in the note on *Perseus, ubi,* l. 27.

In section 6 explain the case of *deō,* 54; of *Andromeda,* 55; of *virgō,* 56. What are the principal parts of *volō?*

---

51. offendō, -fendere, -fendī, -fēnsum, *tr.,* [ob+fendō, strike], offend.

saevus, -a, -um, *adj.,* fierce, savage.

52. dē-vorō, -āre, -āvī, -ātum, *tr.,* swallow, devour.

53. ob, *prep. with acc.,* on account of.

pavor, -ōris, *m.* [paveō, be afraid], terror, alarm.

54. cōnsulō, -sulere, -suluī, -sultum, *tr. and intr.,* consult; consult the interests of (*with dative*).

56. virgō, virginis, *f.,* young woman, maiden, virgin.

fōrmōsus, -a, -um, *adj.* [fōrma], beautiful, handsome.

57. percipiō, -cipere, -cēpī, -ceptum, *tr.* [per+capiō], perceive, feel.

58. ex-trahō, -trahere, -trāxī, -tractum, *tr.,* draw out; extricate, release.

59. imperātum, -ī, *n.* [*p. part. of* imperō], command, order.

7. A Human Sacrifice

Tum rēx diem certam dīxit et omnia parāvit. Ubi ea 60
diēs vēnit, Andromeda ad lītus dēducta est et in cōnspectū
omnium ad rūpem alligāta est. Omnēs fātum eius dēplō-
rābant, nec lacrimās tenēbant. At subitō, dum mōnstrum
exspectant, Perseus accurrit; et, ubi lacrimās vīdit, causam
dolōris quaerit. Illī rem tōtam expōnunt et puellam dēmōn- 65
strant. Dum haec geruntur, fremitus terribilis audītur; simul
mōnstrum, horribilī speciē, procul cōnspicitur. Eius cōnspectus timōrem maximum omnibus iniēcit. At mōnstrum

---

60. diem: in the plural, *diēs* is always masculine, in the singular sometimes masculine, sometimes feminine.

omnia, *all things, everything;* or with *parāvit, made all preparations.*
The masculine plural forms of *omnis* used substantively mean *all men,* as
in l. 53, the neuter plural forms, *all things.*

63. nec tenēbant, *and did not restrain; neque* is regularly used in Latin
for *and not.*

dum . . . expectant, *while they were awaiting;* the present tense with
dum, as in l. 46.

64. accurrit: for vivid effect a past event or situation may be represented as present. The present in this use is called the historical present,
which may often be translated by the English past. Several other examples occur in this section.

67. speciē: the case use is the same as in l. 36.

68. timōrem . . . omnibus iniēcit, *inspired all with the greatest fear;*
literally, *threw the greatest fear into all; omnibus* is a dative with a compound
verb, as in l. 33.

---

60. certus, -a, -um, *adj.* [*p. part. of*
cernō], fixed, certain.

61. dē-dūcō, -dūcere, -dūxī, -duc-
tum, *tr.,* lead away; draw down;
nāvem dēdūcere, to launch a ship.

62. rūpēs, -is, *f.,* rock, cliff.

alligō, -āre, -āvī, -ātum, *tr.* [ad+
ligō, bind], bind to, tie to.

fātum, -ī, *n.* [*p. part. of* for, speak],
fate, destiny.

dē-plōrō, -āre, -āvī, -ātum, *tr.,* deplore, lament.

64. accurrō, -currere, -currī, -cur-
sum, *intr.* [ad+currō], run to,
come up hurriedly.

65. ex-pōnō, -pōnere, -posuī, -po-
situm, *tr.,* set forth, explain; ex-
pose, abandon; set ashore.

66. fremitus, -ūs, *m.* [fremō, roar],
a roar, a loud noise.

terribilis, -e, *adj.* [terreō], dreadful,
terrible.

67. procul, *adv.,* in the distance, at
a distance, far off.

cōnspiciō, -spicere, -spexī, -spectum,
tr., [con-+speciō], look, perceive,
observe.

68. iniciō, -icere, -iēcī, -iectum, *tr.*
[in+iaciō], throw into, hurl upon;
inspire in, cause.

magnā celeritāte ad lītus contendit, iamque ad locum appro-
70 pinquābat ubi puella stābat.

---

69. magnā celeritāte: ablative of manner.

In section 7 account for the tense of *geruntur*, 66; of *stābat*, 70.

---

8. The Rescue

At Perseus, ubi haec vīdit, gladium suum rapuit, et, postquam tālāria induit, in āera sublātus est. Tum dēsuper in
mōnstrum impetum subitō fēcit et gladiō suō collum eius
graviter vulnerāvit. Mōnstrum, ubi sēnsit vulnus, fremitum
75 horribilem ēdidit et sine morā tōtum corpus sub aquam
mersit. Perseus, dum circum lītus volat, reditum eius exspectābat; mare autem intereā undique sanguine īnficitur.
Post breve tempus, bēlua rūrsus caput sustulit; mox tamen
ā Perseō ictū graviōre vulnerāta est. Tum iterum sē sub
80 undās mersit, neque posteā visa est.

---

72. in (*mōnstrum*), *on.*

80. neque: translate as in l. 63.

In section 8 account for the case of *gladiō*, 73; of *Perseō*, 79; of *ictū*, 79. What case is governed by *sub* with a verb of motion? By *in* meaning into? By *circum?* By *sine?*

---

72. tollō, -ere, sustulī, sublātum, *tr.,* lift, elevate, raise; elate; remove.

dē-super, *adv.,* from above.

73. collum, -ī, *n.,* neck.

74. graviter, *adv.* [gravis], heavily; severely; with dignity, impressively.

sentiō, -īre, sēnsī, sēnsum, *tr.,* feel, see, perceive.

75. ē-dō, -dere, -didī, -ditum, *tr.,* give out, put forth; give birth to; exhibit; inflict.

sub, *prep. with acc. and abl.,* under.

76. mergō, -ere, mersī, mersum, *tr.,* plunge, sink.

reditus, -ūs, *m.* [redeō], return.

77. inter-eā, *adv.,* meanwhile, in the meantime.

undique, *adv.,* from all parts, on all sides, all around, everywhere.

sanguis, sanguinis, *m.,* blood.

īnficiō, -ficere, -fēcī, -fectum, *tr.* [in +faciō], stain, dye, color.

78. bēlua, -ae, *f,* wild beast, monster.

80. unda, -ae, *f.,* wave.

9. The Reward of Valor

Perseus, postquam in lītus dēscendit, prīmum tālāria exuit; tum ad rūpem vēnit ubi Andromeda vīncta erat. Ea autem omnem spem salūtis dēposuerat et, ubi Perseus adiit, terrōre paene exanimāta erat. Ille vincula statim solvit et puellam patrī reddidit. Cēpheus ob hanc rem maximō gaudiō affectus 85 est. Meritam grātiam prō tantō beneficiō Perseō rettulit; praetereā Andromedam ipsam eī in mātrimōnium dedit. Ille libenter hoc dōnum accēpit, et puellam dūxit. Paucōs annōs cum uxōre suā in eā regiōne habitāvit, et in magnō honōre erat apud omnēs Aethiopēs. Magnopere tamen cupiēbat mātrem 90 suam rūrsus vidēre. Tandem igitur cum uxōre ē rēgnō Cēpheī discessit.

---

83. terrōre: ablative of cause, App. 42, 16.

86. meritam grātiam rettulit, *made a deserved requital,* or *repaid the favor as it deserved.*

prō, *in return for.*

88. puellam dūxit, *married.* *Dūcō* has reference to that part of the ceremony in which the bridegroom led the bride to his own house. With regard to the woman, the verb for marry is *nūbere,* literally, *to veil oneself,* with the dative of the bridegroom's name.

In section 9 account for the case of *patrī* 85; of *Perseō,* 86; of *annōs,* 88. Point out a complementary infinitive. What cases are governed by the prepositions *ad, ob, apud?*

---

81. exuō, -uere, -uī, -ūtum, *tr.,* take off, remove.

82. vinciō, -īre, vīnxī, vīnctum, *tr.,* bind, fasten.

83. dē-pōnō, -pōnere, -posuī, -positum, *tr.,* set down, deposit; lay aside.

ad-eō, -īre, -iī *or* **-īvī, -itum,** *intr.,* go *or* come up to, come up, approach.

terror, -ōris, *m.* [terreō], terror, fright.

84. paene, *adv.,* nearly, almost.

ex-animō, -āre, -āvī, -ātum, *tr.,* put out of breath, stun, exhaust.

vinculum, -ī, *n.* [vinciō], bond, fetter.

solvō, -ere, solvī, solūtum, *tr.,* loosen, unbind, release; relax; *of ships, with* or *without* **nāvem** *or* **nāvēs,** set sail, weigh anchor.

85. afficiō, -ficere, -fēcī, -fectum, *tr.* [ad+faciō], do to; treat; affect.

86. meritus, -a, -um, *adj.* [*p. part. of* mereō], due, deserved, just.

87. praeter-eā, *adv.,* in addition, besides, further.

89. regiō, -ōnis, *f.* [regō], region, district.

honor, -ōris, *m.,* honor, repute, esteem; **Honor, -ōris,** *m.,* Honor *personified as a god.*

90. apud, *prep. with acc.,* among, with; near; at the house of; on the bank of.

10. Turned to Stone

Postquam Perseus ad īnsulam nāvem appulit, sē ad locum contulit ubi māter ōlim habitāverat. At domum invēnit 95 vacuam et omnīnō dēsertam. Trēs diēs per tōtam īnsulam mātrem quaerēbat; tandem quārtō diē ad templum Diānae pervēnit. Hūc Danaē refūgerat, quod Polydectem timēbat. Perseus, ubi haec cognōvit, īrā magnā commōtus est; ad rēgiam Polydectis sine morā contendit et, ubi eō vēnit, statim 100 in ātrium irrūpit. Polydectēs magnō timōre affectus est, et fugere volēbat. Dum tamen ille fugit, Perseus caput Medūsae mōnstrāvit; ille autem, simul atque hoc vīdit, in saxum versus est.

---

93. sē . . . contulit, *betook himself, proceeded.*

97. quod: a conjunction.

99. eō: an adverb.

100. magnō timōre affectus est, *was very badly frightened.* What is it literally?

102. simul atque, *as soon as;* the same rule as to the tense of the verb applies to this phrase as to *postquam* and *ubi*, explained in the note on l. 12.

In section 10 account for the case of *vacuam, dēsertam*, 95; of *diē*, 96; of *ātrium*, 100; of *Medūsae*, 101. What case does *per* govern? What are the meanings of the adverbs *hīc, hinc, hūc?*

---

95. dē-serō, -serere, -seruī, -sertum, *tr.,* [serō, join], abandon, desert.

96. quārtus, -a, -um, *adj.* [quattuor], fourth.

97. hūc, *adv.* [hic], this way, to this place.

re-fugiō, -fugere, -fūgī, -fugitūrus, *intr.,* flee back; flee away, escape.

99. rēgia, -ae, *f.* [rēgius], palace.

eō, *adv.* [is], to that place, thither; on that account.

100. ātrium, -ī, *n.,* atrium, *the principal room or hall of a house.*

irrumpō, -rumpere, -rūpī, -ruptum, *tr. and intr.* [in+rumpō], burst, break in, rush into, burst into.

102. mōnstrō, -āre, -āvī, -ātum, *tr.* [mōnstrum], show, exhibit; point out.

---

11. The Oracle Fulfilled

Post haec Perseus cum uxōre suā ad urbem Ācrisiī rediit. 105 Ille autem, ubi Perseum vīdit, magnō terrōre affectus est.

Nam propter ōrāculum istud nepōtem suum adhūc timēbat.
In Thessaliam igitur ad urbem Lārissam statim refūgit;
frūstrā tamen, neque enim fātum suum vītāvit. Post paucōs
annōs rēx Lārissae lūdōs magnōs fēcit; nūntiōs in omnēs
partēs dīmīserat et diem ēdīxerat. Multī ex omnibus urbibus 110
Graeciae ad lūdōs convēnērunt. Ipse Perseus inter aliōs
certāmen discōrum iniit. At, dum discum conicit, avum
suum cāsū occīdit; Ācrisius enim inter spectātōrēs eius certāminis forte stābat.

---

106. istud: this word is declined like *ille*, and usually means *that* or
that of yours. Here the force is, *that oracle of which you know*.

107. Lārissam, *of Larissa;* an appositive translated like *Serīphum*, 1. 11.

109. lūdōs fēcit, *gave games*.

in omnēs partēs, *in all directions*.

112. discōrum: the discus was a flat piece of stone or metal.

113. cāsū, *by chance, accidentally; cāsus* is one of a class of very common nouns used without prepositions to express manner.

What cases are governed by the prepositions *propter, ex, inter?* What
is the regular position of *enim?*

---

106. iste, ista, istud, *demonstr. pron.*,
that of yours, that.

109. lūdus, -ī, *m.*, game, sport.

110. ē-dīcō, -dīcere, -dīxī, -dictum,
tr., declare, proclaim, appoint.

112. certāmen, -inis, *n.* [**certō**],
struggle, contest, rivalry.

discus, -ī, *m.*, discus, quoit.

in-eō, -īre, -iī *or* **-īvī, -itum,** *tr.*,
enter; enter upon, form.

113. spectātor, -ōris, *m.* [**spectō**],
onlooker, spectator.

114. forte, [*adv. abl. of* **fors,** chance],
perhaps, by chance.

VOCABULARY FOR PERSEUS

abeō, -īre, -iī (-īvī), -itum, go away, depart

abscīdō, -cīdere, -cīdī, -cīsum, cut off

accurrō, -currere, -currī, -cursum, run to, come up hurriedly

Ācrisius, -ī, M., Acrisius, *grandfather of Perseus*

addūcō, -dūcere, -dūxī, -ductum, lead to, bring; induce

adeō, -īre, -iī (-īvī), -itum, go to, come up, approach

āēr, āeris, M., the air

aes, aeris, N., copper, bronze

Aethiopēs, -um, M., *pl.*, the Ethiopians, *a people of Africa*

afficiō (*or* adficiō), -ficere, -fēcī, -fectum, do to, treat, affect

agō, agere, ēgī, āctum, drive, do; spend, pass

alligō, -āre, -āvī, -ātum, bind to, tie to

Andromeda, -ae, F., Andromeda, *the daughter of Cepheus*

Apollō, Apollinis, M., Apollo

appellō (*or* adpellō), -pellere, -pulī, -pulsum, drive to, bring to

arca, -ae, F., chest, box

at, *conj.*, but

atrium, -ī, N., atrium, *the principal room or hall of a house*

avus, -ī, M., grandfather

beātus, -a, -um, happy

bēlua, -ae, F., wild beast, monster

benignē, *adv.*, kindly

cāsus, -ūs, M., accident, mischance

Cepheus, -ī, M., Cepheus, *a king of Ethiopia*

collum, -ī, N., neck

cōnspectus, -ūs, M., sight, view

cōnsulō, -sulere, -suluī, -sultum, consult

contegō, -tegere, -tēxī, -tēctum, cover

continēns, -entis, F., mainland

Danaē, -ēs, F., Danae, *mother of Perseus*

dēdūcō, -dūcere, -dūxī, -ductum, lead away

dēplōrō, -āre, -āvī, -ātum, deplore, lament

dēpōnō, -pōnere, -posuī, -positum, deposit; lay aside

dēscendō, -scendere, -scendī, -scēnsum, descend

dēsuper, *adv.*, from above

dēvorō, -āre, -āvī, -ātum, swallow, devour

Diāna, -ae, F., Diana, *goddess of the chase*

dīcō, -ere, dīxī, dictum, say, appoint, name

discus, -ī, M., discus, quoit

dolor, -ōris, M., sorrow, suffering, pain

dormiō, -īre, -īvī, -ītum, sleep

dūdum, *adv.*, before, formerly; iam dūdum, this long time

ēdīcō, -dīcere, -dīxī, -dictum, declare, proclaim, appoint

53

ēdō, -dere, -didī, -ditum, give out, put forth

exanimō, -āre, -āvī, -ātum, render breathless, stun

excipiō, -cipere, -cēpī, -ceptum, take out, take up, receive

excitō, -āre, -āvī, -ātum, call out, rouse

expōnō, -pōnere, -posuī, -positum, set forth, explain

extrahō, -trahere, -trāxī, -tractum, draw out; extricate, release

exuō, -uere, -uī, -ūtum, take off, remove

falx, falcis, F., sickle

fātum, -ī, N., fate, destiny

fōrmōsus, -a, -um, beautiful, hand-some

forte, adv., by chance

fremitus, -ūs, M., a roar, a loud noise

frūstrā, adv., in vain, to no purpose

galea, -ae, F., helmet

gaudium, -ī, N., joy, gladness

gerō, -ere, gessī, gestum, carry, carry on; wage

Gorgō, -onis, F., a Gorgon

Graeae, -ārum, F., pl., the Graeae

Hammon, -ōnis, M., Hammon, an Egyptian god

hārēna (or ārēna), -ae, F., sand, shore, beach

horribilis, -e, horrible, dreadful

hūc, adv., to this place

ictus, -ūs, M., blow, stroke

ignāvus, -a, -um, inactive, cowardly

ignōrō, -āre, -āvī, -ātum, not know, be unaware

imperātum, -ī, N., command, order

inclūdō, -clūdere, -clūsī, -clūsum, shut up, enclose

induō, -duere, -duī, -dūtum, put on

ineō, -īre -iī (-īvī), -itum, enter

īnfāns, gen., īnfantis, adj., infant; subst., M. and F., infant, young child

īnficiō, -ficere, -fēcī, -fectum, stain, dye, color

iniciō (iniiciō), -ere, -iēcī, -iectum, throw into; inspire in, cause

īnspiciō, -spicere, -spexī, -spectum, look into, look

īra, -ae, F., anger, wrath

irrumpō, -rumpere, -rūpī, -ruptum, break in, rush into

Larissa, -ae, F., Larissa, a city of Thessaly

libenter, adv., willingly, with pleas-ure

ligneus, -a, -um, wooden, of wood

lītus, -oris, N., sea-shore, beach

magicus, -a, -um, magic

mātrimōnium, -ī, N., marriage

Medūsa, -ae, F., Medusa, a Gorgon

mergō, -ere, mersī, mersum, plunge, sink

meritus, -a, -um, due, deserved, just

Minerva, -ae, F., Minerva, the goddess of wisdom

minimē, adv., least, by no means, not at all

modus, -ī, M., manner, way; limit

mōnstrō, -āre, -āvī, -ātum, show, point out

mōnstrum, -ī, N., portent; monster

nārrō, -āre, -āvī, -ātum, tell, relate

nepōs, -ōtis, M., grandson

Neptūnus, -ī, M., Neptune, *god of the sea*

offendō, -fendere, -fendī, -fēnsum, offend
ōrāculum, -ī, N., oracle

pavor, -ōris, M., terror, alarm
percipiō, -cipere, -cēpī, -ceptum, perceive, feel
perdūcō, -dūcere, -dūxī, -ductum, lead through, lead, bring
Perseus, -ī, M., Perseus, *a Greek hero*
piscātor, -ōris, M., fisherman
poēta, -ae, M., poet
Polydectēs, -is, M., Polydectes, *a king of Seriphus*
procul, *adv.,* in the distance, at a distance, far off

quiēs, -ētis, F., rest; peace, quiet
quousque, *adv.,* till when? how long?

reddō, -dere, -didī, -ditum, give back, return
reditus, -ūs, M., return
referō, -ferre, rettulī, relātum, bring back; **grātiam referre,** make a return, requite
refugiō, -fugere, -fūgī, -fugitūrus, flee back; flee away, escape

rēgia, -ae, F., palace
rūpēs, -is, F., rock, cliff

saevus, -a, -um, fierce, savage
sanguis, -sanguinis, M., blood
sēdēs, -is, F., seat; residence, abode
sentiō, -īre, sēnsī, sēnsum, feel, see, perceive
Serīphus, -ī, F., Seriphus, *an island in the Aegean Sea*
serpēns, serpentis, F., serpent
simul, *adv.,* at the same time
sinus, -ūs, M., bosom
solvō, -ere, solvī, solūtum, loosen, unbind, release
somnus, -ī, M., sleep
speciēs, -ēī, F., appearance, aspect
spectātor, -ōris, M., onlooker, spectator
speculum, -ī, N., mirror

tālāria, -ium, N., *pl.,* winged sandals
tandem, *adv.,* at length, finally
terror, -ōris, M., terror, fright
Thessalia, -ae, F., Thessaly
tranquillus, -a, -um, calm, still
turbō, -āre, -āvī, -ātum, disturb, throw into confusion
turpis, -e, disgraceful, shameful

vinciō, -īre, vīnxī, vīnctum, bind
vinculum, -ī, N., bond, fetter
volō, -āre, -āvī, -ātum, fly